WITHDRAWN

FROM BÜCHNER TO BECKETT

FROM BÜCHNER TO BECKETT

Dramatic Theory and the Modes of Tragic Drama

ALFRED SCHWARZ

OHIO UNIVERSITY PRESS
Athens, Ohio

© Copyright 1978 by Alfred Schwarz
Printed in the United States of America
All rights reserved

Library of Congress Cataloging in Publication Data

Schwarz, Alfred.
    From Büchner to Beckett.

    Includes bibliographical references.
    1. Tragedy—History and criticism. 2. Drama—19th century—History
and criticism. 3. Drama—20th century—History and criticism. I. Title.
PN1897.S3   809.2   77-92255
ISBN 0-8214-0391-5

For Gerry

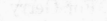

CONTENTS

ACKNOWLEDGMENTS

Sections of this study were first published in the following journals and are reprinted by permission: parts of chapter one, in *Symposium*, 20 (winter 1966); parts of chapter two, in *Modern Drama*, 9 (September 1966); material on Hofmannsthal, in *The Drama Review*, vol. IV, T 7, © 1960 by *The Drama Review*. Reprinted by permission. All Rights Reserved; and the section on Camus's *The Just*, in *Comparative Drama*, 6 (spring 1972), reprinted by permission of the Editors.

I am grateful to the following for permission to use copyrighted material: Oxford University Press for material from *The Oxford Ibsen*, tr. and ed. James Walter McFarlane; The Society of Authors, on behalf of the Bernard Shaw Estate, for material from *Saint Joan*; Constable & Co. Ltd. for material from *Twelve Plays by August Strindberg*, tr. Elizabeth Sprigge; Curtis Brown Ltd. for material from *Six Plays of Strindberg* and from *The Dance of Death*, tr. Elizabeth Sprigge, reprinted by permission of Curtis Brown Ltd., Copyright © 1955 and 1960 by Elizabeth Sprigge; A. P. Watt & Son for material from *The Bond* by August Strindberg, tr. Elizabeth Sprigge, reprinted by permission of The Estate of the Late Elizabeth Sprigge; Harold Ober Associates for material from *When We Dead Awaken and Three Other Plays*, tr. Michael Meyer, reprinted by permission of Harold Ober Associates Incorporated, Copyright © 1960 by Michael Meyer; Yale University Press, Jonathan Cape Ltd, and the Executors of the Eugene O'Neill Estate, for material from *Long Day's Journey into Night* by Eugene O'Neill; Random House, Inc., Jonathan Cape Ltd, and the Executors of the Eugene O'Neill Estate, for material from *The Iceman Cometh* by

The Viking Press, and for material from *After the Fall* by Arthur Miller, Copyright © 1964 by Arthur Miller, reprinted by permission of The Viking Press; Grove Press, Calder and Boyars Ltd, and Editions Gallimard for material from Eugène Ionesco's *Notes and Counter Notes*, tr. Donald Watson, Copyright © 1964 by Grove Press, Inc., *Notes et contre-notes*, © Editions Gallimard, 1966; and Calder and Boyars Ltd for material from Eugène Ionesco's *The Killer*, tr. Donald Watson; Grove Press and Faber and Faber Ltd for material from *Rosencrantz & Guildenstern Are Dead* by Tom Stoppard, and for material from *Waiting for Godot* and *Endgame* by Samuel Beckett. Reprinted by permission of Faber and Faber Ltd; Wayne State University Press for material from *Hugo von Hofmannsthal: Three Plays*, tr. and intr. by Alfred Schwarz; Suhrkamp Verlag, Eyre Methuen Ltd., and Random House for material from Bertolt Brecht's *Gesammelte Werke* (1967), Copyright in the original: © Copyright Suhrkamp Verlag, Frankfurt am Main 1967, Copyright in the translation: © Stefan S. Brecht 1978; and for material from Bertolt Brecht's *Leben des Galilei*, Copyright in the original: © 1955 by Suhrkamp Verlag, Berlin, Copyright in the translation: © Stefan S. Brecht 1978; Eyre Methuen Ltd and Farrar, Straus & Giroux, Inc. for material from *Brecht on Theatre*, edited and translated by John Willett, Copyright © 1957, 1963, and 1964 by Suhrkamp Verlag, Frankfurt am Main. This translation and notes © 1964 by John Willett. Published by Hill and Wang (now a division of Farrar, Straus and Giroux, Inc.). Excerpts from T. S. Eliot's *Selected Essays, The Cocktail Party, Murder in the Cathedral,* and *The Family Reunion* are reprinted by permission of Harcourt Brace Jovanovich, Inc.; copyright, 1935, by Harcourt Brace Jovanovich, Inc.; copyright, 1939, 1950, 1963, by T. S. Eliot; copyright, 1967, by Esme Valerie Eliot. Reprinted by permission of Faber and Faber Ltd.

All translations are mine unless otherwise indicated.

For research support in the initial stages of this work and for support in securing permissions I wish to thank

the Faculty Research Award Program and the Provost's
Office, Wayne State University.

                                                    A. S.

PREFACE

> The most profound question to be asked of a civilization is in
> what form it experiences its tragedies.
>
> *Georg Lukács*

> The desire for a new form is a recognition that our modern
> sense of tragedy is of a new kind, needing radically different
> expression. This should hardly need arguing, but we have in
> fact been oppressed by a traditional persistence, in the defini-
> tion of tragedy, which has often succeeded in persuading us
> that it has a kind of copyright both in the experience and in
> the form.
>
> *Raymond Williams*

In the opening chapters of *Modern Tragedy*, Raymond Williams has set down eloquently the case for a necessary
break with theories and definitions derived from the past if
we are to value ours as a major period of tragic writing and
respond to its distinctive "structures of feeling." He said
what needed saying since Joseph Wood Krutch first an-
nounced the death of tragedy in *The Modern Temper*
(1929). One may hope that his argument will end the futile
debates about the possibility of modern tragedy "after almost a century of important and continuous and insistent
tragic art,"[1] and that instead it will encourage inquiry into
the variety of forms tragedy has taken on the modern stage.
That is the aim of this study.

The "traditional persistence, in the definition of tragedy"
of which Williams speaks is nothing new. It is due to the
conservative bent of the critical mind which feels comfortable among the established masterpieces. Ben Jonson in
his memorial verses claimed that Shakespeare rivaled and
in comedy even outdid the classical dramatists; but in his
more sober mood, as the critic who transmits the classical
theory of drama, he had little to say about Shakespeare's

xiii

modern art except that the man whom he loved and hon-
ored "on this side Idolatry" was inventive, overly facile and
good-natured. Shakespeare's poetic attracted no attention
next to the one that had lasted for two thousand years. Two
centuries later, we come upon the opposite situation. Another playwright-critic, Friedrich Hebbel, remarked in 1852
that revivals of Shakespeare were like taking medicine: the
treatment was necessary, he said, but we must *live* off our
own means.[2] The positions were now reversed. Shakespeare was now the classic model, but his function was
merely restorative. According to the modern critic, the
dramatists must find their own means of responding to the
shifting moral and social pressures of their time. The modern drama can be said to begin and gain momentum with
the critical consciousness, wherever it may first appear and
take hold in the nineteenth century, that a new poetic must
be developed to embody the sense of a new time and that it
must find ways of superseding the old dramaturgy, whether
classical or Shakespearean, whose logic had served another set of ideas. The premise, shared by playwrights and
theorists, was that it made no sense to look for a drama,
and least of all for a tragedy, in any essential way comparable to the classic forms of past tragic theaters.

This sounds like a commonplace notion. Upon it depends
the evolutionist, as contrasted to the still widespread conservative, position among critics. For example, Williams argues that tragedy is "not a single and permanent kind of
fact, but a series of experiences and conventions and institutions. It is not a case of interpreting this series by reference to a permanent and unchanging human nature.
Rather, the varieties of tragic experience are to be interpreted by reference to the changing conventions and institutions. The universalist character of most tragic theory is
then at the opposite pole from our necessary interest."[3]
What is disputed by the conservative critics of our time is
not so much the expected evolution of forms, but the inti-
mation that the new experiences are no less "tragic" than
those based on a different intellectual and ethical framework. The most exclusive is the purist position; but it is no

longer taken seriously because it has used the term "tragedy" virtually as an honorific, reserving it for the grand conflicts between man and the supernatural, the divine power
which defines his destiny. It has also associated tragedy
with the idea of nobility and triumph over calamity and,
like Krutch, leveled an indictment against the modern age
for its triviality and meanness: "The journey from Elsinore
to Skien is precisely the journey which the human spirit has
made, exchanging in the process princes for invalids and
gods for disease."[4] Whereas this is an example of a wholly
emotional conservatism, doing justice neither to *Hamlet*
nor to *Ghosts*, there is the related conservative position
which, examining the historical development of tragedy,
pronounces the patient dead from Enlightenment and Romanticism.

Despite its categorical title, George Steiner's *The Death
of Tragedy* does not belong to this simplistic variety.[5] The
section devoted to the modern situation has a threefold conclusion, and it is not clear that he is committed to any one of
them. First, there is the possibility that tragedy is, indeed,
dead. This judgment is based on the purist position: "Tragedy is that form of art which requires the intolerable burden
of God's presence. It is now dead because His shadow no
longer falls upon us as it fell on Agamemnon or Macbeth or
Athalie" (p. 353). His least plausible suggestion admittedly
is that tragic drama, having indeed died, might come back
to life, perhaps in some communal meadow in China. And
then there is the possibility that tragedy carries on its essential tradition despite changes in technical form. "The
curve of tragedy is, perhaps, unbroken" (pp. 351, 354). Here
Steiner halfheartedly admits a position which Williams
goes on to explore more fully, but Williams rejects the conservative plea that surely the traditional outlook must persist while the changes are only technical. On balance,
Steiner is not a purist, but, if I may borrow the term, a
strict constructionist. He is always aware of the problem of
comparison with the "immense presence" of the *Oresteia,
Oedipus Rex, Hamlet*, and *Lear* (pp. 33-34).

The same attitude can be found in a number of lively dis-

cussions, published over the past dozen years, that are
chiefly concerned with gaining a more rigorous understanding of what is and is not tragedy. The definitions offered may be broad or narrow or variants of Francis Fergusson's tragic rhythm. All of them, however, face the same
problem: to find universally admissible grounds for demanding certain criteria in the definition. The aim is to define authentic tragedy. And the dangers are not unfamiliar
in genre theory. If the criteria are to be derived from recognized tragedies, the critic in order to select his models must
have an idea of tragedy prior to the definition; and the argument becomes circular.[6] If the criteria are chosen only
in order to sharpen our critical terminology, regardless of
traditional conceptions of the genre, as in Robert Heilman's
distinctions between the structure of tragedy and the structure of melodrama,[7] the suspicion arises that the definitions
are made *ex cathedra*, for the sake of clarity in a murky area
of critical discourse, but have no general validity. In practice, both methods arrive at definitions that are normative;
the temptation is to be prescriptive rather than descriptive.
There would be no harm in this except that the categories
of the definitions are liable to impose themselves in the act
of criticism, like an a priori structure, and distort our critical
response.

This is no place to review in detail those recent studies
that try, very usefully, to be more discriminating than the
earlier critical literature had been in defining the realm of
the tragic.[8] What is important to me here is the conception
of genre that is presupposed by those who work from or
toward a definition. Explicit or not, it is that of the strict
constructionist whose dedication is to an original charter,
abstracted from a core of plays generally admitted to be
tragedies. The orientation is toward the past, and depending on the freedom with which he interprets the abstracted
formal pattern or its corresponding structure of experience,
he defines more or less strictly the individual forms he is
willing to admit into the pale. Professor Heilman's charter
is even narrower since he derives it from one kind of experience: "In tragedy, dividedness is inner; in melodrama,

it is outer."[9] His elaboration of this principle is, as one would expect, impartial and richly illustrated. The reader may be momentarily piqued to find that a long admired tragedy, under the new dispensation, has become what Heilman calls a drama of disaster, one of the several variants of melodrama. But the real drawback turns out to be that underneath the persuasive analyses of experience and dramatic form the argument is controlled by the premeditated generic definitions. Critics who rely on a charter deny themselves the opportunities of an evolutionist approach to genre that is descriptive in its emphasis rather than normative, and hospitable to structures of feeling as yet unexplored by past practitioners of the art.

Insofar as it construes its charter too strictly, neither method of definition allows for "possibilities which cannot be anticipated." But suppose we start from the following premise: "The genres serve as ideal forms (or norms) of feeling, from which innumerable particular and actual forms may take their shape, even while these particular forms differ from the norms to which they 'belong'."[10] Our attitude to genre is still a matter of emphasis. But now there is a possible alternative to the method of definition. We may indeed choose to stand by an established generic norm and deal with new individual works in the spirit of taxonomy, that is, creating sub-genres and mixtures of genres when necessary. Or, we may regard the new individual work as "belonging" to a given genre but *modifying our perception of it as an ideal norm.*

The question is, how radically may the particular forms differ from the generic norms? Is *Endgame* an authentic modification of the genre we call tragedy or does it fall outside certain established norms? The former view is acceptable only if our idea of the genre is flexible and hospitable, allowing for what cannot be anticipated, while recognizing its essential function, that of preparing us for the *kind* of experience we may anticipate. As a matter of fact, the concept of genre thus understood made it possible for Ben Jonson to mention Shakespeare in the same breath with Aeschylus, Sophocles and Euripides, despite the radi-

cal differences in the two cultures and the two dramatic
traditions. But when the concept was more narrowly construed, according to norms transmitted from antiquity and
interpreted by the neoclassic critics, the collision with
Shakespeare was unavoidable. Since his immense presence
could not be denied, he had to be assimilated by making the
theory of genres more hospitable. The early history of
Shakespearean criticism demonstrates how the perception
of genre underwent a change as the strict neoclassic theory
confronted and gradually capitulated to Shakespeare's
dramaturgy.

If, then, the idea of a genre is thus modified by the production of new individual works, no single definition (or
"scheme" or set of "principles" or "elements") can ever account for the evolving generic norms. What is needed is a
continual updating, a series of descriptive genre studies to
take stock of the transformations occasioned by the changing intellectual and moral temper of a culture. Similarly, an
individual author's changing conception, in the course of
his career, of what constitutes tragic suffering or tragic
knowledge may radically alter the idea of the genre, the
norms of feeling which we are willing to accept. Could one
construe a single poetic to account for a mere dozen years
of Shakespeare's playwriting career? Between, say, *Romeo
and Juliet* and *Coriolanus*, is it possible to speak usefully of a norm of feeling or a tragic conception that embraces the astounding variety of tragic forms he produced?
A concept of the genre to be adequate must allow for this
variety, as it must also allow for different dramatists in the
same tradition, not to speak of different tragic theaters arising in different cultures. The task of abstracting a generic
norm which has such wide relevance is formidable. One
way is to retreat to a least common denominator, like equating the tragic with what is intolerable (for example,
Goethe's passing remark about Molière's *The Miser*:
". . .what is tragic there, or indeed anywhere, except
what is intolerable?"), or irreparable, or unendurable.
Whereas such norms are obviously too inclusive, those who
attempt strict generic definitions tend to become too exclu-

sive; they generally expose their definitions to few examples. Professor Heilman, on the other hand, keeps his neat distinctions between tragedy and melodrama intact by disposing of the great variety of what used to be called tragic forms under a variety of categories on the side of melodrama. In any case, the rationale of those who resort to definitions of tragedy is to gain precision where precision had been notoriously lacking.

But it may be argued that such precision is gained only by fixing a fairly specific pattern. Such a pattern or rhythm is first inferred from a spectrum of recognized tragedies, but through the effort of proving itself definitive when applied to particular works, especially the more uncertain examples of the genre, it is liable to become rigid and even prescriptive. Moreover, what is important is not the universality of the pattern, but the specific forms it takes in different theaters and in the hands of different playwrights. The point to prove is not that we can construe a definition which will give a generic name to a number of existing plays and enable us to recognize a new play as belonging to one or another genre. The precision which is finally significant, particularly on the assumption that the tragedies of an age are an index to the inner and outer life of a people, is that which takes account of what playwrights have actually done; what structures of feeling and fresh insight they have devised; what technical modifications they have undertaken. Of course, the critic ought to be always aware of the transmitted forms of tragic drama, but at the same time he must be alert to the transformations of the genre as the new playwrights respond to changing conventions and institutions, showing "the very age and body of the time his form and pressure."

In this study, I am therefore not interested in definition, but in tracing the continuing life of the genre in the modern theater. By drawing together dramas that share a common ground of ideas, a pattern of action or type characters developing in a given direction, it is possible to distinguish a number of traditions in the dramatic literature of the last century and a half. Through similarities in conception and

technique certain dramas illuminate one another and at the
same time illustrate the possibilities of a given tragic pattern. They may exemplify the forms in which familiar tragic
motives have reappeared or altogether new kinds of tragic
conflict and destruction, characteristic of our own time,
have emerged. For example, Büchner's *Danton's Death*
represents an idea of historical tragedy and a dramatic
method which sheds light on and in turn is illuminated by
such plays as Shaw's *Saint Joan*, Miller's *The Crucible*, and
Bolt's *A Man for All Seasons*. Each of these plays may be
approached usefully in terms of its immediately pertinent
background, but it is also a fruitful strategy for the critic to
consider them together as defining a tradition of modern
realistic historical drama, and to show how each playwright
has explored a basically similar pattern and adapted it to
his own purposes. By the same method of comparison, it is
possible to show how in Brecht's *Galileo* and Osborne's
Luther the potentially tragic pattern of the individual's
clash with the institution has been deliberately modified so
as to prevent a tragic conclusion. The realm of the tragic is
thus more precisely—because more concretely—delimited
than it is by the predictive categories of a definition.

This essay is not meant to be a history, but a critical study
of the modes of tragic drama on the modern stage. I have,
for example, left out of account Synge's *Riders to the Sea*,
Lorca's poetic tragedies, and the whole subject of Chekhov
because in certain ways these plays are unique. They do
not stem from recognizable modes of dramatic work, nor
did they beget other plays of the same kind and of equal
importance. In an essay so heavily dependent on critical
juxtaposition and comparison, in order to distinguish traditions of outlook and consequently of technique, these plays
had to be omitted.

Chekhov displays a modern sensibility that is the starting
point for the various forms which tragicomedy was to take
on the modern stage.[11] But Chekhov's original recognition
that life can seem unbearable and in the face of it human
behavior can be absurd is radically different from Beckett's
perception that the human situation as such is absurd, that

to exist at all is in one sense tragically and in another sense comically absurd. Chekhov's plays stage an escape from tragedy, whereas Beckett's, if they command credence, seal the death of tragedy. It is the latter event that needs to be looked at closely. Chekhov is determined to be on the side of life despite the unbearable facts;[12] Beckett does not shrink from the facts as he sees them. The path that leads from one to the other traverses the distance—in something less than two generations—between life seen in terms of pain and compassionate laughter, still an affirmative though ambivalent view, and the absolute devaluation of life rendered with wit and learning and in dead earnest.

But Beckett is willing to go further. Even the gradual collapse of being can command a tragic or tragicomic response invoked by the loss of what we value. When the interest shifts, however, from the feelings occasioned by loss, or failure, or destruction to the sheer mechanics of loss, or failure, or destruction, in other words, when the wittily constructed model of an experience begins to interest us more than the experience it stands for, an insidious dehumanization has set in for the spectator himself. Beckett seems to realize that beyond a certain point the spectacle of the diminished life ceases to arouse a tragic or comic response, and he moves from drama to mime. One asks, what feelings can there be left to muster over the human condition after *Waiting for Godot, Endgame,* and *Happy Days?* In *Act Without Words I,* we still discern human desire and the will to act though it is frustrated; but in *Act Without Words II* the mime represents man as automaton and the paradigm of life has been reduced to the sequence of stimulus and response, the goad moving the players inside the sacks to sluggish or brisk activity ad infinitum. Beckett records the debasement of life with fearful honesty and precision, however our fascination with his ingenuity begins to overshadow the human concern. We note the fact of dehumanization without the feeling of outrage.[13]

Thus, Beckett's theater reflects the demise of tragedy, and at the same time it indicates the reason why the idea of tragedy, after adapting itself to social and intellectual changes of all kinds, may have no place in the present state of our culture.

It has often been suggested that the death of tragedy is due to despair. For example, Walter Kaufmann states the argument in this way:

> Tragedy is inspired by a faith that can weather the plague, whether in Sophoclean Athens or in Elizabethan London, but not Auschwitz. . . . Tragedy depends on sympathy, ruth, and involvement. It has little appeal for a generation that, like Ivan Karamazov, would gladly return the ticket to God, if there were a god. Neither in Athens nor in our time has tragedy perished of optimism: its sickness unto death was and is despair.[14]

Moreover, there has been a conscious intellectual revolt against tragedy in the name of knowledge and political action, a revival of Plato's arguments. Shaw and Brecht, two powerful voices from the first half of the century, and Robbe-Grillet, a present-day voice, have tried to show us, in different ways, how to escape the "tragification" of the universe. But what Shaw and Brecht told us was simply that as long as men exploit and destroy each other in predictable ways, the theater should show them what they were doing and how to stop doing it. True, neither one could entirely avert his gaze from instances of unavoidable tragic suffering, but being activist minds they knew where their priorities lay. Robbe-Grillet moves in a different direction. He represents the systematic disengagement from a world that produced idealized nature, myths, recorded its misfortunes in art, and thus created a scale of false values. The human condition, he tells us, is really far less interesting than we had thought. Knowledge—neutral knowledge, *Wissenschaft*—will tell us more precisely what we are and where we stand in relation to the world, and thus we shall avoid the bugbear of tragic suffering.

This attitude reflects a widespread disillusionment as well as hope; and Beckett's automata goaded into activity look like a parody of it. The death of tragedy is due not to despair, but more precisely to the degradation of the human actor, leading to indifference before the spectacle of man made into a thing. Tragedies can still be made out of despair—Ivan Karamazov is the best example—but not in the face of indifference. Returning the ticket to God is a momentous act, and waiting for Godot arouses anguish as well as laughter. But we have moved to the verge of withdrawal from any such emotion. Our heroes explore outer space. The astronauts believe in God; the cosmonauts do not. But it makes no difference, because in either case the human crew has been officially defined as a subsystem—one of thousands which must properly function—and as we were told at a NASA news conference (August 29, 1965) the crew of the Gemini 5 flight was "plugged in" with less preparation than usual. Whether the human being has been reduced to a phantom lost in a metaphysical void or part of a subsystem functioning superbly in a physical void, the fact is that in the first instance he is expendable and in the second, replaceable. Our response to his devaluated existence approaches apathy. We cease to feel, and that is the end of tragedy.

As I have indicated earlier, it is not my intention to account historically for the fortunes of tragedy on the modern stage. The following pages are more in the nature of an inventory, a stocktaking of the forms of tragedy—a morphology of the genre. This is a good point to do so since the postwar burst of dramatic creativity—Ionesco, Genet, Beckett, Dürrenmatt, for example—has slowed to a virtual standstill as far as original ideas and novel techniques are concerned. And as we look back at this body of dramatic work, we discover that it was not, as had been thought, a fresh start leading to a new theater, but a resounding conclusion of the century-and-a-half old traditions of the modern theater. We are therefore at a point that offers an excellent opportunity to view this past critically as a whole.

NOTES

1. Raymond Williams, *Modern Tragedy* (Stanford: Stanford University Press, 1966), p. 46.

2. *Dramaturgische Aphorismen*, 1852, *Sämtliche Werke*, ed. Richard M. Werner (Berlin: B. Behr's Verlag, 1904), XII, 16.

3. Williams, pp. 45-46.

4. Joseph Wood Krutch, *The Modern Temper* (1929; rpt. New York: Harcourt, Brace & World, 1956), p. 90.

5. (New York: Knopf, 1961). Steiner's working title, "The Pursuit of Tragedy," was actually more accurate, if less striking, than the title of the published book.

6. Dorothea Krook, *Elements of Tragedy* (New Haven: Yale University Press, 1969), pp. 4-5, faces the problem of the circular argument by comparing it to the scientific method of testing a hypothesis. The analogy does not hold, however, because the chosen models, unlike a hypothesis in scientific work, cannot be rigorously tested to establish their *validity*.

7. Robert B. Heilman, *Tragedy and Melodrama: Versions of Experience* (Seattle: University of Washington Press, 1968) and *The Iceman, the Arsonist, and the Troubled Agent: Tragedy and Melodrama on the Modern Stage* (Seattle: University of Washington Press, 1973).

8. In addition to Heilman's two books and Krook's *Elements of Tragedy*, I have in mind such works as Oscar Mandel, *A Definition of Tragedy* (New York: New York University Press, 1961), and Geoffrey Brereton, *Principles of Tragedy: A Rational Examination of the Tragic Concept in Life and Literature* (Coral Gables, Fla.: University of Miami Press, 1968). Cyrus Hoy, *The Hyacinth Room: An Investigation into the Nature of Comedy, Tragedy, and Tragicomedy* (New York: Knopf, 1964) and N. Joseph Calarco, *Tragic Being: Apollo and Dionysus in Western Drama* (Minneapolis: University of Minnesota Press, 1968) are more broadly conceived.

9. *The Iceman*, p. 46.

10. Elias Schwartz, "The Problem of Literary Genres," *Criticism*, 13 (number 2, spring 1971), 119, offers an ingenious discussion of the relationship between the individual work and the generic norm. I am here concerned with the continuity of a genre.

11. Chekhov is the centerpiece of J. L. Styan's *The Dark Comedy: The Development of Modern Comic Tragedy*, 2nd ed. (Cambridge: At the University Press, 1968) and the subject of Walter Stein's fine critical challenge in *Criticism as Dialogue* (Cambridge: At the University Press, 1969), pp. 92-102.

12. This is the point of Stein's argument.

13. By an analogous process, erotic art may become pornographic.

14. Walter Kaufmann, *Tragedy and Philosophy* (Garden City: Doubleday, 1968), pp. 165-166.

PART ONE

The Old Drama and the New

1. THE EMERGING POETIC OF MODERN REALISM AND NATURALISM

> When a people does not want to look at human passions any more, it no longer has any of its own.
>
> *Friedrich Hebbel*

> [Shakespeare's] kings are not statesmen: his cardinals have no religion: a novice can read his plays from one end to the other without learning that the world is finally governed by forces expressing themselves in religions and laws which make epochs rather than by vulgarly ambitious individuals who make rows. . . .
>
> There are no villains in the piece. Crime, like disease, is not interesting: it is something to be done away with by general consent, and that is all about it. It is what men do at their best, with good intentions, and what normal men and women find that they must and will do in spite of their intentions, that really concern us.
>
> *G. B. Shaw*

William Archer's influential book, *The Old Drama and the New,* published in 1923, celebrated the coming of age of realism in the modern English theater. Looking back over the past half century, the book was partly a history and partly an impassioned plea in favor of the new movement in the theater. Archer was expert in his demonstration of the outward, formal differences between the old drama and the new. But the critical consciousness of a set of essential differences had emerged much earlier. A radical break with the social and moral basis of the old drama and therefore with its traditional forms had occurred in the 1830s, for example, in Büchner's *Danton's Death* and the dramatic fragment, *Woyzeck* (first published in 1879). And in the course of the nineteenth century a number of thoughtful theorists of the drama, from Hebbel to Strindberg, furnished the details of a specifically modern

3

poetic. They indicated the necessity of abandoning set forms which were no longer expressive of modern subjects and modern conceptions of man's condition in this world. The desirability of a post-Aristotelian and a post-Shakespearean poetic became explicit in these writings.

By comparison, Archer's study of the actual development of the new drama was simple in its argument. It drew a clear distinction between an antiquarian older drama, overlaid with lyrical passion and the rhetoric of feeling, and the purified new drama, mimetic, realistic, and logical. In short, he considered the mastery of surface imitation as a liberation in the development of dramatic technique. Naturally the categories of comedy and tragedy were bound to disappear (a final release, he said, from the fetters of the traditions of prehistoric tribal life) in a sober and accurate imitation of the life we live; for we do not live either in comedy or tragedy—we live in life. In response to Archer's thesis, T. S. Eliot defined the fallacy of an unlimited aim at realism as ending in an "exact likeness to the reality which is perceived by the most commonplace mind."[1] But Archer actually welcomed the "genius of the commonplace" (his term for the work of T. W. Robertson) as a modern phenomenon. Scribe, the great technician, had introduced the new art of plot manipulation and had purified the drama of its extrinsic rhetorical elements. The actual coming of age occurred with Ibsen's impact on the English dramatists, beginning with the last decade of the century. He taught them the art of interpretation through accurate imitation. The "poetry of realism in common life" flourished in Pinero and Granville-Barker; in fact, said Archer in a fit of enthusiasm, *Waste* (1907) was our greatest modern tragedy.[2]

The differences which Archer perceived between the modern realistic social drama and the "barbarous" extravaganzas of the Elizabethan and Jacobean stage were all on the level of technical cunning in creating an illusion of life. But the changes were, of course, more far-reaching. The modernity of the modern drama is a more complex question than Archer's merely symptomatic distinctions would indicate. It has less to do with the technical accomplishments of a Scribe or an Ibsen than with the awareness (which tells the difference between an Ibsen and a Scribe) that the modern playwright must create a specifically modern dramaturgy in order to grasp and express a changed view of the human condition: namely, that man's fate is inextricably tied to his life in society and to his experience of history as a force to be reckoned with. The best theorists and practitioners of the new drama recognized that realism involved more than a technique of imitation; that it had as its presupposition a sense of historical and social change and an essentially secular view of the world. The way was cleared toward a distinctively modern realistic drama when the theater freed itself from religious and moral imperatives. That is to say, as soon as the drama ceased primarily to *exemplify* the *truth* of a religious or ethical world view, as soon as the drama ceased to be orthodox in its social function, it became possible merely to reflect or to *examine* the *reality* of this world as the playwright saw it. Indeed, the naturalistic dramatists went so far as to equate reality with truth.[3] Hence, the emphasis on the historical and social position and the psychological condition of man in his environment.

Actually, the drama began to serve this new skeptical, explorative function as early as the Euripidean theater in one tradition and the Jacobean theater in another. But with few exceptions the traditional forms of drama—plot, protagonist, agon, logical or analogical structure—persisted and served as the conventional tools for the "emancipated" secular dramatists far into the nineteenth century. Only when the modern practitioners discovered that their contemporary versions of man's tragic condition could not be represented in the older forms, did they realize that the new function of the drama—mimetic, analytical, explorative—demanded a new poetic.

1

The call for a new realism came in the middle decades

of the nineteenth century, and it was a call not merely
for a realistic manner, for technical reform. It demanded
a drama of contemporary significance in reaction to the
romantic idealism of the previous generation on the one
hand and the dilettantish, trifling naturalism of the popular stage on the other. A trio of writers in Germany, Hermann Hettner, an academic critic, and Friedrich Hebbel
and Otto Ludwig, who were themselves playwrights, were
eloquent spokesmen of a movement which was to culmi-
nate in the triumph of realism and naturalism on the European stages. They foreshadowed Ibsen's lifework and illustrated in their critical discussions practically all the
modes of the nineteenth-century drama. All three diag-
nosed the ills of the contemporary drama, and in predict-
ing the shape of the new drama they assessed the modern
situation in view of the traditional theaters, and particularly in relation to Shakespeare. Hebbel and Hettner
looked forward to the emergence of a new drama of
ideas, while Ludwig advocated a modern tragedy on the
model of Shakespeare.

Hettner's small book, *Das moderne Drama* (1851),
which Ibsen read early in his career, prophesied that the
times would demand a social drama. Therefore it would
be necessary to transform the two major traditional
genres, the history play and the bourgeois drama, into
genuine social drama; in fact, there lay the possibility of a
modern tragedy. But it must be realistic drama, not romantic, idealistic, or drily moralistic. Its future subject, he
said, will be the dialectic of moral principles. Thus it must
become a drama of ideas. Of course, such a drama must
still be true to human nature; Shakespeare's psychological
realism in the handling of motives and character development would remain exemplary. But the tragedy was to
arise from the dialectic of ideas or principles, from social
questions, and in this sense the bourgeois social drama
would be more historical than the so-called historical
drama. In effect, such a drama must be tragic or else it
would be trivial.

Hettner was fully aware that the modern sense of history as being fateful had furnished the contemporary drama with a new significant subject matter, the transformation of social conditions seen in terms of the historical conflict of moral principles. Thus, the agon was to be external, objective, in the new drama. It did not tear a protagonist to pieces inwardly; it was not a conflict brought on by individual passions nor was it the conflict of an individual pitting himself against the ethical or religious sanctions of his community. He was no outcast, nor a villain. Yet he was sacrificed in the play of external forces. Hettner agreed with Hebbel's dictum that Shakespeare's dialectic of characters would be replaced by a dialectic of the idea.

The most fruitful speculations in Hettner's modern poetic have to do with the transformation of the flourishing bourgeois drama into serious modern tragedy. He recognized the possibility of developing a modern domestic tragedy on the model of classical tragedy, provided its conflicts embodied serious social questions, principles and views that were naturally opposed, and provided the necessary course of such real conflicts was pursued without compromise. The deplorable state of the genre in its current productions prompted Hettner to reaffirm the age-old formal principles of good dramaturgy. For though the drama of Lillo and his imitators was gone from the stage, Lessing, Diderot, Schroeder, Iffland, and Kotzebue were still to be seen. The so-called family dramas had become progressively more prosaic, drily moral, and trivial in their depiction of the miseries of private life. Their popularity rested on their surface realism, on their being topical and homely as well as highly moral; man's destiny in these dramas consisted in bankruptcy and the solution in a *deus ex machina*, the rich relative from Mexico who restored the remorseful family to its prior splendor. Yet the triviality of such drama was not due to the milieu depicted. It was due to the fact that naturalistic imitation for its own sake or for the sake of entertainment was meaningless. Such plays dealt with merely external conflicts, merely temporary errors and misunderstanding.

Yet domestic tragedy was possible if the conflicts were
to be real rather than apparent, necessary rather than incidental. If the dramatist were true to human nature and
handled the dialectic of moral principles with integrity,
the modern subject matter, though externally unheroic,
would yield a moving and elevating tragic drama. Thus,
if the conflicts were deeply moral, fate would be correspondingly great, and where there was an inner necessity
in the fate, there was genuine tragedy.[4]

From this point of view he examined the various possibilities of bourgeois or domestic tragedy and preferred
in each instance the type which embodied, not merely the
painful individual case, but the tragically elevating clash
of universal forces. His sympathies did not lie with the
"Sturm und Drang" imitators of Shakespearean character
tragedy, but with the modern descendants of the classical
drama of moral ideas. Like Hegel, he found Sophocles'
Antigone the ideal tragedy of opposing principles. And
Goethe's *Faust,* in contrast to *Hamlet,* was to him, as to
Friedrich Hebbel, the model for the modern dialectic of
historically perceptible ideas. Though Hebbel's *Maria
Magdalene* had its faults, it too demonstrated the feasi-
bility of a modern domestic tragedy. It was for Hettner the
most significant recent dramatic work, a poetic critique
of narrow morality founded on a serious conflict of principles (pp. 100-106).

Hettner distinguished three types of bourgeois tragedy:
the tragedy of circumstance; the tragedy of passion; and
the tragedy of idea. In describing the possibilities of the
first type, he anticipated the naturalistic milieu drama.
And he pointed to all its drawbacks in comparison with
the third type, for which he borrowed Hegel's name and
which was to be the genuine social tragedy of the future
(pp. 83-94). In talking of the tragedy of human passion,
he had to confront Shakespeare and call on a Hegelian
distinction to help him out. There are two kinds, he said,
the subjective and the objective tragedy, that of the singular, individual passion and that of "substantial" passion
(to use Hegel's corresponding terminology), that is, a

passion sustained by great and general purposes, mirroring the fate and the history of humanity at large. One was psychological character tragedy, like *Othello*, *Macbeth*, or *Wallenstein*; the other a universal tragedy of principles in opposition or of opposite ethical claims. The passionate heroes of the first kind did not come to ruin in opposing a hostile external world, but through faults and weaknesses in their own nature. As in the familiar example of Shakespearean tragedy, the conflict may be an inner conflict or it may reveal itself between two opposing figures. It rests upon certain, specific, incidental presuppositions. There is not, in his view, the unavoidable necessity for tragic conflict in these plays, nor a general or purely human motive in these characters of passion, but rather a touch of the special. He shared Hegel's preference for two opposing passions or purposes which are equally moral and therefore equally in the right (pp. 94-99).

Hettner's implied criticism of Shakespearean tragedy becomes explicit at this point. Though he half apologized for his modernist stand, he maintained that if the hero, for example, were not so jealous or gullible, the necessity of the conflict and the resolution would disappear. He cited Hegel's *Aesthetic* in support of his point: The Shakespearean heroes, lured by external circumstances or out of blindness, hold to their deed by sheer strength of will, and act from a need to maintain their vulnerable position. In short, he applied Hegel's distinctions between the ancient drama and the modern romantic drama to the problems of his own generation. The "substantial" character of ancient tragedy was supposed to become the model for the modern realistic bourgeois tragedy as opposed to the "subjective" character of Shakespearean and modern romantic tragedy.[5] As Hebbel put it, though more modestly, in the preface to *Maria Magdalene*: There is the dialectic of Shakespeare's characters, of emancipated protestant individuals; but then Goethe laid the foundation for another great type of drama, the dialectic of the idea.

What Hettner did not understand was that in the Elizabethan world view the Shakespearean theater exhibited "substantial" passions, not merely subjective, individual cases, and that the moral world of Shakespearean tragedy was universal *by virtue* of its lack of historical consciousness, its timeless quality as allegory, and so could mirror the fate of humanity at large. It was a tragedy of opposite ethical claims, though not of equal validity. Hettner's view rested on the lopsided emphasis of Romantic criticism on Shakespeare as the creator of a gallery of living *individual* characters; hence the misleading phrase "the dialectic of Shakespeare's characters" in opposition to the dialectic of the historical idea. There is a difference, obviously, between the two theaters, but it is not the difference between a merely moving psychological drama of singular human passions and a realistic social drama of historical significance. Rather, it stems from the completion of the process of secularization since Shakespeare's time. The difference is that the modern drama derives its sense of what is *real* from the consciousness of historical processes and therefore fashions its conflicts from historically perceptible forces; whereas the older drama, equally sensible that its conflicts are unavoidable, relies on a cohesive ethical framework for the *truth* of its dialectic play between passionate individuals and the moral order of the universe. Therefore, the moral values which were in the older drama a presupposition, if not always a conviction, are now subjected to examination. What was once an accepted convention, by which dramatic conflicts were "tried" publicly, has become the subject of the drama of social conflict.

Hettner proposed precisely such a "realistic" drama for his time. The tragedy of the idea was to him the highest form of drama because it dealt in conflicts which were unavoidably (that is to say, historically) given by the nature of the two sides; thus all accident and arbitrariness has disappeared (p. 100). The world of this drama was then the world of inner necessity, the world of reason; and accident or misunderstanding (which was the accident of intellect) must be excluded. But there is also a

basic difference between the conception of Aristotle's
Poetics and Hettner's theory of the modern drama.[6] Aristotle insists on the formal logic of the plot, on the law of
probability or necessity, to insure that the course of the
dramatic action will be both surprising and inevitable and
so evoke the proper tragic emotions of fear and pity.
Oedipus Rex is his ideal illustration. Hettner's formula for
the ideal modern tragedy stresses more prominently the
cognitive value of a logical conflict of claims in which
moral or socio-political forces are realistically represented. His rationale is Hegelian and therefore holds up
the example of the *Antigone.* A tragedy which deals thus
profoundly with moral principles in deadly opposition
achieves its artistic effect in proportion to its depth of content, to the substantiality of its passions (pp. 104-105).
Thus Hettner's poetic for the new drama attempted to
supersede both the Aristotelian and the Shakespearean
emphasis on the emotional effect of tragedy; it located
the tragic experience, at least by implication, in the mind,
that is to say, in the social and historical consciousness
of the audience. It predicted the sweep of realistic social
drama over Europe.

In contrast to Hettner's systematic blueprint for a contemporary drama, Otto Ludwig's *Shakespeare-Studien*
and Friedrich Hebbel's *Diaries* were the day-to-day jot-
tings and occasional essays of two professional writers.
Their speculations and reflections are, therefore, more
detailed and of greater practical value. Every page of
aphoristic remarks or more extended pieces of dramatic
theory betrays lively critical minds at work. These two
contemporary critics have been called "hostile brothers," and rightly so. Their contributions to the emerging
poetic of the modern drama complement one another.
Both recognized the need for a theory of realistic drama
in order to overcome the commanding presence of Goethe
and Schiller and to escape the sterile developments of
surface realism and naturalism both in France and in
their own country. Both saw the need for reform, indeed
for a new beginning, to lay the foundations for a mean-

ingful contemporary drama, but conceived in traditional
terms; their knowledge and respect for the great theaters
of the past is everywhere evident. But while Hebbel, himself a major dramatist in the traditions of historical and
bourgeois drama, sensed the possibilities of future developments, Ludwig feared them (for example, in his comments on *Maria Magdalene*) and continued to hold up
Shakespeare as the one sensible model for a contemporary theater of power and ultimate significance.

That Ludwig was wrong in his emphasis, both practically and historically, is beside the point. For our purposes
his critique of the contemporary drama is more valuable
than his conception of a Shakespearean poetic realism.
His dream of a modern theater of passionate heroes who
incur guilt and live out the inevitable course from passion through action to punishment with exemplary psychological verisimilitude remained a dream. But in applying the standard of Shakespeare's tragedies he touched
on the risks and weaknesses of the new poetic which was
in the making. He saw the disadvantages inherent in Hettner's and Hebbel's retreat from the tragedy of passion and
in their conception of a modern social and historical tragedy, dialectic rather than psychological, a tragedy of
ideas rather than men.

Ludwig's critical position toward the drama of his day
can best be summed up in two sets of alternatives:
Shakespeare *or* Schiller and Shakespeare *or* Scribe.
Though the choices would appear to be obvious from the
spectator's point of view, we must remember that Ludwig
was exhorting the contemporary artist to align himself in
his work with one mode of drama or the other. In championing Shakespeare as the supreme model, he tried to
reveal the synthetic falseness, the trickery, of the popular and allegedly realistic drama in France; and he also
tried to reach back beyond the legacy of romantic idealism and the intrusions of modern philosophy to a genuine
"naive" drama, mimetic instead of reflective, representational instead of descriptive, a drama productive of an im-

mediate sensuous impact instead of edifying sentiments. The trouble with the German drama was precisely that it was a literary drama. The action was not represented, but argued dialectically, felt lyrically, and described epically. And so the drama had all but disappeared from the stage. Unlike Shakespeare, the modern poet was seldom the mirror of his time. He did not objectively render the passions and actions of men; he idealized and sentimentalized the image. He was, in short, not the judge, but played the role of defense attorney, and celebrated himself in celebrating the cause for which he was pleading.[7]

Clearly, the dramatic effect must be achieved through the representation itself, not by way of sentiments concerning the represented action (p. 279). That is not to say that reflections and sentiments are altogether improper in the drama. But Shakespeare's exemplary tragedies of passion contain *objective* reflections on the part of the character: "Why should a dog, a horse, a rat, have life, / And thou no breath at all?" whereas the reflections in Schiller's drama, for example, are the poet's (p. 266). Ludwig made the protest against this self-conscious intrusion of the poet between the represented object and the audience in the name of realism. A Sophoclean drama, he wrote, is like a slender palm; a Shakespeare production, like a gnarled oak; but Schiller's is like a christmas tree, with loosely hanging maxims and fruits dangling on the thread of caprice (p. 323).

The attack was sharp because Ludwig sought to eradicate in himself a powerful trend of the times. He was equally aware of the opposite danger, which was easier to combat: the presentation of an "impoverished reality" in the clever productions of the French stage. The distinction between the poetic realism of Shakespeare's drama and the "clockwork" realism of Scribe was crucial for Ludwig. Granted, the modern French playwrights moved their dramatic figures with astonishing skill, but essentially they performed feats of legerdemain for the amusement of their audiences (pp. 349-351, 413-415).

But Ludwig also rejected the idea that the modern
tragedy was to develop typically in the form of realistic
social drama. He would admit that in the hands of a
dramatist like Hebbel the contemporary bourgeois tragedy
and the historical drama were in every respect superior
to the work of the idealist poet who could not or would
not imitate life as it was, and that they were certainly
superior as works of *art* to the flimsy confections of the
pseudo-realists of the French school. Still, they failed as
tragedy and even as drama because they engaged primarily the understanding or the intellect of the audiences, not their emotions.[8] For example, *Maria Magdalene*, an early landmark in the realistic social drama,
struck him as being in many ways commendable, yet he
sensed the coldly calculating poet behind the human
play. Personalities appear to be merely abstract numbers,
or quantities, to the poet, and this frigid attitude trans-
fers itself to the characters. Hence we witness the ineffectual twists and turns of the certain victim (Klara)
which is no longer tragic, but gruesome. The dramatist
ought to act as judge, not as executioner (p. 357). The
necessary passivity of the protagonists in the modern
conceptions of tragedy disturbed him. It was a modification of dramatic form which appeared to him to deny, as
it did later on in the century to Brunetière, the distinctive
quality of the genre. Once we conceive of fate as the unchangeable running down of a clock mechanism, he said
in one of his aphorisms, the victim is caught without deliverance or the possibility of independent action, and the
play is done (p. 412).

In this respect, the difference between Shakespearean
tragedy and modern tragedy was absolute. And therefore, he insisted repeatedly that a modern tragedy was
possible only if the playwright created the basic tragic
tension by conceiving of his hero as a guilty man. He
himself must be the cause of his ultimate fate. The new
poetic of the realistic social tragedy was an evasion of
the stern moral judgments of the Shakespearean theater,
an accommodation to the sentimental temper of the

times. "Our age is frightened of the idea that a man might incur personal guilt" (p. 441). This was due, he thought, to a misunderstood streak of humanity, a general reluctance to pass harsh judgment on one's fellow man and correspondingly a desire to be easy on one's self. The social drama wanted to take refuge in peripheral causes. Not the self-determining individual acted or sinned, but the state, the society, upbringing or schooling, the institution of marriage, the degree of education or a man's cultural status; in short, environmental factors committed the sin through him, and so absolved the individual from guilt. Such sentimentality amounted to immorality in Ludwig's view and virtually precluded the possibility of tragedy in this form on the modern stage (p. 442).

What may be at issue between him, championing a moral and psychological drama of passion, and the proponents of the realistic social drama is the difference in emphasis on the word *realism*. Ludwig interpreted it as freedom from willful philosophical and lyrical distortions; as truth to the moral and psychological condition of man; as an artistic, enriched rendering of a world which contained in itself its own conditions and consequences, a whole recreated world, not an impoverished naturalistic imitation of a slice of reality (p. 458). The moral and emotional effect of such a drama derived from the inner logic, the inevitable tragic nexus of passion, guilt, suffering, and punishment. In the traditional tragic drama, Ludwig reminds us, the demand was for an overwhelming impression by the tragic hero on our senses; nowadays it was sufficient that upon due reflection, the audience found evidence of his philosophical fitness to be a tragic hero (p. 496).

On the other hand, the theorists of the historical and social tragedy insisted on the truth, or objective validity, of the conflict of ideas which they represented. To them, the sheer energy of human passion was less important than its significance as a moral momentum, a viable ethical claim which collides with an equally viable claim, either institutional or personal. To which Ludwig replied,

in effect: Note that Brutus and Cassius nowhere assert
that freedom represents a moral or human right; it appears
rather as the object of their passionate desire. In contrast,
the modern tragedy has become a vehicle for polemic
tendencies which paralyze the effect it ought to have as
tragedy. He was convinced, and stood virtually alone in
his conviction, that a modern tragic theater, modeled on
Shakespeare's and modified according to contemporary
circumstances, but uncompromising in its moral and psychological effects, was possible. He reasoned that a man
who was strong enough to be evil could still arouse pity;
he could still have a fate. But only for an audience which
thought so was tragedy still possible.

2

The similarity between Hettner's compact academic
theory of the modern drama and Hebbel's far-flung entries
into his diaries and letters and his dramatic essays is only
general. Both absorbed the influence of Hegel's teaching
early in their careers; in the mid-forties they met in Italy
and talked about dramatic theory, Hettner, the young
scholar, listening to the theories and plans of the elder
dramatist who had already launched his career with two
admirable productions, *Judith* and *Maria Magdalene.* What
distinguishes Hebbel's critical writing from that of his contemporaries is that its best features grow out of his experience as a working dramatist who succeeded in creating a
genuine tragic theater in his time. His tragedies are an integral part of his poetic; they often showed him what his
theories really came to in the theater, and some of his clearest insights into the nature of tragic drama as he understood it appeared in his commentary on his own finished
work.

His total production, both as dramatic artist and critic of
his own accomplishment, puts him, for our purposes, in an
interesting middle position. On the one hand, he occupies
his place in the line of dramatic poets beginning with
Lessing who form a distinct tradition of tragic writing in
Germany. His plays created a moment of living tragic the-

ater, perhaps the last possible in that tradition. Moreover, he saw himself as the modern representative of a larger European tradition. Contrasting his own poetic with Wagner's esthetic theories, which he thought stood in sharp contradiction to the great European past, he claimed late in his life that his purpose had not been to preach a new gospel; he wished, on the contrary, to reinstate the older dramatic traditions, derived from Sophocles and Shakespeare. In fact, he tried to create a poetic of tragedy, comparable in power, if not in its intellectual foundations and therefore in its precise effect, to those of the traditional theaters.

On the other hand, he realized that to align oneself with a tradition was not the same as simply modeling one's work on its characteristic outlook and formal expression, an anachronism of which Ludwig was guilty in his exclusive critical admiration for Shakespeare as the panacea of all dramatic ills. Though Shakespeare's work was to him "the bible of the drama," yet as an active dramatist Hebbel was equally conscious of his modernity: It was necessary to become as familiar as possible with Shakespeare, but then to keep away from him as far as possible because Shakespeare was the world itself all over again. The new drama must be different from Shakespeare's as far as its moral and intellectual foundation was concerned; in fact, the closest paradigm for Hebbel's tragic view in a theater of the past would (once more) be the *Antigone*, the "masterpiece of masterpieces." The common link between the modern artist and his illustrious forebears might be expressed in Hebbel's phrase describing the task common to all serious drama, past and present: to solve the "two enigmas, human nature and human destiny."[9] But at the same time, if the drama was to amount to more than idle entertainment or the trivial record of the poet's private fantasy, it must be the expression of the human spirit in a given historical and cultural situation; in short, it must have a valid philosophical or historical foundation which makes sense in its own time, a condition *sine qua non* especially for the tragic poet.

In Hebbel's view, the new drama would have to go beyond Shakespeare's in one respect, and that a crucial one.

If it ever came into being, the dialectic of drama would
operate not merely in the characters, as in Shakespeare; it
must get directly into the *Idea* itself so that not merely the
relation of man to the Idea, but the justification of the Idea
itself will be debated (2864 [1843]; II, 299). This remark
clearly illustrates Hebbel's link to the traditional modes of
drama as well as his awareness of a basic difference between the old drama and the new. The complex of meanings
which Hebbel assigned to the word *Idea*, one of several
key terms in his prose writings and more specific than Hettner's use of the term, may create difficulties with certain
passages of his dramatic criticism. But the term becomes
clear once we realize that Hebbel conceived of a tragic
theater, in the tradition of Sophocles and Shakespeare,
which was also founded on the interplay between the individual and a universal order or law of morality from which
the individual has somehow separated himself. As the
highest form of all the arts, the drama must reveal the estate of man and the world at any particular time in their
relation to the Idea, that is, to the moral center which we
accept as the condition of all existence (Preface to *Maria
Magdalene*). It must reflect the conflict inherent in life itself. Thus, the Ideas in the drama are what counterpoint
is in music, nothing in itself, but the basic condition of
everything (5695 [1859]; IV, 136).

The Idea, or the Universal, or Necessity—Hebbel employs
a number of almost interchangeable terms—appears to be an
essentially secular concept corresponding to the Greek notion of *dikê* and to the Christian concept of Providence or
divine justice as the expression of an inviolable order in
Shakespearean tragedy. The difference is that Hebbel's
drama is the product of a particular time when a *change*
takes place in the relation between the individual and the
Idea. It is founded on a philosophy of history whereas the
tragic conflicts in the older drama are single illustrations
of broken order and restored equilibrium in an unchangeable moral universe, independent of time. But the gestures
of self-assertion, trespass, and consequent destruction of
the individual are the same. And Hebbel insisted, also in

the traditional manner, that insofar as reconciliation was at all possible in tragedy, it occurred in the interest of the whole, not of the individual, the hero. He illustrated the process in a vivid metaphor: Life is the great river, the individualities are drops of water, but the tragic ones are pieces of ice which must be melted down again, and to make this possible, they must break and smash one another (2664 [1843]; II, 239).[10] Of course, a character can also become tragic in representing the Idea, in upholding the superpersonal order, like the elder duke Ernst in *Agnes Bernauer* who must sacrifice his son's innocent wife to save the commonweal. But all serious drama, according to Hebbel, must in some way deal with the fateful relation between the individual will and the universal law. Most of his contemporaries produced trivial plays for the lack of such conflicts. There are dramas *without* Ideas, he noted in his diary, in which people simply go for a walk and happen to run into Misfortune (1784 [1839]; I, 399).

So far, in Hebbel's theory, we have a modern counterpart to the dualistic world views on which the older theaters were based. The drama must never content itself with imitating the phenomenal world. But Hebbel also foresaw a radical change which must take place as the drama strives to attain significance as a representation specifically of the contemporary state of the world. It will be necessary to supersede Shakespeare by making the Idea itself the subject of dramatic debate, instead of revealing only the "terrible dialectic" in the characters who have broken away from it in their need for individual self-assertion. As a matter of fact, a general shift of emphasis must come about, away from the dramatic character as free agent and center of interest whose personal destiny is unfolded before us; rather, the modern drama will develop as the highest form of *historical* writing, depicting man in his role as agent and victim of the historical process itself, subject to impersonal forces that are greater than he. Hebbel's prognostication is that the drama, with the complete detachment from its religious origins and from its function as a moral institution in the narrow sense, which in various guises it still claimed to fulfill even in modern times, will eventually no longer be able to assume a "given" moral center. The drama will itself become an examination of the moral ideas and institutions on which society depends; and thus man will be shown as he participates in the evolving dialectic of ideas (Preface to *Maria Magdalene*).

The consequences of this shift of emphasis become apparent in Hebbel's own work and in the developing forms of the new drama. Insofar as the supremacy of the Idea over the individual in their conflict is inherent in the order of things, insofar as this conflict is to Hebbel a fact of life, a historical, not a religious or ethical moment in drama, the categories of good and evil, of obedience and disobedience to a higher Will, fall away. And it follows that the concept of guilt and reconciliation in Hebbel's poetic transcends the narrower, more specific religious concept of sin and retribution or forgiveness. Guilt in this sense is everywhere and always possible, but not inevitable. It derives from want of moderation (*Masslosigkeit*), any form of excess under the given circumstances, however innocent, in deed or even in appearance (like the beauty of Agnes Bernauer), leading to a tragic conflict with more general human or social interests. As soon as a protagonist asserts his individuality in action he jeopardizes his relation to the whole, he isolates himself (*Vereinzelung*), he incurs guilt. And the direction of his will, whether toward good or evil, is immaterial because guilt necessarily accompanies all purely individual action (*Mein Wort über das Drama!*). For Hebbel the highest form of drama deals only with this basic aspect of life, the tragic separation of man as he violates the universal sanctions of his world; and the most moving effect such drama can achieve is to derive tragic guilt from actions which are in themselves good, not unlike the effect of the reversal of a "good" intention in Aristotle's *Poetics*.

One of the differences between the old drama and the new lies precisely in the conception of individual guilt which has nothing to do with positive evil or villainous motives, but is a necessary result of colliding interests.

Thus, as the historical replaces the moral judgment of human action, the question of free will and human responsibility plays a diminished role in the modern social and historical drama. Hebbel prided himself on his ability to deduce logically the most frightful consequences, and tragic conclusions, from the interplay of characters who were all in the right, who committed no evil act, and whose fate was due to the fact that they were just these men and women and no different.[11] Also in his bourgeois tragedy, *Maria Magdalene*, he has been able to derive tragic guilt solely from a characteristically inflexible narrow-mindedness in the household of the village carpenter. In the background of the play, says Hebbel, move the Ideas of Family, Morality, and Honor, both in their clear and their blind aspects, and consequences begin to dawn on us which only in centuries to come will be accepted into the catechism of life.[12]

Similarly, in the Preface to *Saint Joan*, Shaw, in his best tutorial manner, tells his presumably misguided reader that Joan "went to the stake without a stain on her character except the overweening presumption, the superbity as they called it, that led her thither." Both the Elizabethan libels on her and the modern whitewash at the expense of her judges make her into a melodramatic heroine, which she was decidedly not. And in a symposium some years ago, Arthur Miller rejected as *irrelevant* charges of immorality against Willy Loman. In Miller's words, Willy is seeking for a kind of ecstasy in life, of which the machine-civilization deprives people. He is looking for his selfhood, for his immortal soul, so to speak. "Willy embodies some of the most terrible conflicts running through the streets of America today."[13] In all these cases, whether we read the plays as they do or not, the modern playwrights view the tragic action as a historically significant conflict in which man asserts his individuality in a futile effort against the institutions, the moral ideas, or the social mode of his time.

In Hebbel's modern poetic, the drama is by definition a historical drama because it shows us the nature of all human action in the context of our historical consciousness.

In the conflict between the individual and the general will, the human act, expressive of freedom, is always modified and reshaped by the event, the historical circumstance, the exigency, which is expressive of necessity. Therefore, it makes no difference whether the subject and the setting is contemporary or derived from the past. In either case, the most significant dramatic actions can be represented only in the context of the historical crises, the embodied religious and political ideas, which engender them and shape their meaning. In other words, the historical character of the drama does not depend on its subject or material; in that sense, even a dramatic fantasy can be historical. When the poet uses recorded history, he uses it only as a vehicle to make his ideas palpable and so dramatically apprehensible (*Mein Wort über das Drama!*).

Maria Magdalene was Hebbel's only tragedy in a contemporary setting, and he took care repeatedly in his critical writings to point out that his play was not to be confused with the naturalistic milieu drama on domestic themes. His purpose was to restore the tradition of bourgeois tragedy, to show that a "shattering tragic effect" could be achieved within circumscribed limits and in the narrowest walks of life, provided the playwright restricted himself to those elements which rightly belong to that sphere of life (2910 [1843]; II, 324-325). The bourgeois drama was also intended, if it were to be considered serious drama, to illuminate the historical process, i.e., to reflect the changing relationship between the individual and the moral law. It was not to serve narrow documentary purposes, like the so-called social dramas, nor become a sentimental school of practical morality, as it had been under the aegis of the twin "industrialists," the immensely prolific and popular playwrights, Iffland and Kotzebue. Insofar as the action of a drama was in itself meaningful, that is, symbolic of the historical process, it made no difference whether it was set in a higher or a lower social sphere, "whether the hand of the clock was made out of gold or out of brass." What the contemporary practitioners of the bourgeois drama failed to see—and Hebbel considered *Maria Magdalene* exemplary in this respect—was that the tragedy lay in the inherently constricted life of that middle stratum of society in which individuals incapable of dialectic stand opposed to each other, confined as it were, within their narrow circle; hence the resultant constraint, the terrible bigotry, of life which is typically and properly the ground of tragic conflict in the bourgeois or domestic drama (Preface to *Maria Magdalene*).

In making this distinction between the naturalistic drama which represented external social conditions that led to individual misfortune and the bourgeois tragedy proper which had to do with the broadly moral conduct of its characters, Hebbel pointed to the two main types of realistic social drama which all but dominated the European stage in the next hundred years. He obviously regarded the first type as an easy, temporarily fashionable, reflection of the misery of current social circumstances, but in his sense of the word, of no historical importance; whereas, for him, the bourgeois tragedy portrayed the necessary suffering and even the destruction of the human being caught in an insoluble moral dilemma. In other words, the truly social tragedy had to do with a historically significant dialectic of moral claims; it was founded on the age-old law that the assertion of an individual right inevitably causes a tremor of wrong somewhere in the web of social relations. Again, there are no sinful characters; their intentions are valid yet hopelessly inflexible, like the father's in *Maria Magdalene*. Anton's exclamation before the final curtain is characteristic of Hebbel's view of the purpose and the domain of bourgeois tragedy: "I don't understand the world any more!" Hebbel is here a forerunner of Ibsen's social drama of the middle period, particularly of the plays of the 1880s like *Ghosts*, *The Wild Duck*, and *Rosmersholm*, in which the terrible constraint of life represented as a powerful moral claim entails tragic suffering. Ibsen, of course, created a moral dialectic which was characteristically his own and rich in dramatic ironies beyond Hebbel's drier, historical imagination. But essentially he shared Hebbel's point of view and also shunned the documentary form of social play.

Hebbel, moreover, predicted the direction in which the modern drama was ultimately liable to move, given the motive of social protest and the desire for realistic stagecraft as an end in itself. It might move closer and closer toward the banal perception of reality which the common spectator brought to the theater. The ordinary play, he wrote, deals with commonplace circumstances and the most ordinary people. It need not, therefore, struggle to gain credibility since that is granted as a matter of course; you can meet the hero on every street and, what's more, his life's destiny too. But the genuine, "poetic" drama cannot even exist unless it break with this world and build up another in its stead, whether in the sitting room of the ordinary citizen or in the throne room of the king. Thus, unless there was a primitive confusion of art and life, realism could never be an artistic end, but only a means toward illusion, a way of bringing the forms created by the imagination into a certain degree of harmony with reality itself (5996 [1862]; IV, 231). In any case, the purpose of drama was not primarily imitation of reality. And there lay the trouble with the new concept of social tragedy.

Besides, such a drama could never lead to tragedy since it did not admit the question of guilt and reconciliation. As a point of departure, it led rather to the dissolution of tragedy, in fact, to satire which hurls into the face of the moral world its glaring contradictions and paradoxes (6287 [1863]; IV, 344-345). And such a satire could express itself only in the comic mode or in a genre which he called modern tragi-comedy, where the spectator is frozen with horror, while his face twitches with repressed laughter. Hebbel described the new genre as one in which a tragic fate appeared in untragic form, an action in which we have on one side the struggling protagonist in the process of being annihilated whereas on the other side we have, not the rightful, justified, moral power, but a marsh of foul circumstances that swallows up thousands of victims without deserving a single one, in effect a power of senseless evil, giving rise to a paradoxical, even a ludicrous situation. He expressed his fear that certain events in modern times, however important they might be, could be dramatized only in this hybrid form because it alone was capable of producing the effect of terror and absurdity at the same time. It would be necessary to represent, not the conflict between the conviction of one side and the conviction of the other, which could assume tragic form, but rather the struggle against *interests* (Dedication to *Ein Trauerspiel in Sizilien*). In short, he foresaw that a drama based on the relativity of values and exploring the consequently paradoxical nature of human motivation and conduct must become either a wry satirical comedy, if the playwright chose to attack social injustice, or a kind of tragic farce, if he emphasized man's desperate plight in succumbing to his arbitrary fate in a world devoid of any recognizable moral center. From our vantage point a hundred years later, we recognize this as a prophetic account of a theater of the absurd.

Hebbel was possibly the first critic to suggest that we ought to distinguish between the purpose or the end of a dramatic representation and the emotions which it was supposed to arouse. "Aristotle had perhaps a worse effect on the art of drama by his statement that tragedy should arouse fear and pity than by the theory of the unities. And yet the statement is correct if we take it to be only a description of the emotional effect of a genuine tragedy, not a definition of its purpose" (3525 [1845]; III, 68). He himself insisted that the emotional effect, though important, was incidental, and that the dramatic mode was above all suited to reflect the dialectic of historical events. This purpose of giving a realistic account of the condition of man and the world at a given moment in history was also applicable to the drama of contemporary life, as in *Maria Magdalene*. In reviving the bourgeois tragedy, Hebbel felt that it would have to be realistic in this sense, not merely edifying in the narrowly moral sense, like its eighteenth-century ancestors, or sentimentally accommodating to the modern audiences, like the still popular brand of domestic drama.

This way of defining the new function of the drama, and above all of tragedy, in terms of its relation to history was Hebbel's main contribution to the modern poetic. His example gave the serious modern drama a much needed intellectual, even a semiphilosophical, basis which permitted it to make a fresh beginning at a time when the theater had practically lost its function of representing the moral consciousness of the community. He knew, of course, that he was fighting a losing battle since the more popular and entertaining forms of drama were, as always, inundating the stage. The example of Scribe and his progeny, supported by their critical apostle, Francisque Sarcey, would educate the European audiences in the sophistications of the well-made play. But what Hebbel did not know was that Henrik Ibsen, well trained in the brilliant dramatic technique of the school of Scribe, would none the less create a modern theater in terms of the new poetic.

3

The next generation of playwright-critics, Zola and Strindberg, developed the modern poetic in a different direction. They were equally sensitive to the temper of their time, and specifically to the demands of a modern, progressive age upon its lagging theater, which was either hidebound in its romantic conventions or inane in its pursuit of technique. But they were also less conscious than Hebbel of the continuity of the Western dramatic tradition and therefore spoke of the new drama which they envisaged as nothing short of revolutionary. They predicted radical and necessary changes in the art form itself, reflecting the new modes of thought: scientific inquiry, the detailed study of social conditions, observation and experiment. In doing so, they prepared the way for a kind of drama which became the staple commodity of our theaters: technically adroit in giving the illusion of everyday reality and subjecting that reality to sociological and psychological analysis.

Less intelligent as dramatic critics than Hebbel, but pragmatic in their attitude toward the theater, the new generation of theorists and practitioners of naturalism carried certain elements implicit in the modern poetic to their logical conclusion. Hebbel had understood that the modern drama, if it was to be more than synthetic excitement or distraction for a mass audience, must represent the individual's changing relationship to the institutions and moral sanctions of his time. Thus the primarily rational and historical understanding of man in a temporal context was to be the modern equivalent of the mythological and religious view of the human condition in the old drama. The moral exemplum was to be replaced by the historical instance, pretending to the same universal validity though on a naturalistic plane of discourse. In short, Hebbel created a poetic based on a philosophy of history which could satisfy the modern rational mind. But though the modern tragedy had lost its metaphysical perspective, for Hebbel it still retained its character, if not of public ritual, at least of a formal and solemn action rehearsing the recurrent process of tragic conflict in human affairs. He resisted the merely realistic image of life on stage; the truth of his dramatization of the historical moment depended not on verisimilitude, but on a symbolic repetition of the real clash of moral principles seen in historical perspective. The dialectic structure of the drama was of course perfectly suited to the representation of man in his changing relationship to the Idea of his time.

The naturalists went one step further, at least in their theoretical pronouncements, and claimed that the modern drama should reflect life directly, without idealizing the image in any way, either morally or philosophically. The work of art thereby lost its status as symbol of a preconceived tragic vision; rather, it took on the character of a meticulous sociological study, rendered in sharp detail by means of the modern tools of the inquisitive intellect, observation and analysis. An authentic imitation of reality would automatically yield a true image of man and society. In Zola's *Naturalism in the Theater* (1881), the two catchwords have almost become interchangeable: truth (*le vrai*; *la vérité moderne*) and reality (*le drame réel qui se joue sous nos yeux*). This position not only revolutionized the technical side of the drama; it was at the same time a moral judgment which eventually made the secular and naturalistic point of view the norm in modern drama.

As a result, Zola found the term *realism* no longer suitable because as it was then understood it implied for him "a narrowing of the literary and artistic horizon" whereas the word *naturalism* designated a "widening of the domain of observation."[14] The revolutionary spirit of the naturalistic creed appears to have rejected, in theory, anything that might hamper the faithful recording of reality, in keeping with the modern demand for unadorned truth in art as well as life. Hence Zola attacked not only the lies of the romantic drama and the grand spectacles of the historical drama, but also the distortions of the *pièce à thèse* and the false theatrical conventions of the *pièce bien faite* (p. 177). So did the theorists of the previous generation, but they clearly distinguished between realism as a mode of philosophical and artistic perception and as a technique of faithful imitation. The difference between Zola and Hebbel is again instructive. The drama, Hebbel thought, should never lose itself in a banal imitation of reality. "Realism and idealism, how do they combine in the drama? In that the artist heightens the one and diminishes the other. A character, for example, should never act and speak above his sphere of life, but for that which is possible in his world let him find the purest form and the noblest expression; even the character of a peasant."[15] By contrast, the naturalists extended the poetic of the modern realistic drama in the direction of a complete identification of perception and execution, of the real object and its imitation, in order to grasp and express "the unlimited domain" of the life before them.

Zola's critical manifesto was challenging and forceful. His prediction that the general movement of naturalism in science, history, criticism and the arts must finally penetrate the drama came true. But at the same time it was a

naive assumption on his part that, given the proper respect for truth in life and art, the formal problems of art
will solve themselves. Although he considered in passing
the difficulties of "disengaging the simple formula of naturalism from the pell-mell of life" and creating the "true
poetry of humanity" out of the grotesque figure of a citizen of his time (pp. 24-25), in general he overlooked,
or else avoided, the crucial artistic problem brought up
by his identification of truth with reality and of reality
with its faithful imitation in art.

The problem is of particular importance in discussing
the poetic of modern drama because the characteristic
forms of naturalistic tragedy were determined by the
meanings which the modernists associated with the key
term *reality*. Zola was under the impression that to turn
away from the conventions of art was to break out from
a kind of confinement into the open domain of real
life; hence the refusal to be associated with realism which
had itself become a school of art or a conventional style
of expression (p. 147). And he thought that the theater in
particular offered a chance to be "more 'real' than real,
the way the novel never could be"; it invited the virtual
"elimination of its formal characteristics as art."[16] Theoretically, the opportunities were limitless; in effect all that
was needed was a dramatic genius to revolutionize the
theater and so bring it up to date with the other arts,
particularly its modern rival, the novel. Whatever skill
Dumas and Augier may have had, said Zola, they were
dwarfs alongside a man like Balzac (p. 17). The solution
was simple in his program for the restoration of the stage.
The naturalistic approach was undoubtedly the wave of
the future; it brought to art the poetry of real life which
could be found all around us; for "there is more poetry
in the small apartment of a bourgeois character than in
all the empty and worm-eaten palaces of history." This
true poetry of humanity had been brought into being in
the novel; it could also be recreated in the theater. And
Zola concluded his argument with a disarmingly simple
answer: it is only a matter of adaptation (pp. 25-26).

This double demand for a fresh approach to reality,
in keeping with the contemporary scientific mentality,
and an effort to repeat the success of the modern novel
by adapting its methods to another medium had far-
reaching consequences. Insofar as Zola's program for the
revival of the modern drama was realized in practice, it
gave a distinctive character to tragic drama as the naturalists conceived it. His enthusiastic predictions of an unlimited horizon and a wealth of fresh subject matter open
to the artist's observation proved to be too sanguine.
For the "reality" as yet unexplored by the modern dramatists and destined to become the object of their analytic
scrutiny turned out to be not a broad spectrum of human
experience or an action symbolic of modern life in general; it was rather a narrow segment of social life, reflecting the age not in terms of its characteristic moral or
intellectual *conflicts*, but by rendering a detailed picture
of the *condition* of existence in a specific contemporary
milieu. Although by traditional standards this would have
been called an impoverished version of reality, Zola and
his disciples thought that precise observation of man in
his environment, careful analysis of human behavior,
and a highly realistic account of such an "experiment"
greatly enlarged the domain of the art of drama and even
constituted in its own way a scientific conquest of nature.

But undoubtedly the attempt to adapt the drama to this
new analytic function, despite the gain in verisimilitude
and pictorial eloquence, tended to reduce the power and
impact natural to the dramatic mode by abandoning its
distinctive form, that is, physical confrontation, inner
conflict, clash of wills, dialectic of ideas. If Zola was
conscious of the loss, he considered it well worth the opportunity of applying the experimental spirit of his time
in the theater, in imitation of the modern novel. In his
preface to his own early adaptation from a novel, *Thérèse
Raquin*, he noted ruefully that it was dangerous to derive
a drama from a novel since the two modes were absolutely different. But despite the necessary amputations, he
clearly thought that the job could be done; for he began

to collaborate with a professional man of the theater in dramatizing his own novels. Their method was to reduce the novel to a series of *tableaux* which in turn would become the scenario of the new play. Thus the link between the two modes was a crude story line set firmly in visually realized scenes. The resultant conception of a naturalistic drama, adapted from the novel form, was one in which the décor, corresponding to the milieu in which the original characters lived out their lives, played an overriding part in the combination of elements that go to make up a theatrical production.[17]

For, as Zola noted explicitly, the décor has taken on the same importance in the theater which description has held in the novel. Specifically, it explained the characters and their actions; and, in general, it enlarged the domain of the drama by putting nature itself into the theater, demonstrating its effect upon man (pp. 87-88). Obviously the décor was to be henceforth strictly functional and realistic since the actor was to *live* his role *in* the stage setting rather than *play* before the public against a plausible background. An exact setting could at once establish the dramatic situation, locate the characters, and tell something about their habits of life. But a playwright like Scribe did not need a realistic milieu because his people were merely cartoon characters (p. 77). Thus the function of the décor, for Zola, was not merely to increase the illusion of reality on stage; the décor became itself a notable *dramatis persona* in the way it defined and even determined the action of the living characters. And it ought to be condemned only insofar as it abandoned that scientific function, insofar as it failed to play its part in the analysis of the action and the characters (p. 88).

The new awareness of the close relation between character and setting was bound to alter the nature of the modern drama in comparison with the traditional kinds of drama which, however diverse their forms, had this in common, that the story unfolded chiefly through the interaction of the characters, the contest of wills expressed in a series of dramatic conflicts, which did not arise from a specific milieu, but, if anything, created one. That is to say, a primarily moral or psychological conflict between human characters could be played against any convenient background; but now, in the naturalist's perception of reality, the social setting and the concrete details of the physical milieu have themselves become protagonists with an unalterable "will" of their own. Hence, the reintroduction into the naturalistic drama of an element of fatality expressed in terms of the social situation, the facts of existence, the physical circumstances-—in short, the things outside the suffering hero over which he has no control. It is significant that Zola, for example, spoke of *Thérèse Raquin* as a purely human "study" (*étude*) and similarly referred to the modern novel as *cette étude sociale et individuelle.* Theoretically both modes could serve the purpose of submitting human behavior to an exact analysis, to see modern man in the context of a precisely realized milieu. But in practice inevitable difficulties arose. Though Zola may have felt that he succeeded in finding a visual counterpart through realistic décor to the milieu, and even the indefinable atmosphere, of the novel, he still had to make severe reductions in the story line and alter such effects as were expressible only in narrative form.[18]

It became apparent to the proponents of a naturalistic theater that the narrative, descriptive, and episodic form of the novel was in fact more suitable to the study of man in his environment than the existing forms of the drama. The naturalistic playwright found himself in a peculiar dilemma. In his typical subject matter and plan of approach he wanted to represent the slow disintegration of the individual caught in a situation not of his own making; but the tools of his trade handed down to him from earlier times were a theater, geared to didactic fiction or vaudeville amusement, and an art form which apprehended life in terms of make-believe action, conflict, and resolution. He wanted to represent the oppressive force of a character's environment; he wanted to observe the gradual attrition of the modern individual by fateful circumstances. Yet the familiar idiom of his art had to do with passionate acts, villains, plots of intrigue, and rhetorical dialogue. In short, he knew that in the modern tragedy, as Georg Lukács puts it, men are destroyed epically.[19] Therefore, he must revolutionize the technique of the drama in order to grasp this newly discovered reality. The few masterpieces written from a naturalistic point of view succeeded in escaping this dilemma; that is to say, they were masterpieces because the playwrights found ways of dramatizing the recalcitrant material.

Strindberg's opening paragraphs in the preface to *Miss Julie* echo Zola's point, made fifteen years earlier in the preface to *Thérèse Raquin*, that the drama will either die or become modern and realistic. In fact, Strindberg argued that precisely in those countries in which the greatest thinkers reflected the modern temper and the development from "rudimentary and immature thought-processes" to "reflection, research and analysis," namely England and Germany, the drama *was* dead. He thought it not unlikely that "the theater, like religion, might be discarded as an outworn form for whose appreciation we lack the necessary conditions."[20] The words "reflection, research and analysis" seemed to have become a slogan in discussing the inevitable impact of the scientific spirit on modern art. But the value of Strindberg's response to the contemporary revolution of "thought-processes" and method lay in his critical ability to see the effect it must have on artistic form. Thus he was able to amplify and particularize Zola's more general vision of a naturalistic theater. He came to grips with the question of dramatic form in its various aspects: composition, characterization, setting, lighting, acting, dialogue. Whereas in Zola's manifesto we hear the voice of a man of letters, powerfully attracted to the theater as a possible instrument of realistic imitation, Strindberg writes like a man of the theater who has already mastered its possibilities as an instrument for creating different kinds of artistic illusion.

Twenty years after the writing of the preface to' *Miss
Julie*, he was again in the midst of a theatrical experiment. The general outlook of the time, he noted, had
changed from materialistic tendencies, demanding absolute verisimilitude in the theater, to an interest in the
immaterial, suggestive, imaginative side of the dramatic
art; hence, the new emphasis after the turn of the century on the spoken word against a simplified, nonrepresentational background: the experiment with short
uninterrupted "chamber plays" in a small auditorium.[21]
Compared with his fellow dramatists, Strindberg displayed an astounding flexibility; he easily abandoned
the naturalistic formula when the time seemed ripe for a
new approach.

In Strindberg's formulation of a poetic of naturalism,
we observe once more the characteristic shift since the
middle of the century from a historical and moral consciousness of human existence to a primarily sociological,
psychological and even biological interest. Zola had introduced the phrase *l'unique étude psychologique et physiologique des personnages* (*Le Naturalisme*, p. 26). The
tragic sense of historical change in Hebbel's *Maria Magdalene* found expression in the clash between the old and
the new morality, the older generation being unable to
comprehend the inevitable fact of change; the father
remains adamant in his view of life and personifies fate
or the universal law which his daughter may not break
with impunity. But *Miss Julie*, as Strindberg tells us,
represents a clash between the old and the new nobility,
between the modern tragic type, the half-woman, and her
natural superior, the valet Jean, whose "male aristocracy" is only momentarily hampered by social circumstances and his present environment. Although this subject could be conceived from the historical point of view,
Strindberg chose to base the struggle on the sociology and
biology of survival, as if to say that the fact of social

ascendancy and decline was determined by the evolution of a new species of man.

Strindberg was aware, as Zola had not been, that such new ideas and up-to-date subjects demanded a thorough-going revision of dramatic method. He was not content with Zola's facile remark that there was merely the problem of adapting the techniques of the novel to the theater. "As no new form has been devised for these new contents, the new wine has burst the old bottles." Therefore, he devoted the preface to *Miss Julie* to explaining his attempts at modernizing the form in order to meet the demands which may now be made on the art of drama. It is a credit to Strindberg's critical perception that he quickly recognized naturalism both as a philosophical point of view and as a new technique of imitation. He thereby avoided the dilemma of the modernist hampered by a dramaturgy which had evolved from a different conception of life and different conventions of expression. And on the other hand he avoided the sham effect of merely reproducing a grim picture of life to shock or to protest, a purpose to which naturalistic stagecraft without substance or idea behind it lends itself too easily.

In his discussion of the story of *Miss Julie* as a tragic subject, Strindberg did not betray a particularly profound understanding of what was happening to the genre in modern times, even under his own hands. He preferred to tease the reader about the reactions of the modern sensibility to the inevitable downfall of rotting institutions and invalid specimens of humanity. He himself could find "the joy of life in its strong and cruel struggles." Yet his personal challenge of the reader's middle-class mentality contains valuable critical insights into the naturalist's point of view and concept of tragedy. Like the modernists who found the tragic cause in the dialectic of historical events and therefore denied the dramatic motive of human guilt in strictly ethical terms, Strindberg denied the existence of absolute evil as a motive. He reasoned that the downfall of one family was simply the good fortune of another, "fortune being only compara-

tive." Therefore, in this tragedy based on the natural
principle of survival, our feeling of pity for the heroine
was solely due to weakness, in effect to our fear of sharing
the same fate. Pity, says Aristotle, is aroused by unmerited
misfortune. But given Strindberg's robust cosmology of
natural forces, there cannot be any feeling of pity except
in those who are themselves weak. "*As yet* it is tragic to
see one favoured by fortune go under, and still more to
see a family heritage die out. . . . " [Emphasis added.]
As far as he was concerned the effect of such a spectacle
was tonic, joyful, and informative.

Like Zola before him, Strindberg leveled his attack
against outmoded views as well as their conventional
dramatic expression both in the romantic and the realistic
theater. He went so far as to imply that Miss Julie's tragedy
symbolized the dissipation by Naturalism of a "Romantic
inheritance," in that her type revealed "a desperate fight
against nature." The larger historical implication was that
the new outlook, unflinching before the forces of nature
that rule our lives, discovered a distinct modern type of
tragic character. He or she has always existed in real
life, but only in the light of the new naturalistic dispensation did the tragic inadequacy of such a character come
clearly to the fore. Yet the current forms of drama did not
serve his purpose. Strindberg realized that neither the
modern romantic nor the realistic dramaturgy with its
"simple stage characters" and mathematical dialogue
could do justice to the new insights into the complexity of
motivation and conduct. Nor did Ibsen's dramatic technique of the 1880s, beginning with *Ghosts*, seem to strike
a responsive chord, perhaps because he was so bitterly
critical of Ibsen's social ideas.

Significantly, Strindberg associated the lagging development of dramatic technique, the inability of the drama
to reflect the ferment of new ideas, with the long-stand-
ing rule of the middle class over the theater. For example,
character, according to the "middle-class conception of
the immobility of the soul," meant exhibiting a single and
easily apprehensible trait, and "a character came to sig-

nify a man fixed and finished"—a deadening simplifi-
cation of psychology as well as ethics. Strindberg con-
gratulated himself on the multiplicity of motives at work
behind the action and the dialogue of *Miss Julie*.[22] In fact,
in terms of the conventional method of characterization,
his figures might be regarded as "characterless," since
they did not with every word or gesture announce their
individual temperament or play their fixed roles. Having
discovered that in real life an action was generally caused
by a series of motives, the naturalists were bound to be
dissatisfied with the stylized imitations of people and
events on stage. Besides, since the novel was able to render
the "soul-complex" of its persons, it was necessary now to
challenge the old-fashioned ethos and the untrue characterizations of the popular stage. Strindberg mentioned in
particular the documentary (or "monographic") novels,
as he called them, of the brothers de Goncourt in connection with the modern demand of audiences to be taken behind the scenes, as it were; to be made privy to the psychological process animating the action; to be shown, not
only what happens, but how it happens. At times he himself found more freedom as an author in the novel form
than in the theater.

But the ultimate reason for Strindberg's technical
"innovations" was not merely that he wanted to achieve
a complete illusion of life, though his remarks on plot,
character, scenery, lights, and acting were directed to that
end. Rather these new techniques of showing his characters "vacillating, disintegrated, a blend of old and new
. . . conglomerations of past and present stages of civilization" were necessary to his conception of the modern
tragic type, "living in a period of transition more fever-
ishly hysterical than its predecessor at least." The grim
spectacle of the disintegration of such a person in the
context of the modern equivalent of Fate or Universal Law
may be said to constitute a fresh conception and a new
form of tragic drama. The theme of the weak or foolish
giving up their power to the strong is, of course, an age-
old motif in tragic drama. One may think of the struggle

between Richard II and Bolingbroke as being also in part
a matter of sheer survival as the degenerate king must
give way "to the new nobility of nerve and brain" (to
use Strindberg's modern terminology). But the main
question in the older drama is always one of moral guilt,
and therefore the tragic conception and the dramatic
idiom are bound to be different. "The Naturalist," says
Strindberg, "has abolished guilt with God"; consequently,
the modern author-analyst gives us a complex, documentary
drama in which the hero has become entirely the victim
and perishes as a result of his defective personality and
the pressure of outward circumstances.

And the dispassionate, analytical attitude demands a
corresponding leveling down of the language. The naturalistic tragedy is characteristic of the time which produced it, and Strindberg described his time as "skeptical,
unfeeling, and democratic," hence suspicious of large
gestures and emotions. A slight aura of doubt, even
apathy, envelops the modern stage so that, as he says,
King Lear looks unrestrained, and Timon can no longer
arouse pity when he is abandoned by those who had flat-
tered him. Should the time come, Strindberg concluded,
when men will regain their feeling and view the world
in terms other than zoological, the repertoire will also
have to change and it will have to be played differently.[23]

Finally, it is well to remember that the naturalistic
mode, although it brought the author down off his
"stilts" and spoke the flattened language of the "wild
mob" (these are Strindberg's terms), was yet for some
time considered an exclusive, elite theatrical entertainment. For it searched seriously after "nature or reality,
truth" in a place which commonly had been used to dis-
pensing histrionics, versified commonplaces, and awesome outbursts of passion, as well as alcoholic spirits
through the concessionaire during extensive intermis-
sions. By comparison, the naturalist made strenuous demands on the intellect of his audience; he recommended
an intense, uninterrupted evening's experience in a
small theater where nothing could divert the spectator's

attention. A performance of *Ghosts* or even the more sensuously appealing *Miss Julie* would naturally tax an audience accustomed to the conventional theater beyond endurance. The general acceptance of the naturalistic mode was reluctant and slow, but it was inevitable unless the theater was to be abandoned as an anachronism. The poetic of naturalism emerged in response to a crisis in the drama; it pointed to the glaring disparity between the intellectual tenor of the times and forms of drama which had become the meaningless vestiges of an earlier revolution in the theater.

NOTES

1. "Four Elizabethan Dramatists," *Selected Essays* (New York: Harcourt, Brace, 1932), p. 93.
2. *The Old Drama and the New: An Essay in Re-valuation* (Boston, 1923), pp. 305-320, 360.
3. For example, in Zola's *Le Naturalisme au théâtre* the two catchwords, *truth* and *reality*, have become almost interchangeable. See Otto Mann's "Weltanschauliche Grundlagen der gegenwärtigen Situation des Dramas," *Der Deutschunterricht*, 5 (1953), No. 5, 5-19, for a detailed discussion of the changing function of the new drama and the old.
4. *Das moderne Drama*, ed. Paul A. Merbach (Berlin, 1924), p. 80. Subsequent references will be indicated in the text.
5. See Hegel's *Aesthetik*, III, 540 ff., 571-572, *Sämtliche Werke* (Stuttgart, 1954).
6. In a letter to Gottfried Keller, quoted by his editor, Hettner spoke of his task in relation to Aristotle's *Poetics (Das moderne Drama*, p.iv).
7. *Otto Ludwigs Gesammelte Schriften*, ed. Adolf Stern (Leipzig, 1891), V, 53-55. Subsequent references to the *Shakespeare-Studien* will be indicated in the text.
8. Is it the task of tragedy, Ludwig asked with reference to Hebbel's *Agnes Bernauer*, to give explanations to our understanding for that which hurts our understanding, but to which our sensibility remains indifferent (p. 360)?
9. *Tagebücher*, ed. R. M. Werner (Berlin: B. Behr's Verlag, 1903), 1034 (1838); I, 223. Subsequent references to the Diaries will be identified in the text by entry number, year, volume and page in this edition.
10. Compare 2440 (1842); II, 138: "What we call life is the presumptuousness of a part face to face with the whole. . . ."
11. Letter to Eduard Janinsky, Vienna, August 14, 1848, with reference to *Herodes und Mariamne*. Hebbel boasted repeatedly that his drama had no villains and needed no sin to destroy the protagonist. For example, Agnes Bernauer became the "purest victim" of historical and moral necessity. She must be destroyed, he explained to the director

of the first production, since her fate involved her in a conflict between an absolute and a positive claim. She was to him "the Antigone of modern times" (Letter to Franz Dingelstedt, Vienna, January 26, 1852).

12. Letter to Elise Lensing, Paris, December 5, 1843.

13. *TDR*, 2 (May, 1958), 66-67.

14. Emile Zola, *Le Naturalisme au théâtre, Oeuvres Complètes* (Paris: François Bernouard, 1927-1929), XLII, 147. Subsequent references to this volume will be indicated in the text.

15. *Tagebücher*, 5328 (1854); IV, 37.

16. Martin Kanes, "Zola and Busnach: The Temptation of the Stage," *PMLA*, 77 (1962), 115.

17. Ibid., pp. 112, 114.

18. Ibid., pp. 110-111; e.g., in *L'Assommoir* and *Germinal*. Twenty years after Zola had launched his campaign to renovate the theater by bringing it up to date with the novel, Ferdinand Brunetière in his essay, *Le Loi du théâtre* (1894), protested against the blurring of the distinction between these two essentially opposite genres: "The material or the subject of a novel or of a play may . . . be the same at bottom; but they become drama or novel only by the manner in which they are treated; and the manner is not merely different, it is opposite. One will never be able, therefore, to transfer to the stage any novels except those which are already dramatic; and note well that they are dramatic only to the extent to which their heroes are truly the architects of their destiny" (trans. Philip M. Hayden).

19. "Zur Soziologie des modernen Dramas," *Archiv für Sozialwissenschaft und Sozialpolitik*, 38 (1914), 692.

20. "Author's Foreword" to *Miss Julie*, trans. Elizabeth Sprigge, in *Six Plays of Strindberg* (Doubleday Anchor Books, 1956), p. 61. This translation is used for all subsequent quotations from the preface.

21. Compare *Open Letters to the Intimate Theater*, trans. Walter Johnson (Seattle: University of Washington Press, [1967]), pp. 289-290.

22. His debt to "the leading writers of naturalistic fiction in France" and to the "scientific psychological literature of the period" is discussed in B. G. Madsen, *Strindberg's Naturalistic Theatre* (Seattle: University of Washington Press, 1962), pp. 70-80.

23. *Letters to the Intimate Theater*, pp. 138-140.

2. TRAGEDY IN THE THEATER OF REALISM

The great traditional examples of dramatic theory, Aristotle's *Poetics*, Dryden's *Essay of Dramatic Poesy*, Coleridge's Shakespearean criticism, were written after the fact; that is, they looked back upon a body of dramatic work which had proved its power to move and had stood up to the test of experience. In the view of these critics the tragic poet was primarily an artist, a maker, who had the skill (or even the God-given gift) to express the human comedy or tragedy in dramatic form. Therefore, the traditional poetic was largely formal in nature; it was a critical rationale of that skill or, as sometimes in Coleridge's case, an adoration of that imaginative gift. The new poetic, which emerged in the nineteenth century, did not analyze established forms of drama in order to determine their excellence; on the contrary, its aim was to abandon set forms which were no longer expressive of modern philosophical views and modern dramatic subjects. The new dramatic theory was prophetic of things to come. It regarded the playwright not so much as a skilled and inspired artist, as the purveyor of new knowledge.

The modern theorists, from Hebbel to Strindberg, and their eloquent exponent early in this century, Georg Lukács, sought to determine the major features of the new drama on the basis of a changed outlook on life. A new tragic theater would have to come into being, cognizant of modern theories of history, sociology, psychology, and biology. The modern tragedy itself would become a form of inquiry or re-examination of man's estate in the world and thus possess cognitive value. It would extend the range of our perceptions and understanding. And indeed, perhaps the outstanding characteristic of the new drama is that it

41

directs our attention inquisitively and exclusively to the
phenomenal world. The plot, as medium of imitation, no
longer re-enacts an archetypal action, like the Greek legends or the moral allegories which Shakespeare fashioned
out of historical and fictional sources; on the contrary,
the new drama attempts an artistic conquest of external
reality, in an effort to understand the natural and social
forces, the ineluctable fate, to which the modern individual is exposed. From this basic change in the function of
the drama we can derive a number of general characteristics of modern tragedy as the realists and naturalists conceived it.[1]

But we should be clear at the outset that it is realism and
naturalism understood as an intellectual point of view or
attitude toward human existence which determine the
characteristic forms of modern tragedy; realism as a technique of faithful imitation has for the moment little bearing on the questions with which we are concerned. The
distinction is important. It was self-evident to the architects of the poetic of realistic drama in the nineteenth
century. And it allows us, for example, to understand the
difference between two modern plays like Tolstoi's *The
Power of Darkness* and Miller's *Death of a Salesman*. Miller writes in the realistic tradition, although in the staging
of his play there was no attempt at giving a lifelike illusion.
The setting, the lighting, the music, the evocation of Loman's hallucinations were far removed from the conventional practice of realistic production. On the other hand,
Tolstoi's imitation of the daily life of the Russian peasant
is deceptively realistic. He delineates the bestial conduct
of his characters in meticulous detail; few naturalistic
plays can match the shocking presentation of Nikita's
murder of the newborn baby. Yet by the time the last curtain comes down, it is clear that Tolstoi wrote a modern
morality play. Nikita's confession before God and the
community testifies to the truth of a religious conviction;
and the play as a whole exemplifies the traditional pattern
of temptation, sin, the turning from the good angel (father
Akim), deeper sin, despair, and finally the act of con-

trition. Tolstoi reenacts the allegory of the fall and redemption in keeping with a Christian conception of the human condition and in the manner of the old drama, but his *technique* is scrupulously realistic, except that Nikita's sudden illumination of spirit cannot have a rational motivation.

The main impulse of the realistic drama is to see things as they are, to gain a rational understanding of the causes for human suffering in a given situation. Hence the typical role which the realist playwright assumes is that of the historian who dramatizes the significant moment of conflict between the individual and his social milieu. "The dramatic poet is in my view nothing but a historian," said Büchner in 1835; and in a pointed rejection of idealism in art he continued, "His highest task is to come as close as possible to the historical event as it really happened. His work should not be any more nor any less moral than *history itself.*"[2] Hettner and Hebbel, as we have seen, were convinced that the highest form of drama was that which mirrored the dialectic process of history. More recently, Hauptmann maintained the same point of view of the realist with even greater conviction: "Every drama is a historical drama; there is no other."[3] And among our contemporary playwrights, Miller puts himself squarely in this realistic tradition. He cites the cognitive function of the new drama: "Drama is akin to the other inventions of man in that it ought to help us to know more, and not merely to spend our feelings." Every genuine new form of the drama makes possible a "new and heightened consciousness . . . of causation in the light of known but hitherto inexplicable effects." And he too rediscovers the historical function of the modern dramatist: "A new poem on the stage is a new concept of relationships between the one and the many and the many and history, and to create it requires greater attention, not less, to the inexorable, common, pervasive conditions of existence in this time and this hour."[4]

The dramatist as historian perceives the social situation, and more narrowly the physical milieu, as the condition of a tragic action. He is as much interested in the role of the determining historical circumstances as he is in the role of the suffering individual; and he attempts to present the resultant conflict or the inescapable dilemma as a concrete instance of modern man's subjection to time conceived as history or to natural forces beyond his power. The tragic conception need not, however, be fully deterministic, though the purely naturalistic play tends to view the individual as a victim of environmental and hereditary, i.e. psychological or biological, forces. From Hebbel to Miller, there is a distinct tradition of realistic tragic writing which conceives of the individual as a protagonist with a will of his own, which, in other words, allows for the interplay between historical necessity and individual freedom. Yet also in this respect the difference remains absolute between the old drama and the new; for the hero of the new drama is the representative of a moment in history and a distinct stratum of society, whereas the Greek or Shakespearean hero symbolizes the human condition in a timeless context of universal powers. The free act of self-assertion or challenge may appear to be the same, yet in one instance the necessity lies in the way of the world so that the tragedy is the result of conditions at a given time, whereas in the other instance the necessity lies in the inexorable consequences of a moral commitment, where the momentary circumstances do not function as an independent fatalistic power, but only as an instrument of supernatural agencies.

The modern tragic hero, as Hebbel perceived, is the meeting point of clashing ideas. He is witness and victim of a dynamic social or historical change. (This is as true of Danton, Saint Joan, and John Proctor as it is of figures in plays on nonhistorical subjects, like Mrs. Alving, Miss Julie, and Willy Loman.) Consequently, as Georg Lukács has pointed out, a new form of the conflict between generations comes into being. The scene of the new drama is in this case the meeting point between two worlds separated in time, and with the end of each tragedy a whole world collapses since the difference between the generations is a radical ethical difference. The conflict has to do with the relative claims of different values at a given moment of confrontation.[5] Thus, the contrast between a family tragedy like *Maria Magdalene* and *King Lear*. In Shakespeare the fathers' errors unleash evil in the children, causing the destruction of both generations, but every action, whether for evil or good, derives its meaning from the unalterable moral framework which embraces both generations. Therefore the world of Edgar and Albany and Kent stands firm at the end; it is the timeless norm of love, allegiance, and patience in suffering. And the convulsive clash between the generations turns out to be an episode of individual error and sin *sub specie aeternitatis*. But in the modern play Hebbel views the strict morality of the older generation as a historical phenomenon, subject to the pressures of a changing world. He questions its validity in the contemporary social circumstances; and it is precisely because the father raises his fundamentalist convictions to the status of iron law in his household that the conflict between the generations must end tragically.

What interests the modern dramatist is not the tragic change of the hero (*quantum mutatus ab illo*: "O, woe is me/ T'have seen what I have seen, see what I see!") within an accepted frame of ideal moral order, but the tragic role of the individual either as victim of an inflexible, institutionalized social order or as agent and sacrificial victim at the point of collision between old and new ideologies. A thoroughly modern aphorism reads, "In a war of ideas it is people who get killed."[6] Since the fate of the modern hero can be understood only in the context of a historical moment of change or a compelling social milieu, his role is partially defined by factors external to his personality. He suffers before he acts, or as Hebbel put it more accurately, the suffering gives birth to action. Therefore, the modern protagonist, like Hamlet, seems to have lost the cue to independent action or at best tries to escape his dilemma in a desperate final act. He is a passive figure compared with the traditional heroes who suffer in consequence of a free act of commitment, right or wrong; whatever motives for action he has, they are not alone derived from his individual character or from a moral conviction or a specific passion, but are in part given by the situation in which he finds himself.

Hebbel had predicted that Shakespeare's dialectic of characters would be replaced by a dialectic of ideas in the new drama, thus reducing the modern protagonist to the role of agent and victim of forces beyond him; he would have to *react* to circumstances not of his own making. And in the view of the disciples of naturalism, the modern individual could never be (in Brunetière's phrase) "the architect of his own destiny"; he was to be shown as a corporate part of society, placed in a given milieu and suffering under the inescapable facts of modern life. In their determined rejection of all forms of romantic idealism, the realists and naturalists of the latter part of the nineteenth century embraced this bleak view of the human condition as the only honest one. They refused to grant their protagonists resources of energy and inspiration to shape and suffer their own destiny since that would have been a falsification of the actual conditions of existence in modern society.

The typical conception of the hero's role in the new drama was an inevitable result of the task which the realists and naturalists set themselves: to mirror the contemporary world with scrupulous attention to historical, sociological and psychological facts. Hence, on the one hand we have Strindberg's claim that the characterization in his drama is both a more faithful rendering of life and much more complex than that of the older drama. But on the other hand such a conception of character as being the product of multiple external and internal forces also reduces the hero's autonomy; thus it calls into question the possibility of a tragic act and, beyond that, even the possibility of dramatic action and dialogue, which was Brunetière's criticism of the new drama.

Not long after the first flush of excitement over the renascence of the modern drama had worn off, Georg

Lukács worked out the sociological implications and their formal consequences in the development of this new social drama, recognizing the crucial shift of focus in the modern conception of tragedy. If the tragic act is no longer a matter of free moral choice, if, on the contrary, the human agent is so inextricably connected with his background, his time, the ideological atmosphere, and a given social situation that his will cannot be considered autonomous, the relation of the doer to his deed must be called into question. If he is not responsible for his deed, since the motivation has been largely determined by social forces and circumstances around him, can we still speak of tragedy? Lukács clearly saw the risk that naturalism might reduce the human actor to the position of a figure on a chessboard and thus become altogether nondramatic. But in answering this question, he took his cue from Hebbel who faced the same dilemma in his critical speculations half a century earlier. From a realistic, historical point of view, the domination of the character by his situation, of the actor by his act, is undeniable. The problem, then, is "to build a bridge between the deed and the doer," to find another point of view by which, all "scientific" facts to the contrary, the autonomy of the tragic actor can be saved.[7] Hebbel had found it in his conception of tragic guilt, which was for him not merely a "way out" in order to preserve the genre in modern times, but a moral and an artistic insight showing the personal cost of the dialectic war of ideas. Guilt, in Hebbel's view, accompanies all human action insofar as individual self-assertion, representing a single ethical claim, comes in conflict with the general will. In *Maria Magdalene*, for example, he had set himself the task of deriving the idea of guilt without resorting to positively evil motives. Ibsen shared this tragic vision in his social plays, but in his late work, in an effort to overcome the ambiguous motivation inherent in the naturalistic outlook, he resorted to the idea of the demonic, returning to his heroes a measure of autonomy and moral presumption reminiscent of the tragic aura of the older drama.

But Lukács, though he writes incisively about the dilemma of the realistic social drama and the naturalistic
milieu drama, was evidently so intent upon defending
them as new forms of tragedy that he minimized, quite
unnecessarily, the difference between two distinct tragic
experiences. It makes no difference, he says, whether the
will which resists fate originates entirely inside the human
actor or not, whether it is free or determined by circumstances. The conflict of forces in the latter instance is, in
fact, more complex and more interesting so long as the
inner power of resistance lasts. But what of the dramatic
quality of such a conflict? Again Hebbel clarified the
problem for him by his perception that in the modern
situation suffering is equivalent to an inwardly directed
action and that every act in opposition to one's fate assumes the form of suffering. Lukács makes an excellent
case for the tragic stature of the modern hero: his will
is not his own, he is driven to defend himself, he acts from
desperation and necessity—yet the intensity of his commitment is such that he symbolizes the fate of the modern
individual in a conflict of essentially abstract forces. The
new drama demonstrates that an idea or a social value can
serve as a powerful motive, and if it is made palpable
dramatically as a passionate tenacity in suffering and action, it can assume tragic proportions.[8]

Obviously, the nature of the tragic experience is altered
in the modern social drama. In the classic tragic theaters,
whether Greek, Elizabethan, or French, where the moral
order of the universe was predetermined, the hero lost
his autonomy only as a consequence of his freely chosen
course of action. In contrast, the modern drama must
first delineate the complex social order which is to be the
arena of the hero's possible actions; it must each time
create a rational structure of ideas, events, and psychological motives which defines the protagonist and at the
same time foreshadows his sealed fate. Thus it embraces
a wider and more analytic consciousness of the forces
outside the human character which initially formulate his
tragic predicament. This consciousness becomes part of

the tragic experience, as, for example, the dialectic scene between Warwick and Cauchon in *Saint Joan*. The tragic necessity is given at once, in the situation as it unfolds, rather than surmised in the moral consequences of an act disruptive of a universally accepted order. Thus, Strindberg's remark that the naturalists have abolished guilt with God in their dramas is not to be taken as testimony of widespread unbelief; it only shows that the basis of tragic guilt in the new drama is not necessarily ethical. The fourth scene of *Saint Joan* in effect seals the Maid's tragic fate since she cannot swerve from an idea which she embodies, yet neither Warwick nor Cauchon, and least of all Joan herself can be considered guilty in the moral sense.

These new premises of the realistic and naturalistic drama have so changed the conception and the esthetic form of tragedy that not only our intellectual but also our emotional response must be different. Tragic irony in the traditional sense has disappeared. In the Aristotelian view it depended on *peripeteia*, a "good" intention reversed. And since the fate of the legendary heroes was a matter of public knowledge, even the first entrance of Oedipus was a powerful stroke of irony. Beneath the royal robes of the self-confident king the audience must have seen the beggar in exile, groping in the darkness. In the Shakespearean tragedy the audience could recognize the fatal error long before the hero did—an ironic distancing from the hero. But significantly this is not the case in *Hamlet*, in this respect the most "modern" of Shakespeare's tragedies, where from the start the hero is placed in a complex and baffling situation to which he must *react*. Under these circumstances tragic irony in the classic sense is impossible because, as the Romantic critics indicated, we *are* the oppressed hero. Similarly, as an audience of common men, we instinctively recognize the reality of modern life in the caged existence of Woyzeck or Mrs. Alving or Willy Loman. With the loss of tragic irony, however, we also experience the loss of a sense of pity. Since the modern playwrights typically assume the role of advocate or executioner, and not the role of judge (Otto Ludwig), and since we tend to identify ourselves with the realistically portrayed characters, the emotional effect of the new tragic drama is sometimes terror, but more often self-pity.

Of course, different forms of incidental irony are still possible in the new drama, but the pervasive sense of tragic irony predicated on the blindness of the hero is gone. In its stead the modern drama often produces a sense of tragic paradox predicated on the guiltless guilt of the modern hero; the world cannot tolerate his momentary inspirations, his dreams, his gestures of independence, in short his attempts at asserting his individual being, however good his intentions may be. But not only may a personal idea transformed into purpose clash with the impersonal laws of nature or society, sometimes his very being, the fact of human existence, can become a tragic motive. At this point the feeling of helplessness gives way to the feeling of despondency; the best of these dramas, from *Woyzeck* to *Death of a Salesman*, elicit a response which is necessarily distinct from the classic formulation, pity and terror.

Helplessness and despondency are typically private feelings. They are possible because in the modern drama, unlike the traditional theaters, the community has no stake in the tragic action. In fact, the community as the determinant of social values and the ground of moral judgment has disappeared; so has the community as a central consciousness or a body capable of suffering misfortune, as expressed by the theatrical device of the chorus or choric characters. The modern concept of *society*, though it may presuppose the quality of cohesiveness as well as diversity, does not carry the meaning of commonweal in the sense that the audience as a whole responds to the hero's fate. What happens to him may happen to the individual spectator, but his action and suffering make no difference to the society as a whole. That is to say, he is never an object of danger and revulsion or of celebration and pity. He is never expelled from the community or sacrificed for the commonweal.

"The time will demand a social drama," said the nineteenth-century critics. They were correct, and what they meant was that society itself would become an object of analysis. Dramatically, it would become one of the chief actors in a tragic struggle put on view for the modern audience. A great historic struggle may signal a modification in social values, but in general the social structure survives unaffected. Thus society has become a dramatic agent, a stage concept, a given set of imperturbable powers, and our response as single spectators is directed to the private motives, the suffering and the destruction of the individual protagonist. From this point of view, Eliot's *Murder in the Cathedral* is an instructive compromise between the old drama and the new. The society, the temporal power, serves as antagonist, making Becket's martyrdom possible, yet the action and the suffering of the hero is at the same time a communal matter—the women of Canterbury suffer and in their suffering get to know the meaning of Becket's action. Eliot attempts to recreate the fusion of audience and chorus in a communal consciousness.

The developing concept of the social drama, as well as the novel relationship between hero and spectator, brings with it characteristic formal changes. In particular, the function and, therefore, the form of the plot in the new drama adapt themselves to altered purposes. If by plot in its most general sense we mean the arrangement of incidents amounting to an intention (i.e., giving direction to a complex experience), the ends which the playwright has in view will determine his means. If the end of a tragic action is to arouse pity and fear, Aristotle's law of probability or necessity is a reasonable deduction to make as to the best formal arrangement of the incidents; in a "complex" plot it insures the effects of inevitability and surprise. Shakespeare's mixed logical and analogical plot structures serve in turn his view of the drama as *exem-*

plum or as analogue of the fall of man; thus Cassio's temptation and subsequent loss of reputation in the second act prefigure Othello's greater temptation and fall. On the other hand, the end of the modern social drama is to render, not Everyman's disruption of the moral law and his consequent destruction, but every man's potentially fatal involvement with the external and internal forces that shape his life; the end is to explore and, as Otto Mann has said, to interpret reality. But the pattern of such an analytic and mimetic rendering of life need not be logical, nor is it prefigured in myth or any known symbolic action.

The classical conviction that poetry (i.e. tragedy) is more philosophical than history and the Christian humanist corollary that it is morally preferable eventually give way to the notion of the modern realistic writer that the serious drama should be a faithful interpretation of history. For, to him, the historical or sociological event is inescapable fact which needs to be understood in itself as a determinant of the human condition; it is the sum of reality. Thus plot in the traditional sense, which is the imposition of a symbolic pattern upon the recognizable events of life or the logical ordering of moral consequences, is likely to disappear. That is why the "well-made" plot, a pale vestige of the law of probability or necessity, when it is used for serious purposes in the social drama, leaves the impression of disingenuousness. For the explicit aim of realistic drama is to imitate history in the making; consequently, the devices of an irrelevant logic betray the intention of demonstrating a moral lesson or a sociological thesis. Therefore, the realistic and naturalistic playwrights who looked to the possibility of a modern tragic drama avoided this exercise in form without substance. They preferred to analyze inductively the significant relation of character to milieu and the course of a human passion as it would naturally develop.

Ibsen, who was attracted both by temperament and training to the logical plot, converted the formula of the well-made plot to usefulness in his tragic drama by placing the center of gravity in the moral choice of his characters rather than on the fatal play of misstep and accidental discovery. He became, in effect, a classical dramatist, increasingly devoted to the moral and symbolical representation of human failure rather than the strictly analytic and historical representation of reality. The possibility of abandoning the traditional plot structures presented itself to the less conservative dramatists as a result of their new conception of the function of the drama and the example of the novel as a flourishing art form. Hence the tendency toward epic form in the drama, which was due to the effort to trace the process of historical change and the evolution of ideas. Zola tried to reproduce on stage the effect of the physical and social milieu upon the lives of individuals. And Strindberg noted with interest that *Hamlet* was "novelistic." On the assumption that the suffering and the defeat of the modern hero was due to a multiplicity of causes which could be explained in their cumulative effect, the traditional logical plot lost its relevance to this new view of tragic necessity. The modern dramatist as historian, sociologist, and psychologist tends to present his case in its devious, concrete, and intellectual ramifications; he lets the intellectual perception of a tragic dilemma emerge from a sequence of scenes which is no less compelling than the dramatically logical operation of Nemesis. The deterioration of the formal plot in Webster's tragedies anticipates the reflective, self-conscious mode of the modern drama. Evidently Shaw refused to be bound by the strict logic of dramatic form, but preferred to impose his own interpretation in his choice of six scenes and an epilogue to *present* the story of Saint Joan.

Once the tragic focus shifted from the moral and psychological interplay between human agents within a known framework of natural order to the interplay between the protagonist and the forces to which he is exposed in a specific political and social milieu, the drama was bound to break out of its traditional forms. But the power of tradition is strong, and the theater has always been a conservative institution. Therefore, though a great number of plays produced in the last hundred years display

the characteristic outlook of realism and naturalism, they
yet limit their range of perception by adhering to the classic dramatic forms. The landmarks in the history of the
modern drama are those plays which experimentally tried
to find an adequate form to embody new premises of
thought (for example, Büchner's *Danton's Death*) and
those plays which represent the triumph of the experiment.

A composite theory of modern drama, such as I have
outlined in these opening chapters, is largely of historical
value. It shows that there was a consciousness of the
necessity for change, in particular for a new intellectual
basis from which a serious drama of contemporary significance could once more grow. And it describes the major
conceptual, and by implication the formal, differences between the old drama and the new. Its practical use is that
of a rationale, a taking of stock, and of intelligent specu-
lation about the possibilities of the modern drama.

But one must remember that dramatists are notoriously
afraid of theory. It seems to them prescriptive and im-
practical as a guide. The dramatist must himself sense
what a theory tries to articulate. He does what appears to
be right at the time, what is feasible, and what he has it
in his power to do. Yet dramatists also learn from one
another. They experiment and the successful experiments in the same mode form a discernible tradition
productive of occasional masterpieces, which in retrospect
define the mode more precisely. Thus it becomes possible,
and even desirable, for a critic to view the work of a playwright like O'Neill or Miller not merely against the social
and theatrical setting of the last few decades in America,
but in line with related work in the same manner, reaching back a century to the plays of Büchner and Hebbel
and the more recent ancestors, Ibsen, Strindberg, and
Hauptmann.

"A drama worthy of its time," says Miller, "must first,
knowingly or by instinctive means, recognize its major

and most valuable traditions and where it has departed from them" (*Collected Plays*, p. 54). One of the remarkable facts about Miller's most sustained critical reflection on his own work, the general introduction to his *Collected Plays*, is his concern with questions which had engaged the attention of earlier playwright-critics like Hebbel, Ludwig, Zola, and Strindberg. Sometimes he recognizes his traditions knowingly; at other times he evolves his positions painstakingly and with an air of discovery, though of the major forms of his realistic theater, *Death of a Salesman, The Crucible*, and *A View from the Bridge*, each has its distinct ancestry in the drama of the last hundred years. For example, his remark about making society "a power and a mystery of custom and inside the man and surrounding him, as the fish is in the sea and the sea inside the fish, his birthplace and burial ground, promise and threat" (p. 30); or about the necessity of probing into the nature of guilt itself instead of revealing it merely as a ground of fateful retribution (p. 41); or about his decision to use an "engaged narrator" in *A View from the Bridge*, following his "impulse to present rather than to represent an interpretation of reality" (p. 49)—these, as we have seen, were all central points in the evolution of the modern poetic. Since Miller is a serious, critically self-conscious artist and since he understands the premises as well as the implications of the realist's philosophical position, it is not surprising that his best work represents a mid-twentieth century continuation of a still vital tradition. Whether Robert Bolt had a firsthand knowledge of the landmarks of historical tragedy in the realistic manner is beside the point. Obviously they understood the possibilities of the form as they composed *The Crucible* and *A Man for All Seasons*.

Thus it is an illuminating strategy for the critic to draw a hypothetical line from Büchner's two prototypal plays, *Danton's Death* and *Woyzeck*, through the major developments in the historical and the social and psychological drama, to the most recent examples of realistic and nat-

uralistic tragedy. The modern dramatist working in
this tradition must still fulfill these three functions if he
will be true to the realist's conception of man as intimately
involved and discovering his fate in the phenomenal
world: He must be historian, social critic, and amateur
psychologist, and attempt to give a rationally apprehensible account of this tragic involvement. The emphasis,
however, may lie with one or another point of view and
may be dictated by the choice of subject matter. Büchner's
plays, more than a century ago, brilliantly anticipated
the chief possibilities of tragedy in the realistic-naturalis-
tic manner, and therefore I propose to use them as models
for subsequent variations in the form.

Although the tradition of realism ought to be considered
as one since the same basic outlook controls its different
formulations, it is necessary in a discussion of the possibilities of tragic drama in this mode to designate a few
clearly recurrent patterns. One of these, using recorded
history as its material, views man as participating in an
epochal change which a society undergoes. Placed at a
critical moment when a clash of ideas shapes the course
of events in time, the individual experiences history as
fateful, as a loosing of forces beyond his control yet made
meaningful by his action and suffering. Another pattern,
giving the social drama of protest tragic significance, delineates the social animal pitted against the institutions
which define and at the same time destroy his life. Dealing mainly with external causes, a tragedy so designed
must emphasize the apparently unchangeable conditions
of human existence in a given milieu; thus, from the point
of view of the individual protagonist, tragic necessity resides in the laws of society as it does in the laws of nature
and his motive to action is only his will to survive. But
when the arena of the struggle extends to the inner man,
the point of view is broadened to include psychological
motives. The tragic pattern is to analyze the course of a
human passion and the destructive personal relations
between individual human beings. At its most extreme
this form of realistic or naturalistic tragedy resorts to

pathological characters in the process of destruction and self-destruction.

Though for my purposes I distinguish between the social and the psychological motives in order to understand them as elements of a tragic action, there is usually an interplay between the two patterns. With few exceptions, a pure milieu drama as well as a purely psychological drama tends to verge intellectually on determinism and emotionally on sheer demonism or dumb suffering. Yet, as has always been the case in the theater, the most moving effects are sometimes achieved just this side of grotesqueness and outrage. This is true of the moral monsters in Shakespeare, Webster, and Racine as well as of the more clinically presented demons and victims in the modern drama.

NOTES

1. For my present purpose, I ignore the philosophical and technical quarrels between the two schools. As René Wellek says, "the distinction between 'realism' and 'naturalism' was not stabilized for a long time. . . . The separation of the terms is only a work of modern literary scholarship" ("The Concept of Realism in Literary Scholarship," in *Concepts of Criticism*, ed. Stephen G. Nichols, Jr. [New Haven, 1963], p. 233).

2. Letter to his family, Strassburg, July 28, 1835. *Sämtliche Werke und Briefe*, ed. Werner R. Lehmann (Hamburg: Christian Wegner Verlag), II (1971), 443.

3. "Einsichten und Ausblicke," *Das Gesammelte Werk* (Berlin: Suhrkamp Verlag), XVII (1943), 433.

4. *Arthur Miller's Collected Plays* (New York: The Viking Press, 1957), p. 53.

5. Lukács, "Zur Soziologie des modernen Dramas," pp. 334-337.

6. Quoted in a review of Stanislaw J. Lec, *Unkempt Thoughts*, in *TLS*, May 31, 1963, p. 394.

7. Lukács, pp. 338-342.

8. Ibid., pp. 340, 342-345.

PART TWO
Man as Agent and Victim

3. THE EXPERIENCE OF HISTORY AS FATEFUL

As a general rule, the realistic historical tragedy derives its materials from historical records and makes a point of interpreting the records with reasonable fidelity, yet an accurate rendering of history in dramatic form is not its major objective. The realistic dramatist in his role as historian sets himself a task which is more significant than producing chronicles of his country's past or celebrating the national spirit. He also shies away from the anecdotal falsification of history and from its romantic idealization. On this score, Schiller became an easy target for the realists. Büchner argued heatedly against the *Idealdichter* who created "marionettes with sky-blue noses and affected pathos" rather than flesh-and-blood characters. At a time when Schiller's reputation was generally held high, he expressed his sole admiration for Goethe and Shakespeare, and only scorn for Schiller's rhetorical drama. "If I am told that the poet should render the world, not as it is, but as it ought to be, I answer that I don't wish to improve upon God Almighty who surely made the world as it ought to be."[1] Hebbel's subtler critique of Schiller's *Maid of Orleans* was that the maid should not have been allowed to reflect upon herself; she had to plunge into the abyss like a somnambulist retaining her naiveté to the end.[2] And Shaw, of course, preferred his own flesh-and-blood country girl to Schiller's romantic heroine in a familiar passage in the Preface to *Saint Joan*. It should be clear enough from all this what the modern historical tragedy ought not to be.

But there is one further distinction, that between modern historical tragedy in the realistic manner and the history play with a moral bias, which touches on an im-

61

portant question: how should the dramatist, and particularly the tragic dramatist, relate the historical event to the
individual whom he uses as an agent in his drama?
Should he allow the character to shape the event, or should
he think of the unfolding historical event as the condition
of his character's possible action and indeed of his existence? The great example of historical drama written
from a consistent moral point of view is Shakespeare's
cycles of English history plays. Here, a conflict arises
typically from the attempt of the individual will to shape
the world to its own liking in opposition to a higher, inviolable moral order. Shakespeare uses the events "borrowed from history" in order to fashion a politically and
morally edifying dramatic fiction.

The modern realistic view is different. It shifts the emphasis to the dramatic unfolding of the historical event
in order to find its meaning for the society and the individual involved in the change. The operation of a higher
and fateful power is still felt, but it has no spiritual significance. The protagonist in the realistic historical tragedy
represents an idea which is doomed to failure in the
dialectic clash of opposites, i.e. given the momentary historical circumstances. But his claim may be valid under
different circumstances, whereas the tragic figure in the
Shakespearean history play commits a moral error
which would cause evil consequences under any circumstances. Such an action is the result of merely anarchic
personal choices, as in the case of Richard II, and the
destruction of the bonds of human and political relations
entails personal as well as general suffering. Hence
Shaw's charge that Shakespeare manipulates history in
creating "vulgarly ambitious individuals who make
rows" and pretending that the world is governed by them.
The modern conception of historical tragedy asserts
that men who follow their best inspirations must suffer
defeat if their actions separate them from the mainstream
of society at a given historical moment. "Imagine characters," writes Hebbel to a friend, "who are all in the right,
who nowhere diverge into wickedness or evil; their fate

derives from the fact that they are just such men and no other, yet it is a dreadful fate—and you will have an idea . . . of the magnitude of my task."[3]

As we have seen, Hebbel conceived of the protagonist in a historical tragedy as an agent—and ultimately as a victim—of change. The idea against which the agent asserts his rightful claim represents the institutions, the forms and functions of the society of which he is a part; it represents the common weal and is static. If the individual is driven, because he is what he is and cannot act otherwise, to assert his identity as a single and singular spirit, he suffers tragic isolation and incurs the guilt, however justifiable, of his social rebellion. Hebbel called the heroine of his late play, *Agnes Bernauer*, "the Antigone of modern times." In her necessary death he sought to demonstrate how "the common human and the highest social interests run together tragically in an insoluble knot."[4] But it is also possible to conceive of a clash of ideas in which the society, under the impulse of revolutionary change, sweeps beyond the steadfast convictions of an individual who represents an earlier stage of order or balance of power. Such dramas are naturally limited to certain historical settings, like the French Revolution in *Danton's Death* or the Tudor Reformation in *A Man for All Seasons*.

In any case, if the dialectic of opposing forces is made to be so compelling as to amount to a necessary clash, the individual protagonist at the point of collision must be destroyed. In the realistic history play he assumes the role of martyr, or witness, not however to a supernatural, preconceived truth, but to an alternative idea of historical reality. The Maid claims to hear voices in *Saint Joan*, thus threatening the social fabric; Sir Thomas More chooses to die to preserve his individual conscience as well as the social fabric in *A Man for All Seasons*. But neither play attempts to depict the spiritual experience of martyrdom. The religious motives serve only as the expressive forms of an individual inspiration, and the point at issue in both plays is how the Christian society

shall be constituted and how men shall henceforth live.
Both plays are conceived in terms of a dialectic of historical ideas. In one the heroine embodies ideas which are
premature in her time and she must therefore be destroyed. In the other the hero embodies a principle of
spiritual integrity which his society cannot tolerate because it is in the process of radical change; in order to
destroy the principle, it must destroy the man.

Such conflicts become tragic when they are shown to be
unavoidable. Depending on the choice of the historical
moment and on the vision of the dramatist, the interplay
of character and circumstances can be construed into
tragic necessity. Moreover, if the dramatic conflict of opposing impersonal forces grasps the lives of historical
figures about whom we are made to care, the play may
assume tragic stature. The realistic point of view alone
does not, of course, guarantee a tragic interpretation of
the process of history. Tragedy is an artistic construct.
And a dramatic logic less strict than that which produces
the inevitable clash and destruction, or a treatment of
character less compelling than that which produces total
commitment to a course of action, will end in a chronicle
of mere disillusionment and frustration. Unless the protagonist is so engaged that his willful separation from the
society must destroy him—in other words, unless he is
guilty at the moment of his presumptuous insistence on
his individual claim—his sacrifice does not matter; he is
merely bypassed in the course of events. The historical
tragedy, then, demands the concept of strict necessity in
the unfolding of the incidents, unchangeable purpose in
the protagonists and antagonists, and the concept of guilt
in Hebbel's nonreligious sense of the term. It interprets
a conflict of interests, encompassing the whole society in
a moment of crisis, in terms of the fate of one individual.
The tragic quality of the realistic historical drama derives
from the identification of the hero's fate with the issue
of the larger conflict. Consequently, only certain historical subjects lend themselves to such a tragic view. But
the hero may appear only as the chief participant in a

historic action. The emphasis would then rest mainly on
the play of ideas, or the interpretation of the character
and the event, without necessarily involving the hero in a
tragic commitment. Therein lies the difference between
Bolt's *A Man for All Seasons* and Osborne's *Luther*, or
between *Saint Joan* and Brecht's *Galileo*.

1

Georg Büchner's *Danton's Death* possesses the virtues
of both kinds of drama, the objectivity and plausibility
of dramatized history as well as the tragic interpretation
of the historical events leading to Danton's death. It is
the earliest full-fledged realistic historical tragedy and in
many ways the subtlest. The dramatist, Büchner said, was
nothing but a historian, yet he stood above the historian
"by creating history for the second time, by placing us
directly in the life of an age instead of giving us a dry
account of it, and by presenting us with characters instead
of characteristics and living figures instead of descrip-
tions. His highest task is to come as close as possible to
historical events as they really happened. His story must
not be any more nor less moral than *history itself. . . .*"
So much for the criterion of verisimilitude in the realistic
history play. Büchner was trying to vindicate his candid
portraits of the revolutionary leaders, including Danton,
and the indecent vignettes of private life; "after all, the
good Lord did not conceive history to suit the reading
habits of young girls."[5]

But besides his function as an objective chronicler and
recreator of history, the dramatic poet must shape his
materials according to his understanding of the historical
events. Büchner's reaction to his reading in the period of
the French Revolution was intensely personal. In the middle of a letter to his bride, the twenty-year old man bursts
out with this devastating discovery of human impotence
in the face of the iron law of history:

I have been studying the history of the Revolution. I feel

as if I had been annihilated by the horrible fatalism of history. I find a terrible sameness in human nature, an inescapable force at work in the human situation, which is
given to all and to none. The individual—only froth on the
wave; greatness—a mere accident; the sovereignty of genius—a
puppet play; a ridiculous struggling against an iron law; to
recognize it, the utmost achievement; to control it, impossible. . . . *Must* is one of the words with which man was
baptized and damned. The saying: "for it must needs be that
offenses come; but woe to that man by whom the offense
cometh!"—is gruesome. What is it in us that lies, murders,
steals?[6]

In itself this often-quoted passage is of little significance.
Such a reading of history is easily come by, and as a
passionate unreflective outcry against an inhuman force
guiding our every action it may only betray the young
man's despair over the repressive governmental policy
which shortly afterwards sent him into exile. But the
same idea, once he gains artistic distance, serves him
admirably to give tragic meaning to Danton's downfall
and to create in each scene the sense of a situation controlled by necessity.

Although Danton echoes the quoted passage in Act II,
Büchner does not merely transfer his felt horror of the
fatalism of history to the protagonist; that is, his approach is not primarily biographical, nor is it limited to
Danton's awareness of his changing fortunes. His aim is
to render objectively the multiple forms which historic
necessity takes as it sweeps over several individual lives
and especially as it turns Danton, the hero of the September Massacres, into a paralyzed, yet knowing victim of
events. The "iron law" of which Büchner speaks in his
letter, though it makes little sense in a general philosophy
of history, becomes a reality to reckon with in his plausible recreation and interpretation of Danton's fate at the
hands of his political opponents. Robespierre and St. Just
appear as the fit instruments of an impersonal power
which is clearly beyond their control. Yet the play is
more than a document of nihilism as it is sometimes
described. In Danton's initial weariness, in his momen-

tary resistance and final capitulation, it offers, from the point of view of the realist, a rationale of historical conflict and change. The significance of Danton's course of action lies in his gradual realization of the role he must play in the unfolding events.

Because of the mordant irony to which Büchner gives free rein from the very first words of Danton, it is easy to misunderstand the nature of this historical drama. Lukács argued rightly that Büchner does not voice his disillusionment and desperation, but that he sees Danton clearly enough as a man who has lost his direction and who holds a passé world view at a time of violent change. It is the dramatic protagonist who suffers from a fatal incapacity to understand the process of history. In other words, the play is not merely an apocalyptic vision of terror or a gesture of revulsion. Rather, it explores a battle between opposing forces, whether to continue the revolution (Robespierre and St. Just) or to stop it before it becomes senseless murder (Danton).[7]

The tragic quality of the play does indeed depend on such a dialectic of ideas. But Lukács can see it only in political terms; he feels compelled to take sides in the struggle, and to show Büchner politically sympathetic to St. Just and to Robespierre's plebeian revolution. As for Danton, Lukács points out that he does not care for the continuing struggle between the poor and the rich; he exemplifies the apathy, the cynicism, and the *ennui* of the well-fed bourgeois. Yet he is attractive and he has wit, which gains him the sympathy of the audience. Büchner, in short, may feel close to Danton as a man, says Lukács, but in his recognition of historical necessity he is definitely on the side of Robespierre. What else could we expect from a writer who was himself a revolutionary caught in the misery of the 1830s in Germany?[8] This part of Lukács' essay is a discourse in politics rather than dramatic criticism. In effect, he charges Danton (both the historical and the dramatic figure) with a political error for which he suffers death. In comparing St. Just and Danton to Fortinbras and Hamlet, he is saying that the

political realists of this world win in the end. This amounts
to a reduction of the meaning of both plays.

We are moved by Danton's death not merely because he
is attractive and a witty fellow. Büchner penetrates more
deeply into the opposing positions given by the historical
record of the Revolution. He understands that the life-and-
death struggle between the leaders who ride the crest of
the still powerful revolutionary momentum and the dila-
tory hero, who is swept aside in the inevitable clash, has
a moral as well as a political meaning. Danton's tragic
stature derives from Büchner's dramatic restatement of the
dialectic of ideas in just these terms: Is it the purpose of
the Revolution to serve man, or has man become the un-
thinking instrument of an impersonal power? Therefore,
Danton's wit and irony are more than the cynical thrusts
of an effete epicurean and an intellectual dilettante; they
serve Büchner to lay bare the dehumanized politics which
Robespierre conducts in the name of virtue and vice.

If Danton begins to accept himself as a "dead saint"
or a useless relic among the helpless deputies, Robespierre
on the other hand recognizes his tragic isolation as the
self-appointed savior of the people. In his soliloquy at the
end of Act I, Robespierre translates Danton's comic quip
in calling him "heaven's police officer" into tragic terms.
Not unlike Dostoevsky's Grand Inquisitor he compares his
tragic burden with that of Christ, and he sees at least
for a moment the moral futility of his sacrifice: "Truly,
the Son of Man is being crucified in all of us, we all
suffer the agony of Gethsemane sweating blood; but none
of us redeems the other with his wounds. . . . They are
all leaving me—all is void and desolate—I am alone." In his
recreation of the last days of Danton and his followers,
Büchner is not trying to decide the political rightness of
one cause or the other. His vision of the historical process
is tragic in that the victors and the vanquished, as well
as the figures peripheral to the drama, are shown as paying
the cost of the historical struggle. Perhaps the only characters morally unaffected by the events are the cart-drivers
plying their trade between the prison and the guillotine.

In their brief tragicomic dialogue, modeled on that of the gravediggers in *Hamlet*, we learn that they barely feed their children by earning ten *sous* per head.

The dramatic structure of *Danton's Death* is typical of the realistic historical tragedy. Its episodic form reveals the anti-Aristotelian conception of the action. There is no logically ordered plot which carries the action toward the inevitable catastrophe. Instead we are confronted with an almost kaleidoscopic composition, in which each scene brings to life intensely and vividly a moment that is expressive of the violent assaults of the time on men's lives. This gives Büchner every opportunity to explore the effects of the public political struggle on human relations. We get the low-life scenes between Simon and his wife as comic analogies of Robespierre's philosophy of the Revolution, as well as the street scenes, the prison scenes, the pathetic and tragic relations between Danton and Julie and between Camille and Lucile, and even the extended reflections of a prostitute on the pleasure principle in a time of moral disorder. In these scenes Büchner "creates history for the second time" and manages to give it the density of lived experience without a tendentious story line or plot.

At the same time there is a discernible progression in the composition. The panoramic representation of the public and the private life of the two political factions reveals the historical process of change in which the world of Danton is unable to withstand the renewal of the terror and is destroyed along with the proponents of its ideology. The first act defines the critical opposition of the two philosophies of life as they are personified by Danton and Robespierre, and sets the political conflict in motion. In the second and third acts Danton watches the impossible come to pass and begins to understand the inexorable process of change. His reflections as he goes under in the wave of fanatic terrorism are of a general nature; his spirited orations in his own defense before the tribunal seek to place the revolution and his role in it in historical perspective. But in the last act Büchner narrows the scope of his vision, as Shakespeare often does, to present the tragic consequences of his action on individual lives, as the prisoners prepare themselves to die. He emphasizes the grim details of physical death and madness, the tragicomedy of moral indifference and senseless cruelty in the jeering mob and the public servants charged with the handiwork of death. There are reminiscences of *Hamlet* and *Lear* in the elaborate business of getting acquainted with the smell and the finality of death.

The structure of the scenes (or in the Aristotelian phrase, "the arrangement of the incidents") mirrors Büchner's modern tragic conception which is markedly different from the classical and the Shakespearean. It is that of an inevitable progression to defeat and death, without sudden reversal and recognition of a prior error or misconception. There is no need for redemption since the hero did not fall through sin; there is no call for a moment of dignity and special courage since the opponent is an impersonal force; there is no possibility of a final illumination since the hero does not act blindly. Büchner's irony is not the classic tragic irony, predicated on the blindness of the hero to the way the world is governed. It is the modern tragicomic variety by which the hero gradually learns to live with an insoluble dilemma and to die in consequence of it. Danton gains perspective in his frustration and develops the capacity to regard himself ironically, even as he anticipates his execution; in this he reminds us of the stoical villains of Jacobean tragedy. Büchner's hero is a man who has been bypassed by the course of events and watches the process by which he is toppled from his prominence.

To the realist such a process is explicable in terms of ideas which shape men's actions. In the first two acts, Robespierre and St. Just present the rationale of their position, while Danton, who slowly admits the new balance of power, rationalizes his growing helplessness. The two sets of opposing ideas in counterpoint share a common purpose: to determine the meaning of freedom and to shape the course of the revolution in accordance with that meaning. Robespierre's slogan is "the despotism of freedom against tyranny." In his speech to the Jacobin club he reveals his purpose of driving the revolution forward by eliminating the internal enemies of the Republic, namely those who would call a halt to the methods of terror and who imitate the depraved life of the aristocrats. "The weapon of the Republic is Terror, the strength of the Republic is Virtue—Virtue because without it Terror corrupts, and Terror because without it Virtue is impotent" (I, iii).

Robespierre, the Incorruptible, rationalizes the political situation in ethical terms, the most expedient way of removing Danton from his path to absolute power. Yet Büchner's characterization never permits us to interpret Robespierre's action as simply hypocritical or politically astute. He is impelled by a momentum which arises from the situation itself and acts, like the others, "as in a dream, only more distinctly, more accomplished, and defined" (I, vi). He personifies the push of the evolving events, and therefore his confrontation with Danton displays only the difference between their temperaments. "Is there nothing in you which sometimes whispers to you secretly: you lie, lie?" To which Robespierre can only answer: "My conscience is clear." The true motive of his actions lies outside his consciousness. He knows only parrot-like that "the social revolution is not yet complete; whoever leaves a revolution half-finished digs his own grave. . . . Vice must be punished, Virtue must reign through Terror" (I, vi). Gradually, Danton must learn that these sentiments, so alien to his temperament, represent historical reality.

The other half of the job of explaining the "iron law" of history Büchner leaves to St. Just. After Danton's fate has been determined in the proscription scene, in which St. Just parodies the conspirators in *Julius Caesar*—"We must bury the great corpse with dignity, like priests, not like butchers; we must not cut it to pieces, all its limbs must go underground with it"—the necessity for this bloody sacrifice has to be made clear to the assembled deputies. St. Just explains the impersonal process of history in terms of an ancient tragic image: humanity must be dismembered in order to be rejuvenated and rise whole; and in terms of

the modern naturalistic creed: contrary to outworn traditional beliefs, the working of the moral law is analogous
to that of the physical laws of nature.

There seem to be in this Convention a few delicate ears which
cannot stand the word "blood." Perhaps a few general considerations may convince them that we are not more cruel
than nature and time itself. Nature follows her laws quietly
and irresistibly; and man is destroyed whenever he comes
in conflict with them. A change in the components of air, a
flaring up of the telluric fire, an overbalance in a mass of water,
and as a result a plague, a volcanic eruption, a flood bury
thousands. What is the upshot? An insignificant and, seen as a
whole, a hardly noticeable change in physical nature which
would have passed without a trace if corpses were not scattered along the way.
    Now I ask you: shall moral nature in its revolutions be more
considerate than physical nature? Shall not an idea as well
as a law of physics destroy that which opposes it? Why
shouldn't an event, something that alters the whole form of
moral nature, that is to say, of mankind, come about through
blood? The world spirit makes use of our arms in the moral
sphere just as it utilizes volcanoes and floods in the physical.
What does it matter if they die of a plague or the revolution?
    The march of mankind is slow; you can count the steps only
by centuries, and behind each step rise the graves of whole
generations. To arrive at the simplest discoveries and fundamental principles millions have died along the way. Is it then
not clear that at a time when the march of history has been
accelerated a greater number of men should lose their
breath?

*   *   *

. . . Moses led his people through the Red Sea and into the
desert until the old rotten generation was annihilated before
he founded the new state. Legislators! We have neither the
Red Sea nor the desert, but we have war and the guillotine.
    The revolution is like the daughters of Pelias: it dismembers
mankind in order to rejuvenate it. Humanity will rise out of
the cauldron of blood with powerful limbs, like the earth out
of the waves of the Deluge, as if it had been created for
the first time. . . . (II, vii)

Robespierre's and St. Just's elaborate self-justifications are
dramatically necessary, not only as a statement of one side
of the dialectic of ideas, but also as sheer rhetorical de-

vices by which the two men convince themselves and the deputies that they are in the grip of an impersonal power, an iron law, beyond their choosing. As in other realistic historical dramas of the modern theater, *Saint Joan* and *The Crucible* for example, the playwright must show how an idea, assuming the force of an absolute law, may dehumanize characters (modern descendants of Creon in the *Antigone*) by engaging them totally in its service.

The hero in this kind of drama is typically the victim, and he is tragic in terms of the modern realistic drama because he is conscious of the nature of the fatal situation and yet helplessly enmeshed in it. Danton senses the fatalism of history early in the play. He is warned that Robespierre "needs a heavy head," and answers, "Yes, I know—the Revolution is like Saturn; it devours its own children." But this apt figure, suggesting that he is at the mercy of a primordial force which has little to do with human motives and choices, does not yet at this point carry full conviction; for he adds after a moment of thought: "And yet, they won't dare. . . . They never had courage without me; they won't have any against me. The Revolution is not yet ended; they might still need me; they will save me in their Arsenal" (I, v). Thus Danton can feel the renewal of the terror, but he does not yet understand that the revolution must destroy him by its own accelerating power like an avalanche.

Only after his fruitless interview with the incorruptible eunuch, Robespierre, Danton knows that he is a relic of bygone days: "I have achieved it at last; the Revolution has retired me, but in a different way from what I had expected. . . . Robespierre is the dogma of the Revolution; it may not be struck down. Nor could it. We did not make the Revolution, rather the Revolution has made us" (II, i). None of his party understands Danton's paralysis of will; some ascribe it to laziness, others to cynicism and *insouciance*, because he masks his knowledge with irony and wit. But underneath his theatrical pose, offering himself again and again as an image of the doomed hero, not unlike Richard II, he watches his world crumble. While his friend Camille Desmoulins tries to find ways of averting the inevitable fate because he loves life, Danton actively flirts with death as relief from the absurdity of his situation. He is genuinely tired of the Revolution and under the circumstances finds dying easier than living.

He, too, knows that the revolution has not yet ended and that the goal of freedom has not been achieved: "The statue of Freedom has not yet been cast; the furnace glows, and we all may yet burn our fingers in the process" (I, i). But at the beginning of his education in historical necessity, Danton still believes naively that his idea of freedom may be realized by calling a halt to revolutionary politics and establishing a constitutional republic. He is genuinely apprehensive because for too long a time the revolution has been oppressing individual life and now threatens to extirpate the last refuge of a demoralized society, the pursuit of sensual pleasure, in the name of freedom. Büchner's implied criticism strikes both ways. For in his depiction of the anti-Robespierre faction he indicates clearly that their frivolity of speech and action hides a sense of desperation and loss of self-respect. Danton is afflicted with this social disease as is, on the other end of the social scale, the young grisette, Marion; and the easy, comic dialogue of Danton's friends has all the earmarks of *Galgenhumor* which turns into grim sarcasm as their world succumbs to the assault of the opposing party.

Finally, as Danton comes to terms with the reality of his situation, he seeks to escape the curse of necessity by embracing a new freedom, that which is offered by death. Not only the present danger of his enemies without, but also the confrontation of his enemies within, his conscience and his memory, compels Danton to flirt with the idea of absolute peace in nothingness. In two short scenes, the soliloquy in the open field (II,iv) and the night scene in his room (II,v), he wrestles with his nightmare thoughts about the past, particularly his acts as minister of justice during the September massacres of 1792, and finds that his own life provides an image of subjection to necessity. "We are marionettes, and unknown forces pull the wire; nothing, nothing in ourselves! We are the swords with which spirits fight—only you can't see their hands as the fairy tales say" (II,v). Before the tribunal Danton offers a more dignified version of this insight, as he recounts his services to the Revolution: "Fate guides our arms, but only powerful natures serve as her instruments" (III,iv), yet in effect he recognizes that his cause is lost and that he must prepare himself to be killed off "mechanically."

With this moment in the play, Büchner's tragic rhythm is complete. The remainder is essentially an improvisation on the theme of mental and physical dissolution, and the burden of detailing the sense of futility before certain death rests on the victims themselves. They are the most perceptive and articulate observers of their defeat at the hands of the whore Freedom, whose destructive work they view with the detachment of men who have nothing more to do with the affairs of this world. Danton speaks now in accents of complete disillusionment: "Freedom and a whore are the most cosmopolitan things under the sun. She will now handsomely prostitute herself in the marriage bed of the attorney from Arras. But I think she will be his Clytemnestra; I give him no more than six months' grace before I pull him down with me" (IV,v). His former revolutionary ardor had left Danton by the opening of the play. But now that his perception has been schooled in the course of his humiliating defeat, even the idea of freedom which had been the fundamental impulse of the Revolution has been debased in his mind.

Büchner, the realist, chose as his subject that moment of the French Revolution and that segment of Danton's career in order to demonstrate the tragic subjection of a free spirit to historical necessity. For the harshness of his vision he could find support in the historical events themselves, but the spiritual bankruptcy of Danton's cause and the total disillusionment with man-made ideals are the product of Büchner's destructive irony. Paradoxically, he employs his fantastic imagination in the service of realism. Karl Gutzkow, a fellow dramatist and sympathetic sponsor of his

work, recognized Büchner's novel genius, but had to warn
him of the difficulties he must expect from publishers and
audiences who were not ready to exchange their conventional versions of historical drama for his unsentimental
and uncompromising portrait of the unheroic human animal. Büchner himself was not yet satisfied with his novel
achievement. He claimed that he was forced to write the
play in about five weeks, and felt that he had cause to
"blush" at his recreation of history; but he consoled himself with the thought "that, with the exception of Shakespeare, all writers stand before her and before nature like
schoolboys."[9]

The title, *A Man for All Seasons*, points to Robert Bolt's
realistic conception of historical tragedy. The phrase, taken
from a contemporary Oxford grammarian, Robert Whittin-
ton, summarizes Thomas More's life as that of a complete
man, honorable, rational, urbane, learned, orthodox, grave
and gay as the occasion demanded, a man, as Bolt puts
it, "absorbed in his society" and "almost indecently successful." In other words, Bolt's portrait is not that of a saint-
to-be who spurns this world and its corrupt ministers, such
as the timeserving Cromwell or the king himself, whose
will serves only his appetite. More reassures his wife that
he is not of "the stuff of which martyrs are made" (Act
I).[10] And he rejects his reputation among learned men as
"the English Socrates" because he has "no taste for hem-
lock" (Act II). Yet he sets himself against the current of
his time and in so doing courts disaster. But the point is
that, in Bolt's recreation of a historical crisis, More does
this as an individual who separates himself from his society
with the greatest reluctance. He opposes himself to the
whole movement of the times—the Parliament, the bishops,
the universities all understand and support the far-reaching consequences of Henry's "convenience" in changing
wives—and he is amazed that he cannot give in; what's
more, he is afraid and wonders at his own temerity.

It would therefore be false to regard More either as the
unequivocal champion of God's law, assured of his reward

in a better world, or, conversely, as a modern anti-hero, a victim of events beyond his control or understanding. Bolt sees him rather as a reluctant "hero of selfhood" in a world in which men, from Cromwell down to the ubiquitous and protean Common Man, have given up their claim to a separable identity. "What you have hunted me for is not my actions," says More at his trial, "but the thoughts of my heart. It is a long road you have opened. For first men will disclaim their hearts and presently they will have no hearts. God help the people whose Statesmen walk your road" (Act II). He has tried in every way to escape the choice between the dictates of his own conscience and Henry's policy of convenience; through silence he hoped to avoid an act of disobedience and yet to refuse a free declaration of loyalty. The best legal mind in the kingdom, he has tried to seek refuge in the laws of his society. But the guaranteed "shelter" of his society fails him, and he must choose, "to be human at all; . . . why then perhaps we *must* stand fast a little—even at the risk of being heroes" (Act II).

Superficially, the tragic pattern of *A Man for All Seasons* is similar to that of *Danton's Death*. The protagonist in each case is an individual who is overtaken by the course of historical events; he represents a moral or political idea of society which is being swept away in a tide of radical change. In each case the new idea cannot become reality until the old one is discarded so that the presumptuous individual must be "melted down again" in the stream, to use Hebbel's figure, or sacrificed to the new definition of the common weal. Both playwrights, belonging to the same tradition of realistic historical dramaturgy, create a similar objective pattern: a war of ideas in which men get killed. But apart from the obvious difference in the personalities of the two playwrights, which reveals itself in the texture of their dialogue and their sense of humor, there are further and more important differences in their conception of the tragic role of the individual caught in a historical crisis.

Büchner posits his newly discovered "iron law of history"

as the context in which men struggle, pretending that their
individualities matter, whereas they are always subject to
the imperatives of an impersonal force: an outlook in which
Lukács detected an anticipation of the socialist theory of
dialectical and historical materialism. Bolt, on the other
hand, chooses a historical subject in order to illuminate a
present moral and cultural crisis. It too has to do with the
loss of the individual self, with a society of men who "disclaim their hearts" to suit the convenience of their ruler.
But the antagonist here is not the momentum of a revolution already set in motion which in its forward stride makes
either instruments or victims out of its participants. More's
true antagonist is the Common Man who, in his many
guises, serves him as steward, informs against him, jails
him, judges him as juror, and murders him as the hangman. Henry's youthful vanities and his impetuous desires,
translated into reasons of state, may be considered the
occasion for the conflict with Thomas More, but the prolonged struggle itself goes beyond the immediate question
of Henry's "changing his woman." Bolt's purpose is to show
how the society which admires More's qualities this side
of idolatry betrays him and in the process betrays itself.
A Man for All Seasons is a social tragedy based on a situation taken from history which has been reworked into a
moral parable. Like all good historical dramas, it elicits
more than an antiquarian interest. It involves the present-
day audience directly so that the Common Man's parting
speech: " . . . It isn't difficult to keep alive, friends— . . . If
we should bump into one another, recognize me" (Act II)
sounds like a justifiable accusation.

Yet the imputation is not that we are all villains, through
guilt by association. Bolt, like Shaw, wants to write historical tragedy, not a costumed melodrama. He knows that
the most significant conflicts are those in which the claims
of both sides can be upheld. The Common Man, and the
society for which he stands, which includes by implication
our society, is no mere villain. Yet in the trial of a moral
dilemma suddenly thrust upon him, he is guilty as are those
who manage the state. They do not have the strength

to tolerate opposition, and not surprisingly the Common
Man lends his services to the powers that be. "It isn't
difficult to keep alive, friends—just don't *make* trouble—or
if you must make trouble, make the sort of trouble that's
expected" (Act II). Bolt's critique of such a society, caught
in a storm of far-reaching changes, is that it not only evades
choice altogether, it also denies the uncommon man his
independent self and thereby gives up its claim to humanity. A social revolution, set in motion by a war of ideas,
strips men of their personality by making them agents of
a cause which seems more important than their individual
sense of being, and it exacts the ultimate sacrifice from
those who stand in the way. That is the import of Büchner's
as well as Bolt's tragic interpretation of historical forces
at work.

Both heroes are passive in their resistance to the changing pattern of thought and politics which enmeshes them
like a spider's web; but both become fully aware of their
isolation and helplessness in the new order of things. Danton is simply liquidated by the iron men, Robespierre and
St. Just, who, for Büchner, enact the iron law of history;
only Danton's richly ironical reflections give meaning to
the image of animals led to slaughter. Bolt, on the other
hand, throughout the play tests the recurrent question
whether Thomas More is not the architect of his own destruction. Obviously, he is not in the sense in which
Shakespeare conceives of Richard II as a culpable man who
exacerbates the social and political powers of the usurper
until he is overwhelmed. And if More were a saint, as by
popular repute he was taken to be, his "willful indifference
to realities which were obvious to quite ordinary contemporaries" (Act I) would also easily solve the question. But
Bolt's characterization indicates that he was not indifferent
to realities, that, on the contrary, he was the political and
social man par excellence. That is why at one point even
his intelligent and sensitive daughter cannot understand his
persistent silence despite all the pressure from family,
friends, well-wishers and opponents to make him give in.
The necessity of the conflict rests for Bolt on the premise

that in contrast to the society which envelops him Thomas
More cannot deny his self: "I can't give in. . . . You might
as well advise a man to change the color of his eyes.
I can't" (Act II). The implication growing out of his several
efforts to explain his stand is that if he were able to deny
his individuality he would thereby forfeit the possibility
of choosing at all; a man who has no self has no choice.
Bolt's interpretation of such a collision between the self-
assertive individual and a society transformed into a mono-
lith stresses the tragic cost of altering the moral values
by which we live.

In the end More is forced, if he must be true to himself,
to seek the shelter of the "larger society" of the Church
of Christ. But that was not his original intention. Bolt, again
like Shaw, constructs a play which has to do, not with the
making of a saint, but with the tragic issue of a social
revolution. The part of the saint falls in both plays outside
the proper compass of the tragedy. In the one case it is
the tacit conclusion which we append based on our knowledge of history; in the other, it is relegated to an epilogue
which is designed to give the spectator a tragicomic
Shavian perspective of the historical consequences of the
action. "As to the epilogue, I could hardly be expected to
stultify myself by implying that Joan's history in the world
ended unhappily with her execution, instead of beginning
there. It was necessary by hook or crook to shew the can-
onized Joan as well as the incinerated one. . . . So I am
afraid the epilogue must stand" (Preface to *Saint Joan*).
In the plays themselves both dramatists approach their
heroes in historical-realistic terms. They are concerned
with the individual conscience in conflict with the static
or changing idea of society.

2

Shaw prides himself on his recreation of history and on
his realistic approach to Joan's adversaries in the drama,
particularly his conception of the ecclesiastical tribunal in
the final scene. If high tragedy presupposes the view that

"the world is finally governed by forces expressing themselves in religions and laws which make epochs," not by
passionate men whose arbitrary personal conduct affects
the course of events, his bishop and inquisitor must be
shown as "capable and eloquent exponents of The Church
Militant and The Church Litigant." Posing as the objective
historian, Shaw sees himself in the Preface to *Saint Joan*
as arbitrating a conflict of forces, scoring a point on this
side and then again on the other side, and deliberately
making his characters who represent these forces more
intelligible to themselves and to us than they would be in
real life. The playwright as historian must elucidate the
tragic issue of the conflict even while he represents it.
His aim is to "give the essential truth of it," though some
accidental facts may be inexact. And the truth of it for Shaw
is that "the tragedy of such murders is that they are not
committed by murderers. They are judicial murders, pious
murders. . . . " He conceives his historical tragedy in the
same way as Hebbel, in terms of "characters who are all
in the right, who nowhere diverge into wickedness or evil,
[whose] fate derives from the fact that they are just such
men and no other." In his version of the same idea, Shaw
says: "It is what men do at their best, with good intentions, and what normal men and women find that they must
and will do in spite of their intentions, that really concern
us."[11]

The pattern of the conflict in *Saint Joan* is the obverse
of that in *Danton's Death* and *A Man for All Seasons*. Here
a static and securely structured society is being assaulted
by an imaginative individual or genius or rebel or heretic
or witch or saint, depending on the point of view of the
speaker and the impression Joan makes at different stages
of her crusade. She gets a fair diagnosis from the Archbishop in scene II: "Child: you are in love with religion,"
and from Dunois in scene III: "You have the makings of
a soldier in you. You are in love with war." She is a little
startled over the discrepancy, but not unpleased with the
recognition. In time she realizes that she is an agent of
new ideas, but she will never understand the upheaval

they must cause in a rigorously ordered society, just as the ecclesiastical authorities (with the exception of the Inquisitor) do not understand the historical force of her power and see it only as an infectious heresy. The pattern of the conflict makes her clearly the architect of her own destruction.

Though the six scenes of the play are logically connected, Shaw relies on a larger tragic rhythm which can best be expressed in musical terms. It consists of a rising movement as Joan makes her way from Vaucouleurs (scene I) to the court, from the court (scene II) to the battlefield at Orleans (scene III), and finally to the cathedral at Rheims (scene V). A countermovement begins in the tent scene in the English camp (scene IV), in which her fate is sealed in her absence as Warwick and Cauchon join forces against her; it persists and mars the apex of her power in the coronation scene at Rheims (scene V), and at last overwhelms her in the trial scene (scene VI). Her rise is attended by miracles which are conceived in the spirit of comedy, though Shaw is careful to furnish his spectators with the reverent definition of the Archbishop: "A miracle, my friend, is an event which creates faith." During Joan's fall in the last three scenes, however, the tragic dramatist as historian comes to the fore. The tent scene as well as the trial scene determines Joan's tragic destiny in terms of political and doctrinal necessity. Resistance to her actions becomes a public necessity. Moreover, she loses personal contact with her friends after the coronation, and stands alone, choosing her road to salvation, before the court of churchmen.

In the tent scene, the turning point of the play, the dialectic which animates Shaw's historical figures comes explicitly to the surface, and here, in one of his magnificently structured discussions, Shaw the tutor in history is surely in his element. The three participants in the discussion become wholly the representatives of conflicting ideas, and furthermore their lucid negotiation over Joan's threat to Christendom gives *her* a voice and virtually a presence in the debate. The didactic burden of the scene is to explain the clash of interests both from the point of view of the temporal and spiritual leaders of society and, surprisingly enough, from Joan's point of view, though she is absent. Warwick and Cauchon find it convenient to compose their initial quarrel for the sake of their common purpose; they perform a paradigm of the behind-the-scenes political meeting which is dictated by the necessity of self-preservation. Joan's point of view, on the other hand, emerges incidentally as an expression of what Shaw in the Preface calls the Law of Change, namely that saints and prophets are "always really self-selected, like Joan," and that "all evolution in thought and conduct must at first appear as heresy and misconduct" (p. 1018).

> CAUCHON. The Pope himself at his proudest dare not presume as this woman presumes. She acts as if she herself were The Church. . . . It is always God and herself.

*   *   *

> WARWICK. But have you noticed that in these letters of hers, she proposes to all the kings of Europe, as she has already pressed on Charles, a transaction which would wreck the whole social structure of Christendom?

*   *   *

> These two ideas of hers are the same idea at bottom. (Scene IV)

As Warwick and Cauchon begin to see eye to eye, Joan's vision is doomed to extinction at least in her lifetime. The debate in the tent inflicts a defeat on her by the decision that her ideas cannot be tolerated because they are anarchic.

The two following scenes, which complete the motion downward to utter defeat, are analogous to the tent scene; but they bring the conflict from the level of debate and decision to that of enactment. Although scene V, at Rheims, shows Joan in the company of her political and military associates whom she has carried to victory, the same fear of anarchy and the motive of self-preservation cause them to withdraw their support. Scene V exhibits the personal rather than the public (or historical) reasons for isolating the visionary, and scene VI enacts the ritual whereby the society may in good conscience "cut off the dead branch."

Whereas Warwick and Cauchon had defined Joan's actions as a clear threat to the social structure of Christendom, the arguments of Dunois, Charles, and the Archbishop in the aftermath of the coronation have to do with the question of faith and pride. Practically speaking, the court and the military leaders are satisfied with Joan's successful campaigns, therefore they see no reason for taking further risks. But Joan's faith is absolute, and not occasional. Hence in this scene she is defeated by being no longer trusted. Not even Dunois, with whom she has had the closest ties of friendship, can share her unqualified faith in divine guidance. His faith is intensely practical: God helps those who help themselves, therefore there is no use in trying the impossible.

The Archbishop's faith is no less practical: the voice of God on earth is the voice of the Church Militant. Thus both the soldier and the ecclesiastic arrive at the same conclusion: Joan's faith must be merely willfulness, the result of pride. "The old Greek tragedy is rising among us," says the Archbishop. "It is the chastisement of hubris" (scene V). But the comparison is false from Joan's point of view—she simply does not understand the charge of sinful pride because her faith is absolute and has nothing to do with military success or obedience to ecclesiastical authority. The comparison is false also from the spectator's point of view; for though the Archbishop speaks in character, with the voice of the priest who represents the authentic idea of a Christian society, in Shaw's historical perspective the idea itself is on trial and subject to examination. The scene is based on a conflict between two opposed conceptions of faith in God.

In the eyes of her former admirers Joan is steering toward a tragic end because her misguided faith makes her supersede all social and religious offices.

ARCHBISHOP. You stand alone: absolutely alone, trusting

to your own conceit, your own ignorance, your own head-
strong presumption, your own impiety in hiding all these
sins under the cloak of a trust in God. When you pass
through these doors into the sunlight, the crowd will cheer
you. . . . But you will be none the less alone: they cannot
save you. We and we only can stand between you and the
stake at which our enemies have burnt that wretched
woman in Paris. (Scene V)

But in her own eyes, at the end of this scene, Joan can rest
secure in her trust in God. For the moment she can transcend
the terrible prophecy of her fellow mortals.

There is no help, no counsel, in any of you. Yes: I am
alone on earth: I have always been alone. . . . Do not think
you can frighten me by telling me that I am alone. France
is alone; and God is alone; and what is my loneliness before
the loneliness of my country and my God? I see now that
the loneliness of God is His strength: what would He be if
He listened to your jealous little counsels? Well, my loneliness shall be my strength too: it is better to be alone with
God: His friendship will not fail me, nor His counsel, nor His
love. In His strength I will dare and dare, and dare, until I
die. . . .

This doctrinal conflict between the priest and the inspired
country girl produces a third view, that of the historical
dramatist who sees the tragic issue not as a result of the
rightness or the wrongness of her faith, but in the fact
that at this moment in the history of Christendom Joan's
absolute trust in God is a social presumption which must
lead to her death. Shaw understands her "overweening
presumption" or "superbity" in that sense which is different from the Archbishop's charge of pride and impiety.

The judgments of history are relative, a fact which is
viewed tragically in the realistic world of the play and
comically in the fantasy world of the Epilogue. The Inquisitor alone among Joan's opponents understands that
he represents the necessity of the historical moment and
that Joan is innocent, because she is ignorant of its
meaning: "We have proceeded in perfect order. If the
English choose to put themselves in the wrong, it is not
our business to put them in the right. A flaw in the pro-

cedure may be useful later on: one never knows." The
Inquisitor suspects that his judgment might have to be
reversed in future times, yet he also knows that at this
moment he acts to preserve the structure of his society
and that the trial is the only legal means to deal with heresy: "But it is a terrible thing to see a young and innocent
creature crushed between these mighty forces, The
Church and the Law. . . . She did not understand a word
we were saying. It is the ignorant who suffer" (scene VI).
Unlike the Archbishop in the previous scene, the Inquisitor has the historical imagination to see the event tragically, though in his view Joan is purely the victim of circumstances.

But the tables are turned with Joan's recantation and in
the Epilogue. Although for her presumption as a creature
of her time she has been punished by the ecclesiastical
court and the secular arm, she emerges triumphant over
the Law from another conflict in which her judges
suffer for their ignorance. She articulates her natural piety
when she goes back on her recantation:

> . . . Bread has no sorrow for me, and water no
> affliction. But to shut me from the light of the sky and the
> sight of the fields and flowers; to chain my feet so that I can
> never again ride with the soldiers nor climb the hills; to
> make me breathe foul damp darkness, and keep from me
> everything that brings me back to the love of God when your
> wickedness and foolishness tempt me to hate Him: all this
> is worse than the furnace in the Bible that was heated seven
> times.

And paradoxically she chooses death in order to reaffirm her
love of life.

> His ways are not your ways. He wills that I go through the
> fire to His bosom; for I am His child, and you are not fit
> that I should live among you. That is my last word to you.
> (Scene VI)

By this final act of social presumption and willful self-isola-
tion she delivers herself from the mighty forces of the
Church and the Law. De Stogumber, the bigoted English

chaplain, first suggests her new identity when he returns from the execution: "I am no better than Judas: I will hang myself." And the disgraced Cauchon, in the Epilogue, completes Shaw's ironic reflections on the tragic roles which history assigns to men: "Must then a Christ perish in torment in every age to save those that have no imagination?" Shaw recognizes that at the trial the tragic clash could not be avoided because "what men do at their best, with good intentions," can never be enough in historical tragedy which deals precisely with the limited consciousness of historical personages caught in unavoidable conflicts; their imagination which guides their actions is necessarily circumscribed by the institutions that define their historical roles. On the other hand, the comic perspective of historical conflicts is given to us in retrospect in the Epilogue when we share the expanded consciousness of the gods: ". . . the angels may weep at the murder, but the gods laugh at the murderers" (p. 1031).

There is no conceivable place for the comic perspective in *The Crucible* because Miller detected the use of diabolism as an instrument of authority in our own society.[12] Thus, the play was for him an *exemplum*, using a notorious event in American history as a meaningful subject for the theater of his own time. Yet it does not depend for its significance today only on the specific allusions to the political climate of the early fifties; even now these allusions need to be explained in footnotes for the younger readers of the play. Rather, it depends on our recognition, as always in tragedy, that the conflict *is* exemplary and remains tragic even from our vantage point in history. It is not true that Shaw's Epilogue is entirely conceived in the comic perspective of an expanded consciousness; for when Joan threatens to rise from the dead, all the disembodied spirits leave her one by one, not yet, nor ever, ready to receive the saint. Though each tragic conflict is predicated on the shortsightedness of the characters directly involved in the crises of their time, a historical tragedy retains its significance only if the modern spectator finds in it an analogy to a conflict of ideas as yet unresolved in his own time. "Since 1692," writes Miller, "a great but superficial change has wiped out God's beard and the Devil's horns, but the world is still gripped between two diametrically opposed absolutes. The concept of unity, in which positive and negative are attributes of the same force, in which good and evil are relative, ever-changing, and always joined to the same phenomenon—such a concept is still reserved to the physical sciences and to the few who have grasped the history of ideas" (Act I). From this point of view both plays, dealing with heresy, are historical tragedies relevant to our time. Each is a drama of ideas which challenges, from the point of view of modern realism, the long tradition of interpreting history morally and melodramatically.

The affinities as well as the differences between the two plays are most instructive in considering this particular type of historical tragedy. There is, first, the rigid structure of the society, the political scene in the largest sense of the word, against which the tragedy is set. Miller explains the New England theocracy, "a combine of state and religious power," as an idea of society designed for self-preservation in a hostile environment and therefore alert to heresy, i.e. a show of any kind of disunity. Shaw's medieval hierarchical society, in which the secular and the ecclesiastic leaders suspend their enmity for the sake of self-preservation, acts to preserve its order in a similar way, except that, being more firmly established and surer of its power, it is less given to hysteria in the face of disorder. Joan is tolerated until she becomes a political nuisance even to her friends in power, whereas in the New England setting the paranoia inherent in the view of life as a constant battle against evil easily transforms the scene from precarious orderliness to total disorder. Miller's historical reading of the situation, however, holds for both plays:

When one rises above the individual villainy displayed, one

can only pity them all, just as we shall be pitied someday.
It is still impossible for man to organize his social life without repressions, and the balance has yet to be struck between
order and freedom. (Act I)

But beyond the overt pattern of the individual's threat to
the established idea of society, there is a remarkable
difference between the two plays. In *Saint Joan* the maid
is the pure theocrat. She proposes an alternative idea of
society as if it were directly sanctioned by God. She bases
her political ideas (loyalty to a supreme head of a national
state and a citizen army fighting wars for the preserva-
tion of national boundaries) as well as her religious ideas
(a clergy to teach and to minister, but not representing
the ultimate voice in matters of faith) on a direct communion with the will of God. And it is against this threat
of disorder that the pragmatic leaders of her society band
together as the authorized interpreters of God's will. In
The Crucible, however, the pure theocratic idea is embodied in the power structure of the society, and Abigail,
the hysterical adolescent "doing God's work," becomes
its voice; that is why "four judges and the King's deputy
sat to dinner" with the accusing girls. The challenge in
this play comes from the opposite direction, namely John
Proctor's effort to retain his individual identity both in
life and death against the alleged voice of heaven which
speaks through the children. Abigail is the saint of Salem
at the height of the witch hunt because through her
the society hopes to cleanse itself of heresy. In the clear
dialectic between good and evil "a person is either with
this court or he must be counted against it, there be no
road between," as the deputy governor says (Act III), so
that Proctor can break the power of theocracy only
through discrediting the accuser by admitting his own
guilt. Proctor dies to make reason prevail against the dangerous ethic of his theocratic society. Joan must die because her theocratic ethics and politics appear dangerous
to the reasonable leaders of her society. The conflict between order and freedom is thus illuminated from differing
points of view.

But though Joan finds support in her supernatural
voices whereas Proctor must find his freedom in himself,
they are both protestant souls in their resistance to the
authority which would call their identity as individuals
into question. Both are excommunicated, and both tear
up their confessions. They forfeit life, "God's most precious gift," in order to bear witness to the truth of their
vision and to the fraudulence of the law. Unlike Joan's
activist role in the first three scenes of the play, Proctor
is drawn into the crisis against his will. Despite his
brusque way with hypocrites and small men in authority,
he does not initiate a challenge against the foundations of
the Puritan community, but once he is forcibly involved in
the hysteria, he must decide on opposition to its authority. The community creates its own crisis yet is unable
to deal with it in its own way, through exorcism and
purge, since Proctor disrupts the process by his tragic
self-sacrifice.

Lion Feuchtwanger had some years earlier written a
play on the same subject. *The Devil in Boston*[13] is not,
however, a tragedy because the action remains largely on
the level of abstraction. Cotton Mather represents the
idea of theocracy and harbors the same Abigail Parrish,
the "instrument of God," in his house. His authority in
the colony is opposed by Dr. Thomas Colman, the skeptical scientist and man of common sense. Mather is finally
defeated, though he holds to his principles unswervingly.
But since the dramatic conflict never enters into the
conscience of either man in the form of a struggle for
life and identity against the opposing power, as it does in
the case of Proctor, we are left with an obsessed autocrat
and the memory of his victims. At best, the play is a
psychological study of Cotton Mather's mentality which
has its counterpart in the climate of fear in the New England community.

Miller, by contrast, complicates the clash between the
power of the state and the individual by making his hero
vulnerable and indeed responsible for his own implication in the witch hunt. He goes beyond the simple scheme

of historical tragedy by introducing the moral complication of Proctor's adultery and relating the personal sense
of guilt to the public cause of defeating the mass hysteria
of the community. Unless Proctor confesses the sin of
lechery, his wife, accused of witchcraft, must die for him.
Ironically, his moral flaw becomes his strongest weapon
with which to break the power of Abigail. Thus Proctor
must overcome his loathing of his own weakness and
learn to forgive himself before his act of resistance to the
official persecutions can have any meaning at all. In making this connection between the private agony and the
larger historical event, Miller shows his understanding of
the way in which essentially impersonal ideas must be
transformed into a personal dilemma if the conflict is to
issue in a tragic choice. Unlike the other victims of the
Salem tragedy, Proctor becomes an agent in the struggle
and concentrates in his private suffering the historically
documented crisis of a whole community.

Miller's presentation of the theocratic idea translated into political reality is particularly powerful in the third
act. In this "sharp" and "precise" time, the deputy governor himself comes from Boston to take the prosecution
out of the hands of the local "inquisitors." The matter
has become the case of the state against the Devil's assault
on Salem: "Do you know, Mr. Proctor, that the entire
contention of the state in these trials is that the voice of
Heaven is speaking through the children?" (Act III). Giv-
en such an assumption, the inquiry will extend beyond
the evidence of facts into the secret motivations of the
accused. So complete is the identification of the judgment
of the court with the judgment of God that all human responsibility is lifted from the shoulders of the witnesses
and the judge. The situation stands in contrast to the established procedures of the Church Litigant in *Saint
Joan*; it is analogous rather to the deliberately irrational
prosecution of Danton in the name of the Revolution.
Hence the fear of anyone's desire to undermine the authority of the court which is solely an embodiment and the
chief instrument of the theocratic idea. Miller drama-

tizes the unquestioned priority of the idea at the moment in the play when the deputy governor turns to question Abigail's veracity, and suffers a rebuke for his fleeting assumption of individual responsibility in the case.

> ABIGAIL, *in an open threat*: Let *you* beware, Mr. Danforth. Think you to be so mighty that the power of Hell may not turn *your* wits? Beware of it!

And the ensuing "crying out" returns absolute power to the pure theocrat until Proctor resorts to his last weapon: "It is a whore! . . . I have known her, sir. I have known her" (Act III).

This is the turning point of the play. Proctor's self-accusation, the sacrifice of his good name, does not succeed, however, in breaking down the judicial procedure of discriminating between absolute good and absolute evil, especially since his own servant girl takes up the cry of diabolism. For a moment Miller allows his hero to sink in a desperate acceptance of the devil's power: "I say—I say—God is dead!" But his interpretation of the devil's real power now brackets the judge with the accused:

> A fire, a fire is burning! I hear the boot of Lucifer, I see his filthy face! And it is my face, and yours, Danforth! For them that quail to bring men out of ignorance, as I have quailed, and as you quail now when you know in all your black hearts that this be fraud—God damns our kind especially, and we will burn, we will burn together. (Act III)

With this confession and insight Miller has redrawn the line which separates the saints from the sinners in preparation for Proctor's final choice, whether to admit the law's lie or to restitute his tarnished name. Joan would not deny her voices when she had to make the ultimate choice. But Proctor's dilemma has an added tragic dimension since he is burdened with the private sin of having been faithless to his wife:

> I cannot mount the gibbet like a saint. It is a fraud. I am not that man. My honesty is broke, Elizabeth; I am no

good man. Nothing's spoiled by giving them this lie that
were not rotten long before. . . . Spite only keeps me silent.

But in the end he cannot commit the far worse sin of dis-
honoring his name by a false confession: "Because it is
my name! Because I cannot have another in my life!"
(Act IV). There is an imputation here, as there was in
Saint Joan and *A Man for All Seasons*, that the choice is
dictated by pride, but his self-recognition: ". . . I do
think I see some shred of goodness in John Proctor,"
echoed by his wife, "He have his goodness now. God
forbid I take it from him!" establishes the meaning of his
tragic struggle in forgiving himself and preserving his
integrity against the power of theocracy in Massachu-
setts.

3

In each of the historical tragedies which we have examined, the playwright focuses on a moment of political
crisis signaling a change of direction in the evolution of a
society. In each the pattern is that of a confrontation between those in power, representing an established or a
temporarily enforced idea of social organization, and an
individual who in his opposition to authority either holds
fast to a displaced order of society or anticipates a change
that would entail the destruction of the present order.
To the historical dramatist writing in the tradition of
realism, this appears to be the typical tragic action which
is, however, as we have seen, capable of all kinds of variation. The conflict for the realistic playwright does not
involve a clear choice between good and evil; he care-
fully excludes villainy as a motive. Nor must the resistance of the hero appear to be an act of willfulness; his
vision of an alternative idea of social order must be founded
on historical possibility. Given the strength of character to
separate himself from the body politic and to persist in his
lonely role as a self-assertive individual, the hero of modern historical tragedy represents one side of an unavoid-

able clash of ideas. In such a drama the concept of necessity derives from a virtual identification of the hero's
singular spirit and purpose with the idea which gives it
shape.

On the other side, the society which cannot harbor this
foreign body in its organism is equally determined in preserving its static or evolving identity. Hence the inevitable
destructive collision. But in *The Crucible* we hear of a
community which is able to avert destruction. Andover,
so it is rumored, will have no part of witchcraft and has
thrown out the court which would perpetuate theocracy
and purge the town of rebels. Drawing the comparison,
Miller is justified in speaking of the *tragedy* of Salem
since even a whole society can suffer the consequences
of its inflexible exercise of power:

> Excellency, there are orphans wandering from house to house;
> abandoned cattle bellow on the highroads, the stink of rotting
> crops hangs everywhere, and no man knows when the harlots'
> cry will end his life.

Or else the cost of the conflict may be the destruction
of the spirit of a community as in Thomas More's prophecy: "It is a long road you have opened. For first men
will disclaim their hearts and presently they will have no
hearts. God help the people whose Statesmen walk your
road." But though the victors as well as the vanquished
must pay the cost of the historical struggle, its tragic significance resides not so much in the damage to the established institutions as in the agony of the individual protagonist because his suffering results from a personal
commitment in a crisis of historical dimensions; in his
unique dilemma and resultant fate both sides of the tragic
conflict are included. Mere resistance to injustice and
poverty on the part of an oppressed group, as in Hauptmann's *The Weavers*, cannot produce a tragic effect because the struggle involves no moral choice; the alternatives are either resignation or violent protest.

Other types of historical drama may be set against the
four examples of realistic historical tragedy in order to

clarify its characteristic structure. Anouilh's *Becket* is an entertaining dramatic pageant. I draw attention to it only to show the faulty conception of its central conflict. Superficially it may resemble a genuine historical conflict of ideas which is embodied in the confrontation between Henry II and Becket after the king appoints his dearest friend Archbishop of Canterbury. But Anouilh remains fascinated with the psychology of their relationship and therefore steers toward a catastrophe which is incommensurate with the nature of the conflict. The king becomes the antagonist out of sheer jealousy, because he feels his love scorned on account of Becket's newly found devotion to God. And therefore the test of Becket's commitment to the "honor of God" is irrelevant in this context. That is to say, the conflict which Anouilh construes is not between opposite forces of the same order. The choice is not between God and King or eternal justice and political convenience, as in Bolt's play about the testing of Thomas More's conscience. The alternative which Henry II offers to Becket is a return to the position of boon companion. Eliot's Thomas à Becket undergoes a spiritual battle with the four tempters, of whom he finds that only the last one offers a relevant agon before his martyrdom. Anouilh's Becket has no opponent either in his own conscience or outwardly in the king's claim on him. The knights who kill him are no more than agents of persecution. We may admire Becket for his steadfast devotion in the face of brutal power, but this play does not engage us in the moral predicament which might have been brought about by the relative claims of king and priest.

Osborne's *Luther* and Brecht's *Galileo*, on the other hand, are two far more instructive instances in which the potentially tragic pattern of the realistic history play can be found. But in these two dramas it has been deliberately truncated or modified to prevent a tragic conclusion. The conflict with authority in each case profoundly involves the fate of the protagonist, yet each playwright in his own way seeks for a nontragic effect. Osborne locates the struggle entirely within his hero. The historically

verifiable confrontations with the church are there, but
Osborne chooses to interpret the events of Luther's career as externalizations of an internal crisis of identity,
of the very private question, "How can I justify myself?"
Luther's appearance before the papal legate has to do
with his own struggle for certainty rather than his role as
an instrument of change in his society. In a perfectly serious sense, his repeated fits of physical suffering, traceable
to choked bowels, symbolize Osborne's emphasis on the
personality of the man. The play is a moving psychological study of Luther's love-hate relationship with God
and his fellow men, and it is this personal agony which,
for Osborne, determines his public actions. Thus restricted
in its emphasis, the drama is never intended to carry
to completion a tragic clash of ideas over the reformation
of the church.

Brecht gains his desired nontragic effect in the opposite
manner. Instead of concentrating on the personality of
his protagonist, he concentrates on the life of an idea.
His dramaturgy is the ultimate development of Hebbel's
theory that the modern drama would debate not merely
the relation of man to the idea of his time but the justification and validity of the idea itself. The realistic historical tragedy depicts the conflict of ideas in terms of the
suffering and the fate of an individual; therefore, it retains our interest in the emotional dilemma of the individual. Brecht abstracts a logical dilemma from a potentially
emotional dilemma, and, in keeping with his program
for an epic theater, transforms the spectator from a participant into an observer and judge of the problem unfolding before him. The emphasis is always on the idea of a
new scientific dispensation, not on the character of the
man propagating the idea. Consequently Brecht shows us
Galileo responding to the authorities in the spirit of
calculation rather than in the spirit of tragedy. Galileo's
disciples hope for a tragic act of defiance after his arrest,
in the manner of the heroes of the historical tragedy, but
he recants under pressure. At this point, Brecht affirms

his belief in the irrelevance of tragedy in human affairs in the following exchange:

ANDREA. Unhappy is the land that has no heroes!

*   *   *

GALILEI. No. Unhappy is the land that needs heroes.

Galileo's role as the proponent of a "new age" for mankind becomes, then, the object of investigation.

Brecht's method is an extension of Büchner's in *Danton's Death*. He too dramatizes discrete moments, constructing each scene for itself rather than for the sake of the following scene, and using them cumulatively like building blocks to exhibit the "case history" of Galileo as the man of the new science in the medieval society of his time. But instead of Danton's ironic self-contemplation, Galileo creates distance between himself and the spectator by speaking and acting only with reference to the new force which might alter the lives of men. For example, while the plague rages around him, he explains his new discoveries to his apprentice who is still weeping over his stricken mother, a scene which is simultaneously shocking and illuminating. It directs us, like other scenes, to an *understanding* of Galileo as totally absorbed in his work of discovery. Thus, his insatiable scientific curiosity at the outset enhances the possibilities of the idea of a new age supplanting the old, whereas his recantation checks the progress of the idea. In short, Brecht tries to limit our interest in Galileo as an individual man, which is a difficult feat in a staged performance, by equating his life with the rise, the progress, and ultimately the frustration of an idea.

Such a view subordinates the potentially tragic to the strictly historical interest, in Brecht's particular sense:

Historical events are unique, transitory events bound up with particular epochs. The behavior of the persons in them is not something purely human, unchangeable;

it has certain peculiarities because of the progress of history; it has obsolete aspects and aspects that can be made obsolete, and it is subject to the criticism of whatever epoch happens to follow. Constant development alienates us from the behavior of those born before us.[14]

In one sense, this is comparable to Shaw's conception of history in *Saint Joan*; as a general rule, Shaw would share Brecht's polemicist view that in a developing world human action may become obsolete and irrelevant, and therefore cannot be purely tragic. And if we are by definition "alienated from the behavior of those born before us," historical tragedy becomes impossible. Applied to this play, Brecht would have us judge Galileo's behavior and its consequences for our time; obviously the meaning of his recantation is liable to change as the function of science as a force in society changes. Brecht details Galileo's "social failure" in the extended confession to Andrea in scene 14 as well as in the added notes written from the vantage point of the atomic age. By retracting his doctrines and their implications before the inquisition and by pursuing his studies secretly like a mystery and "like a vice," divorced from any public function, Galileo "robbed [the] sciences of the greater part of their social significance."[15] But that failure may be reprehensible; according to Brecht's theory, it is not tragic in the commonly accepted use of the term.

NOTES

1. *Sämtliche Werke und Briefe*, II (1971), 444.
2. *Sämtliche Werke*, ed. R. M. Werner (Berlin: B. Behr's Verlag, 1904), XI, 192.
3. Concerning *Herodes und Mariamne*. Letter to Eduard Janinsky, Vienna, August 14, 1848.
4. Letter to Georg Gottfried Gervinus, Vienna, December 11, 1852.
5. *Sämtliche Werke und Briefe*, II (1971), 443.
6. |Giessen, 1834|. Ibid., II, 425-426. Büchner quotes *Matthew* 18:7.
7. Lukács, "Der faschistisch verfälschte und der wirkliche Georg Büchner" (1937, on the 100th anniversary of his death), in *Deutsche Realisten des 19. Jahrhunderts* (Berlin: Aufbau-Verlag, 1952), pp. 77, 83.

8. Ibid.

9. Letter to Gutzkow, Darmstadt, February 21, 1835.

10. Robert Bolt, *A Man for All Seasons* (New York: Random House, 1962).

11. Preface to *Saint Joan*, in *Nine Plays* (New York: Dodd, Mead, 1948), pp. 1029-1031.

12. *The Crucible* (New York: Viking, 1953).

13. *Wahn; oder, Der Teufel in Boston* (Los Angeles: Pazifische Presse, 1948).

14. "Kurze Beschreibung einer neuen Technik der Schauspiel-kunst, die einen Verfremdungseffekt ˙ hervorbringt," *Gesammelte Werke* (Frankfurt am Main: Suhrkamp Verlag, 1967), XV, 347.

15. "Preis oder Verdammung des Galilei?" (1947), ibid., XVII, 1108.

4. SOCIETY AND HUMAN PASSION AS A TRAGIC MOTIVE

1

When we think of the century-old tradition of realism in the modern theater, we tend to think directly of the social drama and Ibsen, the finest practitioner in this mode. Indeed, in the popular mind, the realistic theater is equated with the form of the social dramas of Ibsen's middle period and the many imitations in every part of the western world. We are thoroughly familiar with this type of play. But there is one strain in the developing realistic tragedy which Ibsen does not take up (excepting the earlier instance of *Brand*) until he enters upon his last series of plays beginning with *Rosmersholm*: human passion as tragic fate. When he combines this idea with his social thesis, he creates a unique tragic vision going·beyond the moral and social dilemmas of his preceding plays. The discussion of Ibsen's late plays which transcend the conventional social drama belongs in a subsequent chapter. The combination of social and psychological motives outside of Ibsen's work, however, takes another form for which Büchner's *Woyzeck* will serve as our prototype. It is a theater of passion in which the protagonists appear as subject to the impulses of their animal nature and to a social milieu that only aggravates their pathological readiness to destroy and be destroyed.

Passion as a tragic motive has a distinguished history in the drama, from the Greek theater through Shakespeare, the Jacobean dramatists, and Racine to Kleist's *Penthesilea*, which is often cited as an immediate forerunner of the moderns. Yet Büchner's version is radically different from all these and introduces elements into the tragic conception which will later also characterize the work of Zola, Strindberg, Hauptmann, Wedekind, O'Neill, and Miller in the same type of drama. The difference does not lie in the supposedly expanded awareness of psychological motivation. It is a critical commonplace that the great theaters of the past, even without the benefit of the romantic and modern emphasis on depth psychology, display an unparalleled insight into the workings of human passion. The difference lies primarily in the social context in which the passion is shown to overwhelm and take its toll of a human life. The clinical detail, if I may use the phrase, is no less true to experience in Euripides, Shakespeare, Webster or Racine than in the moderns. But in the modern playwrights the destructive course. of the passion which grips the protagonist is always linked with a particular social context that exerts an additional pressure on him. The older dramatists view man as a microcosm, himself the scene of an agon between the aberrant passions and the virtues requisite to a civilized life; hence the protagonist's behavior creates a social world about him which responds to his actions. But the modern realistic dramatists posit a social environment which acts at once as the hero's antagonist and the scene of his destruction. Their aim is to explore the fatal interplay between the passionate individual and the complex external reality of life, the tragedy of man as social animal.

In Shakespeare's middle tragedies we can see the classic treatment of tragic passion as a moral failing: the betrayal of love, piety, or reason, and the consequent ruin. Consider, for example, Othello's distortion of Desdemona's love, culminating in the "brothel scene" (IV,ii), and his final confession that he has thrown away a pearl like the base Indian and assaulted the Christian state like a Turk. The passion runs its course freely in the immediate domestic and professional world of the military commander which is merely suggested as background. As for the larger social context, it virtually disappears after the first night on Cyprus and reenters only with the embassy from Venice. It stands for the norms of civilized life by which we may be able to measure the enormity of Othello's crime. The case is, of course, more ambiguous in *Antony and Cleopatra* since the immoral lovers live out their passion in a world which itself has no moral authority except that of military efficiency. Shakespeare now celebrates the sheer power of the sexual passion, though not condoning its destructiveness; in the end even Octavius must pay his respects when he views Cleopatra's royal way of linking love and death. Without giving up the moral judgment of the two lovers, Shakespeare displays his obvious fascination with love and lust as a psychological phenomenon.

In the modern drama human passion becomes a psychological fact to be explored. It is not opposed to any moral norms, but rather placed in the social context, and, as we have noted, the potential force of passion within the protagonist actually derives its destructive power from the force of circumstances impinging on him. The playwright shows the combination of psychological and social forces operating as man's fate. Therein lies the difference between a drama like Kleist's *Penthesilea* (1808) and *Woyzeck*, our prototype of the realistic social and psychological tragedy. To be sure, Kleist does regard the Amazon's passion for Achilles as a fact to be reckoned with rather than an evil to be judged, and in that sense he has replaced the moral with the purely psychological view. In his precociously modern handling of unrestrained sexual passion he has anticipated the psychopathic behavior of stage heroines from Strindberg to Albee. But the play lacks the contributing social context of the realistic drama. Based on an episode from classical mythology, it does not connect the way of life in a given society with the fate of the heroine. The action takes place on the battlefields near Troy, where each military confrontation serves as a grand metaphor for the battle of the sexes; and the context of Penthesilea's suffering is rather the exotic customs of her tribe of female warriors than the recognizable life of human society.

Woyzeck, on the other hand, shows the interplay of psychological and social forces in an original way. That is the mark of its modernity. Significantly Büchner assumes the point of view, not of the social norm, but of the suffering individual. The captain, the doctor, the drum major, and even Marie appear like grotesque versions of the world as antagonist, because the center of consciousness is that of the virtually inarticulate specimen of human nature who serves Büchner as his protagonist. This is the artist's deliberate reversal of the journalist's point of view. The bare facts of the crime of passion committed by the real Johann Christian Woyzeck, who was executed in Leipzig in 1824, could be reported only as an offense against society. For the purposes of his play, however, Büchner transforms the insane murderer into the victim driven insane by the society. Though the fragmentary, unfinished drafts which he left at his death do not permit us to draw any certain conclusions about the sequence of scenes, it is clear that the dramatic sketches carry the subject beyond the simple plot of unfaithfulness, jealousy, and murder.[1] Marie's affair with the drum major fits into a larger design in which Woyzeck suffers the moral superiority of the captain, the scientific mania of the doctor, and the brute power of the drum major. Reduced to a demented beast, with his last possession taken from him, and driven by his paranoiac hallucinations, there is nothing to restrain his animal nature from retaliating in a final act of revolt. The play explores a total situation, from the hero's vantage point, fusing the world within and the outside world in a phantasmagoric perception of his disintegration.

Despite the unfinished state of the manuscript we may surmise that Büchner was again, as in *Danton's Death*, experimenting with an episodic structure. Aristotle insisted that an episodic structure cannot arouse the emotions of tragedy because it fails to impose a logic upon the incidents of the story. Shakespeare's episodic history plays are held together by the continuity of his ideas on legitimate kingship and usurpation, government and chaos; the arrangement of the incidents, the story line, is therefore guided by the morally significant selection of events. But

when Büchner assumes the role of contemporary social
historian, in his effort to create history "for the second
time," he chooses to create a mosaic of dramatic events.
Plot or story line is not useful to his tragic conception.
His purpose is to present a composite portrait of an incredibly wretched individual, the common soldier Woyzeck,
who experiences oppression in all relationships that make
up his circumscribed life. In exploring this situation in a
series of discrete scenes, the play at the same time describes a process of attrition that strips the hero of the last
vestiges of manhood. It demonstrates the inescapable result of total deprivation from a psychological, sociological,
and even physiological point of view. Woyzeck commits
the murder in a veritable state of trance; he performs a reflex action.

This is exactly what Strindberg thought naturalism in
art should properly do: to bring into play the ultimate
motives of human behavior and to analyze them in detail
in order to render the brutality and true complexity of life.
Woyzeck is the first modern play in which the human being is anatomized according to naturalistic principles.
Büchner places before us unaccommodated man, not like
Poor Tom abandoned on the heath, but one of the army of
wretched small men, a born underling in a society which
is not a shelter to him but a purgatory and just as surely
degrades him to being "no more but . . . a poor, bare,
forked animal." My allusions to *Lear* are intended to recall another world in which men reach the least common
denominator of human existence even from the highest
ranks in the social scale. After Hamlet's philosophical
disquisition on "What a piece of work is a man!" Shakespeare poses a related question, this time in naturalistic
terms, "Is man no more than this?" and conducts the
search for an answer in the open country. The scenes on
the heath which constitute the nadir of Lear's pilgrimage
stand in suggestive relation to Woyzeck's whole world,
the provincial garrison town in which he undergoes a
trial of body and soul that he cannot endure.[2]

In both plays the scenes of trial are at once naturalistic

and expressionistic in form, allowing us to view the disintegration of personality from the point of view of the
victims who reveal to us the experience of a progressive
alienation from the world. Both heroes find themselves
exiled, thrown upon their own resources in the struggle
to survive, and both transform the natural setting of their
affliction into a nightmare world. Thus their version of
reality is both distorted and true; but whereas Lear re-
creates his recent traumatic experiences of conflict which
as a king he cannot absorb in his consciousness, Woyzeck
receives the blow of each damaging encounter in dumb
submission, giving only indirect symbolic expression to
his deranged feelings. The usefulness of this analogy is,
of course, confined to detecting a similar atmosphere in
Lear's natural world of storms, beasts, and lunatics and
Woyzeck's world with its eerie landscape (*Open Field* and
particularly *The Pond*, at the scene of the murder), the
variety of animals that provoke comparison with the human race, and the psychological misfits that inhabit it.
Needless to say, it is a mark of the difference between the
two plays that Lear's descent into the natural world is
only an episode in his spiritual journey at the end of which
stands Cordelia, "who redeems nature from the general
curse"; in Shakespeare's total view, however dark it may
seem, Lear's assessment of Poor Tom as a worm, a poor,
bare, forked animal, is only true insofar as Edgar represents the possible degradation of humanity, but Edgar's
true role will be to lead his father out of despair. Lear's
belief on the heath that man is "no more than this" is
false, whereas Woyzeck's belief inside his purgatory that
the brutal world of nature unredeemed is the only world
for the likes of him is true. The antinomy between the
state of nature and the ordered moral life is at the heart
of both plays. Only Büchner demonstrates the impossibility of the second alternative for his representative man
from the lowest stratum of society.

Woyzeck's tenuous hold on the civil life is broken by the
confluence of two currents which lend each other force
to sweep him the short distance back into savagery. His

inner feverish confusion, emanating in images of desolation and in apocalyptic hallucinations, is augmented by
each encounter with the social world around him, causing
him finally to lose the saving grace of his basically good-
natured temperament. As in *Danton's Death*, Büchner's
irony, directed at the powers in human shape that press
upon his hero, increases the fierceness of his protest;
not that the play is a dramatized tract against the times,
but the satiric and hyperbolic treatment of the persons
who bait the miserable outcast gives them a monstrous
character. As in a dream, the grotesqueness only enhances their ineluctable force. Woyzeck's mind grasps
the fact that he has nothing, but it falters before the realization crowding in upon him that he *is* nothing. Büchner
"locates" his drama in that marginal area of the consciousness where the natural world has died, the social
world resembles an obscene witches' Sabbath, and the
mind struggles with the insistent question, Is man no
more than this? He records the tragic process of dissolution
as surely as any of the great tragic writers of the past.

"Friedrich Johann Franz Woyzeck, militiaman, fusileer
of the Second Regiment, Second Battalion, Company D, b.
the Feast of the Annunciation, July 20—today I am 30 years,
7 months, and 12 days old." Disposing of his last effects
before the murder, Woyzeck reads his military registra-
tion as if to determine his minimal identity, and even that
ironically is marred by a wrong date for Lady Day. The
stripping away of all the outward appurtenances of civilized life and even of the qualities that distinguish man
from beast goes on throughout the play. The captain, a
comically sentimental idealist, offers the first challenge
to Woyzeck's distracted behavior, which he ascribes to a
bad conscience. But as Woyzeck explains, in defense of
his illegitimate child, moral virtue is a luxury for the rich.
"The likes of us lack all blessings in this world and the
next. If we ever got into heaven, I think we'd have to lend
a hand with the thunder. . . . You see, we common people,
we have no virtue; the feeling just comes over us—it's nature. But if I were a gentleman and owned a hat and a

pocket watch and an Anglaise and could speak like people of quality, I'd be virtuous too. It must be a fine thing, sir, this virtue. But I am a poor fellow." The tone of Woyzeck's apology is that of genuine regret for his failure to measure up to the "higher" morality which the captain upholds with comic complacency, exactly as if it were a thing that all decent people ought to possess.

But if, in this scene, Büchner sardonically excludes Woyzeck from the sham community of morally decent men, he quickly goes one step further in testing his hero's claim to belonging to the human race at all. In the first of the two scenes with the doctor, whose chicanery he suffers in the name of science, as he had suffered the captain's in the name of morality, Woyzeck must once more apologize for the irresistible power which nature has over him. The analogy made by the barker at the fair between his trained animals and the social animals gaping at the spectacle prepares us for the doctor's medical experiments upon Woyzeck, the paid guinea pig. Woyzeck disappoints the doctor by being unable, like the performing horse, to resist the claims of nature: he is caught voiding against a wall. The horse exhibits its unexpected intelligence at the side show as well as its subordination to the laws of nature. But Woyzeck cannot keep his agreement, for three pennies a day, to retain his urine for scientific purposes. Hence the doctor's contempt: "It's nature, nature, nature! Haven't I proved once and for all that the *musculus constrictor vesicae* is subordinate to the will? Nature! Man is free, Woyzeck: man's individuality is transfigured into freedom. Not to be able to hold in one's urine!" The doctor reduces Woyzeck to the role of biological specimen, and a not very useful one at that. But in the second scene he is able to use Woyzeck to demonstrate to his medical students the effects on the human organism of a sustained diet of peas, and Woyzeck, though slightly embarrassed, even moves his ears in the cause of science.

Still, the moral and physical degradation, which will become the hallmark of the naturalist's study of man, is as

nothing to the decisive psychological crisis that lends
Woyzeck's struggle for survival the quality of a nightmare.
His estrangement from the world expresses itself at first
as a general delusion of persecution; through his hallucinations he invests nature with phantom objects and voices
that make him shrink with fear. But when they disappear,
"all is quiet as if the world were dead." His behavior is
that of an animal on the run, the object of a perpetual hunt.

> DOCTOR. Woyzeck, you have the most beautiful *aber-
> ratio mentalis partialis*, second species, a wonderfully pro-
> nounced case. An extra allowance for that, Woyzeck. Second
> species, monomania with a generally rational conduct. Do
> you still go about your work as usual, like shaving the cap-
> tain?
> WOYZECK. Yes sir.
> DOCTOR. Eating your peas?
> WOYZECK. Yes sir, regularly. The money goes to my wife for
> housekeeping.
>
>   *   *   *
>
> DOCTOR. An interesting *casus*. You get an increased allow-
> ance, Woyzeck. Keep up the good work! Let me see your
> pulse. Ah, yes.

Woyzeck's general susceptibility to the condition of paranoia, however, finds its specific occasion in Marie's unfaithfulness. Since she is all he has left in the world, his
unspecified suspicions and fears are channeled into one
torrential passion. The two short scenes, *Street* and *Marie's
Room*, develop an intensity of anguish which matches
that of the corresponding "brothel scene" in *Othello*. Woyzeck reacts physically to the torment of jealousy, goaded
by the captain's obscene hints: " . . . the earth is hellishly
hot—I am ice cold, ice cold—hell must be cold, I'll bet on
that.—It is impossible! . . ." But his greatest anguish is
the look of innocence on the sinner's face: "A sin so thick
and gross—the stench might smoke the little angels out of
their heaven. You have red lips, Marie. No blister on them?
Marie, you are as fair as sin itself—can mortal sin be so
fair?" Yet he can see nothing to give adequate proof to
his feelings: "Every man is an abyss; it makes one dizzy
to look down." By the time Woyzeck watches Marie and

the drum major dancing in the tavern, his bewilderment and disgust envelop the whole creation: "On and on! Spin and wallow together! Why doesn't God blow out the sun so that all may couple and tumble helter-skelter, man and woman, man and beast. Do it in the middle of the day, do it like the gnats on the back of the hand! —Wench—the wench is hot, hot!—On and on, round and round!" The echo of "Let copulation thrive" rings in our ears. There is method also in this madman's passionate, half-articulate outcry against the so-called rational world.

But the tragic power of *Woyzeck* does not depend alone on Büchner's radical analysis of the hero's anguish. As is the case in the darkest tragedies, the world of the play is itself in the grip of an inescapable disintegrating force. It is filled with people who express fear, guilt, remorse, despair, nihilism, as they move before us with brief dramatic gestures. Büchner summarizes their sense of total estrangement in the old woman's story of the abandoned child who searches the earth and the sun and the moon in his loneliness, but finds the whole universe deserted and in a state of decomposition, whereupon "he sits and weeps, and he still sits there and is all alone." At the conclusion of this prose Song of Experience, Woyzeck appears on the scene to conduct Marie to her death.

> WOYZECK. Marie!
> MARIE (frightened). What is it?
> WOYZECK. Marie, let us go. It's time.
> MARIE. Where to?
> WOYZECK. Who knows?

It takes the devil in human shape to reduce Othello to a fool, a beast, and finally a murderer, and Shakespeare plays upon the Christian prejudices of his audience in causing a baptized moor to commit a crime of passion. Still, the distance between his best image of the man and his worst is considerable. But our latter-day slave of passion appears to begin with in a state of psychological and social deprivation. There is no moral temptation to make him swerve from his better self; he has no choice at all. What Büchner

shows us is the slow cumulative pressure which causes
him to revert to the primitive life of instinct.

However great the difference between the tragic heroes
of the old drama and the new, both possess that which
makes them susceptible to undergoing their fate. They are
endowed with an energy that is needed to activate the fateful machinery of destruction. That is obvious enough
in a drama concerned with characters who are forced to
make moral choices, or in a drama in which the complication arises from a definite act of commitment. But the
naturalist playwright must also provide an inner force that
will credibly engage his hero in a life-and-death crisis and
lend him that will to persist which is his indispensable
claim to tragic stature. What was once a *donnée* for the
tragic dramatist, who used mythological or historical personages, kings, soldiers, or civic heroes, must now be replaced by intention. Not only the modern dramatists but
also the tragic novelists, like Dostoevsky, Conrad, and
Faulkner, invest their characters with an energy that is
yet compatible with their private worlds and their less
splendid station in life. The equivalence to "greatness of
soul" in the modern psychological and social drama may
be sheer tenacity, the will to survive, sexual passion (either
undisguised or in various forms of sublimation), or it may
be a compulsive idea, that is, an idea which has become a
felt obsession in the life of the character. In the phrase
"greatness of soul" I include the notion of hubris, "a mysterious dynamic" as Richard B. Sewall calls it;[3] the dynamic of the obsessed characters in the modern drama
is neither heroic nor mysterious, but it is equally powerful
as a motivating force. In *The Life of the Drama*, Eric Bentley summarizes the change in another way: "If Beauty in
the classic sense was allowed to die, a *terrible* beauty was
born. If the Noble and Heroic were excluded *ex hypothesi*,
the ignoble and unheroic revealed a wider range and a
deeper humanity than they could ever have been thought
capable of. . . . A modern tragedy is all that Schiller's
Mary Stuart is not: its movement is simply and steadily

down to defeat. Schiller's era ended, and the modern one began when Büchner wrote *Danton's Death*."[4]

In his last plays, Ibsen sought to reinvest his protagonists with "a mysterious dynamic," in this instance a quality of demonism which would make them, in the manner of the classic tragedy, the architects of their own destiny through commitment and individual guilt. But the majority of the psychological and social dramas remained on the level of naturalism. They permit their protagonists a sufficient stubborness of will or passionate feeling to lay themselves open to destruction. On the other side, the deadly trap is always poised, and it is its machinery which interests the modern dramatist. He analyzes from a social and psychological point of view the struggle between the generations, the battle of the sexes, the conflict between instinct and fixed codes of behavior, or the fight for self-preservation in an indifferent environment. Strindberg, Hauptmann, O'Neill, and Miller belong in this tradition which Ibsen felt he must transcend by implanting a dionysiac element in his middle-class heroes. In this chapter I shall be concerned with such tragic figures as Miss Julie, Eddie Carbone, and Willy Loman rather than their relatively grandiose counterparts, Hedda Gabler, Halvard Solness, and John Gabriel Borkman.

2

We are justified in speaking of a tradition, I believe, because there are recurrent tragic patterns in the work of these nineteenth- and twentieth-century playwrights which appear to them to be true to experience in the modern world. Willy Loman can be recognized as a twentieth-century middle-class version of Woyzeck, whether Miller knew Büchner's play or not when he wrote *Death of a Salesman*. And the affinities of *Streetcar Named Desire* to *Miss Julie* are no less striking, though the psychological interplay between Blanche and Kowalski lacks the full complication of the class conflict raging between Miss

Julie and Jean. The necessary adjustment of the social
relations to contemporary realities both in *Salesman* and
Streetcar does not alter the basic similarity in pattern to
the earlier plays. These playwrights display the naturalist's interest in the sociology and biology of survival in a
changing society; the novelty of Büchner's play is that in
the 1830s he chose as his protagonist a figure like Woyzeck
and was able to anticipate the naturalistic approach at all.
If Miss Julie and Blanche represent the typically modern
tragic type of the "half-woman" perishing in "a desperate
fight against nature," as Strindberg diagnoses the case, a
variation of the pattern is observable in the pathological
behavior of vampires like Hedda Gabler and, in a different
fashion, Wedekind's Lulu, who cannot come to terms
with reality either, and consequently try to reshape it.

   The battle of the sexes between husband and wife is, of
course, Strindberg's specialty. If his own tortured life
caused him to return to the subject with obsessive regular-
ity, as artist he was able to transform the conflict into a
variety of dramatic confrontations and tragic resolutions:
for example, the suffering captain in *The Father* becomes
the shrewd Baron in *The Bond* and eventually the demonic
captain in *The Dance of Death*. But the basic pattern
which Strindberg perfected is that of defeat by attrition,
the wearing away of the possibility of normal human relations. The metaphor here is not the trap of inexorable
social forces closing in from the outside, though these
forces always play a part in naturalistic tragedy; for his
strictly psychological conflicts Strindberg, rather, invented
the self-created prison, in which the life-or-death struggle
between the protagonists resembles a siege from within.
It is a tragic vision common to otherwise different types
of plays. Eric Bentley's generalization is especially pertinent here: "Modern tragedies are all journeys into night."[5]
The Dance of Death or The Journey into Night (or whatever metaphor we may be able to substitute) takes place
in a physically isolated locale which symbolizes the confinement of the actors to the arena of their conflict. A
granite fort, surrounded by the sea, holds the captain and

his wife, Alice, in Strindberg's play; a summer house surrounded by fog, the Tyrone family in O'Neill's play; a whitened sepulchral interior encloses Bernarda Alba and her daughters. But the true bond linking the actors in a danse macabre is the need for mutual laceration, as is the case also in Hauptmann's early psychological drama, *The Festival of Peace* (*Das Friedensfest*, 1890), which he subtitled, "A Family Catastrophe." The larger social context in these plays exerts its influence only marginally through the past failures and frustrations which played a part in making these characters what they are; their present agony is explored in purely psychological terms.

Thus, however powerfully moving Strindberg's marital battles may be in plays like *The Father, The Bond,* or *The Dance of Death,* the dramatic inquiry into motives and consequences stops short of penetrating to the broader social and moral causes that produce such characters and therefore such human misery. In each of these dramas, in a climactic moment, Strindberg poses the same question and gives virtually the same inconclusive, vaguely transcendental answer. As the captain lies helpless in a strait jacket, Laura's shawl reminds him of their courtship:

> When you were young, Laura, and we used to walk in the birch woods. There were primroses and thrushes— lovely, lovely! Think how beautiful life was then—and what it has become! You did not want it to become like this, neither did I. Yet it has. Who then rules our lives?
> LAURA. God.
> CAPTAIN. The God of strife then—or nowadays the Goddess! (*The Father,* Act III)[6]

And towards the conclusion of *The Bond:*

> BARON. . . . and you have no one but yourself to blame.
> BARONESS. Myself? Yes, but did I make myself? Put the evil tendencies, the hatred and wild passions into myself? No! Who denied me the power and the will to fight them? When I look at myself at this moment I feel I should be pitied. Shouldn't I?
> BARON. Indeed you should. We should both be pitied. . . . Do you know with what, do you know with whom we strove? You call him God, but I call him Nature. And that power in-

cited us to hatred, just as he incites mankind to love. And
now we are doomed to lacerate each other so long as one
spark of life remains in us. . . .
BARONESS. . . . I shall wander about the roads and in the
woods, so as to hide myself and be able to scream—scream
myself tired against God who has put this devilish love
into the world to torment mankind. . . .

Part I of *The Dance of Death* ends in a momentary truce
from sheer exhaustion.

ALICE. And now I am to be your nurse?
THE CAPTAIN. If you will.
ALICE. What else is there for me to do?
THE CAPTAIN. I don't know.
ALICE *slumps down in despair.*
ALICE. These are surely the everlasting fires! Is there no end?
THE CAPTAIN. Yes, but we must have patience. Perhaps
when death comes, life begins.
ALICE. Ah, if that were so . . . ! (Act II, scene 2)

And after the captain's death in Part II, Alice modulates her
expression of immense and cruel relief into a "requiem":

. . . For while we have been talking here, I've had a
vision of him when he was young. I saw him—I can see him
now—as he was when he was twenty. . . . I must have loved
that man.
KURT. And hated.
ALICE. *And* hated. . . . Peace be with him! (Act II)

The paradoxical love-hate relationship reflects Strindberg's
conviction that there is an inherent impasse in the marital
situation: instinctive wickedness on the part of the woman
and cunning on the part of the husband to retain his vestige
of masculinity. The captain in *The Dance of Death* fights
like a cunning beast, by his own testimony, to hold his
own in the hell which he and Alice have made of their fort,
before they become "garden manure for the wheel bar-
row." They contemplate themselves as instruments of an
absolute evil and talk of it as if it existed outside of themselves: "But everyone who comes near us grows evil and
goes his way. . . . Kurt was weak and evil is strong" (Part

I, Act II, scene 2). This is as far as a predominantly psychological inquiry can go.

Strindberg's naturalistic parables of marital conflict (and unwholesome child rearing) have to do with the narrow sociology of family life: the clash of wills, shifting balance of power, and the ultimate battle for survival. In contrast to *Miss Julie*, in which the conflict involves the "laws of nature" but also the laws of society, the social context in these plays serves merely as a frame or a setting for the cannibalistic battle between the sexes. The captain's generous nature and intellect in *The Father* are wrenched by his compulsive distrust, allowing Laura legally to take advantage of it, "a little innocent murder that the law cannot touch." The emphasis of the developing action is on the emasculation, the loss of his role as father and husband. Strindberg's paradigm of the clash of animal passions in a domestic setting, divorced from the life of society beyond the front door, set the direction for a number of playwrights who have tried to emulate his achievement as amateur psychologist. But, though the autobiographical element in Strindberg's art is evident, his imagination transmuted his experience and his prejudices into a spare dramatic statement which is universal rather than topical in its appeal; whereas in the same mode the plays of O'Neill, Williams, Inge, and Albee betray an increasing concern with merely idiosyncratic and psychopathic behavior. The captain's self-generated doubts about paternity, taken as a realistic reflection of human behavior, are surely eccentric; but the question itself has classic validity as a comic or tragic motive. In contrast, Albee's phantom child which is "killed" in the early morning hours of *Who's Afraid of Virginia Woolf?* is merely a product of neurotic minds; it has little to do with the archetypal games and battles of married life.

Strindberg's *The Father* succeeds against all odds. It is an almost purely psychological inquiry, omitting the larger social and moral context from which audiences ordinarily derive a generally shared meaning. A basic conflict of this sort, the battle between Man and Woman, succeeds

only if it embodies a significant tragic *action*. Human passion as such is meaningless in the drama unless the release
of energy in action is directed according to choice or purpose—"ethically," in Aristotelian terms. And the purpose
here is to destroy the erstwhile partner in marriage. But
a bare *situation* of psychological conflict, as in *The Dance
of Death* or *Long Day's Journey into Night*, can only de-
teriorate. The modern playwright who spurns the logic of
the social drama, the inescapable clash with the laws and
institutions of society, concentrating on psychological
relationships alone, may consign himself to writing variations on the Dance of Death. He runs this risk by separating the private from the social life of his characters. *The
Father*, a drama of pure passion leading to a tragic issue, is
a singular tour de force in the modern theater. The true
prototype, however, is the drama which, like *Woyzeck* even
in its unfinished form, fuses the psychological and social
motives with powerful results.

Arthur Miller's remarks in connection with the two versions of *A View from the Bridge* touch directly on this
point. Years later, they sound like a critical dialogue in
which he convinces himself that his gravitation toward the
form of the social drama was a correct choice. In the original one-act version of *A View from the Bridge* (produced in
1955), Miller also thought that he had a subject which demanded a classical simplicity in its presentation, purified
of all social concerns. When he first heard the story he mar-
veled "how directly, with what breathtaking simplicity, it
did evolve." As he recounts then in a Note, "It seemed to
me, finally, that its very bareness, its absolutely unswerving
path, its exposed skeleton, so to speak, was its wisdom and
even its charm and must not be tampered with."[7] The
semi-abstract set, the characters seen purely in terms of
their action, and the introduction of Alfieri as a chorus
speaking in verse—these created an "atmosphere . . . in
which nothing existed but the purpose of the tale," and a
tragic hero whom, in retrospect, he saw as a phenomenon,
"a figure, a force," suffering from an aberration.[8] "In this
instance," Miller continued in his original Note, "to cleave

to his story was to cleave to the man. . . . [The] *qualities* of the events themselves, their texture seemed to me more psychologically telling than a conventional investigation in width which would necessarily relax that clear, clean line of his catastrophe" (Note, 1955, p. 17). In other words, his original conception was tantamount to a retreat from the realistic, exploratory form of his preceding plays. The tale would have to stand as it was told, as fact or a synoptic version of reality; "when a character entered he proceeded directly to serve the catastrophe" (Introd., 1960, pp. vii-viii). For once, Miller wanted to see "a fine, high, always visible arc of forces moving in full view to a single explosion" (Note, 1955, p. 17).

The play stresses the universality of Eddie Carbone's dilemma and repeatedly guides the imagination to the distant, ancestral Mediterranean past. He was attracted to the clear, self-contained sequence of the events, "the myth-like march of the tale," in reaction to the staged psychodramas which had become fashionable in the New York theaters. But he also recognized the lack of a wider social context, the remote world in which Eddie lived out the course of his overwhelming passion, so that, given the opportunity of a second production in London, he revised the play with a view to placing Eddie "squarely in his social context." There is little doubt that Miller came to feel more at home in the full-length version of the play. The reasons he gives are instructive. They appear in several related essays published within a short span—"On Social Plays" (introducing the two one-act plays, *A Memory of Two Mondays* and *A View from the Bridge*, 1955), "The Family in Modern Drama" (first printed in the *Atlantic Monthly*, 1956), the Introduction to the two-act version of *A View* (1960), and the general Introduction to the *Collected Plays* (1957)—in which, incidentally, he demonstrates the progress he has made toward a theory of tragedy for our times, since the publication in 1949 of the very personal and critically unsophisticated statement, "Tragedy and the Common Man."

Miller notes with justified alarm the tendency of the mod-

ern theater to concentrate more and more on the life of the
individual psyche, as he pointedly phrases it, "retreating
into an area of psycho-sexual romanticism" (Introd., 1960,
p. vi), producing an antisocial drama suffused with feeling.
In opposition to this exercise in emotionalism and, at
worst, voyeurism, he proposes his idea of a modern social
drama, "the drama of the whole man" ("On Social Plays,"
p. 7), which is predicated, like the Greek drama, on the
notion that "the human being can live as a naturally political, naturally private, naturally engaged person" (p. 8) and
that his fate is most meaningful to us when we learn to
understand its causes in his private and in his social life.
In such a situation, i.e. *if* Miller's plea is reasonable that
"history has given the social drama its new chance," the
modern drama can break out of its perennial theme of frustration; "the new social dramatist . . . must be conscious
at least of the futility of isolating the psychological life of
man lest he fall always short of tragedy. . ." (p. 12). Miller
is a keen diagnostician. His essays deal, as they must,
not only with the shortcomings of the contemporary drama,
but also with the malaise of a society which is at once
the subject and the spectator of the futile Dance of Death.

But whether his projection of a new social drama modeled on the Greek community theater is anything more than a
fanciful theory can be proved only by his own work and
the work of those who share his optimistic democratic humanism. His statements range between what is feasible in
the theater and what is desirable in twentieth-century ur-
ban life. Describing the playwright who works under ideal
conditions, he says: ". . . what we call social matters become inseparable from subjective psychological matters,
and the drama is once again whole and capable of the
highest reach." The last hundred years of playwriting in
the best realistic tradition prove that this is feasible. Miller
knows however that today it is even difficult to imagine
"an individual fulfilling his subjective needs through social
action, to think of him as living most completely when he
lives most socially" (p. 6); and yet he predicts a new social
drama which "will be Greek in that the 'men' dealt with

in its scenes—the psychology and characterizations—will be more than ends in themselves and once again parts of a whole, a whole that is social, a whole that is Man" (pp. 14-15). Twenty years later, this prediction sounds incredibly cheerful. But the implication is there, and it is important, that the playwright working from such an assumption may possibly revive our consciousness of an inseparable private and social life, that only by making such an assumption he is able to ask the right questions about man in a pluralistic society, and that thus he may fulfill his highest function as artist and social critic.

At any rate, Miller's position with respect to the questions posed earlier is clear: "The social drama, as I see it, is the main stream and the antisocial drama a bypass. I can no longer take with ultimate seriousness a drama of individual psychology written for its own sake, however full it may be of insight and precise observation" (pp. 7-8). In the essay, "The Family in Modern Drama," Miller directs his attention to the way familial and social relationships govern dramatic form. Although his initial speculations are not particularly novel or fruitful, again he arrives at his best formulations when he abandons his penchant for general dramatic criticism and decides to put down his own experience and aims as a playwright. The question, "How may a man make of the outside world a home?" is Miller's own insistent way of perceiving and interpreting the condition of man in our society, and it leads him to the conception of a new social drama which may bridge the split between the private life of man and his social life. Insofar as the artist does not merely reflect the prevalent feelings of alienation, rootlessness, and frustration, but engages the spectator in a meaningful action involving the private and the social life, he realigns himself with the practice of tragic writers as different (in other respects) as Ibsen, Büchner, Shakespeare, and the Greeks. The modern version reads like this:

> . . . A serious work, to say nothing of a tragic one, cannot hope to achieve truly high excellence short of an investigation into the whole gamut of causation of which society is a mani-

fest and crucial part. Thus it is that the common Realism of
the past forty or fifty years has been assaulted—because it
could not, with ease and beauty, bridge the widening gap between the private life and the social life. Thus it is that the
problem was left unsolved by Expressionism, which evaded it
by forgoing psychological realism altogether and leaping over
to a portrayal of social forces alone. Thus it is that there is
now a certain decadence about many of our plays; in the past
ten years they have come more and more to dwell solely upon
psychology, with little or no attempt to locate and dramatize
the social roles and conflicts of their characters. For it is
proper to ascribe decay to that which turns its back upon society when, as is obvious to any intelligence, the fate of mankind
is social.[9]

Evidently he thought of both versions of *A View from the
Bridge* as social dramas in spite of "the mythlike feeling of
the story" (Introd., 1960, p. ix). Why then the expansion
of the social context in the revised play? He speaks of the
fortuitous circumstances of the London production, the
possibility of hiring more actors, the work of the British director, the fuller naturalistic set, suggesting the enveloping presence of a neighborhood world—all these created the
opportunity of making a more explorative full-length play
out of the earlier one-act version (p. viii). But a careful pe-
rusal of the various introductions shows that the alteration
was not quite so casually conceived. In his Note to the original play Miller emphasizes the mythlike character of the
story to the point of attributing archetypal qualities to it:
"When I heard this tale first it seemed to me that I had
heard it before, very long ago. After a time I thought that
it must be some re-enactment of a Greek myth which was
ringing a long-buried bell in my own subconscious mind.
. . . The thought has often occurred to me that the two
'submarines,' the immigrants who come to Eddie from
Italy, set out, as it were, two thousand years ago." And he
characterizes the motives as arising not from any comprehensible causation, but from unchallengeable determinant
passions: "There was such an iron-bound purity in the
autonomic egocentricity of the aims of each of the persons involved that the weaving together of their lives
seemed almost the work of a fate." No wonder that he ridi-

cules the notion that the "hard" and "objective" shape of the story could be tampered with, that is to say, brought closer to realistic observation: "It would be ripe for a slowly evolving drama through which the hero's antecedent life forces might, one by one, be brought to light until we know his relationships to his parents, his uncles, his grandmother, and the incident in his life which, when revealed toward the end of the second act, is clearly what drove him inevitably to his disaster" (Note, 1955, pp. 16-18). The tone of parody disappears in the following year when he actually added "significant psychological and behavioral detail" to make the play more human, warmer and less remote (Introd., 1960, p. x).

He has come to realize that "the mind of Eddie Carbone is not comprehensible apart from its relation to his neighborhood, his fellow workers, his social situation. His self-esteem depends upon their estimate of him, and his value is created largely by his fidelity to the code of his culture" (p. viii). Thus his earlier "sense of having somehow stumbled upon a hallowed tale" (1955, p. 18), or, in formal terms, "an unbreakable series of actions that went to create a closed circle impervious to all interpretation" (*Collected Plays*, pp. 47-48), gave way now to his practiced skill as a realistic playwright in placing the hero among his people, in providing simple human motivation, in short, in allowing Eddie to live out "his horror in the midst of a certain normality" (p. viii). And the New York setting, a platform representing Eddie's living-dining and "a Grecian-style pediment overhanging the abstract doorway to the house," gave way to a tenement building with fire escapes, passageways, suggested apartments, "bringing the people of the neighborhood into the foreground of the action" (*Collected Plays*, pp. 50,51). In the Introduction to the *Collected Plays* (1957), Miller describes the process of revision as stemming from a growing realization that the story was no longer something outside himself to be regarded with passionate detachment, but that it expressed a very personal preoccupation, that in the writing his life had created it. This growing intimacy

also meant that he must learn to understand it in his own
way, which was in terms of his conception of realistic social tragedy.

Miller's experience with the two versions of *A View from
the Bridge* provides us with a model for the psychological
and social mode of tragedy on the modern stage. His "reading" of the significance of the one-act version is practically an abstract of those plays which emphasize the psychological analysis of the human condition. "That reading,"
says Miller, "was the awesomeness of a passion which,
despite its contradicting the self-interest of the individual
it inhabits, despite every kind of warning, despite even
its destruction of the moral beliefs of the individual, proceeds to magnify its power over him until it destroys him"
(*Collected Plays*, p. 48). Strindberg, O'Neill, and Miller,.
at their best, manage to preserve that awesomeness in
their depiction of a passion-ridden individual disintegrating under the force of his own aberration or a psychologically crippled character collapsing under the force of
more robust specimens. But this type of drama has its obvious limitations. Looking inward into the psychological
and sexual dilemmas and minimizing the social role of its
protagonists, it transforms them into victims and leads,
in the hands of less gifted playwrights, to that characteristically modern genre, the theater of frustration.

The social drama, which Miller pronounces to be in the
main stream of the tradition, involves the individual with
the forces of his interior life as well as those forces, ideas,
codes, and concepts which define him as a social being.
Eddie's act of betrayal, prompted by the passion which
grips him, destroys him as a social being. Miller says of
the revised version: "What had seemed like a mere aberration had now risen to a fatal violation of an ancient
law" (Introd., 1960, p. ix). The tragic vision appears to
him to be of a different order in the two plays. That difference, as I have suggested earlier, is actually more pronounced in Strindberg's two naturalistic tragedies, *The
Father* and *Miss Julie.*

3

Strindberg's work—his plays as well as his theoretical remarks—remains exemplary in this mode. Underneath the realistic surface of his marital dramas (the captain's life in a house full of women, the divorce court proceedings in a Swedish village) he abstracts, in the conduct of his dramatic action, the schematic blows and counterblows of the battle between the sexes. In such short plays as *The Father* and *Miss Julie* we get only a momentary sense of the ordinary cadences of life, even as the plots move swiftly toward the extinction of the victim and the survival of the victor. The outcome is determined by the comparative strength, ruthlessness, and cunning of the combatants. It is a psychological (one is tempted to say, zoological) struggle for survival played against the domestic setting.

That, Strindberg seems to be saying, is the true center of interest for the modern dramatist, not the social and moral crises which the bourgeois mentality fabricates in response to the cruel facts of existence. Hence the ironic allusion to Ibsen's tragic heroine, Mrs. Alving. The obtuse doctor in *The Father*, who is virtually in collusion with the captain's wife, protests his neutrality in the marital battle:

> And I should like you to know, Captain, that when I heard that Mrs. Alving blackening her late husband's memory, I thought what a damned shame it was that the fellow should be dead.
>
> CAPTAIN. Do you think if he'd been alive he'd have said anything? Do you think if any husband rose from the dead he'd be believed? (Act II)

From the midst of the dramatic situation of *The Father*, Mrs. Alving's case appears to be a false version of the marital conflict. Her fault must have been greater than what she admits in her confession; and her suffering resulting from her hypocritical concealment of the "excesses" of her late husband appears to be an implausible subject for a tragedy. For Strindberg, it is the unflinching con-

frontation of the natural impulses ruling our behavior and
thus our lives that is the tragedian's task. *Ghosts* seems to
be out of focus, as his allusion indicates, because one of
the combatants is dead and Mrs. Alving struggles only
with the consequences of having given in to social pressure.

The battle for survival is inevitable, in Strindberg's
view, because it is waged instinctively, as in the animal
kingdom.

> KURT. . . . Do you know why you hate one another?
> ALICE. No, it's a quite unreasoning hatred. It has no cause,
> no object, but also no end. (*The Dance of Death*, Part one,
> Act I, scene 1)

This view of an unconscious motivation strikes the final
note of terror in *The Father*. As Laura approaches the
helpless reclining figure of her husband, she gives the woman's rationale of the battle she has just won:

> LAURA. But I didn't mean this to happen. I never really
> thought it out. I may have had some vague desire to get rid
> of you—you were in my way— and perhaps, if you see some
> plan in my actions, there was one, but I was unconscious of
> it. I have never given a thought to my actions—they simply
> ran along the rails you laid down. My conscience is clear,
> and before God I feel innocent, even if .I'm not. You
> weighed me down like a stone, pressing and pressing till my
> heart tried to shake off its intolerable burden. That's how
> it's been, and if without meaning to I have brought you to
> this, I ask your forgiveness.

Even the alleged cause of the conflict fades to insignificance after the battle has been won:

> LAURA. Your suspicions about our daughter are entire-
> ly unfounded.
> CAPTAIN. That's the horror of it. If they had some founda-
> tion, there would at least be something to catch hold of, to
> cling to. Now there are only shadows, lurking in the under-
> growth, peering out with grinning faces. . . . Reality, how-
> ever deadly, puts one on one's mettle, nerves body and
> soul for action, but as it is . . . my thoughts dissolve in fog,
> my brain grinds a void till it catches fire. . . . I'm cold.
> I'm terribly cold. (Act III)

The captain's doubts about his paternity are merely the occasion of the life-and-death struggle for power and as such they are both ridiculous and tragic. For the captain's orderly, Nöjd, who is accused of fathering an illegitimate child, the question is pragmatic; why should he slave all his life to bring up what may well be another man's brat? But the captain's idealistic attitude towards fatherhood, the atheist's bid for immortality, makes him vulnerable on both counts. His uncertainty amuses the old nurse, who takes the familial relationships with matriarchal equanimity: "Well, goodness me, you're all some woman's child, aren't you?—All you men, big or small . . . Lord, what a silly boy you are! Of course you're your own child's father. Come along and eat now. Don't sit here sulking . . . " (Act I). And Laura finds the question at first ridiculous, until she discovers its usefulness as a cruel device in the power struggle between them. As for the captain, he understands the ridiculousness of any man's claim to fatherhood on natural grounds alone, yet at the same time he is aware that his own position is tragic because his lack of certainty undermines his self-esteem and reduces him to the figure of a man-child. Viewed in its practical aspect, the plot shows how, step by step, Laura maneuvers him into a state of legal and physical impotence. But psychologically it traces the concurrent process of his self-induced disintegration. Strindberg clearly marks the stages which lead the captain from his obsessive ideas of the male-female relationship to his virtual emasculation.

The sequence begins in the first act when the captain affirms, perhaps even flaunts, his socially approved male authority over the household. The talk here is about his responsibility for financial matters and the religious education of the child. The woman "sells her birthright by legal contract and surrenders all her rights. In return the husband supports her and her children."

LAURA. So she has no rights over her own child?
CAPTAIN. None at all. When you have sold something, you don't expect to get it back and keep the money too. (Act I)

But the literal reading of the law, without the mutual trust which makes any contract or bond meaningful, is bound to become a power struggle. Laura perceives this opportunity at once: "Can't one tell who a child's father is? . . . Then how can the father have those rights over the mother's child?" and she is ready to drop the first doubts "like henbane" into the captain's ear. She has effectually shifted the argument from the question of legal rights to that of power. She has, says the captain, a fiendish power of getting her own way, "like all people who are unscrupulous about the means they employ," a judgment which is corroborated by the pastor who openly admires his sister's feral personality.

By the time of their second confrontation, in Act II, the captain's uncertainty about the child's parentage has become an irresistible preoccupation and has been generalized into an obsession with the ludicrous position of all fathers:

> CAPTAIN. Is it true that if you cross a mare with a zebra you get striped foals?
> DOCTOR, *astonished*. Perfectly true.
> CAPTAIN. And that if breeding is then continued with a stallion, the foals may still be striped?
> DOCTOR. That is also true.
> CAPTAIN. So, in certain circumstances, a stallion can sire striped foals, and vice versa.
> DOCTOR. That would appear to be the case.
> CAPTAIN. So the offspring's resemblance to the father proves nothing.

Strindberg is now able to abstract the contest for power between male and female on the basis of their different biological functions and the psychological advantage accruing to the female on account of the difference. In the open warfare which follows, Laura needs only to make the best of her advantage, unfeelingly to pursue her interests, since the captain's view of his own position drives him logically to the breaking point. The opening skirmish had occurred earlier:

> CAPTAIN. I find the whole thing tragic.

LAURA. Which makes you still more ridiculous.
CAPTAIN. But not you?
LAURA. No, we're in such a strong position.
CAPTAIN. That's why we can't fight you.
LAURA. Why try to fight a superior enemy?
CAPTAIN. Superior?
LAURA. Yes. It's odd, but I have never been able to look at a
man without feeling myself his superior.
CAPTAIN. One day you may meet your master—and you'll
never forget it.
LAURA. That will be fascinating.

Laura's sarcastic rejoinder reflects her instinctive consciousness that she is the superior enemy in a psycho-sexual contest. And the events prove her right.

The captain's suspicions typically feed "on trifles light
as air" until, convinced of an enormous deception, he
descends to the argument of his orderly, only on a grander
scale: "You women, who were so tender-hearted about
freeing black slaves, kept the white ones. I have slaved for
you, your child, your mother, your servants. . . . I have
had seventeen years of penal servitude—and I was innocent.
How can you make up to me for this?" His rage and Laura's reply, "Now you really are mad," mark the point of no
return in his growing impulse to prove the reality of his
idée fixe. Her assessment of his self-wrought passion is
correct: "If I say it isn't so, you still won't be certain, but
if I say it is, you will believe me. You must want it to be
true." And he does, because he is caught in the trap of his
own logical mind: the first supposition cannot be proved,
while the second can. Thus the debate cannot be carried
further. Laura cannot, even if she would, free him from
doubt because his assessment of her character is his undeniable premise: as a woman seeking to gain the upper
hand, and as a mother, she would commit any crime for
her child. Sensing his defeat the captain is reduced to
tears, begging for mercy on his life. Strindberg now modulates the dialogue into a new key, to investigate the peculiar sexual relations of the modern couple, the "incom-
plete" man and the wife posing as mother-mistress. He
was interested in the contemporary psychological research, but in his imaginative analysis of the causal rela-

tionship between the past and present in the life of the
psyche he anticipates twentieth-century psychiatry.

Two relationships originating in the past are now alternately acted out as in a charade. Stripped of his manhood,
the captain reverts to the first: child-mother-friend.

> CAPTAIN. Can't you see I'm helpless as a child? Can't you hear
> me crying to my mother that I'm hurt? Forget I'm a man, a
> soldier whose word men—and even beasts—obey. I am
> nothing but a sick creature in need of pity. I renounce every
> vestige of power and only beg for mercy on my life.

Laura's feelings respond with automatic certainty to the
evocation of this relationship.

> LAURA. Weep, then, my child, and you shall have your mother
> again. Remember, it was as your second mother that I came
> into your life. You were big and strong, yet not fully a man.
> You were a giant child who had come into the world too
> soon, or perhaps an unwanted child.

But the other relationship—lover-woman-enemy—is the one
which she recalls with revulsion:

> . . . I loved you as if you were my little boy. But didn't you
> see how, when your feelings changed and you came to me
> as a lover, I was ashamed? The joy I felt in your embraces
> was followed by such a sense of guilt my very blood seemed
> tainted. The mother became the mistress—horrible!
> CAPTAIN. I saw, but I didn't understand. I thought you de-
> spised my lack of virility, so I tried to win you as a woman by
> proving myself as a man.
> LAURA. That was your mistake. The mother was your friend,
> you see, but the woman was your enemy. Sexual love is con-
> flict. (Act II)

Having laid bare the causes of strife, Strindberg can
produce his dramatic climax. Making a last effort, the captain resumes the test of strength until he finds that he has
been outwitted. Only then, in an act of violence, throwing
the lighted lamp at Laura, he resorts to the only desperate
means left to him to strike back at his tormentor, and
Laura gains the last piece of evidence needed to have him
certified as insane. She describes her objective signifi-

cantly in biological terms: "Now you have fulfilled the unfortunately necessary functions of father and bread-winner. You are no longer needed, and you must go. . . ." To all intents and purposes the point of the play has been made, but Strindberg is not writing a thesis play. He needs to demonstrate, and have the audience experience, the physical detail of the captain's decline to impotence. Only now, in the last act, since Laura stands revealed as the mortal enemy, it is the old nurse who revives the actual memory of the child-mother-friend relationship as she slips the strait jacket over her "dear little boy."

As in the earlier parts of the play, Strindberg maintains his attention simultaneously to naturalistic surface detail and to symbolic action. The combination is powerful. It allows him to show that the gestures of civilized life only cover the brutal struggle for existence. The entire last act has to do with the preparations and the execution of the plan to secure the captain for shipment to an asylum. He has been imprisoned in his own house, and the people around him, though emotionally upset, perform their appointed tasks in this outrageous scene with moderate efficiency. Neither the pastor's well-bred remonstrance nor the nurse's fanatic piety has any relevance to what is going on. And when the captain calls to Nöjd for help, even the common soldier is on the side of civilization.

CAPTAIN. What? You can't manage one woman?
NÖJD. I could manage her all right, but there's something stops a man laying hands on a woman.
CAPTAIN. What is this something? Haven't they laid hands on me?
NÖJD. Yes, but I just can't do it, Sir. Same as if you was to tell me to hit Pastor. It's like religion, it's in your bones. I can't do it. (Act III)

The normalcy of these reactions and Laura's mindless denial of all responsibility—"But I didn't mean this to happen"—stand in sharp contrast to the captain's agitated search for literary analogues to his situation. To support his earlier suspiciousness he had found Homer and Ezekiel and Pushkin among his library volumes. And now, strapped and helpless on the sofa, he seeks to invest his defeat with meaningful precedents. Omphale comes to mind—"Playing with the club while Hercules spins your wool"—and Eve—"Shame on you, woman of Satan, and a curse on all your sex!"—but the effect is pathetic as he sinks back on the lap of his old nurse: "Ah, that's warmer! Lean over me so I can feel your breast. Oh how sweet it is to sleep upon a woman's breast, be she mother or mistress! But sweetest of all a mother's" (Act III).

His invocation of myths to account for his condition cannot alter the fact, proved by the last tableau, that he was doomed to extinction as a man unequal in a test of strength with the opposite sex. Strindberg underlines this naturalistic view of the struggle as a recurrent biological event. At the end of Act II Laura had dismissed the captain: " . . . You are no longer needed, and you must go. You must go, now that you realize my wits are as strong as my will—you won't want to stay and acknowledge my superiority." And in the final moments of the play the parable of married life ends—

> LAURA. Adolf, tell me, do you want to see your child?
> CAPTAIN. My child? A man has no children. Only women have children. So the future is theirs, while we die childless. O God, who holds all children dear!

—the mortal combat has been won. After the captain loses consciousness, Bertha runs to Laura.

> BERTHA. Mother! Mother!
> LAURA. My child! My own child!
> PASTOR. Amen.

Years later, Strindberg still wrestled with the subject in a one-act tragedy, *The Bond*, and a long drama in two parts, *The Dance of Death*. It is significant, I think, that both the one-act play, which takes about an hour in production, and the long drama, which should take between three and a half and four hours, exhibit the same limitation, the same narrowness of scope, inherent in the type. All the Strindbergian elements of sexual warfare are present. The antagonists face each other in a continuous psychological confrontation probing for the well-known weaknesses in the opponent, answering each vileness in kind, trying to gain the decisive advantage. But they are well-matched opponents in these plays, and therefore the agony is drawn out. "Falsehood persists like original sin," says the skeptical old pastor, in his warning to the inexperienced judge in *The Bond*. The evil is ineradicable for those who are bound to each other as are the Baron and the Baroness by a child who will survive their divorce, and the captain and Alice, in *The Dance of Death*, by the hatred which keeps them alive: ". . . We are welded together—we can't escape. Once we *did* separate—in our own home—for five years. Now only death can separate us. We know it, so we wait for him as the deliverer." The limitation of these plays is that they represent, not an action which defines the fate of the characters, but rather a series of ingeniously varied acts of mutilation, like a large canvas depicting damned souls tormenting each other without reprieve. In *The Father*, however, the antagonists do not wait for death. They battle for absolute superiority until the inevitable end. The conclusion may be fairly drawn that in a naturalistic tragedy of this type a definitive action—the survival of the strong, the extinction of the weak, or the self-destruction of the man of uncontrollable passion—must emerge from the observed psychological conflicts. The conflicts in themselves represent only a static situation, as Strindberg's occasional imagery indicates:

> BARON. We have torn one another as bloodily as wild beasts; we have laid bare our shame before all these people who rejoice at our ruin. . . .

> *　　*　　*

> BARONESS. . . . It is as if we have been dragged into a mill and got our clothes caught in the wheels. And all these malicious people stand looking on, laughing. What have we done? What have we done in our anger? Think how they will enjoy it, all these people, seeing the Baron and Baroness stripped and scourging one another. Oh, I feel as if I were standing here naked!
> *She fastens her cloak again.*

Yet the Baron and the Baroness as well as the Captain and Alice resume their danse macabre. The figure is apt for Strindberg, since he seemed almost doomed to reiterate compulsively the pattern of his own dance of death.

4

O'Neill performs a similar, cathartic, task in *Long Day's Journey into Night*, enabled, as he says, "to face my dead at last."[10] As with Strindberg, his repetition-compulsion, the effort to rehearse and thereby control his painful memories, extends over a number of his late plays. It also operates, as it does in Strindberg, within the single drama like a circular narrowing spiral. The same accusations recur like musical motifs and are intensified with each repetition until they threaten to become unbearable, except that the four tortured souls consign themselves to the stupor of whisky and drugs to speed the journey into night. But, as in the case of the dance of death, intensification can lead only to a worsening of an existing situation. It does not effect a change of fortunes which illuminates the tragic fate of man. Although *The Iceman Cometh*, which O'Neill finished two years before *Long Day's Journey*, insists heavily on the pattern of repetition and although the play ends where it began as far as the derelicts of Harry's bar are concerned, it does present a distinct dramatic action which derives its meaning from the desperate, but sober, choices made by Larry Slade and the evangelical salesman of death, Hickey. The difference between these two plays illustrates once again that the exploration of psychological conflict, whether between persons or within the mind of an individual, has only limited possibilities in the tragic drama unless it serves an ulterior purpose beyond its immediate sensational interest.

The similarity of O'Neill's workmanship in the two plays —the almost leisurely building up of an atmosphere of psychological crisis which the characters begin to shut out from their consciousness as the suffering becomes too intense—should not blind us to the difference in the conception and the structure. The ordering principle of *Long Day's Journey* is linear, chronological, describing the process of straight deterioration as the fog and the night close in. The momentary hope of redemption—"some day when the Blessed Virgin Mary forgives me and gives me back the faith in Her love and pity I used to have in my convent days, and I can pray to Her again" (Act II, scene 2)—is a helpless show of rhetoric under the given circumstances. It cannot possibly alter the course of events as O'Neill has conceived them. Hickey's intrusion, on the other hand, forces the inmates of Harry's saloon to experiment with his idea of freedom from illusion in order to gain peace. Dramatically he causes a classic reversal of intention, which makes the ordinary alcoholics come back to their collective dreams of well-being, since they cannot bear very much reality, while Larry Slade becomes his only real convert to death. At the end of the play, Larry sits in isolation in his chair by the window, staring in front of him, oblivious to their racket. Forced to participate in the life he thought he had given up and being witness to the death of the spirit in himself, he has achieved tragic consciousness. The Tyrone family, without a challenge to the spirit to *choose* hopelessness, slip gradually into exhausted resignation.

Both plays differ from Strindberg's tragedies, as well as O'Neill's earlier *Desire Under the Elms*, in their preoccupation with guilt. Instead of the naturalistic assumption of forces arising from social and biological necessity, which are reflected in predatory relationships, these plays deal with the idea of inexpiable guilt. Therefore, the characters rummage in their past, trying either to refashion it into an acceptable reality by deluding themselves or to sever its effects in the present through the use of opiates. Since each character is exposed to the watchful eye of another and all know the truth in their moments of sobriety, the relationships are alternately painful and compassionate. The amoral logic of the naturalistic plot, based on the relative strength of the opposing forces, gives way to a mellower pattern among the victims (there are no victors) of flaring resentment, followed immediately by remorse, pity, even sentimentality, on their common journey into night. Contrary to Strindberg's characters, who bluntly exploit each other's faults and weaknesses, O'Neill's characters thrust and parry, exposing and recovering their pretensions, which gives the dialogue a hide-and-seek quality in these late plays. Albee is indebted to both playwrights in *Who's Afraid of Virginia Woolf ?*: to O'Neill for the effects achieved by his characters through whisky and the consciousness of personal failure and to Strindberg for the grotesque, hysterical animosities of a permanent family quarrel.

The key difference between *Long Day's Journey* and *The Iceman Cometh* may be illustrated by the characters' awareness of time. The problem for all of them is how to redeem the failures of the past. The Tyrones, caught in a network of painful interrelationships, are unable to surmount the remembered wrongs which are still imprinted in their personalities. Edmund's birth and present illness, Jamie's cynicism, and Tyrone's cheapness are all connected with Mary's drug addiction; it is actually her journey into night which we witness and metaphorically the three men's, as they watch her slip away where, as Edmund describes the fog, "life can hide from itself." The present in this play is irredeemably tied to the past. Such a view may yield, on the simplest level, the kind of detached pathos that Mary is capable of voicing:

> But I suppose life has made him like that, and he can't help it. None of us can help the things life has done to us. They're done before you realize it, and once they're done they make you do other things until at last everything comes between you and what you'd like to be, and you've lost your true self forever. (Act II, scene 1)

Or,

> TYRONE. Mary! For God's sake, forget the past!
> MARY, *with strange objective calm.* Why? How can I? The past is the present, isn't it? It's the future, too. We all try to lie out of that but life won't let us. (Act II, scene 2)

In response to Mary's fatalism and her only way out—to kill
the pain, to "go back until at last you are beyond its reach.
Only the past when you were happy is real" (Act III)—the
three men are forced into the crosscurrents of love and
hatred which are the substance of the drama. Ultimately,
only two alternative attitudes are open to the dramatist
who treats the relation of past to present with such unqualified determinism. In deciding to write the play and making his presence felt in each agonizing encounter, O'Neill
assumes one attitude, that of facing his dead nobly and
courageously. But for his characters, seen objectively by
the audience, he must assume the opposite attitude toward
the past: resignation and escape into obliviousness. Thus,
in one way, the play is a magnificent act of the private conscience. Seen in another way, as an objective dramatization of four wretched characters who rehearse their family
history to the point of attrition, it cannot get beyond the
logic of its simple postulate—that the past is the present
and the future, too. Hence the pattern of a steadily in-
tensifying dance of death.

The chorus of devotees to the "pipe dream" in *The Iceman Cometh* share the same fate, except that they delude
themselves sufficiently with respect to the past and the
possibilities of the future to keep up the appearance of
life, or, to put it another way, to preserve an eternal present precariously balanced between their false dreams of
the past and the future. "I've never known more contented
men," says Larry Slade. "It isn't often that men attain the
true goal of their heart's desire" (Act I).[11] The remark is,
of course, ironical, colored by Larry's cynicism about life
in the outside world and his pity for the living dead in the
back room of Harry Hope's saloon. Supposedly free from
illusion, being through with life in the cannibal world, he
can act as O'Neill's raisonneur in the opening portion of
the play, and it is through him that we learn of each man's
threatening past, which brought him to this place. "No one
here has to worry about where they're going next, because
there is no farther they can go. It's a great comfort to
them."

But in this play O'Neill breaks the repetitive pattern of illusion, despair, escape-into-forgetfulness and back to illusion. In the central action of the play he examines the effect of erasing the past and the future, the possibility of finding true peace, i.e., freedom from guilt and remorse, by living in a today severed from the burden of yesterday and the nagging obligation of tomorrow. This promise of salvation is held out to the tortured souls; if only they would agree to test their false dreams by leaving their refuge, they would return confirmed in their hopelessness and therefore at peace with themselves. But at the center of this experiment in the psychology of despair O'Neill places the fantastic story of the false messiah, Hickey, who unravels, bit by bit, his own search for peace. It is O'Neill's way of enacting allegorically the murder of the human conscience, the death of the spirit. At the end of each act, Hickey reveals fragments of his own quest for peace, which is somehow connected with his wife's death. Meanwhile, our attention is caught up in his crusade to free Harry Hope and his guests from their illusory dreams. In doing so, proving them incapable of joining the world of the living, he kills the last spark of self-esteem and the will to live in each of them. Harry Hope looks like a corpse after his unsuccessful sally out into the street, and Joe, the negro gambler, epitomizes their total collapse, "Scuse me, White Boys. Scuse me for livin'. I don't want to be where I's not wanted," as he joins his white brothers in the death-watch, all of them trying to pass out. But, paradoxically, they cannot because Hickey's presence has even taken the "life" out of the booze.

Not until Hickey completes his confession in the final act do they understand the cost of the peace which he tried to bring to them. His tale is the personification of the soul choosing death over false hope or the self-destruction of the psyche. No wonder that his recitation of the murder of his wife Evelyn becomes excruciatingly painful to his listeners so that they try to drown out the climax of his story by pounding their glasses on the tables and grumbling in chorus, "Who the hell cares? We want to pass out in peace!" They see in Hickey's story the image of their own plight. Since they cannot overcome their past failures and lack the strength of will to return to the world outside, they ought to accept Hickey's peace of death. But the instinct of self-preservation is strong. The first suggestion that Hickey might have been insane allows them to explain away their own behavior and to resume their old ways. So much for the chorus; they have felt the touch of death but in the end the whisky has its old kick again, blotting out their consciousness of Hickey's deadly experiment.

But Hickey's exemplary act, freeing himself from guilt and hope and thereby making time discontinuous, leaves a profound impression on Larry Slade.

> HICKEY (*With a strange mad earnestness*) Oh, I want to go, Officer. I can hardly wait now. . . . You've got me all wrong, Officer. I want to go to the Chair.
> MORAN Crap!
> HICKEY (*Exasperatedly*) God, you're a dumb dick! Do you suppose I give a damn about life now? Why, you bonehead, I haven't got a single damned lying hope or pipe dream left!

*   *   *

> LARRY (*His eyes full of pain and pity—in a whisper, aloud to himself*) May the Chair bring him peace at last, the poor tortured bastard! (Act IV)

Although Slade is the first to recognize that Hickey's gift of peace is poison and that the great Nihilist has "started a movement that'll blow up the world," his own position undergoes a significant change even as he taunts Hickey's evangelical zeal and elicits his piecemeal confession. Slade's original pose is that of the intelligent nihilist, free from worldly greed, hope, and illusion, cut off from his past and peaceful at the bottom of a bottle.

> Forget the anarchist part of it. I'm through with the Movement long since. I saw men didn't want to be saved from themselves, for that would mean they'd have to give up greed, and they'll never pay that price for liberty. So I said to the world, God bless all here, and may the best man win and die of gluttony! And I took a seat in the grandstand of philosophi-

cal detachment to fall asleep observing the cannibals do their
death dance. (Act I)

But thus located out of time, in a today without a yesterday
and a tomorrow, as Hickey would have it for the other tor-
mented souls, Slade finds himself confronted with an in-
truder from the past. His defenses hold against the prompt-
ing of his memory and his conscience until Hickey completes the revelation of his desperate act to still his own
conscience. Then Slade recognizes the kinship between
the Great Salesman of death and the young traitor, Don
Parritt, whose own desperate act demands punishment to
ease his guilt. He is drawn back into an awareness that the
past and the present cannot be severed, not because he
believes in retribution but because his pose of detachment
is flawed by the involuntary pity in his heart. Thus he
sends Parritt to his death with a curse for his act of betrayal, but modulates it into a kind of blessing which echoes his final tribute to Hickey:

> LARRY (*Pleads distractedly*) Go, for the love of Christ,
> you mad tortured bastard, for your own sake!
> PARRITT . . . Jesus, Larry, thanks. That's kind. I knew you
> were the only one who could understand my side of it.
> (Act IV)

Now Slade is the deathbringer, waiting with eyes shut for
the thump of Parritt's body hurtling down from the fire escape, while the company at the other tables drink heavily
to get "paralyzed." If they celebrate the loss of consciousness, a radical metaphor for the human condition, he, the
lone protagonist of these lower depths, beset by bad
dreams, has gained a clarity of consciousness which comes
only with a tragic act of commitment.

> LARRY . . . God rest his soul in peace. (*He opens his
> eyes—with bitter self-derision*) Ah, the damned pity—the
> wrong kind, as Hickey said! Be God, there's no hope! I'll
> never be a success in the grandstand—or anywhere else! Life
> is too much for me! I'll be a weak fool looking with pity at
> the two sides of everything till the day I die! (*With an in-
> tense bitter sincerity*) May that day come soon! (*He pauses*

startledly, surprised at himself—then with a sardonic grin)
Be God, I'm the only real convert to death Hickey made
here. From the bottom of my coward's heart I mean that
now! (Act IV)

Compared with *Long Day's Journey*, O'Neill's view of the ineluctable pressure of the past is no brighter nor less deterministic in this play, but he is able to explore its impact
on the reluctant human conscience with greater sophisti-
cation. In their individual monologues, the four Tyrones
achieve a certain lucidity about their lives, but essentially
each laments over the loss of what might have been. Thus
the psychological stalemate of *Long Day's Journey* pro-
longs the dull ache of suffering toward ultimate resignation, which is basically a pre-tragic experience; like Alice
and the captain in *The Dance of Death*, the Tyrones can
only wait for death. But Hickey and Larry Slade enact an
existential drama, a modern morality play about the life
and death of the human spirit. Slade's act is not merely a
gesture of resignation to the commonplace pattern of suffering and self-delusion; it is an unqualified and therefore
tragic acceptance of hopelessness as the moral and psychological condition of man. *The Iceman Cometh* is a
more meaningful play than *Long Day's Journey into Night*.

We should not be deceived in our judgment by the lurid
setting and by characters who barely maintain their hold
on the outer edge of existence. It is true that the Tyrones,
in their purgatory, represent a more immediately recognizable image of a family conflict, involving strongly individualized characters. The play is undoubtedly a virtuoso
performance. Yet *The Iceman Cometh*, like *The Father*,
despite the hyperbolic and paranoiac behavior imputed
to the characters, bespeaks the human *condition* in one
of its aspects, whereas *Long Day's Journey* offers a minutely drawn picture of a family *situation*. To put the distinction in another way, the autobiographical, confessional character of the latter play allows us, the spectators, to
generalize from particulars; but the Tyrones remain
O'Neill's people (evoking an attitude of embarrassed respect and compassion as if we were trespassing in a family

mausoleum), just as Alice and the captain represent
Strindberg's particular version of marital "infighting,"
however much they may remind us of people and situations that we know. In contrast, the individuality of the
captain and Laura in *The Father* and the particularity of
their life-and-death struggle are fused in and embody the
idea of the eternal battle between the sexes. Similarly,
The Iceman Cometh, by virtue of the central action involving Hickey's ill-conceived bid for freedom and Slade's
conversion to the peace of death, presents an archetype
of the human struggle to escape the past and the future
that make the present so unbearable. Each play rises
above the imitation of fixed and recurrent psychological
conflicts to explore, in a clearly defined tragic action, the
drastic consequences of an idea relentlessly pursued. The
characters in these plays, as Coleridge said of Shakespeare's, may be termed ideal realities. "They are not the
things themselves, so much as abstracts of the things,
which a great mind takes into itself, and there naturalizes
them to its own conception."[12]

5

The plays of Strindberg and O'Neill discussed in the preceding sections do not exactly fall into the category of
"anti-social" drama. But there is little doubt that they
exemplify the gap between the private life and the social
life which Miller detected in the modern realistic drama.
One would not conclude on the basis of these plays that
"the fate of mankind is social." The characters, as we have
seen, are deliberately set apart from the larger social context, to fight their private battles of passion and conscience. Their arguments dredge up failures and weaknesses involving their former lives outside; but the
accusations and postures of forgiveness and remorse which
constitute the drama before us have no bearing on the
outside world. The social vacuum around the Tyrones, for
example, represents no doubt a fact in O'Neill's past; but
it also characterizes the drama as a deliberately introverted
psychological exploration. The summer house is surrounded

by fog, not by the outside world of men and women playing a part in the fate of the Tyrones.

Miller's characters are, of course, also entangled in passionate psychological conflicts. The difference is that Eddie Carbone's "awesome" passion in *A View from the Bridge* matters to the community of longshoremen in which he has his identity as a social being. His act of betrayal is an infraction of the law by which they live and, therefore, at the same time the destruction of the moral foundation of his own life. He is a creature of his society. So is Willy Loman, though in a different sense. The city pressing in on the small home left standing from another era could not care less about Willy's futile struggle to maintain his place in society. But though it is indifferent, or rather because it is indifferent, the society affects the personal relations between Willy and his family, particularly the relation between father and son. *Death of a Salesman* resembles O'Neill's two plays in that the past penetrates the present both as a sentimental memory of happiness and the ground of the mounting failure "to make a home of the outside world." In Miller's play, however, the psychological conflicts in the family stem from that failure on the part of the father and his sons to find their identity in the world outside. O'Neill's people are, to begin with, cut off from the world; they concentrate on their guilty consciences and flirt with narcosis and death. O'Neill stresses the pain of the mind's journey into night, whereas Miller dramatizes the truncated life of a man rejected by society. Like Büchner's Woyzeck, the common man in Miller's plays is a victim both of inner forces which distort his vision and the pressure of an unappeasable society from without.

Zola, who wrote a preface to the French translation of *The Father*, was profoundly impressed by the play, but he sensed something of the gap between the private and the social life when he complained that the characters lacked *un état civil complet*. He could not have made the same complaint about *Miss Julie*, where the social milieu so conditions the behavior of the characters that the battle of the sexes is inflamed by the class conflict. (Laura's social and intellectual inferiority to the captain is not an explicit theme in *The Father*; on the contrary, it only helps to underline the biological advantage of the female regardless of her status.) The tragic pattern of the plays to be considered in this and the next section is one in which human passion, whether in the form of sexuality or a compulsively pursued desire, seeks to break through the tribal codes and regulative sanctions which are the way of the world. Successful or not, the attempted assertion of instinct over alien rule or custom is self-destructive. It must be an index to our Western social values that the majority of such plays center on the passionate or pathological female: *Miss Julie, Hedda Gabler, Earth Spirit* and *Pandora's Box, Magda, The Passion Flower, The House of Bernarda Alba, Desire under the Elms, A Streetcar Named Desire*. In fact, Eddie Carbone is the exceptional male protagonist, who is gripped by sexual passion and wrenched by his deed beyond the pale of his society.

Unfulfilled passion, impulse, desire thrust the character into the arena of tragic conflict. Since the antagonist is society itself, we are witnessing not merely the psychological disintegration of an individual, but his destruction by the punitive force of the law, which does not tolerate the errant or defective personality. Whether the law by which people live in community is moral or merely brutal, the fate of the individual in these plays is social. This is not true of *The Father*, which is Strindberg's demonstration, fundamentally, of the law of nature and therefore depends on the exclusion of the social context; Laura uses the civil law only for pragmatic purposes, to further her design, and the onlookers, the doctor and the pastor, must either cooperate or acquiesce in the methodical destruction of the captain.

If Strindberg's and O'Neill's dramas focus on the battles of the private conscience and stress primarily the psychological crises, some of Hauptmann's naturalistic plays may be the best illustrations of the opposite emphasis. After two early dramas, *The Festival of Peace (Das*

Friedensfest) and *Lonely Lives* (*Einsame Menschen*), which
also explore the psychological frictions of family life,
Hauptmann shifted his attention to the oppressive system of industrial employment in *The Weavers*. He goes
beyond social protest drama, showing how conditions of
extreme misery alter the humanity of individual men and
turn them into a mob. But it is a perspective view of men
coalescing into a group and suffering from forces external
to themselves. Similarly Hauptmann's best version of the
tragedy of sexual passion, *Rose Bernd*, takes as its vantage point the peasant heroine's exposure to male lust.
Her beauty makes her a hunted animal, driven to infanti-
cide. She is simply the victim of unrestrained desire,
blackmail, and her father's blind piety. Hauptmann com-
passionately demonstrates how common people, subjected
to forces that disrupt their small, well-ordered lives, may
be driven to despair. The difference between this conception of the social drama and that of Strindberg and Miller
should become clear in the following discussion. Hauptmann describes the impact of the outside world on the
lives of helpless individuals. But the true combination of
psychological and social drama amalgamates the private
and the social roles in the action and suffering of a single
dramatic figure.

Strindberg captures the combination in an image following the seduction and short scene of vulgar recrimina-
tions between Miss Julie and Jean:

JULIE. Go on hitting me.
JEAN, *rising*. No. On the contrary I apologise for what I've
said. I don't hit a person who's down—least of all a woman.
I can't deny there's a certain satisfaction in finding that
what dazzled one below was just moonshine, that that fal-
con's back is grey after all, that there's powder on the love-
ly cheek, that polished nails can have black tips, that the
handkerchief is dirty although it smells of scent. On the
other hand it hurts to find that what I was struggling to
reach wasn't high and isn't real. It hurts to see you fallen
so low you're far lower than your own cook. Hurts like
when you see the last flowers of summer lashed to pieces
by rain and turned to mud. [Trans. Elizabeth Sprigge]

The ruin of the flower late in the season of its bloom points to
the coincident fate of the individual and the species too
frail to weather the storm, and Jean half regrets the collapse of position and pride. Miss Julie's fall is at once a
private catastrophe and a social displacement which
leaves her no way out except concealment and death. In
the end, it is the service bell and the speaking-tube leading from the kitchen to the count's quarters upstairs that
send Julie to her death and return Jean to his station as
the count's manservant in the highly structured household.

In *A Streetcar Named Desire*, which I wish to use as a
foil to *Miss Julie*, there is a contrasting image, summing
up Blanche's pathetic view of the individual exposed to
the inclement conditions of the unsheltered life.

> BLANCHE [with reference to the candles on her birth-
> day cake]: You ought to save them for baby's birthdays.
> Oh, I hope candles are going to glow in his life and I hope
> that his eyes are going to be like candles, like two blue candles
> lighted in a white cake!
> STANLEY [*sitting down*]: What poetry!
> BLANCHE: His Auntie knows candles aren't safe, that candles
> burn out in little boys' and girls' eyes, or wind blows them
> out and after that happens, electric light bulbs go on and
> you see too plainly. . . . (Scene 8)[13]

The touch of sentimentality and self-pity, so reminiscent
of Mary Tyrone ("None of us can help the things life has
done to us"), is due not merely to Williams' characterization of Blanche as a neurasthenic personality; it is, by extension, his own simplified conception of the interplay
between psychological and social forces in the world of his
play. As John Gassner has pointed out, he "muddled the
social basis for Blanche's drama" and thereby "reduced
potential tragedy to psychopathology."[14] Like the play as
a whole, the image constitutes a retreat into the subjective world of suffering and so blurs the conflict, empha-
sizing only the vulnerability of the "soft people" in a world
dominated by the "hard ones." Thus, too, Williams' stage
direction to scene 3, *The Poker Night*, for example, is writ-

ten from a point of view and sensibility akin to that of Blanche DuBois. The description suggests a feeling of superiority to, and a fear of, the poker players whose brightly colored shirts symbolize their uncomplicated animal grasp of life.

Not that Strindberg minimizes the psychopathology of his heroine. She is the half-woman brought up to despise her own sex and grown into a man-hater, who trains her fiancé to jump over her riding-whip. In the scene in which Jean kills the greenfinch on the chopping-block, she is unable to control her sadistic reaction:

> JULIE, *going to the chopping-block as if drawn against her will.* No, I won't go yet. I can't . . . I must look. Listen! There's a carriage. *Listens without taking her eyes off the board and chopper.* You don't think I can bear the sight of blood. You think I'm so weak. Oh, how I should like to see your blood and your brains on a chopping-block! I'd like to see the whole of your sex swimming like that in a sea of blood. I think I could drink out of your skull, bathe my feet in your broken breast and eat your heart roasted whole. You think I'm weak. You think I love you, that my womb yearned for your seed and I want to carry your offspring under my heart and nourish it with my blood. You think I want to bear your child and take your name.

But Strindberg does not get lost in the subjective exploration of her personality. He knows that the portrait of a woman of her type is ancillary to the larger conflict between a degenerate aristocrat, stripped of honor, and the energetic entrepreneur, trying to build his future out of the ruins of the old society. Hence at all times Miss Julie is aware of her dual role:

> . . . You think I want to bear your child and take your name. By the way, what is your name? I've never heard your surname. I don't suppose you've got one. I should be "Mrs. Hovel" or "Madam Dunghill." You dog wearing my collar, you lackey with my crest on your buttons! I share you with my cook; I'm my own servant's rival! Oh! Oh! Oh! . . . You think I'm a coward and will run away. No, now I'm going to stay—and let the storm break. My father will come back . . . find his desk broken open . . . his money gone. Then he'll ring that bell—twice for the valet—and then he'll send for the

police . . . and I shall tell everything. Everything. Oh how
wonderful to make an end of it all—a real end! He has a stroke
and dies and that's the end of all of us. Just peace and quiet-
ness . . . eternal rest. The coat of arms broken on the coffin
and the Count's line extinct . . . But the valet's line goes on
in an orphanage, wins laurels in the gutter and ends in jail.

Despite her scandalous family history, Miss Julie has a tradition of name and honor to lose, whereas Blanche DuBois
tries to parade a tradition that is not only no longer hers
but is gone from the world. "Belle Reve" is an apt name
for the plantation which is an empty reference for her pretensions of gentility. Williams' social conflict is unwork-
able, not because modern America has no counterpart to
the breakdown of social stratification—witness the tragicomic rise of the Snopes family—but because he is more interested in the clash of incompatible personalities and,
quite arbitrarily, identifies Stanley Kowalski with the brutal aspect of society at large.

> STELLA: You needn't have been so cruel to someone alone as
> she is.
> STANLEY: Delicate piece she is.
> STELLA: She is. She was. You didn't know Blanche as a girl.
> Nobody, nobody, was tender and trusting as she was. But
> people like you abused her, and forced her to change.
> [*He crosses into the bedroom, ripping off his shirt, and
> changes into a brilliant silk bowling shirt.*] (Scene 8)

The Streetcar named Desire has brought Blanche, as she
says, to where she is not wanted and where she is ashamed
to be. She is in her sister's house because she has no money to go elsewhere. Still, the confrontation with Stanley
is accidental, and her rape, resulting in her complete mental breakdown, is gratuitous rather than necessary. (The
public transportation route—take Desire, transfer to Ceme-
teries, and get off at Elysian Fields—is at best a premonition; it does not correspond to a logical dramatic sequence.) Williams appears to have been aware that
Blanche's fate depends on his choice of a thoroughly incompatible environment. And since it is important to make
the contrasts effective between neurosis and quick animal

nature, he bends over backwards to picture the house in New Orleans as a vulgar but healthy place, where violence is followed by sexual satisfactions so enviable that they amount to parody. Strindberg knows better. There is an element of sneakiness and falsehood about Jean's alleged life of sexual conquests. But the significant difference lies in Strindberg's preparation of Miss Julie's downfall. The fortuitous circumstances are also there: the absence of the count, the festivities of midsummer night, the necessity to hide in Jean's room. Yet it is Miss Julie's character, with its multiple physiological and psychological motivations, which Strindberg points to in the Preface, that drives her to her destruction. Blanche appears on the scene in a state of exhaustion; her sickly flirtations are motivated only by the pitiful necessity to "shimmer and glow" in order to gain another night's shelter from the storm. Williams' "law of nature" is that "the lady must entertain the gentleman—or no dice." By contrast, in the first dialogue between Jean and Kristin, we learn that Miss Julie is "in heat." Her natural impulse makes her trespass the safe limits of her world and initiate a struggle which she is not equal to. Sexual intimacy, the great leveler, makes her social superiority ineffectual, and as a woman she does not have the strength of character which would permit her, like Kristin, to deal with Jean on equal terms.

Both plays have at their center a triangle of characters representing similar types: the neurotic heroine, the potent male and his natural mate. The opportunities for psychological and sexual entanglements are open to both playwrights, and both avail themselves of the strongest theatrical effects possible. But Strindberg, unlike Williams, concerns himself not only with the process of his heroine's defeat but also with its consequences. This is apparent in the way the two plays end. Jean has the advantage as soon as he and Miss Julie emerge from his room. The second half of the play is, in effect, a visionary elaboration of the rise of the enterprising servant to bourgeois wealth. The sexual union has freed him psychologically from the habit of servility, and the stolen money, according to his plans, will gain him admission to the free market place, to rise by his own skill and shrewdness. In other words, the end of Miss Julie's world is to be the price of his new life. In his Preface, Strindberg advances a particularly sanguine view of Jean, the new hero, speculating beyond the confines of the play about his role as a race-builder and a successful hotel-keeper, whose son will go to the university and perhaps become a county attorney. He stands for the "new nobility of nerve and brain" to which Miss Julie, the relic of the old warrior nobility, is now giving way. "Sexually he is the aristocrat because of his virility, his keener senses and his capacity for taking the initiative." Strindberg's zeal as a naturalist writer whose mission it is to tell the unvarnished truth runs away with him in this portion of the Preface. He finds the spectacle of the transfer of power so bracing that the death of Miss Julie sounds, according to his description, merely like a tragic interlude. What is important to him is that next time Jean will escape his servitude. "His inferiority is mainly due to the social environment in which he lives, and he can probably shed it with his valet's livery."

But, of course, the play ends differently. Miss Julie's decision to commit suicide, though she needs to be ordered to go off-stage in a hypnotic trance, is more than a conditioned response to "that innate or acquired sense of honour" inherited "from Barbarism or Aryan forebears, or from the chivalry of the Middle Ages," as Strindberg would have it. "And so the valet Jean lives on," he continues, "but Miss Julie cannot live without honour. This is the thrall's advantage over the nobleman, that he lacks this fatal preoccupation with honour." The fact is that, in the play, Miss Julie takes stock of her situation and proudly accepts the consequences of her impulsive act of indiscretion:

> JULIE. . . . Whose fault is what's happened? My father's, my
> mother's or my own? My own? I haven't anything that's
> my own. I haven't one single thought that I didn't get from
> my father, one emotion that didn't come from my mother,

and as for this last idea—about all people being equal—I got that from him, my fiancé—that's why I call him a cad. How can it be my fault? Push the responsibility on to Jesus, like Kristin does? No, I'm too proud and—thanks to my father's teaching—too intelligent. As for all that about a rich person not being able to get into heaven, it's just a lie, but Kristin, who has money in the savings-bank, will certainly not get in. Whose fault is it? What does it matter whose fault it is? In any case I must take the blame and bear the consequences.

At this point the service bell rings twice sharply, and it is Jean who reverts to the role of the cringing lackey. Miss Julie wakes from her trance, according to Strindberg's explicit stage direction, once she has forced Jean to whisper his order in her ear. She falters once more, draining Jean of what self-possession is left to him.

> JEAN. Don't think, don't think. You're taking my strength away too and making me a coward. What's that? I thought I saw the bell move . . . To be so frightened of a bell! Yes, but it's not just a bell. There's somebody behind it—a hand moving it—and something else moving the hand—and if you stop your ears—if you stop your ears—yes, then it rings louder than ever. Rings and rings until you answer—and then it's too late. Then the police come and . . . and . . . *The bell rings twice loudly.*
> JEAN *flinches, then straightens himself up.* It's horrible. But there's no other way to end it . . . Go!
> JULIE *walks firmly out through the door.*

It is difficult to see "the thrall's advantage over the nobleman" in this conclusion, or the virility and initiative of the new aristocrat. However true Strindberg's prophecies of social change may have turned out to be in the long run, the situation which he set up in this play demanded its logical conclusion, which is that, given their social roles, Jean's strength ends in paralysis and Miss Julie's weakness, in self-destruction. In short, the outcome of the sex duel between the strong unscrupulous male and the weak hysterical female depends as much on social rule as it does on the law of nature.

The ending of *A Streetcar Named Desire* reflects Williams' continuing uncertainty about the meaning of his heroine's fate. She moves into a private world of spectral forms and sounds; she dresses herself in a faded gown and tiara in order to efface, like Mary Tyrone, the unbearable present reality. Williams has launched her too on a journey into night, except that it is attended by violence. His conception of her fate in the hands of an alien world is perhaps not unfairly illustrated in the brief struggle with the "sinister" matron from the state institution.

> MATRON: These fingernails have to be trimmed. [*The* DOCTOR *comes into the room and she looks at him.*] Jacket, Doctor?
> DOCTOR: Not unless necessary.
> [*He takes off his hat and now becomes personalized. The unhuman quality goes. His voice is gentle and reassuring as he crosses to* BLANCHE *and crouches in front of her. As he speaks her name, her terror subsides a little. The lurid reflections fade from the walls, the inhuman cries and noises die out and her own hoarse crying is calmed.*] (Scene 11)

Since she has no other place to go to, she is handed from Stanley, the personified force of the alien world, raping her, to the authorities of a public institution.

A Streetcar Named Desire is not a social drama in the sense that *Miss Julie* is. Blanche does not have a social role as Miss Julie does. She tries to project an image of herself as if she had a private and a social identity. But in reality her moorings have long since been cut; she has memories, but neither name nor place in which to find refuge. Judging by his sympathetic, yet critical portrait of Blanche, Williams could have produced an excellent psychological drama, focusing on the vanity and the self-torture of such a character in a closed setting like that of *The Glass Menagerie*. As it is, he transplants his trembling heroine to a hostile environment, ostensibly to give his play a social dimension, which however he can manage only on the simplest level. The final image that Williams offers of the society which resents her meretricious make-believe world is brutality and physical restraint.

6

Blanche DuBois is one of the "fugitive kind,"[15] an outsider, suffering her own self-created torments as well as the savagery of the social world in which Williams deliberately places her. Perhaps because the brutal aspects of life were on the surface in the South of Williams' youth, he re-enacts the persecution complex over and over again; but that does not produce social drama. Unless the tragic heroine (like Miss Julie) is herself part of the social order or has a stake in the fixed customs and rules of conduct by which a functioning community resolves its tensions, the result can only be a collision, as in Blanche's case, a mutual rejection.

> BLANCHE: Will Stanley like me, or will I be just a visiting in-law, Stella? I couldn't stand that.
> STELLA: You'll get along fine together, if you'll just try not to—well—compare him with men that we went out with at home.
> BLANCHE: Is he so—different?
> STELLA: Yes. A different species. (Scene 1)

A truly tragic dilemma resulting from the unavoidable clash of impulse with the rules of a society presupposes involvement. Only if an individual has shared the prior commitment to a social order does his infringement of its rules or his violation of its taboos make any sense. An outsider's rebellion may have political significance, but it does not isolate him tragically from the society. The protagonist who has a stake in the life of his society and yet is compelled to violate its laws becomes a tragic figure, not because the body politic takes brutal measures against him, but because by his act of rebellion he has made himself homeless. As we shall see in a subsequent chapter, the concept of existential revolt transcends social conflict altogether.

Property, specifically the New England earth which is a grudging source of life, is at stake in O'Neill's *Desire under the Elms*. It dehumanizes the men who till the land, making them hard and lonesome like the unloving God whom Ephraim Cabot worships in his own image. In his struggle to survive on the rocky soil Cabot subjugates all living things on the farm to the rigid law of self-preservation. He himself has become a force of nature, imbued with greed and lust, holding his own regardless of human wants and desires in others. The two elder sons are able to escape to

freedom in the West by selling their birthright, leaving the
youngest, Eben, and their father's young bride, Abbie, to
play out their drama of possession and desire. But neither
their animal passion, tainted as it is in the beginning by ulterior motives, nor their love which grows from it and
unites them in the shared guilt over the murdered child, can
prevail against the stone walls holding together the property which Cabot had wrested from the inhospitable land.

> God's hard, not easy! God's in the stones! Build my
> church on a rock—out o' stones an' I'll be in them! That's what
> He meant t' Peter! (*He sighs heavily—a pause*) Stones. I picked
> 'em up an' piled 'em into walls. Ye kin read the years o' my life
> in them walls, every day a hefted stone, climbin' over the hills
> up and down, fencin' in the fields that was mine, whar I'd made
> thin's grow out o' nothin'—like the will o' God, like the servant
> o' His hand. It wa'n't easy. It was hard an' He made me hard
> fur it. (Part II, scene 2)

In the end, ironically, his own fleeting impulse to escape to the
gold mines in the West is defeated by the loss of the money
which Eben had given to his brothers, in return for their
share of the farm. Thus it is the land which dominates the
lives and dictates the fate of the three principal characters. "It's a jim-dandy farm, no denyin'," says the sheriff
who has come to make the arrest. "Wished I owned it!"

Cabot's tyrannical behavior toward his sons and wives is
an extension of the tyranny of the land which exacts sub-
missiveness to the laws of survival from those who would
own it and pass it on to the next generation. As in the case
of Lorca's despotic old woman, Bernarda Alba, it would be
a mistake to attribute the tragic violence only to the out-
break of youthful passion against the arbitrary rule of a self-
willed tyrant. The glimpses we get in *The House of Bernarda Alba* of the Spanish village, the obsession with sex
flaunted by the men and stifled by the women, the hidden
suffering a subject of common village gossip, the sporadic
bestialities erupting into the street, all these bits which
Lorca fuses into a sinister environment, not seen but known
and felt inside the house, suggest also that Bernarda has
good reason for carrying out a harsh code of conduct to

protect the family honor. This is not to deny that Bernarda, like Cabot, is characterized as an extravagantly domineering individual, blinded by her own strength of purpose. Essentially, however, she stands for the ritual behavior by which women of her social standing have traditionally dealt with the natural calamities that flesh is heir to. That is to say, she is a monumental embodiment of the strict conventions whereby death and the continuation of life, the anarchic urge to reproduce, may be taken on without jeopardy to the family and to the family's place in society. In Lorca's "drama about women in the villages of Spain" (which is the subtitle of his play) this is no easy task. Above all the obvious individual differences between them, Bernarda and Cabot represent a character type whose experience of life has schooled him to retreat behind the safety of stone walls and a moral austerity in order to control the wayward desires of human nature.

Bernarda's autocratic rule is thus also an extension of the tried codes of conduct in the provincial communities of Spain. "Needle and thread for women. Whiplash and mules for men. That's the way it has to be for people who have certain obligations" (Act I).[16] But while her inhuman discipline serves her well in facing up to the responsibilities which her husband's death has thrust upon her, she is unable to repress the smouldering sexual passions of her daughters.

> . . . For the eight years of mourning, not a breath of air will get in this house from the street. We'll act as if we'd sealed up doors and windows with bricks. That's what happened in my father's house—and in my grandfather's house. Meantime, you can all start embroidering your hopechest linens. I have twenty bolts of linen in the chest from which to cut sheets and coverlets. Magdalena can embroider them. (Act I)

The time-honored rule which brings life to a standstill only accentuates the desire to escape and in the case of the youngest daughter, Adela, to offer her body to her sister's suitor. Thus Lorca develops two extreme and opponent forces in the house, mutually exacerbating and bound to clash violently.

Bernarda views a woman's life as an exercise in self-control, whether she is to follow the prescribed formalities of burying a husband or preparing for marriage. The termination of life as well as the desire of bringing a new life into the world is, to her, mainly an event fraught with social consequences; it affects the family fortunes, but has nothing to do with grief at the mortality or joy at the fecundity of the human body. Bernarda's rule, designed above all to preserve the good name of her house, disrupts the natural rhythm of human life. Lorca pictures the life of frustrated desire as affecting all the women in the house with the single exception of Bernarda. It exhibits itself in the earthy wit of the old servant, La Poncia, and the mad sexual fantasies of Bernarda's eighty-year old mother, in the hopelessness and cynicism of the older daughters and the fierce hatred of Adela's rival, Martirio. But the fatal opposition originates in Adela's passion, which gives her authority at least momentarily equal to Bernarda's. The growing tension is best understood, not as a contest between the strict matriarch and the rebellious daughter, but more abstractly as the rigorous power of social custom obviating the instinctual desire of the body to fulfill its biological function. This is the tragic sense of Lorca's "photographic document."

Bernarda derives her power over her imprisoned daughters from her own obedience to a way of life sanctioned by the social experience of generations past, though, to be sure, her immoderate enforcement of the inherited laws aggravates the tension to the point of disaster. Yet the code remains intact:

> BERNARDA. . . . Cut her down! My daughter died a virgin. Take her to another room and dress her as though she were a virgin. No one will say anything about this! She died a virgin. Tell them, so that at dawn, the bells will ring twice.
>
> *   *   *
>
> Tears when you're alone! We'll drown ourselves in a sea of mourning. She, the youngest daughter of Bernarda Alba,

died a virgin. Did you hear me? Silence, silence, I said. Silence! (Act III)

But the tension remains unresolved as we may judge by Martirio's remark, "A thousand times happy she, who had him."

Adela, the tragic victim of life in the villages of Spain, is likewise endowed with a power which is not to be accounted for in terms of her dramatic character alone. She is beautiful and young so that her expectations have not yet been crushed through prolonged and repeated frustration. This makes her a likely candidate to challenge the destiny in store for her. But the strength to resist which she is able to muster derives from the passion which entirely possesses her. It is a desire for consummation which spurns every warning. There is Poncia's uncharitable advice to wait until her narrow-waisted sister dies in childbirth: "Then Pepe will do what all widowers do in these parts: he'll marry the youngest and most beautiful, and that's you. Live on that hope, forget him, anything; but don't go against God's law." The brutality and hypocrisy of the social mores only strengthen Adela's conviction that her surrender to passion is right and therefore irresistible.

ADELA. Save your advice. It's already too late. For I'd leap not over you, just a servant, but over my mother to put out this fire I feel in my legs and my mouth.

* * *

Bring four thousand yellow flares and set them about the walls of the yard. No one can stop what has to happen.
PONCIA. You like him that much?
ADELA. That much! Looking in his eyes I seem to drink his blood in slowly.
PONCIA. I won't listen to you.
ADELA. Well, you'll have to! I've been afraid of you. But now I'm stronger than you! (Act II)

All the imagery associated with Adela's wild passion, in this scene and throughout the rest of the play, shows that

Lorca meant to depict something other than the apotheosis
of love. Adela's consciousness of immense strength—". . . a
wild horse I could force to his knees with just the strength
of my little finger"—suggests a chthonic power in her which
is broken only by the false report of her lover's death. At the
moment when she snatches her mother's cane and breaks it
in two the conflict reaches its symbolic climax. The question to be decided is whether by her act of defiance she can
liberate herself from the established order of family and
village life and yield freely to the natural dominance of the
male lover. The contest between the two authorities is revealed in the accompanying dialogue.

> MARTIRIO. (*pointing to Adela*) She was with him. Look
> at those skirts covered with straw!
> BERNARDA. (*going furiously toward Adela*) That's the bed of
> a bad woman!
> ADELA. (*facing her*) There'll be an end to prison voices here!
> . . . This is what I do with the tyrant's cane. Not another
> step. No one but Pepe commands me!
>
> *   *   *
>
> I'm his. . . . Know that—and go out in the yard and tell
> him. He'll be master in this house.
> ANGUSTIAS. My God!
> BERNARDA. The gun! Where's the gun? (Act III)

Of course, Bernarda's inflexible administration of the social ethic must prevail, and there is no alternative to the
prospect of a life of sterility for Adela except suicide.

It is not the fear of dishonor that sends Adela to her
death. Like Yerma, though for different reasons, she is denied the fulfillment of an overpowering desire. The difference between the frustration of these full-blooded women
(including Abbie Putnam in *Desire under the Elms*) and
that of a sexual adventuress like Miss Julie provides us with
an understanding of two variant patterns of the tragic conflict of individual desire with the inhumane priorities of
social life. Lorca's female protagonists are the "bearer of
all passion and earthly reality," as Edwin Honig puts it; and
"because their humanity is such an extremely procreative

answer to life, they threaten to disrupt the mere man-made machinery of social law, which is, finally, a substitution for life."[17] The point at issue seems to be clear between the elemental demands of instinct and the opposing purposes of social organization. Our emotions as spectators are caught up in the resultant tension, but they are not ambivalent. The case is more complicated in *Miss Julie* because Strindberg's heroine, the neurotic half-woman, is no passionate rebel against the social law; in fact, by her suicide she confirms the social order which curbs her escape. The outcome is indeed so depressing, from the psychological and social points of view, that Strindberg, whose experience always frustrated his search for the magnificent life-giving female, gave vent to his pent-up feelings in the Preface by declaring Jean the winner. As the sense of the violent endings is different, so is the tragic pattern in these plays. Miss Julie's suicide is an act of *noblesse oblige* forced upon her, whereas each of the other women commits a crime of passion.

Finally, in this context, we ought to consider Frank Wedekind's unique experiment with a completely emancipated heroine whose scandalous rise in the bourgeois world is unopposed since she and her male victims (plus one tortured lesbian admirer) agree to operate outside the social conventions. What happens when the pursuit of desire outstrips not only the public morality of the bourgeois world but even such privately held concepts as love, loyalty, and gratitude, which, as Wedekind has it, are logically untenable?[18] Lulu's sexuality is murderous and ultimately self-destructive. In other words, Wedekind turns his back on the accepted idea of social tragedy. In his celebrated play, *Spring's Awakening (Frühlings Erwachen*, 1891), which he called a tragedy of youth, he had dealt specifically with the turbulence of adolescent sexuality and its suppression by that notoriously illiberal syndrome of power, parental authority and the middle-European school system working in concert. Despite the episodic structure, the pervasive irony (so reminiscent of Büchner), and the surrealistic ending that permits Wedekind to lead his youthful protagonist, who had been accused of "moral insanity," back to a more wholesome apprehension of life, the play follows the basic pattern of conflict between natural impulse (however innocent in this instance) and the rigidly observed norms of social behavior. But in the two Lulu plays, *Earth Spirit* (*Erdgeist*, 1893/94) and *Pandora's Box* (*Die Büchse der Pandora*, rev. ed. 1906), the public morality of the bourgeois world is there only by implication, as a foil to Wedekind's true purpose—to show the behavior of the untamed beast in a cosmopolitan setting.

In making the life of animal instinct preeminent over the bourgeois mentality, Wedekind knew that he must render a picture of human nature and the predatory world which would go beyond the limits of the naturalistic theater. In fact, he complained that the conventions of the naturalistic stage in Germany distorted his conception of Lulu as a magnificent specimen of womanhood into a monster of unnatural malevolence. His purpose was to picture her body in the words she speaks, to portray unabashedly an object of desire, and to represent the one man she loves as possessing the brutal intelligence of a beast of prey.[19] Lulu's moral superiority rests in her being a biological, phenomenal fact of life beyond the categories of good and evil. She is intoxicated by her own beauty and deeply, narcissisticly, in love with her own image.

> LULU. When I saw myself in the mirror, I should have liked to be a man . . . (*interrupting herself*) the man who married me!
> ALWA. You seem to envy your husband the happiness you bestow on him. (Act IV, scene 7)

Instead of calling the play *Earth Spirit*, says Wedekind, he might just as well have entitled it "Realpsychologie," in the same sense in which we speak of "Realpolitik."[20]

Lulu makes her entrance in the famous prologue, after the animal trainer, equipped with a pistol and a whip, has one by one advertised the wild, beautiful, undomesticated animals to be seen in his show and never seen before. A stagehand carries Lulu in Pierrot costume from the circus tent and exhibits her as the Serpent, "created to cause ruin,/ to tempt, seduce, and poison—/to murder without pain," the archetypal female who answers to many known names in her career—Mignon, Nelli, Eva, Lulu—but always remains the same. In the second play, however, her fatal sexuality overtakes her; still triumphantly promiscuous at the outset, she ends her days as a common prostitute, murdered by her criminally insane counterpart of the demimonde, the legendary figure of Jack the Ripper. Wedekind himself played the part in the Karl Kraus production of 1905 in Vienna.

The painted likeness of Lulu in her Pierrot costume, a reminder of her triumphant career, reappears in the grimy London attic, and before it kneels her single remaining lover, the lesbian countess. The image underlines Lulu's steep descent from luxury to rags and the gratuitous nature of her death. But the effect is by no means didactic. On the contrary, the ending of this two-part tragedy carries Wedekind's premises to their logical conclusion. The soulless creatures which the animal trainer had brought before the audience to be looked at with "lascivious pleasure and chilling dread" have played their parts brilliantly and without inhibition. These are not the half-men and the half-women of the naturalistic stage or the problematic literary characters of Ibsen's theater, which Wedekind disliked vehemently. To him, the tragic spectacle of modern times was to be found in the reckless pursuit of pleasure and power, presupposing a social life in which only the keenest minds and the most rapacious natures survive.

NOTES

1. The Hamburg edition, *Sämtliche Werke und Briefe*, ed. Werner R. Lehmann, vol. I, furnishes the first drafts and preliminary versions as Büchner left them, as well as a provisional sequence of scenes for the stage and the study, and in addition medical and legal source materials about the case of Johann Woyzeck.

2. George Steiner, in his discussion of *Woyzeck* in *The Death of Tragedy*, concentrates on the striking echoes of speech. His stylistic analysis is finely attuned to the peculiarities of the language in Lear's mad scenes and in Woyzeck's rising passion: "Woyzeck's powers of speech

fall drastically short of the depth of his anguish." But is this really "the crux of the play"? Danton approached his extinction blessed witn an enviable fluency and subtlety of speech. Woyzeck's comparatively inarticulate yet highly suggestive speech pattern surely denotes a difference in the tragic conception, but it only partially explains the tragic power of the drama which is due to other elements as well.

3. *The Vision of Tragedy* (New Haven: Yale University Press, 1959).

4. *The Life of the Drama* (New York: Atheneum, 1964), pp. 338-339.

5. Ibid.

6. In this and all subsequent quotations I use the translations of Elizabeth Sprigge, *Twelve Plays by August Strindberg* (London: Constable, 1963).

7. Note to the published play, *A View from the Bridge* (New York: Viking, 1955), p. 17.

8. *A View from the Bridge*, a play in two acts, with a new introduction (New York: Viking, 1960), pp. viii-ix.

9. *Modern Drama: Essays in Criticism*, eds. Travis Bogard and William I. Oliver (New York: Oxford, 1965), p. 230. Ironically, the common reaction to *After the Fall* was that Miller had foisted his own private misery on the American public. But that was a shortsighted view of the play, based on the immediate impression of the New York playgoer and reviewer whose aesthetic tastes had been conditioned by a diet of theatrical and journalistic "psycho-sexual romanticism."

10. *Long Day's Journey into Night* (New Haven: Yale University Press, 1956).

11. *The Iceman Cometh* (New York: Random House, 1946).

12. *Shakespearean Criticism*, ed. Thomas M. Raysor (New York: Dutton, 1960), II, 125.

13. *A Streetcar Named Desire* (New York: New Directions, 1947), Third Printing, p. 129. Blanche's second speech was subsequently cut from the text. It does not appear in the Fifth Printing, 1947, nor in *The Theatre of Tennessee Williams* (New York: New Directions, 1971).

14. "*A Streetcar Named Desire*: a Study in Ambiguity," rpt. from *The Theatre in Our Times* (1954) in *Modern Drama*, eds. Bogard and Oliver, pp. 376-377.

15. Gerald Weales's phrase, adopted from Williams himself. See *Tennessee Williams* (Minneapolis: University of Minnesota Press, 1965), pp. 18 ff.

16. *The House of Bernarda Alba: A Drama about Women in the Villages of Spain* (1936) in *Three Tragedies of Federico García Lorca*, trans. Richard L. O'Connell and James Graham-Luján (New York: New Directions, 1947).

17. *Garcia Lorca* (New York: New Directions, 1944). See *Essays in the Modern Drama*, ed. Morris Freedman (Boston, 1964), pp. 245, 246.

18. *Prosa, Dramen, Verse*, ed. Hansgeorg Maier (München: A. Langen—G. Müller), I (1954), 945.

19. "Albert Steinrück," ibid., I, 867.

20. Ibid., I, 945.

5. AFTER THE FALL

1

Arthur Miller has remained true to his dictum of the mid-fifties that the fate of mankind is social. But his idea of society has changed. In *After the Fall*, Quentin experiences what may be called a growing sense of complicity in the paradigmatic murder of Abel by the hand of Cain. Eventually he learns to understand the connection between the single act of betrayal when we turn away from another, consigning him to death, and the organized mass murder of men reduced to objects in extermination camps. The recognition of the changing outlook on man's role in society comes early in the play.

> QUENTIN: . . . It sounds foolish, but I feel . . . unblessed. And I look back at when there seemed to be a kind of plan, some duty in the sky. I had a dinner table, and a wife, a child, and the world so wonderfully threatened by injustices I was born to correct! How fine! Remember? When there were good people and bad people? And how easy it was to tell! (Act I)[1]

"Injustices I was born to correct!" By the end of the first act, Hamlet had his own premonitions that after the fall we are all unblessed because we all become involved in the perversion of love.

> The time is out of joint. O cursed spite
> That ever I was born to set it right!

The traditional pattern of the social drama can be found in Miller's earlier plays, a confrontation between the individual, led by his private vision of justice, and the society inexorably enforcing its unwritten laws. The protagonist's

161

vision may be distorted as it is in Willy Loman, who ex-
hausts his life in his effort to conquer the indifferent jungle
of the city, or in Eddie Carbone, who risks the loss of his
good name because of "a passion that had moved into his
body, like a stranger." On the other hand, the protagonist
may be the voice of sanity pitted against mass hysteria, as
in *The Crucible*. But in each instance, whatever the moral
complexities, the litigants are clearly separated so that
Miller's all-purpose formula for the social play, "How may
a man make of the outside world a home?" is adequate to
his conception.

But the dehumanization of society already apparent in
Death of a Salesman and *The Crucible* becomes progressively worse in the plays of the 1960s. It becomes worse
as Miller, under the pressure of his private and political
experience, redefines the relation of the individual to those
about him. The focus is no longer on the protagonist confronting the outside world which has an impersonal, institutional ethos of its own. The question is no longer why a
hard-working drummer lands in the ash can like all the rest
of them, or why a man must choose to sell his soul or die a
martyr's death. In the plays of the sixties the conduct of the
one is the key to the behavior of the many. Society in *After
the Fall* is the self *and* the others, acting in complicity and
therefore responsible for each other's acts. The form of the
play is that of an inquiry, a trial, and a self-judgment, seeking to discover the possibility of a social life based on that
knowledge. The sustained analogue of the concentration
camp, whose tower is a visible reminder throughout the action, becomes the prime subject of the next play. In *Incident
at Vichy*, Miller goes a step further in his endeavor to understand the almost inconceivable event of modern history,
the systematic extermination of European Jews. Here is
the ultimate image of the victim, stopped for a moment at
the gates of a man-made hell, to learn that he is condemned
to extinction without cause or appeal. What for Quentin in
his social experience had been a shocking revelation—"It's
like some unseen web of connection between people is simply not there. And I always relied on it, somehow; I never

quite believed that people could be so easily disposed of. And it's larger than the political question. I think it's got me a little scared"—has become an overwhelming fact. A whole society, master of a continent, has organized its immense resources for the purpose of genocide.

With these last two plays, Miller has radically altered his concept of the social drama. In the 1940s and 1950s it was still possible to picture society (in the manner of Zola) vaguely as the matrix of a man's life, "a power and a mystery of custom and inside the man and surrounding him, as the fish is in the sea and the sea inside the fish, his birthplace and burial ground, promise and threat."[2] The individual prospered or perished as he did or did not find a home in this world. If Miller's plays written during these years prompted his remark that the fate of mankind is social, it has now become clear to him that a closer look at our experience during and since the war must rouse our concern with the reverse side of the proposition: the fate of society is mirrored in the nature of man. Though *All My Sons*, produced in 1947, and *Incident at Vichy* in 1964, deal with aspects of the same war, they are separated by something more than twenty years of added reflection. Neither play approaches Miller's best work in the theater. The point of the comparison is that he has moved far beyond questions of guilt and responsibility, which a court could adjudicate, to those which stagger the human conscience. In the last two plays, exorcising the spirit of Cain in man is the only hope of salvation for mankind.

A consideration of Miller's dramatic work in the middle decades of the twentieth century returns us to our point of departure. In many ways Georg Büchner's brilliant performance in the historical and the psychological and social drama has not been surpassed. Nearly a century and a half ago, the world goaded his secular, liberal intelligence to ask questions concerning the fate of the individual and of society, which our serious dramatists still recognize as the fundamental questions determining the quality of our lives today. Like Miller, he understood the relationship between man and the power of society in two ways. Studying the

history of the French revolution, he saw the connection between the "terrible sameness of human nature" and "an
inescapable force at work in the human situation." He pon-
ders the frightening certainty in St. Matthew's warning:
"Woe unto the world because of offenses! for it must needs
be that offenses come; but woe to that man by whom the
offense cometh" and asks ingenuously, "What is it in us
that lies, murders, steals?"[3] The modern secular dramatist can only reveal the connection and disguise his horror
with irony as Büchner does in *Danton's Death* or learn to
live with this revelation as Miller does in *After the Fall*.
The second way in which Büchner anticipated the structure of the modern social drama is demonstrated in Woyzeck's psychological and moral degradation and his exclusion from human fellowship. In this view individual human
nature is not the clue to the collective behavior of men;
there is no discoverable complicity in the crimes which
society perpetrates, no analogue between turning one's
back to another like a stranger and the terror of the French
Revolution or the systematic persecutions of our century.
Rather there is conflict on a smaller scale with a society
which defines the individual's existence and, at the same
time, through indifference or hostility, interdicts his claim
to a separate personal identity.

As Miller says of Eddie Carbone in the revised version of
A View from the Bridge,

> . . . However one might dislike this man, who does
> all sorts of frightful things, he possesses or exemplifies the won-
> drous and humane fact that he too can be driven to what in
> the last analysis is a sacrifice of himself for his conception,
> however misguided, of right, dignity, and justice. . . . He
> was seen in context, as a creature of his environment as well
> as an exception to it; and where originally there had been
> only a removed sense of terror at the oncoming catastrophe,
> now there was pity and, I think, the kind of wonder which it
> had been my aim to create in the first place. It was finally
> possible to mourn this man.[4]

Despite the glaring differences between the utter deprivation and passivity of Woyzeck and Eddie's vehement passion or Willy Loman's obsessive pursuit of an idea, *A View*

from the Bridge and *Death of a Salesman* are modern versions of the tragic social drama as Büchner conceived it: the isolated hero driven to a desperate act of self-assertion. It is the vain effort to recover some measure of freedom of control over his own life, no matter what the consequences, and thus to retain the integrity of his person. Büchner's determinism did not permit him to grant his hero more than a reflex action—to repossess Marie in the only way possible, by killing her. Woyzeck's response to the steady encroachment of alien forces upon his simple nature is elemental. Miller, however, rejects determinism as being contradictory to the very idea of drama. "[A man's] will is as much a fact as his defeat."[5] Yet his embattled heroes in these two plays are as far from being masters of their fate as is Woyzeck. The difference is that they guard their private life of feeling and self-delusion in a futile effort to make it prevail over the contrary order of things. Their persistent challenge of the realities of social life is the cause of tragedy.

It is a serious and not uncommon misunderstanding to regard this type of drama as a piece of tendentious writing. The fault lies in the myopic critic, who feels called upon to take sides, who dismisses Willy Loman as a pathological liar and Eddie Carbone as a common informer blinded by his illicit sexual desires, or, to reverse the position, feels nothing but outrage at the brutally authoritarian world of *The Crucible* or, for that matter, of *Woyzeck*. Such political and moralistic judgments may be an appropriate response in a baldly conceived thesis play, but they mask the essential struggle at the center of the tragic social drama. That is why Miller, for example, has been at pains to find the technical means to let the conflict develop in its proper perspective. The hallucinatory interludes in *Death of a Salesman*, as well as in *Woyzeck*, are not short cuts to a faulty dramatic motivation, but rather a necessary device to get us to see the outside world astigmatically from the point of view of the protagonist. Obviously, the point of these plays is not the banal observation that the individual cannot realistically adjust to the pressures of his social environment, or, as in the case of *The*

Crucible and *A Man for All Seasons*, that he should not give in to them because the right is on his side. What the playwright wishes to show is the urgent need inside the man to keep his spirit alive against all odds, even if he has to embark on a self-destructive course of action.

This is to see the balance of moral claims in a nonrational light. What does it feel like, asks Büchner, to lose one's recognition as a human being? On a higher rung of the social ladder, Willy Loman ends his life in a state of physical and psychological exhaustion, yet convinced that at least in death a man can still amount to something in this world. The felt experience, which Miller asks us to share, is the accumulated pain and disappointment of a lifetime that the world cannot be conquered in this way, which is, however, the only way Willy Loman knows. That he labors under a foolish and dangerous delusion is nowhere denied. In fact Miller underlines this dramatically whenever the stereotyped ghost of Willy's "successful" brother Ben is conjured up to renew and support the quixotic joust with the unseen enemy. But again, the point is not that Willy is a confused and unstable person or that the myth of the land of opportunity is a hoax. The tragic moment comes when Willy fears the truth that he has no name or place in his society and that he will die without having planted seeds in the inhospitable soil.

It was for political reasons that the initial production of *The Crucible* was misunderstood, even though—or rather because—the evil effects of mass hysteria were made so unmistakably clear. What was lost to the audience, in Miller's words, was "the real and inner theme, which, again, was the handing over of conscience to another, be it woman, the state, or a terror, and the realization that with conscience goes the person, the soul immortal, and the 'name'. That there was not one mention of this process in any review, favorable or not, was the measure of my sense of defeat, and the impulse to separate, openly and without concealment, the action of the next play, *A View from the Bridge*, from its generalized significance. The engaged narrator, in short, appeared."[6] Robert Bolt solved the problem by creating the timeserving Common Man in *A Man for All Seasons*, who functions openly as *metteur en scène*, narrator, and foil to the uncommon man, presenting to us the tragic figure of Thomas More in his role of the reluctant "hero of self-hood."

A View from the Bridge is the last in this group of social dramas, in which Miller is concerned with the individual's tragic struggle to retain the freedom to be himself, to remain true to his vision, without losing his identity in relation to his society. The Brooklyn waterfront is Eddie's natural habitat; he understands and lives in harmony with the unwritten law which regulates the special privileges and taboos of this cohesive segment of society. The local law has an unquestioned priority over the public law, whose interpreter for the neighborhood community is Miller's narrator, the lawyer Alfieri. But once Eddie's unacknowledged passion for his niece is challenged by her love for the young immigrant Rodolpho, it grips him with a force far greater than that of any social prohibition.

> ALFIERI. I heard what you told me, and I'm telling you what the answer is. I'm not only telling you now, I'm warning you—the law is nature. The law is only a word for what has a right to happen. When the law is wrong it's because it's unnatural, but in this case it is natural and a river will drown you if you buck it. Let her go. And bless her. . . . You won't have a friend in the world, Eddie! Even those who understand will turn against you, even the ones who feel the same will despise you! *Eddie moves off.* Put it out of your mind! Eddie! *He follows into the darkness, calling desperately.* (Act II)

The law referred to here is Alfieri's legal code which cannot satisfy Eddie's passionate sense of wrong, and it is also the superimposed code of loyalty which protects illegal immigrants like Marco, who has come to save his family from starvation, and Rodolpho, who wishes to start a new life. But Eddie is irrationally driven to risk ostracism and death to assert his sensual revulsion toward the marriage of his niece.

In doing so he has lost his name both as a man in his

family and as a respected member of the community. The
concluding scene of the revised version brings out the double humiliation.

> EDDIE. I want my name! . . . Marco's got my name and
> . . . he's gonna give it back to me in front of this neigh-
> borhood, or we have it out.
>
> *   *   *
>
> BEATRICE. You want somethin' else, Eddie, and you can
> never have her. (Act II)

It is a staggering revelation to have his buried desire thus
brought out into the open. And therefore the duel with
Marco is fought, not merely to clear himself of the accusation of being an informer, but also to expunge the truth
which his wife has at last flung in his face. Eddie is called
"animal," both on account of the motivation and the
deed, the unnatural love for his foster child and the act of
betrayal to prevent her marriage to Rodolpho. In place of
the simpler conflict of the one-act play between passion
and loyalty, Miller is now far more explicit about the sexual relationships between Eddie and his wife and niece.
"Whatever happened," says Beatrice in this version, "we
all done it, and don't you ever forget it, Catherine."

Alfieri's epilogue also shows Miller's reinterpretation
of the significance of the tragic action. In the earlier play
he insists again on the archetypal, mythlike quality of the
story.

> Most of the time now we settle for half,
> And I like it better.
> And yet, when the tide is right
> And the green smell of the sea
> Floats in through my window,
> The waves of this bay
> Are the waves against Siracusa,
> And I see a face that suddenly seems carved;
> The eyes look like tunnels
> Leading back toward some ancestral beach
> Where all of us once lived.
>
> And I wonder at those times

How much of all of us
Really lives there yet,
And when we will truly have moved on,
On and away from that dark place,
That world that has fallen to stones?

But in the full-length play, the emphasis rests on the predicament of the modern man who can only live by the truth of his feelings and, paradoxically, by being true to his deepest impulse forfeits his social conscience and loses his name. Miller stands rightly in awe before the destructive course of this man's passion. A view from the bridge is an overhead view of Eddie's life and death inside the community that produced him and cast him off. Looking back on the complete chain of events transpiring inexorably, Alfieri, in the revised epilogue, eulogizes the tragic hero of the social drama who has paid with his honor and his life to vindicate his singular passion.

Most of the time now we settle for half and I like it better. But the truth is holy, and even as I know how wrong he was, and his death useless, I tremble, for I confess that something perversely pure calls to me from his memory—not purely good, but himself purely, for he allowed himself to be wholly known and for that I think I will love him more than all my sensible clients. And yet, it is better to settle for half, it must be! And so I mourn him—I admit it—with a certain . . . alarm.

2

The relatively long interval following *A View from the Bridge* appears now to be indicative of a turning point in Miller's experience of our time. At first sight, the new play, *After the Fall*, may have seemed like a capitulation to the school of dramatists who exploit our morbid interest in amateur psychologizing; and, besides, it left tracks for the hunters after scandalous biographical details. But a more serious critical consideration of the play, which is possible after the gossips and journalists have turned their attention to the next fashionable topic, makes it clear that Miller has not joined the ranks of the purveyors of "psycho-sexual romanticism." The theme transcends the ordinary psychological exercises in the theater. Miller is talking about murder, in the sense in which Dostoevsky understood it, both as physical and spiritual violence, as the betrayal of another and thereby of one's self, leaving an ineradicable mark of guilt on the soul. That he makes use of real-life material and refuses to disguise the fact does not make the play less authentic. But it is the cause of a structural fault, which is that the relationship between Quentin and Maggie is disproportionate to the theme of the play. The murderous denial of another's existence has been illuminated from all sides in the first act; it is demonstrated in Quentin's relations with his family, in his first marriage, in the world of business and politics, and always in his preoccupation with the millions of victims of Nazi persecution. But the theme of betrayal is not made more precise by the extended recall of his affair with Maggie and their subsequent marriage. Miller sees it as the severest test and therefore the central episode in Quentin's self-examination. A more objective view of this pilgrim's progress would indicate that the experience of the man in this instance overtook the judgment of the artist.

After the Fall starts with the assumption of guilt as a fact of existence. Technically it merges the roles of engaged narrator and main actor, fusing subject and object (percipient and perceived) in a complex act of cognition, so that the play cannot be said to be *about* the failure of love, guilt, and self-forgiveness; it is rather a confessional monologue conducted in the form of a dramatic inquiry, a quest for clearer knowledge and feeling bringing into the light of consciousness the hidden motives of our behavior toward one another. It begins in despair, "the endless argument with oneself, this pointless litigation of existence before an empty bench," and moves circuitously through memories, associations, and ruthless introspection toward at least a rejection of fear if not an ethically plausible modus vivendi. In the end, at least, Quentin need not shrink from the prospect of linking his life to that of another person, since he is no longer "a stranger to [his] life."

There is a break here with Miller's earlier conception of tragic social drama. The heroes of the preceding group of plays sought to maintain their independence, to hold inviolate their distinctive personalities and private visions of life, against the alien demands of their social environments. They were concerned with their own individual freedom of choice even if it entailed the sacrifice of their lives. The pattern was that of an encounter with society conceived of as a monolithic power. In *After the Fall*, Miller examines the social life as a fabric of interpersonal relations, the giving and withholding from another the freedom to be himself. The question, therefore, is no longer how to preserve the self as a distinctive entity by refusing to hand over one's private conscience to another; it is rather the delicate realization that the individual conscience must embrace the lives of others if it is not to be plunged in guilt and implicated in the nightmare event of our era, the wholesale denial of life to millions of human beings.

The change is discernible in Miller's retrospective critique of *The Crucible* four years after the writing of it, and in particular his handling of the problem of evil. The dilemma he faced was that the unmitigated dedication to evil on the part of the judges, the prosecution, and certain members of the Salem community, which he saw in the historical record, could not be accounted for by the enlightened concept of social and psychological motivation on which the modern realistic drama is based. "Had I this play to write now, however, I might proceed on an altered concept. I should say that my own—and the critics'—unbelief in this depth of evil is concomitant with our unbelief in good, too. . . . I believe now, as I did not conceive then, that there are people dedicated to evil in the world; that without their perverse example we should not know the good. Evil is not a mistake but a fact in itself." Miller has become dissatisfied with the naturalistic rationalizations of evil and the morally neutral concept of man as the center of analyzable forces which account for his behavior.

The remainder of the passage from the Introduction to

the *Collected Plays* (1957) is prophetic of the changed
outlook which separates *After the Fall* from the earlier
plays.

> I posit no metaphysical force of evil which totally possesses
> certain individuals, nor do I even deny that given infinite wis-
> dom and patience and knowledge any human being can be
> saved from himself. I believe merely that, from whatever
> cause, a dedication to evil, not mistaking it for good, but know-
> ing it as evil and loving it as evil, is possible in human beings
> who appear agreeable and normal. I think now that one of the
> hidden weaknesses of our whole approach to dramatic psy-
> chology is our inability to face this fact—to conceive, in effect,
> of Iago.[7]

It is not clear how one can conceive of Iago without posit-
ing a "metaphysical" force of evil, nor is there any indication in Shakespeare that infinite wisdom and patience
could save the sullen devil from himself. Nonetheless Miller's timely extension of his sensibility is welcome since
it promises to open new areas of experience to his art. He
has not abandoned his commitment to the idea that modern tragedy is necessarily a form of social drama, but he
has found that the tragic motif may be a pervasive evil at
the core of all human relationships rather than a clear-cut
conflict between the private autonomous conscience and
the public sense of justice.

He has learned, moreover, that these fresh explorations
require a more objective awareness and a heightened consciousness on the part of the hero. The problem was there
in *The Crucible*: "I believe that the very moral awareness
of the play and its characters—which are historically correct—was repulsive to the audience. For a variety of reasons
I think that the Anglo-Saxon audience cannot believe the
reality of characters who live by principles and know very
much about their own characters and situations, and who
say what they know. Our drama, for this among other reasons, is condemned, so to speak, to the emotions of sub-
jectivism, which, as they approach knowledge and self-
awareness, become less and less actual and real to us."[8] The
burden of consciousness was borne by the narrator in *A*

View from the Bridge. But when Miller produced *After the Fall* he met this technical demand in full. Quentin, in the act of remembering, watches and minutely examines the evasions of his own mind until its moral perplexities stand revealed.

With his newly acquired belief in the fact of evil as a motive in human relations and the discovery of a stream-of-consciousness technique to give it voice, Miller has reshaped the social and psychological drama, making it commensurate with the particular knowledge of our unblessed condition which we have gained in our lifetime. *After the Fall* is not a religious play. It is an expansion of the ideas and techniques of the theater of realism in order to analyze our most deeply felt moral anxieties, but it does not step beyond the bounds of the phenomenal world. Unlike the professed Christian playwrights of our century, for example Eliot, Claudel, or Hofmannsthal, Miller finds the biblical version of the unblessed condition of man less useful to his inquest than the actual memory of the Fall of Man in the twentieth century. Thus a certain naiveté attaches to Quentin's speculations about innocence and evil, as if these things had never been rehearsed before, but for the same reason his hard-won insights have been honestly earned; they are the bounty of a fresh conquest of reality.

Quentin's abrasive honesty, his persistent striving not to overlook the smallest lie, brings him, at the close of the play, face to face with the irreducible facts on which his conscience must rest. He knows the ways of other men who escape the menace of their own frailties:

> . . . Maybe there is only one sin, to destroy your own credibility. Strength comes from a clear conscience or a dead one. Not to see one's own evil—there's power! And rightness too! So kill conscience. Kill it.
> Know all, admit nothing, shave closely, remember birthdays, open car doors, pursue Louise not with truth but with attention. Be uncertain on your own time, in bed be absolute. And thus, be a man . . . and join the world.

But for him, as one might put it, responding to the rhythmic

echo of Poor Tom, this is no way to assuage the foul fiend
Flibbertigibbet. And as for true innocence, it is only for
those who have no choice. Quentin recaptures the meaning
of original sin painstakingly out of his own experience and
without reference to the Christian dogma. His Eden was
the time, perhaps a generation ago, when social injustices
could be clearly defined and boldly opposed. But now he
has discovered the enemy within, a universal sense of
guilt which touches every man who has not deliberately
killed his conscience.

The affair with Maggie teaches him to distrust the pretensions of innocence and the illusion of the sufficiency of
human love.

> QUENTIN: Maggie, we . . . used one another.
> MAGGIE: Not me, not me!
> QUENTIN: Yes, you. And I. "To live," we cried, and "Now," we
> cried. And loved each other's innocence as though to love
> enough what was not there would cover up what was. But
> there is an angel, and night and day he brings back to us
> exactly what we want to lose. And no chemical can kill
> him, no blindness dark enough to make him lose his way;
> so you must love him, he keeps truth in the world. You eat
> those pills like power, but only what you've done will save
> you. . . . (Act II)

Only the German woman, Holga, who accepts responsibility for what she did not know and gives free release to her
feelings of pity and remorse, bringing flowers to the site
of the concentration camp, seems to be able to resist the
guiles of innocence and the temptation to erase the past.
But her recurrent dream of the idiot child terrifies Quentin
when he hears her tell it early in the play:

> . . . I had the same dream each night—that I had a child; and
> even in the dream I saw that the child was my life; and it
> was an idiot. And I wept, and a hundred times I ran away,
> but each time I came back it had the same dreadful face.
> Until I thought, if I could kiss it, whatever in it was my own,
> perhaps I could rest. And I bent to its broken face, and it
> was horrible . . . but I kissed it.
> QUENTIN: Does it still come back?
> HOLGA: At times. But it somehow has the virtue now . . . of

being mine. I think one must finally take one's life in one's arms, Quentin. (Act I)

The concentration camp tower, as it keeps reappearing, begins to symbolize all that threatens the community of men. But not until his love for Maggie has turned to murderous hate does Quentin understand the link between his individual consciousness of guilt—"My innocence, you see? To get that back you kill most easily"—and the most monstrous betrayal of all, which is symbolized by the "fierce, implacable" tower. And only now does he understand the relevance of Holga's twice-repeated sentence: "No one they didn't kill can be innocent again." Its meaning reaches into another country and another language, and it sears the mind of a man who had shown no more than the concerned tourist's grave interest in the history of the Nazi period.

> QUENTIN: . . . What love, what wave of pity will ever reach this knowledge—I know how to kill. . . . Or is it possible . . .
> *He turns toward the tower, moves toward it as toward a terrible God.* . . . that this is not bizarre . . . to anyone? And I am not alone, and no man lives who would not rather be the sole survivor of this place than all its finest victims? What is the cure? Who can be innocent again on this mountain of skulls? I tell you what I know! My brothers died here . . .
> *He looks down at the fallen Maggie.*
> . . . but my brothers built this place; our hearts have cut these stones! And what's the cure!
> *Father and Mother and Dan appear, and Lou and Mickey; all his people are in light now.*
> . . . No, not love; I loved them all, all! And gave them willingly to failure and to death that I might live, as they gave me and gave each other, with a word, a look, a truth, a lie —and all in love! (Act II)

What is the cure? Miller poses the question from the vantage point of the social dramatist who now sees the fate of society as the corollary of the individual's conscience. Dostoevsky's answer for those who betray another's life through consent or indifference was the mystery of Christian love, but he knew enough about the recurrent vio-

lence of life to regard the ministry of love as a means of
healing the individual soul rather than a promise of harmony enveloping a whole society. Sartre's existentialist
answer aligned politics with morality, as Orestes strides
out of Argos with his own and his people's accumulated
guilt upon his shoulders. These are heroic solutions. By
comparison Miller's answer is diffident, skeptical, tenta-
tive. He is stopped by an insurmountable tragic paradox.
"We are all separate people," and yet we are responsible
for each other's deeds. Nor can we emulate Jesus' love
which raised Lazarus from the dead. "God's power is love
without limit. But when a man dares reach for that . . .
he is only reaching for the power. Whoever goes to save
another person with the lie of limitless love throws a shadow on the face of God" (Act II). Human love will not overcome the Cain in us. Thus he ends Quentin's trial with a
question mark because after the second Fall, linking the
burning cities and the human slaughterhouses with the
death of love in mid-Manhattan, what promise of salvation
is left?

> QUENTIN: . . . Is the knowing all? To know, and even hap-
> pily that we meet unblessed; not in some garden of wax fruit
> and painted trees, that lie of Eden, but after, after the
> Fall, after many, many deaths. Is the knowing all? And
> the wish to kill is never killed, but with some gift of courage
> one may look into its face when it appears, and with a
> stroke of love—as to an idiot in the house—forgive it; again
> and again . . . forever? . . . No, it's not certainty, I don't
> feel that. But it does seem feasible . . . not to be afraid.
> Perhaps it's all one has. . . . (Act II)[9]

Incident at Vichy is a less complex and a less satisfying
play. No doubt, Miller felt that he had to understand and
articulate his understanding of the ineffable crime which
demands a public reassessment of the diminished image
of the species man. "What a piece of work is a man!" The
old categories will hardly suffice; the mind buckles under
the weight of the recorded facts. As Quentin describes his
reaction to the silent walls and the tower: "I guess I
thought I'd be indignant, or angry. But it's like swallowing

a lump of earth." The relevance of the place to his own life only begins to dawn on him as he first identifies himself with the nameless victims:

> Why do I *know* something here? Even hollow now and empty, it has a face; and asks a sort of question: 'What do you believe . . . as true as this?' Yes! Believers built this, maybe that's the fright—and I, without belief, stand here disarmed. I can see the convoys grinding up this hill; and I inside; no one knows my name and yet they'll smash my head on a concrete floor! And no appeal.
>
> Yes! It's that I no longer see some last appeal, and here there was none either! (Act I)

In *Incident at Vichy* Miller transports us into that world where the conscience is dead among the agents of extermination and no last appeal is left to the victims. This is the ultimate terror of a society organizing itself to perpetrate mass murder.

But to dramatize this astounding discovery of what is possible years after the event has actually happened is to compete with reality (to say the least) on unequal terms. Every adult mind knows by rote the methods which were used in the rounding up, processing, and liquidating of millions of human beings. Miller is able to impress upon us the horror of the first step, the transformation of individual men into nameless units of cargo. And we sense, as we do not in the previous play, that the abdication of individual responsibility, which keeps the machinery of destruction functioning, is no longer covered by the legend of the Fall of Man. But the Eichmann trial has brought this home to us with greater force. The "banality of evil" (in Hannah Arendt's phrase) did not originate in the Garden of Eden; it is a modern sequel, and its social consequences in our time are incalculably greater than those of Adam's sin. They are summed up in George Steiner's epigraph for the present age: "Men are accomplices to that which leaves them indifferent."[10]

Miller brings his play to a climax by means of two confrontations which deal with the question of responsibility. The first is between Leduc and the "decent" army major, who has no stomach for these proceedings, but proves by a

specious bureaucratic logic that just as the victim has no
duty to make a gift of himself to the sadism of his perse-
cutor, so he has no duty to make a gift of himself to his
superiors. In the second encounter, Miller attempts to
transcend the corrupting logic of the smoothly functioning
organization. Reversing Quentin's chilling insight in *After
the Fall* that possibly "no man lives who would not rather
be the sole survivor of this place than all its finest victims," he concludes this play with an implausibly heroic
gesture when the Austrian prince, von Berg, makes a gift
of his life to enable Leduc to escape the efficient machinery
of death. According to the last stage direction, the major
and the prince stand facing each other *"forever incomprehensible to one another, looking into each other's eyes,"*
as four fresh prisoners are brought into the detention
room. Whether or not there really existed one such man
or a dozen, Miller's conclusion is borrowed from another
genre, the secular miracle play. It does not grow out of the
original, realistically conceived, vision of a closed system
in which in our day and age the process of dehumanization
was set in motion, unperturbed by the humane ideals
which have brought the race out of the condition of savagery.

Perhaps Miller is as yet too addicted to the liberal tradition in politics and ethics to be able to "conceive of Iago"
and Iago's capacity to reshape the world in his own baleful
image. Büchner, who wrote the first modern social drama
in this vein, anticipated the idea of a closed system without
the possibility of escape. Without equivocation he sent
both the highly civilized and urbane political leader, Danton, and the ignorant, helpless soldier, Woyzeck, to their
inevitable doom. Any gesture of resistance in the name of
humanity would have been inconsistent with his rigorous
conception of the exercise of power by unscrupulous
men. Yet he reminds us of the alternative humane vision
of life, not by tampering with the plot, but through the
irony of his dialogue.

At the other end of the tradition of the social and psychological drama, Ionesco provides the mid-twentieth cen-

tury version of Iago in *The Killer* (*Tueur sans gages*, 1959). Without the motive of Satan's jealousy and hatred of life, the modern killer does his work methodically and senselessly. He is the principle of destruction behind its many forms in contemporary life. The notable difference is that his victim, the "average, middle-aged citizen" Bérenger, cooperates with the killer, not because he is deceived as to his true identity and purpose, but because he cannot marshal adequate arguments to justify his existence. "In fact," says Ionesco, "Bérenger finds within himself, in spite of himself and against his own will, arguments in favour of the Killer." Or, as Ionesco suggests when Bérenger at last comes upon him, "possibly there is *no Killer at all.* BÉRENGER could be talking to himself, alone in the half-light."[11] He pleads with the chuckling figure (or phantom) in every conceivable vocabulary which the human intelligence has developed—philosophy, religion, psychology, economics, ethics, politics—and finally in the language of a hopeless supplicant, but he is incapable of persuading the Killer or himself that life is worth preserving. Ionesco issues the following instructions to the director and the actor: "BÉRENGER should be pathetic and naive, rather ridiculous; his behaviour should seem sincere and grotesque at the same time, both pathetic and absurd. He speaks with an eloquence that should underline the tragically worthless and outdated commonplaces he is advancing." The implication here is that Bérenger's naiveté is not alone responsible for his collapse. His arguments are "outdated" and no trained intellect using the same approach could have done any better.

Actually, his premises are the point in question. Like the prisoners in the detention room in Miller's play, he assumes that an innocent man should not have to justify his right to live. As they examine their own lives for a clue to the meaning of their impending fate, so Bérenger tries to guess the motives of the Killer. The Nazi death-machine is the historical counterpart of Ionesco's abstract conception of the Killer. In both plays the burden of proof rests on the victims. But the sanctity of human life is merely an assump-

tion which can be swept away. "There are no persons any
more, don't you see that?" says the Major in *Incident at
Vichy.* "There will never be persons again. . . . " Miller
created the Austrian prince to disprove this prophetic assertion, to show that the human spirit can survive the
darkest episodes of history.

Ionesco's pessimism is absolute. He carries to its tragic
and grotesque conclusion the idea that a man has no justification for existing. *The Killer* is also a parody of the social
drama. It deals with the modern polis and the failure of the
city planner and the social engineer to create anything
more than the empty showcase of the "radiant city." Ionesco's civic landscape is filled with the ignorant, apathetic,
shabby inhabitants who pursue their comic-pathetic hum-
drum lives in the tenements of the old city, whereas the new
breed of Civil Servant, the inhumanly efficient Architect,
presides over the calculated order and beauty of the radiant
city. But though the Killer waits regularly at the gate of
the city in ambush for his victims, there is a general indifference toward his reign of terror. Since it is a hopeless
task to catch him, the Architect-Police-Superintendent
comforts himself with the knowledge that the Killer never
attacks those who are connected with the Civil Service.
Bérenger's tubercular friend inexplicably carries the Killer's diaries and his timetable in his briefcase, but he is not
surprised because he has never examined its contents. He,
too, is almost indifferent toward Bérenger's crusade to hunt
down the Killer, as are the enormously tall policemen, who
worry more about traffic control than homicide.

Everyone knows about the Killer and appears to accept
him as an irremediable condition; the tools of his trade
could conceivably be found in anyone's unexamined briefcase. Only our bourgeois hero, Bérenger, cannot accept this
metaphysical flaw at the center of life. And so he proceeds
in his bumbling way toward the prefecture to do something
about the "fate of mankind."

> BÉRENGER: . . . Once he's arrested, bound hand and foot,
> out of harm's way, the spring will come back for ever, and
> every city will be radiant . . . I shall have my reward.

That's not what I'm after. To have done my duty, that's
enough. . . . I must stop the rot. Yes, yes, I know I can.
Besides, I've gone too far now, it's darker that way than the
way I'm going. . . . (Act III)

Ionesco locates the meaningless death-in-life of society in
the "vacuity" of the ideas by which we justify our private
and communal existence. He demonstrates the logical
supremacy of the idea of nonbeing over the well-meant
but ridiculous aspirations of Bérenger for a flawless life
in the scientifically planned city. At the conclusion, the futility of reason and discourse opens the way to attempted
violence, but Bérenger lowers his "two old-fashioned pistols": "What good are bullets even, against the resistance
of an infinitely stubborn will! . . . Oh God! There's nothing
we can do. What can we do . . . What can we do. . . ."

With this play we have come to the outer limit of this
dramatic mode. Beginning with Büchner's plays we have
looked at some of the transformations of the tragic social
drama on the modern stage and the different emphases
of individual playwrights. Nearly all of them addressed
themselves to the problematic relation of man to his social
environment, examining the causes of failure and breakdown in the individual and exploring the viability of interpersonal relations and of social life itself. But Ionesco's
play, though it is clearly an offshoot of these explorations,
takes us in another direction. It dispenses with the familiar
psychological, social, and moral conflicts (except in the
satiric vignettes which are inserted here and there) because
it tries to deal with a more radical predicament than those
which afflict the protagonists of the social drama. In other
plays, like *Rhinoceros* and *Exit the King* (*Le Roi se meurt*),
Bérenger also plays the role of the modern everyman, but
what happens to him in those allegorical fantasies is commonplace compared with his discovery of a mysterious an-
tagonistic force, lodged inside him, which renders him physically and mentally inert. Ionesco's skepticism as to the de-
fensibility of the individual life and consequently the possibility of a communal life is the ultimate denial that the
social or the psychological drama is in any way relevant

to us. Bérenger's professed interest in the fate of mankind is easily recognizable as a wry joke in the experimental postwar theater. But there are other voices which have sustained tragedy in the modern theater, avoiding the stalemate position of universal skepticism.

NOTES

1. *After the Fall* (New York: Viking, 1964).
2. Introduction, *Collected Plays* (New York: Viking, 1957), p. 30.
3. See chapter 3, note 6.
4. *Collected Plays*, pp. 51, 52.
5. Ibid., p. 54.
6. Ibid., p. 47.
7. Ibid., pp. 43-44.
8. Ibid., pp. 44-45. Miller's point is not the same as Shaw's, who says it is historically incorrect, but dramatically necessary to make the figures "more intelligible to themselves than they would be in real life; for by no other means can they be made intelligible to the audience." For Shaw this is mainly a question of *explaining* their attitudes and institutions to the twentieth-century audience (Preface to *Saint Joan*).
9. When Miller returns to these questions of innocence and guilt, the nature of evil, love and forgiveness, and does so explicitly in *The Creation of the World AND OTHER BUSINESS* (New York: Viking, 1973), there is, if anything, greater skepticism about the human prospect. He tries, incongruously, a comic approach to the Fall of Man and the murder of Abel, but the frivolity of his treatment, time and again, precludes a full dramatic exploration of these questions. We are left with the puzzle of man—Cain killing for pride and power in the name of love—and, in the end, with Adam's desperate prayer for mercy.
10. "A Kind of Survivor," in *Language and Silence* (New York: Atheneum, 1967), p. 150.
11. Eugène Ionesco, *Plays*, III, 9, 98, trans. Donald Watson (London: John Calder, 1960).

PART THREE

Tragic Theaters of the Will

6. THE DEMONIC WILL IN A BOURGEOIS SETTING

Ibsen's transition from the social problem play to his late dramas exemplifies a deliberate rejection of naturalism as a way of perceiving and accounting for man's tragic predicaments. He recognized its confining logic and the threat it posed to the autonomy of the tragic protagonist. Instead, he created a unique theater of the demonic will in action and paralysis. The adverse reactions he received from the run-of-the-mill reviewers are a notorious episode in theatrical history. Those who heaped abuse on him because of his frank disclosure of erotic motives and ruthless behavior were of no consequence; they exhibited only the shock of recognition. But occasionally Ibsen proved "difficult" and obscure, even slightly mad, to those who had earlier hailed him as a social reformer. He "presents human life in a distorted form, and is entirely without intelligible purpose," wrote one English reviewer about the production of *The Master Builder* at the Trafalgar Square Theatre in 1893. Though Ibsen himself had long since learned to accept a storm of protest with each new production, he was "particularly concerned," as he wrote in a letter to Edvard Brandes, thanking him for a favorable review, "to have the characters . . . correctly interpreted and elucidated, and to see emphasis placed upon their realistic qualities, in the way you have done" (27 December 1892). He wanted the freedom to move beyond the conventions of the realistic theater, to detect trolls and demons, vikings and birds-of-prey, in the make-up of his characters, but at the same time he was concerned to leave the impression that his view of life was realistic and the conduct of his characters psychologically true. The greatest practitioner of the social drama, he changed his dram-

185

aturgy relatively late in his career, in response to a fresh
understanding of tragic reality. The plays of his last period
stand in vivid contrast to his realistic social drama. At the
same time, they may serve us as a convenient introduction to a variety of tragic theaters which share a common
quality, namely that the hero asserts his prominence, by
virtue of an awakened inner power, over the confining
external circumstances of his life.

In the social and psychological drama, as we have seen,
the external world seals the fate of the individual. The
stress lies as much on the operative historical and social
forces as on the psychological susceptibility of the affected
individual. From the beginning, for example in *Danton's
Death* and *Woyzeck*, this mode of tragic drama assumed
that in his confrontation with the world the protagonist's
role would be passive, the conflict pointing toward a condition of absolute defeat to which he must resign himself
or which he brings about through a final act of desperation. Carried to its extreme form, as in *Incident at Vichy*
or *The Killer*, it reaches a point of impasse by denying the
validity of the concept of the individual and even the reason for existing at all. A tangential development of this
major form of the modern drama has gone in the direction
of tragic farce or black comedy, the so-called theater of the
absurd. Here the playwrights insist on man's grotesque
failure to reach others in some form of communal understanding and emphasize his inconsequential existence as a
passive, solitary figure, unsafe in the menacing worlds
within and without. Both kinds of drama contemplate man,
not as a whole being, but in his truncated form, i.e. as victim of unpredictable forces beyond his control. When his
suffering is no longer reducible to material and moral
causes and the illusion of a normative order of events disappears, he is shown to be absurdly at a loss in a world of
senseless dangers and paradoxical contradictions. In other
words, Woyzeck's inner life, his paranoiac tendencies by
themselves, constitutes the foreground in this new drama
as if his distorted vision, which in Büchner is the result of

his suffering, were the sole reality, causing a state of ano-
mie. Both kinds of drama treat the individual like an object with no visible priority over the inanimate objects and
social forces that impinge on his life. That is why *Waiting
for Godot* is the classic parody of the human situation
viewed naturalistically. It is the modern tragicomedy par
excellence because Godot does not reveal himself except
through messages which prolong the false hope that some
day man may escape, or at least understand, his limited,
pointless existence.

An alternative vision in the modern theater is to invest
the protagonist with freedom of choice and the burden of
individual responsibility, in order to reassert the will of
man as a power to be reckoned with, even in defeat. The
dramatic situations which serve this end are commonly
taken from history and legend or are invented to display
a heroic quest for self-realization. Contrary to the realistic
social dramatist, who must rely for effectiveness upon factual observation and logical analysis, the tragic writers
with whom we are now concerned manipulate the external dramatic situation more freely in order to symbolize
the inner lives of their tragic characters. Of necessity they
must be prepared to abandon the techniques of the strictly
representational stage in order to remain faithful to their
conception of a hero whose will is the motive force carrying the drama to its tragic conclusion. Beginning with Ibsen, who supersedes the naturalistic view in the tragic
dramas of his last period, each of the theaters to be treated
in the following chapters rediscovers a philosophically
viable cue to action. The hero's autonomy is restored. He
is impelled to act purposefully from an inner need to determine his own fate, or to assent freely to tragic necessity. Whether secular or religious, however different their
particular objectives may be, the playwrights writing in
this mode produce tragedies in the traditional manner,
involving exceptional men that are larger than life by virtue of their aspirations, their commitments, and the guilt
they are willing to incur.

1

Ibsen is a prime example among modern playwrights of the tragic poet who seeks to enlarge the scope of his stage in order to accommodate a larger than ordinary image of life. Technically there is little change. It is the spoken word in the late dramas which opens up new worlds to our imagination and lifts the dramatic action beyond the plane of naturalism. Embodying new forces at work, other than social and hereditary, which lie deep in the personality, he developed a powerful modern tragic theater out of the original narrower vision.

When Ibsen, in mid-career, turned his attention to the social scene before him, he sought there precisely the kind of subject which Hermann Hettner had recommended twenty years earlier. Hettner's criticism, with which Ibsen was familiar, had been directed against the dilettantish naturalism of the contemporary drama, the prosaic offspring of the bourgeois drama of the previous century: the topical, homely, highly moralized play of family misery. It was a concoction of accidents, he argued, which was not truth to nature. "The bourgeois drama must be tragedy or it is trifling." Only if the dramatist dealt with principles that were naturally opposed would he be able to create tragic situations in which he could develop the hero to a significant completion of his inner life, rather than make do with a forced external compromise. Such absolute conflicts, he thought, were possible in the bourgeois world, in family life and social life. The dialectic of moral principles was to be the future subject.

Ibsen's last historical drama, *Emperor and Galilean* (1873), was truly such a dramatic conflict of principles, of ideas and morals, and not a chronicle play; he had chosen the historical subject to fit his present purpose. Turning to his own time, he also found such absolute conflicts for a serious modern social drama. For example, his "Notes for the tragedy of modern times," which precede a preliminary scenario for *A Doll's House*, reveal the poet's dialectic conception of the social problem. "There are two kinds of moral law, two kinds of conscience, one in man and a

completely different one in woman. They do not understand each other; but in matters of practical living the woman is judged by man's law, as if she were not a woman
but a man." The remaining remarks focus on the conflict
between the woman's natural inclination and her social
environment, a true opposition of principles which Ibsen
saw in modern life. "The wife in the play ends up quite
bewildered and not knowing right from wrong; her natural instincts on the one side and her faith in authority on
the other leave her completely confused." And he ends
with a technical note to himself: "The catastrophe approaches, ineluctably, inevitably. Despair, resistance, defeat."[1] He is evidently convinced of the tragic possibilities
in such a conflict, provided he can establish dramatic necessity, an inexorable logic of events. In *A Doll's House*
a realistically observed social situation results in a care-
fully prepared clash and an open rift in the institution of
marriage. The mechanics of the well-made play carry Ibsen's thesis admirably.

But in his next drama he fashions a tragedy out of the
contemporary scene in which the purpose of a lifetime,
indeed all hope of life, is demolished before our eyes. As
far as the subject of marriage was concerned, Ibsen agreed
in a letter that further than *Ghosts* he then dared not go.
"But *Ghosts had* to be written; I couldn't remain standing
at *A Doll's House*; after Nora, Mrs. Alving of necessity had
to come" (24 June 1882; V, 477). The far more devastating
effect of the second play is due to the technical mastery of
a new phase of realism. In causing the hidden past to bear
on the present moment with an ineluctable force, he has
devised a way of dramatizing a naturalistic concept of fate.
He has discovered tragic necessity in the mechanics of
cause and effect. In the notes he mentions a favorite theme
of his: "Nemesis is invited upon the offspring by marrying
for extrinsic reasons, even when they are religious or moral—" (V, 467); and the finished play is a demonstration of
this thesis. But the power of retribution is, of course, not
supernatural. It is a relentless force which has a logically
conceivable origin and proceeds to overtake its victim in
calculable ways. Thus, he has (in Hettner's terms) devel-

oped the heroine to a completion of her inner life, as far as the naturalistic premises of his fable will allow.

Certain critics, notably Francis Fergusson, have remarked on the discrepancy between the potential tragic rhythm of the play and its abrupt ending in obedience to its mechanical perfection. The comparison of Mrs. Alving's quest with the tragic rhythm of *Oedipus Rex* sets up expectations which Ibsen's play cannot possibly fulfill. Hence her quest seems to be "truncated"; it fulfills its function only as thesis play and thriller. In the context of his larger argument in *The Idea of a Theater*, this is exactly the point Professor Fergusson wants to make. But Oswald's physical collapse, the sudden cutting off of what was left of Mrs. Alving's life, is not merely "sensational," nor is it plausible to suggest that Ibsen, unable to "dissociate himself from his rebellious protagonist and see her action in the round . . . broke off in anger, losing his tragic vision in the satisfaction of reducing the bourgeois parlor to a nightmare, and proving the hollowness of a society which sees human life in such myopic and dishonest terms."[2] Since the naturalistic playwright pretends that the logic of his plot is the logic of life, the comparison with the tragic rhythm of *Oedipus* is actually misleading. Mrs. Alving's action is not a quest like that of Oedipus. She does not seek out Oswald's revelations; they are forced to the surface. Rather, she seeks to free herself of the secrets which she already knows. And when the play opens she thinks that she is at the point of succeeding. In terms of the naturalistic view of man's tragic fate, she suffers a harsh defeat, for which Ibsen's dramatic logic accounts, even the last gratuitous blow which ends her life of action. In other words, Ibsen's stage did not cramp him. It suited his early limited tragic vision perfectly.

What is disappointing, and even outrageous, in the exhibition of the final stages of Oswald's disease is the *deliberate* narrowness of vision. Ibsen seems to be saying: This symbolizes my view of the human condition; these are the sources of a human destiny laid bare. Mrs. Alving's struggle against the ghosts of dead conventionality, of

which her confession of guilt is the noblest part, is suddenly terminated by an event that is extrinsic to her moral
bid for freedom and yet linked to her life. It is patently incorrect to say, as Shaw says, that "the ideals have claimed
their victim." For though Mrs. Alving conceived her son
after returning to her depraved husband, we do not rationally connect the inherited disease with Mrs. Alving's
cowardice before religious and social authority. If then
she cannot take *that* guilt upon herself, the last curtain is
a powerful but almost gratuitously painful ending. She is
overtaken by a pathological accident, and in the context of
the play, the quality of this "retributive justice" is poor.

On the other hand, one ought to keep in mind that naturalism as a way of seeing and representing the workings of
human destiny differs from Aristotle's "law of probability
or necessity" which describes the internal logic of a well-
made plot. The naturalist reasserts the dependence of art
on real life, using the plot as an instrument of enlightenment, of social education. "The play will be like an image
of life," says Ibsen in his notes; but the objective is to show
that "Everything is ghosts" (V, 467). In this sense, the hidden truth of Oswald's disease presses out of the past upon
the present action, as it well might in real life, and is, to
Ibsen's way of thinking, a legitimate reversal of Mrs. Alving's purpose. Thus, her quest is indeed "brutally truncated." But that is in the nature of Ibsen's theater. He develops the social and moral predicaments of his characters with impeccable logic. But it is also part of his dramatic method to find physical equivalents for moral crises,
and for these he must rely upon probable medical causes
in order to safeguard the surface illusion of reality.[3] Oswald's ruin may be more probable in real life than in the
context of the play. In any case, it shows the pertinence of
James's remark that Ibsen's "great quality, the quality that
makes him so interesting in spite of his limitations, so rich
in spite of his lapses [is] his habit of dealing essentially
with the individual caught in the fact."[4]

It was Ibsen's serious purpose to convert the didactic
problem play into a moment of tragedy. He succeeds bril-

liantly. *Ghosts* is as good an example in this kind as one can find. In it are adumbrated the themes and to some extent the technique of his later plays. But in the light of the later plays one can also see that, in time, Ibsen understood its limitations and the necessity of transcending the literalism of his fatalistic view of life. In *Ghosts* Mrs. Alving rises to tragic stature as we learn of her struggle to pursue her impulse toward a free life. In her decision to take all responsibility upon herself, she reaches a high point. But then Ibsen with one blow paralyzes her will; he turns his tragic heroine into a helpless victim. This maneuver indicates, I believe, an abrupt shift from a personal interest in the fate of his protagonist (her heroic attempt to shape her own destiny) to an impersonal, objective judgment of her situation (the vain endeavor to escape from the ghosts of the past). It is impossible to say whether Ibsen acted from anger or conviction. The important point for my present argument is that he reversed the emphasis in his later plays, for example in *Rosmersholm* and *The Master Builder*. In these plays the failure is not reducible to a quasi-moral operation of an impersonal fate; it is rather a foreshadowed condition of the attempt. In other words, the human will behind the intention or purpose is flawed. The plot becomes once again a classic imitation of an action, the awakened desire for liberation tragically reversed.

In the social problem plays there is always a clearly articulated thesis anterior to the plot so that the protagonist does not act as if on his own account; instead he exemplifies a specific mode of action the consequences of which the dramatist is at pains to show us. Ibsen regards truth and falsehood objectively and invites us to evaluate character and conduct rationally in the light of his skillfully timed revelations. The difference between the honest person and the hypocrite or the self-deceived person is the point at issue. He can build tragic situations out of the interplay between truth and lie, though, as we have seen, the illumination of the "problem" is still uppermost in his mind. In the series of plays from *Pillars of Society* through *The Wild Duck* he explores the possibilities of this opposition by asking the same question in different forms: What happens when the hidden truth is revealed to upset a situation built on lies? And the answers depend on the specific situation or problem before us.

In *An Enemy of the People* the champion of truth is portrayed sympathetically, but comically. Ibsen fiercely attacks the "compact majority." Yet he can afford to smile at Dr. Stockman's self-important righteousness because his struggle against the forces of "evil" may cause him discomfort but can never impair his spirit. Unlike Mrs. Alving, he need not battle the lie inside himself. Gregers Werle's portrait in *The Wild Duck* is that of an unhappy youthful meddler whose personal motives may arouse our sympathy (as in the scene between him and his father), but whose frantic idealism, because it is effectual, merits our scorn. Ibsen poses moral riddles for us under partly ambiguous circumstances so that we are forced to choose a lesser of two evils: in the one case truth, no matter what the economic consequences to the town, in the other the "life-lie" in order reasonably to preserve what there is of life in the Ekdal household. That is to say, we are asked to see the moral ideal primarily as a social good or a social ill, in the nature of a problem demanding a thoughtful decision. Ibsen pursues the risk of truth-telling to its macabre conclusion in *The Wild Duck*, and Gregers is his instrument. But Gregers is not personally involved in his moral ideal; he hawks it like a professional reformer. Significantly, he rebels only peripherally against his own life. Nor is Hjalmar possessed by the "claim of the ideal"; rather, he falls easily into a romantic-heroic pose—eating bread and butter all the while—until it is too late. In short, this is not the demonic pursuit of an ideal which we find exemplified in *Brand* and in the later plays. Only the young girl, Hedvig, is capable of such a passionate absolute commitment. She responds seriously to the demand for sacrifice, but, in the world of *The Wild Duck*, to no avail.

The difference between Gregers' motive and Hedda Gabler's or Rebecca West's gives us an idea of the difference between the anti-heroic world of the problem plays and the more fiercely resolute world of tragedy. There is a surface similarity in the action of several plays, a type action which interests Ibsen: the attempt to interfere in the life of another person, to reform or to remold it. But the motive for such an attempt becomes more and more subjective and elusive from play to play, until the agent and the person acted upon appear to shape a symbolic act of the will in tragic collusion.

Gregers Werle, in the first two acts, learns how his father has woven a web of lies around the life of Hjalmar Ekdal to protect his own good name. His "mission" is then, to begin with, personally motivated. But in the latter half of the play, the personal motive all but disappears, and the action develops into a comic-pathetic climax as Gregers inflexibly pursues the ideal of absolute truthfulness over every kind of falsehood. Both Gregers and his friend theorize about principles in the abstract; when they act, they act not from need but from principle, and the damage is done. But their failure does not destroy them. Within the year, as Relling prophesies, Hjalmar will use his daughter's death as a theme for declamation and self-pity. As for the idealist, Gregers, Ibsen sends him off with mockery: "If *you* are right and I am wrong, life will no longer be worth living." The statement is hollow and deserves Relling's bitter retort: "Oh, life wouldn't be too bad if only these blessed people who come canvassing their ideals round everybody's door would leave us poor souls in peace" (Act V). In the faltering world of the Ekdals, Dr. Relling seeks to preserve the lifesaving lie. That does not make him necessarily Ibsen's spokesman, or even a trustworthy raisonneur. But he is worldly-wise and therefore a proper dramatic foil to the empty heroics of Gregers and Hjalmar.

On the other hand, the last scene of *Hedda Gabler* presents us with the opposite situation. When Hedda shoots herself in the temple, all worldly wisdom crumbles. Judge Brack, so sure of his hold over Hedda one moment before, sinks into his armchair, half-fainting: "But, good God Almighty . . . people don't do such things!" The contrast between these two endings is symptomatic of the difference

in the conception of the two plays. Obviously, Hedda
Gabler's motive and action are not subject to the kind of
judgment which we may make of Gregers' and Hjalmar's.
Both her desire to have a human life in her power and her
failure and suicide confound the rational judgment. Like
Rebecca West and Hilde Wangel, she is possessed by a vision in which she is herself deeply implicated. Thus the
outcome of her "thrilling" venture is decisive; she does not
merely fail, she dies of its failure. Ibsen is no longer concerned merely with the objective value of truth over falsehood in a concrete dramatic situation. In a sense, both
Gregers and Hedda attempt to actualize an ideal, to raise
a human life to the truth of its own moral (or in her case,
amoral) potentiality. The same is true of Rebecca's and
Hilde's work of interference. But the difference lies in the
quality of the ideal. Gregers starts with a moral principle
which he pursues tenaciously, blindly. The case presents a
problem, and Ibsen shocks his audience by calling attention, with some straining of effect, to its partly comic,
partly tragic result. Relling's anti-idealist remark at the end
is a straight piece of editorializing upon a problematic
situation. The pathos of the situation is that with the exception of Gina, the mother, no one in the house (including Relling) can bear to face reality. But this theme
is subordinated to the didactic moment of the play.

Hedda's ideal is of a different sort. It has nothing to do
with what is true and what is false in an objective sense;
we are not faced with an ambiguous ethical problem.
Hedda's motive is highly personal, for it is the conflict of
her own life which she is acting out in her attempt to transform another life. Unable to face the commonplace existence in store for her, yet by temperament a moral coward,
she gives free rein to a wild dream of an uninhibited life
and, if necessary, a self-determined, noble death. And she
will have it vicariously. But the struggle rages inside herself, and consequently her life ends with her failure to
achieve her purpose. With the destruction of her ideal, she
has no reason left to continue living at all. The suicide itself
is merely her public assertion of failure. She has the capac-

ity to act where Gregers remarks grandiosely: "If *you* are right and *I* am wrong, life will no longer be worth living." The crucial shift of the battleground into the personality of the protagonist had been made earlier, in *Rosmersholm*, which is Ibsen's first tragic play in the new vein.

2

In fact, after *The Wild Duck* we can no longer speak of social problem plays in the sense of *Pillars of Society* or *A Doll's House*, or even *Ghosts* though Mrs. Alving's struggle with the ghosts of her own past points in the direction of the later tragedies. After the mid-eighties the conflict is subjective in nature. It explores the options of an individual trying to steer his life toward an ideal destiny which he considers ultimately meaningful. This struggle to achieve an exhilarating freedom by overcoming all inward obstacles is not the same as the struggle against social convention and institutional hypocrisy. Mrs. Alving is engaged in both. She thus stands midway between Nora and Rebecca West. The difference between Nora and Rebecca is instructive in the light of Ibsen's preliminary notes to *A Doll's House*:

> A woman cannot be herself in contemporary society, it is an exclusively male society with laws drafted by men, and with counsel and judges who judge feminine conduct from the male point of view.
> She has committed a crime, and she is proud of it; because she did it for love of her husband and to save his life. But the husband, with his conventional views of honour, stands on the side of the law and looks at the affair with male eyes. (V, 436-437)

Nora represents the predicament of the modern woman in contemporary society, raising doubts about the unresolved conflicts of marriage as a social institution, whereas Rebecca's crime is the source of *individual* guilt which destroys the hoped-for life of innocence and freedom at Rosmersholm. Although Ibsen was always guarded in his scattered remarks about his work, two passages concerning *Rosmersholm* and *Hedda Gabler* indicate the conscious shift of his attention at this time to the inner conflicts in his characters.

> . . . [*Rosmersholm*] deals with the struggle that every serious-minded man must wage with himself to bring his way of life into harmony with his convictions. The different functions of the spirit do not develop uniformly or comparably in any one individual. The acquisitive instinct rushes on from one conquest to the next. Moral consciousness, however, 'the conscience', is by comparison very conservative. It has its roots deep in tradition and in the past generally. From this comes the conflict within the individual. But naturally the play is first and foremost a work about people and their destiny. (Letter of 13 Feb. 1887; VI, 447.)
>
> In this play [*Hedda Gabler*] I have not really intended to treat so-called problems. The main thing for me has been to depict human beings, their humours and their destinies, *against a background* of certain operative social conditions and attitudes. [Italics are mine.] (Letter of 4 Dec. 1890; VII, 500.)

Social problems may appear incidentally in Ibsen's theater after the mid-eighties, but the plays never again rest mainly on the moral dialectic of right and wrong or truth and lie. For it is not alone the unforeseen consequences of a hidden wrong or a social lie which press upon the present life with an inescapable logic. Nor is the past which now reaches into the present moment merely a web of human mistakes and unworthy compromises rendered fateful in a causative, naturalistic manner. The pressure in these plays comes from within the individual; an inherited temperament, a habitual way of life, a vivid consciousness of past events now act in the course of the drama with the power of fate. The protagonists of Ibsen's later tragedies must cope with a past inside them which acts as a force running counter to their desire to live a free life. They carry the cause of their own destruction within them, but not like the fact of Oswald's disease, an impersonal yet punitive power which reaches out of the past and demolishes two lives. It is rather a moral force that holds the individual bound to his past. It defines his character and conduct with a subtle authority; and in the end he must capitulate to it. Thus Oswald's inherited disease may be regarded as a natural, however unforeseen, consequence of the past, whereas the master builder's acrophobia suggests a complex of personal causes which contribute to his tragic fall. It raises the question whether the master builder dare not, or cannot, climb as high as he builds.

The difference is significant. What is new in Ibsen's tragic theater is that the human will has been set in motion. The external logic of the naturalistic drama, whereby the factual past as it is uncovered determines with objective certainty the distressing present situation, has been replaced by the unpredictable action of the human will, as the mind confronts its own experience and interpretation of the past. It is Rebecca's second confession, and not Kroll's suspicions, which alters the course of the drama toward suicide rather than escape; and it is Solness' unbearable private sense of indebtedness, not the accusations of his employes, which kindles his desire to climb above the ruins of his life. We witness a secret struggle between the power of the past which fetters the individual and a strange deep power within which impels him to seek deliverance. This in its most generalized form is the potentially tragic conflict in which Ibsen becomes more and more interested; which is not to say, of course, that the later dramas are basically all alike. There is a rich differentiation of motives and action in the contending play between these claims which produces in each drama a particular version of this typical conflict and a unique world of tragedy.

Yet, as Ibsen insisted, we must look at his plays in relation to each other in order to understand his work as a whole. For example, in a series of three plays—*Rosmersholm* (1886), *The Lady from the Sea* (1888), and *Hedda Gabler* (1890)—he deals with three women, Rebecca West, Ellida Wangel, and Hedda Gabler, alien in their environment, each of whom brings with her a particular vision of elemental freedom and a will to achieve it which is demonic. The three plays are undoubtedly correlative treatments of the same general motif, but in each Ibsen develops it differently. And from the last decade of his active career there are the three powerful dramatic figures, the master builder Solness, the financier John Gabriel Borkman, and the sculptor Rubek, who represent Ibsen's final account of the price of total self-realization and the release from the bonds of human relationship.

In *Rosmersholm* we have in Rosmer himself the clearest example of the clash between the past, what Kroll calls "the Rosmer tradition," and the desire to break with it. But Rosmer's apostasy runs its course in the first half of the play, and significantly only on the level of ideas; he does not act. Morally secure, he ventures to proclaim his idea of intellectual and political emancipation. Despite the shocking reversals of Act II, in the three scenes with Kroll, Mortensgaard, and Rebecca, he upholds his new position well enough. What he cannot withstand are the inroads on his conscience, as certain fragmentary revelations about his wife's suicide are made. And with the loss of his certainty of innocence, the whole fabric of noble ideas crumbles. This is, however, only one sequence in the complex design of the play. Its true importance lies in the stake which Rebecca has in Rosmer's defeat. For it is her free spirit which has precipitated the clash and which is broken in the event.

The two appearances of the quixotic Ulrik Brendel illuminate Rosmer's failure with sardonic humor. Rosmer's old teacher has also reached a turning point in his life; he, who had never been willing to profane his pure ideals, his "golden dreams," is ready to give them to the world, a sacrifice on the "altar of liberty." For the moment Rebecca appears to be stirred by Brendel's romanticizing. "You are giving the most precious thing you have," she says; and (looking significantly at Rosmer) "How many are there who do that? *Dare* do that?" And though Rosmer himself is not blind to Brendel's bankruptcy, he can only admire the old man's "courage to live his life in his own way" (Act I). His second appearance in the last act, as we shall see, opens Rosmer's eyes to the cost in human sacrifice of a life of ideals.

Rosmer's will to enact his purpose of ennobling the hearts and minds of men is paralyzed before he can take a single step. The dead cling to the last living heir of Rosmersholm, both the ancestors in their moral uprightness and his unhappy wife accusing him of faithlessness. The real tragic conflict occurs in Rebecca, who pits her free spirit against Rosmersholm and suffers a double defeat. She fails in freeing Rosmer and loses her own courage, too, which is crushed by a tradition that is alien to her. But Rebecca fights her losing battle with far more determination than her partner. With an unnatural calmness, as Rosmer observes, the calmness of resolution, as she chooses to call it, she first confesses her guilt of Beata's death in front of Kroll, a desperate attempt to save Rosmer. By giving him back his innocence, she hopes to preserve at least Rosmer's new vision of life. But she has underestimated the hold of Rosmersholm on his spirit; she is not so much frightened by his rejection of her, as by the fact that he still refuses to cross the millstream, the scene of Beata's suicide.

She had "chosen" between Beata's life and his, but in vain. "That choice," says Rosmer with justifiable severity, "was not for *you* to make." And that should be the end of the matter. In the previous play, *The Wild Duck*, Ibsen had dealt with a similar theme, the attempt to reshape other people's lives. He ended the play with a strong statement condemning the idea of Gregers' mission, a point comparable to Rebecca's recognition of her failure at the end of Act III. In *The Wild Duck* he had said all he wanted to say on the topic of Gregers' brand of idealism. But here Ibsen is not alone concerned with a demonstrably harmful experiment in moral idealism, though Beata was clearly the innocent victim of Rebecca's "horrible game." The dramatic action of *Rosmersholm* begins *after* the memory of her death has been softened and just when "Pastor Rosmer was nice and settled." It has to do, rather, with the process by which a formidable will power is gradually forced to yield to an alien law of conscience. Rosmer's failure to grasp his freedom is the failure of Rebecca's fearless will in action. At the end of Act III she admits to the housekeeper that she has become afraid of the white horses of Rosmersholm, and therefore she must go "north by boat." Though she has no human ties anywhere, she instinctively prepares to return to her spiritual home. There, as she remembers later, the passionate life within has at least its counterpart in the reality of a storm at sea that "takes hold of you . . . and carries you away with it . . . for as long as it lasts[;] it never occurs to you to resist."

The proof that Ibsen has extended the scope of his drama and embarked in the direction of a new tragic theater comes in the final act of *Rosmersholm*. Rebecca's unsuccessful intrusion into the stronghold of Rosmersholm does not end with her confession of guilt and her admission of failure. The tragic resolution, going beyond the logic of her having been found out and left to her own devices, consists of three essential scenes: her second confession, Brendel's reappearance as the tragic Fool, and the final doom session. Reviewing a production of the play in 1908, Max Beerbohm wrote a remarkable analysis of the problem of acting the part of Rebecca, which at the same time sheds light on her role as the tragic heroine of Ibsen's play:

> Rebecca is essentially a vessel for implicit, rather than a vehicle for explicit, emotion. She is a woman who has passed through tortures of the soul, and is now serene. At the beginning of the play the actress impersonating her must not let her serenity deceive us as to the past. And again, when Rebecca has to pass through yet greater tortures, and still, despite them, is calm and self-contained, the actress must not let her own restraint blind us to Rebecca's agony. The part is a very subtle and difficult one, a convoluted one, needing an intellect to grasp it, and extreme skill to express it. Such skill would not, however, suffice. Forthright emotion on the stage can often be expressed merely by artificial means. But secret emotion can be suggested only through a genuine emotion that is in the player. . . . [Miss Kahn] is . . . the most naturalistic of actresses; and when Rebecca is merely folding up her knitting, or giving an order to Madam Helseth, or doing nothing in particular, it is—or rather seems to be—just as a real woman in a real room would do such things. And yet, I know not how, one is kept mindful that Rebecca is something more than the lady residing at Rosmersholm. She never lacks the mystery that the poet left on her when he conjured her from the North.

The poet's idea, the signification in her of something strange
that has happened, and of something terrible that will happen,
is never lost for us.[5]

A sympathetic (almost histrionic) understanding of the inner drama of the will, played against the background of the
conventional life style of Rosmersholm, is here far more
helpful than the exercise of the rational intelligence that
was adequate for the dialectic propositions of the social
plays.

Rebecca's first, semi-public confession (she deliberately
asks Kroll to stay) of the way she "took action" to lure
Beata to her death is a recital of her outward actions, the
way she ventured forward step by step, until Beata leapt
into the millstream. Only at the end of the scene do we get
a glimpse of the inward struggle between an uncontrollable, demonic will power and her conscience:

> But do you think I set about these things deliberately in cold
> blood! I was different then from what I am now, standing
> here talking about it. And besides, it seems to me a person
> can want things both ways. I wanted to get rid of Beata, one
> way or another. But I never really imagined it would ever
> happen. Every little step I risked, every faltering advance, I
> seemed to hear something call out within me: 'No further. Not
> a step further!' . . . And yet I could not stop. I *had* to venture
> a little bit further. Just one little bit further. And then a little
> bit more . . . always just a little bit more. And then it hap-
> pened. That's the way things like that do happen. (Act III)

Rebecca is by no means trying to exonerate herself. She is
rather trying to explain the irrational springs of action in
human nature of which Rosmer and Kroll cannot conceive.
(By the time Halvard Solness makes his confession of how
willing a thing insistently, ruthlessly, can make it happen,
Ibsen will have provided him with a sympathetic and dangerous interlocutress, a demon in her own right; and that
marks a new departure in his tragic theater of the will.)
Rosmer shrinks from such an image of irresistible self-
assertion. But there cannot be a parting of ways. For Rebecca's second confession lays bare the facts of her inward
struggle with the power of the Rosmer way of life, so that
Rosmer finds himself once more deeply implicated in the

commission of Rebecca's crime. She *had* loved him with an uncontrollable passion, and that, she now confesses privately, was the motive for "freeing him." "Yes, it was like a fight to the death between Beata and me at that time." This revelation clarifies the past events at Rosmersholm, and fixes Beata's death as an inexpugnable accusation against them both.

But it is not remorse that reduces Rebecca to despair. The tragic theme of *Rosmersholm* is not primarily guilt and expiation. She recounts rather the gradual disintegration of her independent spirit following the outward victory over Beata. Life at Rosmersholm, or at any rate living with Johannes Rosmer, has so transformed Rebecca's passion that she cannot grasp the prize of life now that she has gained it. Ironically, the moral sense of her own past cuts her off. Her will is paralyzed.

ROSMER. How do you explain what has happened to you?
REBECCA. It is the Rosmer philosophy of life . . . or in any case *your* philosophy . . . that has infected my will.
ROSMER. Infected?
REBECCA. And made it sick. Made it a slave to laws that had meant nothing to me before. You . . . being together with you . . . has given me some nobility of mind. . . .
ROSMER. Oh, if only I could believe that!
REBECCA. You need have no doubts about that. The Rosmer philosophy of life ennobles all right. But . . . [*shakes her head*] . . . but . . . but . . .
ROSMER. But what?
REBECCA. . . . But it kills happiness, Johannes. (Act IV)

Ibsen has left it to this scene in the last act to reveal the reason for Rebecca's conduct from the moment Kroll enters the house. Rosmer's ideal of freedom, based on a clear conscience and issuing in self-denying love, has long since prevailed over her unscrupulous self-will. When Rosmer finds this out, he is eager to hear more about Rebecca's transformation; were it true, it would vindicate his ideal of ennobling human beings. And Rebecca, for her part, is eager to offer the destruction of her free spirit as proof of his success. This is her second attempt to save Rosmer's sense of mission, and now even his reason for living. But words are not enough to restore his faith in "a broken dream" and thus to efface their common guilt; the past is irredeemable. "I have no faith in myself any more," says Rosmer. "No faith either in myself or in you" (Act IV).

If Ulrik Brendel's first appearance is a comic parallel of Rosmer's knight-errantry in the cause of political and intellectual emancipation, his second appearance in the last act foreshadows the tragic alternatives in store for Rosmer and Rebecca: separation and perpetual doubt, death of the spirit, or an act of complete self-denial, unmistakable proof of a great and selfless love. Brendel speaks in parables; and only after they themselves have reached the point of nothingness, complete moral bankruptcy, as he has, can they understand the Fool's wisdom. There are those who live their lives without ideals, like Peter Mortensgaard, the "lord and master of the future," who can do whatever he will because he never wills more than he can do. That, Brendel has found, is the secret of action and victory. But if you must dream of carrying forward a great cause, the cost of victory is sacrifice. The life of ideals is only for selfless martyrs. Let, then, Rebecca, the "enchanting little mermaid," prove her love by hacking off her dainty pink and white little finger and slicing off her incomparably formed left ear. It is the only way out of the emptiness and the paralysis of their lives.

In the late plays, beginning with *Rosmersholm*, Ibsen manages to introduce into the mundane parlors, work rooms, and bathing resorts an idealism as rigorous as that which drove Brand, the priest-hero, from his vicarage into the jaws of death; and he maneuvers the lives of his characters intricately so that they find themselves in stalemate situations which call for the absolute choice: Nothing or All. The All in *Rosmersholm*, as in the other plays, becomes for the protagonists a momentous experience of self-fulfillment which the spectator can only surmise as he witnesses their mounting infatuation with themselves and their private vision. But in the eyes of society their choice must be regarded as irresponsible since they leave behind them the scene of their social commitments, their guilt and their defeat.

The conclusion of *Rosmersholm* presents Ibsen's first variation, to be followed by others, of just such an ambiguous treatment of the individual in quest of the absolute freedom to judge himself and so choose his fate. The dead Beata dominates this scene because it is her example that mesmerizes even Rosmer's sober imagination. Although he and Rebecca lure each other, step by step, in a deadly game toward the decision, their dialogue is not that of desperate guilty creatures trying to glorify an act of atonement. The comfortable, old-fashioned living room with the portraits of robed clergymen and uniformed soldiers is not an unlikely place for Rebecca to have to undergo her supreme test. "As if impelled against his will" Rosmer asks the question. Does she have the courage, the will, gladly and for his sake to go the same way that Beata went? True to character, Rosmer is fascinated by the *idea*; but he leaps up in fright when she slowly puts her white shawl over her head, ready to take him at his word. Rebecca's decision is tragic in the traditional sense of the word, for she consents freely to the necessity of her death. She chooses, without illusion, to do what she must do. And her double motive reflects the ambiguity of victory and defeat in her deed.

On the one hand, she goes to her death voluntarily, to give Rosmer actual proof that his own life has not been vain:

> REBECCA [*slowly takes up her shawl, throws it over her head, and says with composure*]. You shall have your faith back again.

On the other hand, she knows that she has been forced to this by the infectious climate of Rosmersholm:

> ROSMER. But I do not want to see you defeated, Rebecca!
> REBECCA. There will be no defeat.
> ROSMER. There will. You'll never bring yourself to go the way Beata went.

REBECCA. Don't you think so?

ROSMER. Never. You are not like Beata. You are not in the power of some twisted view of life.

REBECCA. But I am in the power of the Rosmersholm view of
life . . . *now*. Where I have sinned . . . it is right that I
should atone.

ROSMER [*looks fixedly at her*]. Is *that* how you see it?

REBECCA. Yes.

ROSMER [*resolutely*]. Well then, I give *my* loyalty to our emancipated view of life. There is no judge over us. Therefore we
must see to it that we judge ourselves.

What is tragic in Rebecca's end is not the fact of her death
in expiation of her crime; there is justice in the exact repetition of Beata's suicide. The tragedy of her defeat is that
Rosmersholm has broken her and now effectually nullifies
her supreme sacrifice. For Rosmer, in order to prove his
emancipation at last, must step out on the footbridge with
her and do justice upon himself.

Ironically, his one independent decision is to die with
her. But first the questioning in reverse to clarify Rosmer's
double motive.

ROSMER. If you go . . . I go with you.

*   *   *

REBECCA. As far as the bridge, yes. You know you never dare
go out on it.

ROSMER. Have you noticed that?

REBECCA [*sadly and brokenly*]. Yes. That was what made my
love hopeless.

ROSMER. Rebecca . . . now I lay my hand on your head . . .
[*does so*] and take you to be my truly wedded wife.

REBECCA [*takes both his hands and puts her head on his
breast*]. Thank you, Johannes. [*Lets go.*] And now I go gladly.

ROSMER. Man and wife should go together.

REBECCA. Only as far as the bridge, Johannes.

ROSMER. Out on it, too. As far as *you* go . . . I too go with you.
For now I dare.

*   *   *

REBECCA. Suppose you were only deceiving yourself. . . .
Suppose it were all a delusion . . . one of those White
Horses of Rosmersholm.

ROSMER. It could well be. We can never escape them, we of this house.
REBECCA. Then stay, Johannes!
ROSMER. The husband shall go with his wife, as the wife with her husband.

Here again is the tragic paradox of choosing freely what must be. Ibsen gives the concluding lines to Madam Helseth, the housekeeper, but she is there to present, by way of emphasis, only the "outside" view of the catastrophe:

. . . God forgive the sinful creatures! Putting their arms round each other! [*Screams.*] Oh . . . over the side . . . both of them! Into the millstream! . . . No, no help there . . . the dead woman has taken them.[6]

At the beginning of the play Rebecca observed: "They cling long to their dead here at Rosmersholm." And Madam Helseth had answered: "It's my belief it's the dead that cling to Rosmersholm, miss." Ibsen has exploited the full power of that remark. But the double suicide, it turns out, suggests more than fitting retribution. It emulates the suicide of the passionate and childless wife both as an act of self-deliverance and as a voluntary payment of a moral obligation. This is the measure of their victory in death: that they save themselves from Brendel's fate, the bankrupt monarch of ideals, and from the ignominy of Mortensgaard's view of life; and that in consenting to their fate they are able to salvage from their broken lives a sense of their own worth. Ibsen's high regard of this momentary fulfillment is unmistakable in the symbolic wedding scene and the remaining moments of the play.

ROSMER. For now we two are one.
REBECCA. Yes, now we are one. Come! Let us go gladly.[7]

3

Critics who used to come to Ibsen's work with a bias in favor of the "naturalism of his psychology," and found their approach justified by the meticulous logic of the earlier

social plays, felt acutely uncomfortable about their playwright's excursion into "mysticism" in the later dramas,
like *Rosmersholm, The Lady from the Sea*, and *The Master Builder*. His conception of the free human will as a demonic power and particularly the idea of transformation
through sacrifice, brought into the bourgeois living room,
left them incredulous. Archer had recognized the shift, but
accounted for it simply as the emergence of the poetic
imagination through the rigorous prose structure.[8] Others
have refused to consider such embarrassingly supraration-
al moments in the late plays, either by taking refuge in
strictly technical discussions or designating them as re-
grettably unsuccessful exercises in symbolism. But the
comparatively recent revival of interest in Ibsen's last period has taught us that he did not always feel himself
bound by what is probable or even plausible according to
a naturalistic psychology and common logic. The fact is
that he recognized certain preternatural forces at work in
human conduct and decided to introduce them, more or
less ostensibly, into his outwardly realistic situations.

He becomes more and more skillful in retaining the surface impression of everyday reality, while defining an action and preparing a dramatic climax which go far beyond the subject matter and the technical management of
the naturalistic theater. Hedvig's self-sacrifice in *The Wild
Duck*, though evidently necessary to his moral, is hardly
compatible with the prevailing tone of the play. To try to
make her resolution psychologically plausible may be
construed as an act of kindness to Ibsen's craftsmanship.
But it seems better to admit that a deed of such spirit was
meant as a shocking intrusion into a world of compromise
action and thought. By contrast, the double suicide in *Rosmersholm* and Hedda Gabler's pistol shot are amply prepared for, since both plays have dealt with the failing
attempt of the human spirit to free itself. The most notorious examples of the demonic eruption in natural sur-
roundings occur in *The Master Builder* and in that parable
of the human will, *The Lady from the Sea*.

Ibsen's technique is to introduce us to the tragic protagonist in a situation of confinement. He has a hundred ways of creating a stifling atmosphere, through the setting, through small gestures of body and speech, and through the revealing phrase.[9] At the same time, he presents the details of the protagonist's alternative image, the rebellious spirit bent on determining his own destiny and that of other lives. And it is this powerful impulse inside the individual to realize his potential as a free (almost godlike) agent which sets off the tragic action. In short, Ibsen tries to recreate heroic tragedy in his bourgeois setting. His new heroes and heroines do not merely run afoul of the laws of the community; they stand apart from the community. They are in effect self-willed anarchists, whose dream either fails or ends in self-destruction, which is the price of attempting to redeem its promise.

By deliberately reversing the pattern in *The Lady from the Sea*, Ibsen precludes the tragic resolution. Though Ellida Wangel also finds herself cruelly confined in her new home, like Ballested's painting of the mermaid who is dying in the brackish waters of the fjord, unable to find her way back to the open sea, Ibsen treats her instinctive longing for the sea as if it were a disease to be overcome. The main action of the play rests entirely on this metaphor of the limitless sea and the strange sailor who comes to reclaim his betrothed. Ellida's will is captive in Ibsen's view; she cannot help herself. "The sea possesses a power to affect one's moods," he notes in his draft manuscript, "which operates like the power of the will. The sea can hypnotize. Nature at large can do this. The great secret is the dependence of the human will on 'the will-less' " (VII, 450). But unlike the mermaid, the woman can overcome her mysterious impulse and transform herself into a land creature. Ibsen is so fascinated by his dramatic metaphor that, as Henry James pointed out, he comes nearer here than anywhere else to "playing with an idea from the simple instinct of sport."[10]

But it is detrimental to the drama that he plays with the

idea explicitly, allegorically. "I'm beginning to understand you . . . little by little," says Dr. Wangel after Ellida has made her choice.

> You think in images . . . your mind works in visual terms.
> Your yearning for the sea . . . your attachment to this
> man, this stranger . . . these things were nothing more than
> an expression of your growing desire for freedom. That's all.
> (Act V)

There is the contrast of the more moderate and conventional ways of flirtation, courtship, love and escape among
the "acclimatized" land animals. Finally, Ellida herself is
released from her "passionate impulse" through the husband's act of love. Her wayward spirit is exorcised; when
she is free to choose, she can reject it.

Ellida both desires and dreads "the demonic pull of the
completely unknown" (Draft manuscript, VII, 455), as
Ibsen calls her mysterious affair. It represents, however
vaguely and uncertainly, the idea of freedom to her. And
because the vagueness and the mystery are there until the
very end—for no single character in this play is as articulate
as Rebecca West about her inner life—the allegory of the
wayward will redeemed through love seems so pat. The
impression one gets is that Ellida's spirit has been domes-
ticated, rather than transformed, and that she simply has
escaped a bad romantic dream. Still, the play is relevant
to our discussion because Ibsen deals here with ideas characteristic of his work and they are only thinly veiled. Ellida, the dying mermaid longing to be released, though in
the end choosing the safety and peace of the fjord, is yet
kinswoman to the tragic heroines, Rebecca West and Hedda Gabler, and to her young stepdaughter, Hilde Wangel,
whose impossible dream will destroy the master builder.
The will to freedom in these women, it should be noted
however, is of a different order from that of Mrs. Alving or
Nora, whose gestures of revolt were wholly in response to
social lies and hypocrisy. *Ghosts*, says Ibsen, only points
out "that nihilism is fermenting under the surface, at home
as everywhere else. And that must inevitably be the case.

A Pastor Manders will always provoke some Mrs. Alving or other into being" (Letter, 6 Jan. 1882; V, 476). The alluring and potentially destructive power which has possession of the human will becomes a motive force only in these later plays.

In Ibsen's heroines it is as ruthless as in the male egomaniacs, Solness, Borkman, and Rubek, but because of their dependent social position it is in the end thwarted, or transformed. Only Hilde, who is an emissary from that world of demonic females, consummates her irrational desires in a moment of ecstasy because Solness responds to them (as Rosmer could not to Rebecca's passionate impulse). In fact, he more than responds to her unencumbered will power; he invites and accepts her gift of youth as a sign of the destined awakening of his own dormant energies.

> HILDE [*utterly serious*]. Something inside me forced me, drove me here. Drew me, tempted me, too.
> SOLNESS [*eagerly*]. There you are! There you are, Hilde! There's a troll in you, too. Just as in me. And it's the troll in us, you see, that calls on the powers outside. Then we *have* to give in—whether we like it or not.
> HILDE. I rather think you are right, master builder.
>
>   *   *   *
>
> HILDE. Tell me, master builder—are you sure you have never called to me? Inwardly, I mean?
> SOLNESS [*quietly and slowly*]. I rather think I must have.
> HILDE. What do you want of me?
> SOLNESS. You are youth, Hilde.
> HILDE [*smiling*]. That youth you are so afraid of?
> SOLNESS [*nods slowly*]. And to which in my heart I am drawn so sorely. (Act II)

It is, then, the male protagonist of the last dramas who is roused once more late in his life, after a career of high success and near asphyxiation in a society of less exuberant souls, to seek his former self and the fulfillment of an early promise.

With the exception of *Little Eyolf*, which treats guilt as a prelude to renunciation, Ibsen's last dramas of the 1890s are variations on the theme, When We Dead Awak-

en. With John Gabriel Borkman, who spends the years
following his prison sentence in self-imposed isolation,
he dwells emphatically on the condition of death-in-life,
while Rubek becomes fully aware of his condition only
when he meets Irene and learns the exact nature of his
crime. Solness, though still vigorous and at the top of his
profession, is obsessed with his fear of retribution.
"Chained alive to a dead woman," allegedly the price of his
success, he now merely defends his position against the
younger generation like an animal at bay. In all three
plays there is a motion toward the desired resurrection
from the dead. The hero's imagination vaults beyond the
present consciousness of guilt to revive the half-remembered idea, and partly composed image, of a different self.
But the attempt to recapture the original vision of life and
to earn a second chance through an act of renewed commitment fails. The dead may wake to find what it is that
they have lost, but it is not given to them to make good the
loss. Hauptmann once remarked that Ibsen saw tragedy
only in the life that lay in ruins; the greater tragedy, he
thought, was that which struck in the fullness of life.[11] It is
a blunt critique of the playwright as an old man. With regard to the last plays, however, it should be observed that
Ibsen's preoccupation with the ruined lives of his characters has a special (and other than autobiographical) significance.

Ibsen writes the tragedy which is implicit in the nineteenth-century conception of the hero as superman. He is
intent on putting the theoretic idea to the dramatic test,
showing the moral and social upheaval caused by the supreme egoist and defining his character as his tragic fate.
In contrast, Shaw's *Man and Superman* is a comic-didac-
tic exposition of the idea rather than a trial against the experience of life. Unlike the Shavian life force, the troll that
calls on the powers outside is a force which at once enhances and destroys life. It takes such demons ruling the
will to make a man break his natural bonds and social obligations in order to follow the dictates of his unfettered
genius. Thus in his best moments the builder, the indus-

trialist, the artist is capable of great accomplishments but at the cost of ruined happiness and shattered lives. Each bears the responsibility for having pitilessly destroyed human love. On the other hand, each is virtually possessed by the demon inside him, and as Solness confesses, "we *have* to give in—whether we like it or not." The tragedy of such a personality is that he cannot renounce his will. "It is a question," says Ibsen, "not of willing this or that, but of willing what one absolutely must, because one is oneself and cannot help it."[12] The work of the troll is something which the character may understand but cannot resist.

The heroes of the last plays are living "a kind of posthumous existence" (to use Kenneth Muir's excellent phrase), having once paid the price for their total commitment to the self and its overpowering aspiration. Ibsen depicts the world of these living dead, their victims of former times, and a frantic younger generation trying to break loose. As his heroes rise from their graves, the gesture is imposing but futile. They climb upwards for a momentary glimpse of their lost vision and then plunge. In Ibsen's view, the man who builds must be an independent spirit; he is destined to forfeit his humanity in order to create and serve. Moreover, the nineteenth-century hero, the "chosen" artist or builder, cannot repent for the wreckage he has caused. "Don't you understand?" Solness exclaims in desperation. "There's nothing else *I* can do! I am what I am! And I can't change myself!" (Act I). He can only suffer the stifling knowledge that he is immensely indebted to those whom he wronged. And the only release for each of these men lies in the last attempt to leave behind the recalcitrant world and to recapture the failed glory and the kingdom.

The relation between the past and the present is now altered. In the earlier plays the dramatic present was the day of reckoning when the compromises and self-deceptions of the past must be unequivocally faced. In these last plays, however, the present moment, in which the protagonists are burdened with the sense of guilt and indebtedness, appears to them an unendurable distortion of their true being, in effect an enforced compromise with the world as it is. Now the past harbors an ideal image of what they are, and it is that which by the strength of their will they must dare to restore, in order to find deliverance from the realm of the dead. This transvaluation is common to all three plays, but Ibsen explores significant alternatives in the tragic movement of each play.

He does this by using a number of parabolic actions and dramatic metaphors. The symbols in Ibsen's plays, seen or alluded to, have been competently discussed by several critics. The orphanage, the pistols, the steeple are objects which derive their meaning from the plays and return it enriched to the developing action. But the use of parable and metaphor in the later plays is a poetic technique of greater scope, determining the shape of the dramatic action itself. It is a statement of one side of a suggested comparison, the other unspoken, in terms of which the play is conceived. For example, the symbolic white horses of Rosmersholm derive their effect from what we know of the place and the attitudes it breeds. But the story of Beata's suicide off the bridge into the millstream, and the repetition of this action at the end of the play, is a dramatic metaphor that explains to us the transformation of the love relationship between Rosmer and Rebecca. Similarly, the sea in *The Lady from the Sea* is not merely illustrative of Ellida's turbulent inner life; it is itself the object of her turbulence, "the dependence of the human will on the 'will-less'." And the ghostly Stranger who comes for her twice in the course of the play is an embodiment in parable form of her struggle with demonic forces.

4

The most common thematic ideas which Ibsen varies and explores in parable form in his last period are: the transformation through the agency of another, the idea of a mutually dependent fate; the experience of guilt and indebtedness, living by the destruction of another's happiness; the reawakening from the dead and the impulse toward a "resurrection," the will to regain a former freedom and truth of being. These motives are present in *Rosmersholm*; only now Ibsen develops them in several distinct ways. The passive would-be reformer assumes a more heroic stature in the older characters, Solness, Borkman, and Rubek, who look back upon a career of potential greatness and bitter failure. Each must confront the woman whose soul he murdered to achieve his ambition. These plays begin at a point where Rosmer has lost his naive faith in his innocence and discovers his involuntary complicity in the death of his wife. Finally, the figure of Rebecca reappears in different guise, in keeping with the unique purposes of the two related plays, *The Master Builder* and *When We Dead Awaken*. Hilde Wangel frees the master builder and destroys him in the process. Irene combines the roles of Beata and Rebecca; she returns from the dead, but the spirit of revenge turns to momentary ecstasy as she joins Rubek in their suicidal climb toward the light above the mists. If Rosmer's and Rebecca's embrace in death is overshadowed by the manner of their suicide, Rubek's "wedding feast" on the mountain peak with the woman whose soul he had killed is surely meant to be a less equivocal conclusion. "As though transfigured" (in Ibsen's stage direction) Irene follows him freely and willingly as his bride to their certain death.

Ibsen clearly refuses to be confined by the realistic conventions of plot structure and character motivation. He is at his boldest in *The Master Builder* and *When We Dead Awaken*, inventing fables of the human will and tracing its enigmatic behavior without regard to psychological or dramatic probability. This, I take it, is the meaning of Joyce's tribute: "Ibsen's plays do not depend for their interest on the action, or on the incidents. Even the characters, faultlessly drawn though they be, are not the first thing in his plays. But the naked drama—either the perception of a great truth, or the opening up of a great question, or a great conflict which is almost independent of the conflicting actors, and has been and is of far-reaching importance—this is what primarily rivets our attention."[13]

John Gabriel Borkman is the least audacious and the bleakest of the three. The *danse macabre* sounding from Borkman's upstairs drawing room may be regarded as the leitmotiv of the play as a whole. It represents the "howls" of the "sick wolf" to those belowstairs whom he has sacrificed to his ambition and failure; but to Borkman himself it is a reminder of the music of the mines, of the singing iron ore as the hammer blows set it free to serve mankind. His career, embracing near greatness and stubborn pride even in failure and death, is best described in Santayana's paradigm of tragedy: the idea in its lyrical state, the hero's original inspiration, turns into dogma and obsession when it enters the world of conflicting interests. All flexibility lost, it involves him in a tragic clash of force against counterforce. Like Solness, Borkman was conscious at the outset of an irresistible commandment within him to which he had to respond "because I was myself—because I was John Gabriel Borkman—and no one else." Thus even in defeat, a maimed Napoleon, he is able to vindicate his actions and remain insensible to the accusations of the two old women whose love he had sacrificed to the single purpose of his life.

The final scene of *John Gabriel Borkman* is remarkable because it has an outward resemblance to the concluding ritual of the other two plays—the invitation to ascend the mountain top to see the kingdom that might have been his— but it ends the play on a note of unrelieved frustration. Borkman speaks of making his way back to freedom and life and humanity, and Ella climbs with him to a remembered lookout over the landscape and the fjord. But she does not share his illusory vision of harnessed power and wealth beneath them. And though he knows himself that his dream has remained a dream, its lyrical force is undiminished:

> ELLA: Ah, but it's a cold wind that blows from that kingdom, John.
> BORKMAN: To me it is the breath of life. It is a greeting from the spirits that serve me. I feel them, those buried millions. I see those veins of iron ore, stretching their twisting, branching, enticing arms towards me. I've seen you all before, like shadows brought to life—that night when I stood in the vaults of the bank with the lantern in my hand. You wanted to be freed. And I tried to free you. But I failed. Your treas-

ure sank back into the darkness. (*Stretching out his hands*) But let me whisper this to you now, in the stillness of the night. I love you where you lie like the dead, deep down in the dark. I love you, treasures that crave for life, with your bright retinue of power and glory. I love you, love you, love you. (Act IV)[14]

The inspiration of a lifetime has become a futile obsession, in effect his nemesis, as a hand of iron grips his heart. But to the sisters who stand over his body, it was the coldness of the heart that had killed him long ago and turned them into shadows. Throughout the play the main figures are frozen and inflexible in their attitudes until their time runs out. Only in the end Ella Rentheim and Borkman's wife join hands over the man they both loved.

As for the younger generation, Borkman's son and Frida Foldal, Ibsen assigns them a dubious form of escape—to live, no matter how, away from the house of death. The dramatic contrast between youth and age is considerably sharpened in *When We Dead Awaken:*

RUBEK. Poor Maja. So we spend most of our time sitting by the fire and talking about *your* interests.
MAJA. Lord, I've no interests to talk about.
RUBEK. Well, perhaps they are rather trivial. Still, time passes, Maja. Time passes.
MAJA. True enough. Time passes. It's running away from you, Rubek. I suppose it's that that makes you so uneasy.
RUBEK *nods vigorously.* And so restless.
Shifts on the bench.
No, I can't stand this miserable life much longer. (Act II)

By the end of the play, Rubek and Irene go up above the mists, while Maja escapes downward in the arms of a Nordic satyr, Squire Ulfhejm, celebrating her safety and newfound freedom. Again Ibsen draws a clear demarcation between those whose time has run out and the young, who value the enjoyment of life above all else. In this play, however, the contrast enhances the meaning of the choice which Rubek and Irene make in the final scene. But the most daring encounter between youth and age occurs in *The Master Builder*, which deals with a younger man, though

well past his prime, who gives in to the tempting possibility of blotting out the present. Solness undergoes a moral
rejuvenation under the tutelage of Hilde Wangel and so
overcomes his fear of youth. But at the same time as the
reawakened demon inside him hardens his conscience, he
is tempted to do the impossible—to climb as high as he
builds, to redeem his promise to his equally demonic princess.

The transformation of Solness—from the moment Hilde
knocks on his door, virtually a stranger to him, until at the
end of the second act she has persuaded him that his diz-
ziness, like the failure of his naturally robust conscience,
can be overcome through an act of will—is a daring dramatic
tour de force. As his deepest desires are touched, Solness
agrees to a version of the past which he cannot remember.

> HILDE [*looks intently at him*]. Is it true, or isn't it?
> SOLNESS. That I get dizzy?
> HILDE. That *my* master builder dare not . . . cannot climb
>   as high as he builds?
> SOLNESS. Is that the way you see it?
> HILDE. Yes.
> SOLNESS. I'm beginning to think no part of me is safe from you.
> HILDE [*looks towards the bay window*]. Up there. Right up
>   there. . . .
> SOLNESS. You could live in the topmost room in the tower,
>   Hilde. . . . Could live there like a princess.
> HILDE [*flatly, between earnest and jest*]. Yes, that's what you
>   promised me.
> SOLNESS. *Did* I, in fact?
> HILDE. For shame, master builder! You said I was to be a prin-
>   cess. That you would give me a kingdom. And then you took
>   me and . . . Well!
> SOLNESS [*cautiously*]. Are you quite sure it isn't some kind of
>   dream . . . some fantasy that's taken hold of you.
> HILDE [*sharply*]. You mean you didn't do it?
> SOLNESS. Don't really know . . . [*More quietly.*] But one thing
>   I do know now, and that is that I . . .
> HILDE. That you . . . ? Say it!
> SOLNESS. . . . That I ought to have done it.
> HILDE [*bursts out gaily*]. You could never be dizzy!
> SOLNESS. Tonight we'll put up the wreath . . . Princess
>   Hilde. (Act II)

If over the years Borkman's dream has turned into an

obsession impossible to realize, Solness, on the contrary, has been tormenting himself to identify a forgotten experience. When Hilde enters, not to storm his house and his position, but to reawaken his former integrity of will, he recognizes her as the conscienceless, ruthless Viking spirit of his own youth. During the long dramatic sequence in which Solness recovers the meaning of his promise which he had allegedly made to the girl at Lysanger and which alone can make him whole and happy again, Ibsen underlines their identical thought and feeling. Imperceptibly the unscrupulous professional man and the unconventional young woman from the country merge their will and character. At the outset Hilde wanders about his work room *"her hands behind her back,"* looking at this and that while Solness stands by the table, *"also with his hands behind his back,"* following her with his eyes. They discover that they have similar bad dreams of falling from heights; that they appear slightly mad in other people's eyes; that they no longer read books, which, at any rate, do not solve the puzzle of existence; and, finally, that they share the same egomaniac thought: nobody but Solness should be allowed to build, and he should do it all alone. Thus Hilde becomes not merely his ally in the struggle against his tortured conscience; by bringing back his youthful spirit she allows him to overcome the fear of retribution through a fresh act of self-assertion. He can now give the young assistant Ragnar his professional independence since he is ready to repeat the challenge of Lysanger—to climb to the top of the steeple and to renew his litigation with God.

As with Rebecca West, there is a moment in the last act when Hilde, having learned the full negation of life in her interview with Mrs. Solness, wants to leave. "I've just emerged from a tomb," she says; " . . . the frost has seized my bones." But the troll within overcomes the momentary pangs of conscience; to dare what one wants betokens a healthy conscience. She has only one last misgiving: "Castles in the air—they're so easy to take refuge in. So easy to build, too. . . . Particularly for master builders with . . . weak nerves." She will insist on the actualization of the ideal, to show that the impossibility willed *can* be achieved. By putting the metaphorical idea of castles in the air to the test, Ibsen comments on the tragic dilemma of the demonic hero. In order to build, in order to enact his private vision, he must exceed the social norms and even the human norms by which ordinary mortals live. In trying to do the impossible, he finds deliverance as a free, almost godlike agent, but falls to his death.

We can never know whether the achievement is genuine except through the testimony of Hilde, but she, like Irene in *When We Dead Awaken*, is enraptured by the climactic moment of triumph and death—and rightly so. Ibsen has, in each case, presented the final act of commitment as a necessity growing out of the desperate situation of the protagonist; therefore, the calculating question whether the act was worth the price becomes irrelevant. Rosmer and Rebecca confirm, and yet overcome, the guilt that had killed them by choosing to die in each other's arms. With the help of Hilde, Solness reenacts his youthful challenge in order to regain his self-possession and independence as the only *master* builder. He transcends his paralyzing fear and guilt through an act fraught with symbolic meaning for himself and his youthful alter ego. Rubek, "before all else . . . the artist . . . sick with a longing to create the one great work of [his] life," *The Day of Resurrection*, had used Irene's young body as a model and had then discarded her. This betrayal of a human life had also killed his artistic inspiration and made him into a cynical producer of society portraits. Now, in remorse and exultation, they willingly enact the resurrection of their squandered lives "for one short hour," before going down again into their graves.

Based on the same general pattern, Ibsen's tragedies of his last period supersede the realistic problem plays in that they focus the attention, not on the moral and social conflicts which produce tragic disorder, but on the inhibitions and the guilt which destroy the human personality. Ibsen's master builders are destined to forfeit their humanity in order to create. But their conscience plagues them, as Solness explains in this striking metaphor:

Who called on the helpers and servants? *I* did! And they came and did my bidding. [*In rising excitement.*] That's what people call being lucky. But let me tell you what that sort of luck feels like! It feels as if my breast were a great expanse of raw flesh. And these helpers and servants go flaying off skin from other people's bodies to patch *my* wound. Yet the wound never heals . . . never! Oh, if only you knew how it sometimes burns and throbs! (Act II)

The wound is self-inflicted and betokens a ruined life, which only a promethean act of the will can resurrect. Ibsen's judgment of the failure of their lives is relentless, yet he grants his mortal heroes (with the exception of Borkman) the demonic capacity, in one last moment of self-fulfillment, to master their fate.

NOTES

1. *The Oxford Ibsen*, trans. and ed. James Walter McFarlane, V (New York: Oxford, 1961), 436-437. All subsequent references to this edition will appear in the text.

2. *The Idea of a Theater* (Princeton: Princeton University Press, 1949), p. 156.

3. See John Northam, "Ibsen's Search for the Hero" in *Ibsen: A Collection of Critical Essays*, ed. Rolf Fjelde (Englewood Cliffs, N.J.: Prentice-Hall, 1965), for a discussion of the analogous relationship between Nora and Rank. Nearly every play thereafter has instances of such symbolic physical and mental ills.

4. Henry James, *The Scenic Art. Notes on Acting and the Drama: 1872-1901*, ed. Allan Wade (New Brunswick, N.J.: Rutgers University Press, 1948), p. 255.

5. Max Beerbohm in the *Saturday Review*, quoted by Michael Meyer, trans. *Rosmersholm* (London: Rupert Hart-Davis, 1966), pp. 122-123.

6. Michael Meyer underlines the contrast between fated retribution and free choice by adding the word *fallen* in his version of Madam Helseth's last lines: "Ah! They've fallen—both of them! Into the millrace! . . . No help. The dead mistress has taken them."

7. Psychoanalytic theory cannot take such moments at face value. Freud finds the key to the puzzle in Rebecca's reenactment of the Oedipus complex, while James E. Kerans ("Kindermord and Will in *Little Eyolf*," *Modern Drama*, eds. Bogard and Oliver [1965]) detects in several plays "concealed maneuvers that drive toward disastrous cancellations of will, toward despair and death, through which friction is set up against the more assertive and, to be sure, far more interesting maneuvers of the upper or conscious levels of the plays or their attendant responses" (p. 207). But these are really the maneuvers of Ibsen's psyche in the process of composition and, as usual, they shed more light on the artist than on the work of art.

8. I am using Hermann Weigand's terminology to indicate a general critical attitude. See Weigand's *The Modern Ibsen* (New York: Henry Holt, 1925), pp. 203, 208, 246, and William Archer, *Collected Works of Henrik Ibsen* (New York: Scribner), IX (1908), xvii.

9. See John Northam, *Ibsen's Dramatic Method* (London: Faber and Faber, 1953).

10. *The Scenic Art*, p. 248.

11. *Einsichten und Ausblicke*, XVII, 434.

12. Quoted by Brian W. Downs, in *Ibsen: The Intellectual Background* (Cambridge University Press, 1946), p. 89, n. 4, from *Breve* (Copenhagen, 1904), I, 208; June 11, 1870.

13. James Joyce, from a review article on *When We Dead Awaken*, *Fortnightly Review*, n.s., 67 (1 April 1900), 575-590; rpt. in *Ibsen: The Critical Heritage*, ed. Michael Egan (London: Routledge and Kegan Paul, 1972), p. 387.

14. Michael Meyer, trans., *When We Dead Awaken and Three Other Plays* (Garden City, N.Y.: Doubleday, 1960).

7. THE PURGATION OF THE WILL: TRAGIC THEATER IN THE CHRISTIAN TRADITION

"It is the risk and the glory of our time, the aged Ibsen standing on its threshold, that we have again come far enough to have to prove ourselves in allegory."[1] Hugo von Hofmannsthal wrote this in 1912, apropos of *Jedermann*, his revival and adaptation of the medieval morality play. A dozen years later T. S. Eliot remarked (in "Four Elizabethan Dramatists") that "the theatre has reached a point at which a revolution in principles should take place." He was concerned with the effects of an unlimited aim at realism, and he saw that without a form to arrest the flow of spirit, without unrealistic conventions, the English drama was bound to end in an "exact likeness to the reality which is perceived by the most commonplace mind." Perhaps in only one play, namely *Everyman*, we had a drama within the limitations of art.[2]

Toward the end of his life, having thought a good deal about the problems of the poetic drama in our time and having produced Christian verse dramas of his own, Eliot wrote two prefatory notes to the Bollingen edition of Hofmannsthal's dramatic work in which their kinship is recognizable. In one he links Hofmannsthal, Yeats, and Claudel as "the three men who did most, in the same age, to maintain and re-animate verse drama"; and in the other he calls special attention to Hofmannsthal's poetic drama, *The Tower*, "the most important single piece in the present collection," expressing symbolically "not only the author's suffering . . . but also his ultimate Christian hope."[3] The reference is to those years of composition in which Hofmannsthal experienced the first world war and its aftermath in central Europe, the vision of a world in dissolution, a tradition demol-

223

ished. Actually, in the revised theater version of *The Tower*,
Hofmannsthal changed the concluding acts of the play,
leaving himself and his audience no hope that the spirit of
man can prevail over brute force. "Bear witness, I was
here," says the dying prince, "though no one has known
me," and the kingdom reverts to mob rule. This unflinching
historical testimony sets the play apart from the Christian
dramas of Eliot and Claudel, as we shall see. Yet in the conception of the world as the great stage on which mankind
plays the drama of life, in the idea of *theatrum mundi*, these
three modern playwrights share a common tradition and a
common outlook and method. Moreover, they approach the
drama as a re-enactment of the tragic moments in the life
of the Christian hero: the struggle of the will to purge itself,
the escape from passion and despair, the necessity of sacrifice, the acceptance of the martyr's role.

It is a remarkable fact that these three dramatists who
chose to explore the human condition in the traditional idiom of the Christian theater, while the realistic drama dominated the commercial stage, have been accorded fresh
recognition in our time. I. A. Richards, in *Science and Poetry* (1926), described "the transference from the Magical
View of the world to the scientific," which, in his opinion,
entailed a drastic reorganization of our attitudes. If the contemporary poet cannot confront or chooses to evade the
changed world picture, Richards concludes, he runs the risk
of being obsolete in his own lifetime. But these dramatists
neglect this confrontation in their work not merely from
personal conviction, but also for artistic reasons. The scien-
tific-naturalistic view of the human condition strikes them
as being an unwarranted reduction of what they perceive
in the human personality. "Situations are symbolic," says
Hofmannsthal; "it is the weakness of our time that we
treat them analytically and in so doing dissolve the magic."[4] They envision a drama which enacts before us the im-
palpable life of the soul, testing the creature under the
eyes of the creator. Since the essential dramatic conflicts
entangle human motives with the divine will, they must in
their plays deliberately assume a point of view transcend-

ing the business being transacted on the stage. Hofmannsthal does this explicitly in his modern mystery play, *The Salzburg Great Theater of the World* (*Das Salzburger Grosse Welttheater*, 1922), and Eliot and Claudel in more or less indirect ways. The characters represent not real men in action, but rather players in symbolic situations drawn from the theater of real life, and they are guided toward their destiny by supernatural agents or unwitting instruments of the divine will, angels, voices, tempters, or lovers, who incite the human will toward a supreme act of commitment.

Like the last tragic dramas of Ibsen, the Christian theater of Hofmannsthal, Claudel, and Eliot is also concerned with the crises of the human will and the risks and fulfillment to be found in the radical act of transforming the self. Such a theater bypasses or subordinates the uses of psychological realism because it presents the typical situation, not individualized character.[5] For the Christian dramatist, the acts of the unregenerate and the purged will constitute the most significant agons of life because they are, to him, the central determinants of the fate of man. In the first act of *The Cocktail Party*, Edward Chamberlayne reflects on the tedium and futility of his life. Although as yet uninstructed, he has a premonition of his own helplessness and the potential regenerative power in others:

> I see that my life was determined long ago
> And that the struggle to escape from it
> Is only a make-believe, a pretence
> That what is, is not, or could be changed.
> The self that can say 'I want this—or want that'—
> The self that wills—he is a feeble creature;
> He has to come to terms in the end
> With the obstinate, the tougher self; who does not speak,
> Who never talks, who cannot argue;
> And who in some men may be the *guardian*—
> But in men like me, the dull, the implacable,
> The indomitable spirit of mediocrity.
> The willing self can contrive the disaster
> Of this unwilling partnership—but can only flourish
> In submission to the rule of the stronger partner.
>   (Act I, scene 2)[6]

From the vantage point of Edward's unheroic position, we may interpret "the rule of the stronger partner" in two ways. On the one hand, it may be the obstinate, the tougher self, expressed in the demonic will power of Ibsen's heroes, or the Marlovian self-confidence of Tête d'Or (the hero of Claudel's first play), or the fatal ancestral will embodied in Hofmannsthal's Elektra. On the other hand, there are the few, the "chosen" witnesses, who have that within them which responds to the greater temptation (in Claudel's phrase) of losing their will in the will of God. Rodrigue, the hero of Claudel's *The Satin Slipper* (*Le Soulier de Satin*) travels the road from one extreme, the pursuit of desire and conquest, to the other, when at the end of the play "all else but God has been withdrawn" and he is taken by a mendicant sister to become a servant in a convent of Mother Teresa of Jesus. *Délivrance aux âmes captives*!

Deliverance from the powers that fetter the soul of man— Ibsen's parables of the human will describe the self-determined road to personal freedom and deliverance from guilt and unbearable confinement. The demonic heroes and heroines of Ibsen's tragic theater rise momentarily above the ruins of their lives by creating their own transcendent experience through self-judgment and self-forgiveness. They are witnesses to their own vision of freedom even if their resurrection is an intensely private and transitory experience. As spectators we can only surmise the significance of the moment of self-fulfillment. It is an ecstatic moment for those who participate, particularly in *The Master Builder* and *When We Dead Awaken*, because it signifies the actualization of an idea. But the demonic will of Ibsen's heroes answers only to itself and rejoices only in its own acts.

Yet there is a tragic exultation also for those who choose to give up "the self that wills" to find peace in martyrdom and for those who seek to transform themselves, to accept the dictates of "the obstinate, the tougher self." Both slough off the feeble creature that can say 'I want this—or want that' in order to answer the mandate of a more determinate will. Thus, Thomas à Becket must learn the mean-

ing of his own words, which the Fourth Tempter flings
ironically back at him:

> You know and do not know, what it is to act or suffer
> You know and do not know, that acting is suffering,
> And suffering action. Neither does the actor suffer
> Nor the patient act. But both are fixed
> In an eternal action, an eternal patience
> To which all must consent that it may be willed
> And which all must suffer that they may will it,
> That the pattern may subsist, that the wheel may turn
>   and still
> Be forever still. (Part I)

Ibsen's heroes are subject to the rule of the will which delivers
and destroys them but which they cannot renounce. "It is a
question, not of willing this or that, but of willing what one
absolutely must, because one is oneself and cannot help
it."[7] The Christian hero loses his will in the will of God. In
either case, acting is suffering and suffering action, and to
those who look on, the act of commitment, whether it
stems from the Christian's consent in the eternal pattern or
the demonic assertion of the self, is a terrifying choice to
make.

1

The evolution of Hofmannsthal's drama toward the
Christian mystery play, and beyond, illustrates his search
for a theater in which to represent the tragic act of commitment in the most meaningful way for our time. He was concerned with the problem of action and specifically the enigma of the tragic act for a number of reasons. Like Eliot, he
came to the theater with the credentials of a successful lyric
poet, one, moreover, who had grown suspicious of the
magic power of language as an unreal bond between the
solitary individual and society. In a theater of tragic action
he hoped to find the one instrument of expression whereby
he could resolve the antinomy between speech and action.
In his early lyric dramas he had depicted the isolated pre-
existential hero who leads an exquisitely private and sen-

suous life, but becomes cognizant of the transitoriness of
things and the tenuous bond between his egoistical consciousness and the world outside. He understood that (in
Yeats's words) "tragedy must always be a drowning and
breaking of the dykes that separate man from man, and that
it is upon these dykes comedy keeps house." That is to say,
it must resolve two other antinomies: that of solitude and
community and that of passing time and permanence. Unlike the heroes of his lyric theater, the tragic protagonist
would undergo the experience of time and yet remain devoted to his sense of timelessness; his action and his suffering would reunite him with the community.

But the great enigma for Hofmannsthal was the final
question. By what sanctions does the tragic hero act?
What are the sources of human destiny, what are the demons or perhaps the guardian spirits inside the chosen, the
tragic personality, which impel him to do the deed which
at once delivers and destroys? At first he turned to subjects
from the Greek mythology. The story of Electra's revenge
for the murder of Agamemnon and the story of Oedipus
fulfilling, step by step, the Delphic prophecy appeared to be
perfect examples of the workings of tragic necessity.

> Wisely
> Respond the gods where we question foolishly.
> They despise the questions which we ask
> With our lips; but that which sleeps within
> Our inmost depths and has not waked to question
> Yet; to that their monstrous voice responds
> Beforehand.

Oedipus and Jocasta, in Hofmannsthal's play, know and
do not know that the dream of Delphi is real, and that the
sensual reality of the widowed queen and the passionate
youth is only delusion. Yet suspecting the delusion and
knowing the darkness, they still surrender themselves, and
so fulfill their destiny. Hofmannsthal's Electra embodies
the doom on the house of Atreus. All moral and social contingencies are stripped away from the situation. The question of right or wrong has no place in this portrait of a
personality in the grip of a demonic will power. Only the

necessity of revenge, and the superhuman effort to achieve it, fills our imagination. She rejects Orestes' conventional remark that the gods have imposed this deed upon him. To her the murder of Clytemnestra is a self-willed necessity, revenge and self-immolation in one. Both plays, *Electra* (1904) and *Oedipus and the Sphinx* (1906), turn upon such an act that is unmotivated ethically but expressive of the will to become what one is, a tragic acceptance and fulfillment of the self.

Voluntas superior intellectu—thus Hofmannsthal describes the conception of a heroic personality who (echoing Ibsen and perhaps Kierkegaard) "wills what he must because he is what he is and cannot act otherwise."[8] His distinctive personal character is itself the law of his actions, and his commitment, therefore, is a total commitment. In tragedy such total commitment reunites the isolated sufferer with humanity, but at the cost of destruction and self-destruction. This is provisionally the answer to the problem of tragic action, which Hofmannsthal gives in terms of a modern theater dedicated to Dionysus, the invisible god inside the human animal.

It is a conception of heroism not unlike that of Claudel's promethean hero, Tête d'Or, whose strength of will derives from his invincible sense of his own destiny. Returning as victor and savior of the kingdom, he receives the homage of the court: "I thank you, Sire./ And all of you. Who am I? What have I done?/ That which must be already exists. Who does not know that?" (Part II). On account of this fatalism, his appetite for power and conquest is insatiable until he falls in battle at the gateway to Asia, the king of men, the illustrious child whom Nature has lent to perform his task among men, like an elemental force (Part III). Tête d'Or's almost religious devotion to the self as a superhuman power is jolted by the accident of war—"I am not a god"—but he makes of his death an apotheosis: "I die. Who shall relate/ That dying, arms stretched out, I held the sun upon my breast like a wheel?" (Part III). The scene on the high mountain pass between the continents, when even in death Tête d'Or subdues the Princess (whose father he had mur-

dered) to the force of his vision, reminds one of the self-
created exaltation of Rubek and Irene climbing above the
mists toward the light in *When We Dead Awaken*. But
Claudel's, like Hofmannsthal's, idea of how men master
their fate and thereby achieve their freedom was to develop
in another direction. It is adumbrated in the lament of the
fallen hero: "Creatures who rejoice in your omnipotence,
look upon me in this unholy place, a wretched man shed-
ding my blood! . . . O earth! earth that I cannot conquer!"
(Part III).[9] Deliverance in the Christian theater comes to
those imprisoned souls who recognize the vanity of even
their grandest desires.

In a lecture in 1916 Hofmannsthal attempted to demonstrate a common idea behind his conception of the Greek
myth of Electra and of his Christian Everyman. In both, he
said, the concept of individuality undergoes trial and question. Faced with ultimate demands, it dissolves. What does
remain when the creature is totally stripped of the incidents of individuality? when all that is left is the lonely soul
in need of deliverance? In both instances the answer lies in
the word *fidelity* or devotion (*Treue*) to that which abides,
to an absolute law, to the realm of Being. In a world in
which everything is conceptualized in terms of becoming,
or historicity, the poet must search for that which abides.
But what makes all the difference between Hofmannsthal's
Greek theater and the Christian theater, as he develops it
in the postwar years, is the definition of that realm of Being
or the Law. In the one, deliverance comes to the tragic hero
by way of fidelity to the self, to what he is; the Law, or the
source of his destiny, lies in the hidden self, and the dream
of Delphi discovers the gestures of the ancestral blood. In
the other, deliverance comes by way of fidelity to the superpersonal, to the Christian order. The problem is to remember the forgotten law which death recalls: the Law is the
Word. In both conceptions, the human act, motivated by
such fidelity, causes suffering and delivers the patient. Actor and patient are one; priest and victim are one.

Hofmannsthal's Greek dramas, as well as Ibsen's theater
of the will, create this tragic ritual and attempt to give it a

quasi-sacramental value. While Orestes kills Clytemnestra and her paramour inside the palace, Electra performs a "nameless" ecstatic dance of victory in the dusky court-yard and at this tense moment of her triumph she falls senseless to the ground. Oedipus ceremoniously receives his prize, the hand of Jocasta, at the cave of the Sphinx. Solness and Hilde, Rubek and Irene, are equally triumphant as if they were consecrating themselves to become their own sacrificial victims. The Christian dramas, on the other hand, imitate the prefigured religious ritual in symbolic terms, a celebration of the transition from sin to redemption. This too is a theater of the will, but it has to do with the recalcitrant will being schooled in the discipline of self-sacrifice, with the transformation of human passion, in short, with the struggle for salvation. Mesa and Ysé in *Break of Noon* (*Partage de Midi*) and Rodrigue and Prou-hèze in *The Satin Slipper* enact such a drama as do the Beggar in Hofmannsthal's *The Salzburg Great Theater of the World* and Celia in *The Cocktail Party*. As the Christian drama focuses on the moment of conversion, spiritual re-birth, so the other focuses on the moment of self-transfor-mation, rebirth out of the self. Beyond this, such modern miracle plays as *The Tidings Brought to Mary* (*L'Annonce faite à Marie*) and *Murder in the Cathedral* turn the drama virtually into a sacred rite. Martyrdom, as Becket explains in his Christmas sermon, reaffirms "in a smaller figure" the incarnation and passion of Christ, fulfilling the design of God and giving rise to mourning and rejoicing in the death of the martyr. This drama attempts to show the delicate renunciation of the will, allowing the chosen actor and pa-tient to "become the instrument of God, who has lost his will in the will of God, not lost it but found it, for he has found freedom in submission to God."

The human will in the Christian theater is not frustrated or defeated by any external social forces. It is rather tested in an existential crisis. The protagonist discovers its inan-ity in the prison of time; he is remorseful over the past, re-sponds without direction to the exigencies of the present, and is apprehensive of the future. For the Christian play-

wright the conditions of existence are essentially the same
now as always: man in the wilderness, unaccommodated
man, Adam expelled into the world, or whichever way one
may wish to phrase it. Choice and action are demanded of
him in virtual ignorance. He is a captive of his own shape-
less impulses, subject, in Eliot's phrase, to the "final deso-
lation/ Of solitude in the phantasmal world/ Of imagination, shuffling memories and desires" (*The Cocktail Party*,
Act II). The idiom of the Christian drama is particularly
suited to the task of identifying the forlorn condition of
man. But at the same time the diagnosis is part of the metaphorical structure of the drama: in his solitude and hopelessness man is shown to be in a state of deprivation resulting from his lack of faith in a providential order. The
Christian playwright views the historical event and man's
moral choices always in relation to that order.

> Those who put their faith in worldly order
> Not controlled by the order of God,
> In confident ignorance, but arrest disorder,
> Make it fast, breed fatal disease,
> Degrade what they exalt. (*Murder in the Cathedral*, Part I)

That is why Claudel finds fault with Shakespearean drama, because he fails to see on that stage, as clearly as he
would wish, "the third dimension, the Vertical direction."[10]
What Claudel missed in the Shakespearean drama is the
effectual transformation of human passion, albeit after
much suffering, in consonance with God's benevolent design to bring men back to His ways. But to demand that
would be tantamount to altering Shakespeare's conception
of tragedy. Claudel's orthodox drama does not negate the
disordered passions and events of this world, but it shows
them always as integral to a larger, and specifically a redemptive, design. Eliot, speaking only generally of an ideal
toward which the poetic drama should strive, points in the
same direction.

> For it is ultimately the function of art, in imposing a credible
> order upon ordinary reality, and thereby eliciting some per-
> ception of an order *in* reality, to bring us to a condition of se-
> renity, stillness, and reconciliation; and then leave us, as Virgil

left Dante, to proceed toward a region where that guide can avail us no farther.[11]

The most emphatic way of demonstrating "the intersection of the timeless with time" (Eliot's phrase in "The Dry Salvages") in the theater is to make the ancient metaphor of *theatrum mundi* literally operative. Hofmannsthal did this at the Salzburg festival in his production of *The Salzburg Great Theater of the World*, borrowing the idea from Calderón's Corpus Christi play, *El Gran Teatro del Mundo*. Ernst Robert Curtius reminds us that Calderón was "the first poet to make the God-directed *theatrum mundi* the subject of a sacred drama. . . . The theatrical metaphor, nourished on the antique and the medieval tradition, reappears in a living art of the theater and becomes the form of expression of a theocentric concept of human life which neither the English nor the French drama knows"[12]—until it is revived in the Christian theater of Eliot, Claudel, and Hofmannsthal. In *The Salzburg Great Theater of the World*, the stage structure does not merely serve as a magic mirror for the visible world and its invisible order, as it did in *Jedermann*, but the idea of man as a player on the world's stage becomes the very principle of the mise en scène. God, the master, speaking from the top of the scaffold, actually orders the World to produce a play under his eyes, featuring man, who is to act out his part on earth.

Six unborn souls are brought forward to be invested with their individual roles in life. Created free and in the image of God, each must face his destiny. It is an improvised play, the plot undetermined. Only its title is given: Act righteously! God is above you! But before the production gets under way, the World, as stage manager, has a bit of trouble assembling her cast. Five of the actors accept their parts willingly and submit to their incarnation as King, Rich Man, Farmer, Beauty, and Wisdom; only the soul destined to be the Beggar, having looked over his difficult role, refuses to take part in the drama of life. He throws aside the patched rags which are to be his costume and tries, though in vain, to tear his parchment scroll into shreds.

At once the Adversary, dressed in the habit of a scholarly

logician, stands at the rebel's side and makes a formally
legal demand for the natural equality of destinies. Why
should, of two guiltless souls, one be created Jacob and
another Esau? The question in behalf of the rebellious soul
is crucial, though we understand that the devil should know
better than to ask it so ingenuously. An angel must intervene, speaking from the upper stage, and he succeeds at
last in instructing the rebellious soul in the mystery of human freedom: What the actor *does* gives meaning to his
part. The free human choice, the deed alone, creates above
creation itself. For though there are these words in the beggar's part: my God, why hast Thou forsaken me?—there is
also this line: not my will, but Thine be done. And so the
soul accepts his costume and his role with resolution.

But as soon as the play gets under way on the lower level
of the stage structure, all the actors except Wisdom forget
the theatrical condition of their existence; they are caught
up so completely in their earthly roles. For the spectator,
however, the two worlds of passing time and eternity, or of
playacting and reality, are always spatially juxtaposed.
Hofmannsthal suggests the significant connection between
them in terms of the human act, the transcendent deed,
which delivers the actor. The Beggar's miserable role in
the world has brought him understandably to the point of
desperation and rage. His murderous axe swings high over
his head, an instrument with which to demolish the visible
order of injustice. But it is the dramatic moment of a mis-
deed averted, the moment of conversion, by which the
Beggar transcends the mundane order of creation.

By an act of grace—Saul responding to the blinding sheet
of light from heaven—the Beggar suddenly sees the *whole*
stage of life again illuminated. In terms of the world's play,
his part has been the least; but in God's eyes it is Jacob's
part. The King who has corrupted God's order on earth
strides for a brief moment across the world's stage; he is always a player king. But it is the Beggar who recollects that
he is playing in a borrowed costume which must soon be
returned; he remembers the mise en scène of life. There-

fore, he drops the axe and withdraws into the forest, choosing the Franciscan contemplative life. And as the passage of time, translated into a rhythmic dance of death, destroys beauty, wealth, and power, the hierarchy is reversed. When Death calls the actors one by one to leave the world's stage and to resign their costumes, it is the Beggar who leads the disembodied souls up before the palace of the Master, while the Rich Man kneels below. The Beggar's decision amounts to a denial of the reality of any time-bound order which distorts the image of the eternal order. In refusing, by his sudden illumination, to destroy the world's false authority, he transforms the potentially tragic temporal moment into divine comedy.

In Hofmannsthal's allegory the ironic condition of play-acting is always held before our eyes. The double perspective on man's action on the World's stage affords us a kind of reassurance, for the cosmic setting of the mystery play allows us to judge the doings of man in time by the eternal order of God and his angelic spokesmen. The converted Beggar can simply withdraw from the scene of human folly and injustice and outlast the bonds of time until he is called before God in whose sight all children are equal and free. But if half of the theatrical metaphor "The world is God's stage" disappears, if the top level of the scaffold is dismounted, the drama loses its magical property of subsuming before our eyes the personal ambitions and social struggles in an eternal pattern of divine justice. Then the platform mirrors only that "terrifying stage, reality"[13] as we know it, where in our fallen state we must act in virtual ignorance and blindness. The formal allegorical figures become mere actors (whose strength, as Prospero says in his Epilogue, "is most faint") playing their tragic roles in a historical setting caught in the narrow logic of time. Then only an act of faith, preceded by a struggle against every kind of temptation, can restore to the Christian hero the truth of the metaphor that the world is God's stage and so redeem his understanding of the part he must play in the historical event and in time.

2

Since in the Christian drama the eternal pattern is the
foreshadowing and the end of all action and suffering in
the world, the idea of *theatrum mundi* is the natural metaphorical device adopted by all three playwrights. Whether
in more explicit ways, as in Hofmannsthal and Claudel, or
less explicitly, as in Eliot, it is the best means of showing
the hand of Providence in the affairs of men. It is indispensable as a dramatic method for making credible the interplay between the ineluctable divine order and the wayward
purposes of man so that the saint as well as the common man may learn what it means to consent to salvation
through sacrifice. Unlike Eliot who tries to avoid the incur-
sion of the supernatural into the world of his plays or resorts to subterfuge, as in *The Cocktail Party*, Claudel does
not hesitate, when it appears necessary, to break into the
"historical" surface action. This gives his plays a deliberately fostered theatrical quality as if they were meant to be
direct imitations of the world conceived as God's stage.

Particularly in the book version of *The Satin Slipper*,
Claudel specifies that the scene should be set in full view
of the public and that the whole operation should look provisional, disordered, as if *improvised* on the spur of the moment and enthusiastically. Providing an approximate historical setting, he takes in practically all the parts of the
globe known to imperial Spain at the end of the sixteenth
century. But there is a constant ironic tension between
the political events of the far-flung empire and the private
longing for love and salvation arising from the idea of the
Christian universe. His actors become players in a huge improvised show, gambling their lives for temporal and eternal stakes. The lost "letter to Rodrigue" is surely a tragicomic parody of the role of chance in the Spanish intrigue
drama, and the "investiture" of Rodrigue as viceroy of
England despite the defeat of the Armada is the ultimate
mockery of the ambitious hero as well as the political and
military rituals of the state. Claudel's irony is unabashedly
didactic as he exploits the theatrical metaphor of life. "For
nought but a comedy of the race of man is all this life,"

says St. Augustine, "which leads from temptation to temptation."[14]

In a prefatory poem addressed to the readers of the English translation of *Le Soulier de Satin*, Claudel explains his panoramic theater of the world:

> When the wind blows, all the windmills turn at once,
> But there is another wind, the Spirit that sweeps the nations,
> And once unchained after a long stillness, it sets our whole
>   human landscape in motion!
> Ideas from one end of the world to the other catch fire like
>   a parched field!
>
>   *   *   *
>
> The movements may be different, but it is the same wind
>   that blows!
> And that is why I have painted this canvas including
>   everything in it.
> But there is that point, the vital center, around which
>   everything falls into place,
> Try to grasp that, dear readers! Too bad if it slips through
>   your fingers like a flea!

Rich variety in unity, as in the theaters of Lope de Vega and Shakespeare (whom Claudel acknowledges as his masters in this respect), is the principle of composition, but the unity is a doctrinal unity expressed in Claudel's epigraph, the Portuguese proverb, "God writes straight with crooked lines." The other epigraph, Saint Augustine's *Etiam peccata*, further characterizes his conception of the Christian theater of the world. Even sin serves God's purpose. Claudel's actors suffer the pangs of desire; reminiscent of the English devotional poets of the seventeenth century, they must be lured, hooked, pushed, pulled into the arms of God. The road to salvation is violent and it leads through the tortures of the body and the false byways of conquest and desire. What makes them capitulate is the longing for a greater love. Shakespeare's Troilus expresses the earthly agony well: "This is the monstruosity in love, lady, that the will is infinite and the execution confin'd, that the desire is boundless and the act a slave to limit" (*Troilus and Cressida*, III, ii). Claudel's drama provides for his lovers the

greater temptation of finding fulfillment in the infinite love
of God. And for their physical suffering and spiritual drama
the whole world is the stage.

Here again, a comparison with Eliot's Christian theater
is in order. Although Eliot admires the metaphysical and
devotional poets and certain Jacobean dramatists for their
unified sensibility ("A thought to Donne was an experience; it modified his sensibility"), he was able only intermittently to transfer that "essential quality of transmuting
ideas into sensations, of transforming an observation into a
state of mind" from his poems into his verse dramas. It appears in *Sweeney Agonistes*, in the choruses of the Women
of Canterbury, and in certain passages of dialogue in the
later dramas. But it does not penetrate the structure of his
dramas which remains stubbornly discursive and classical.
He prefers to let ideas propel the action. That is why so
many readers, though prepared to accept the dramatization
of religious experiences, have found to their disappointment that Eliot has turned the experience back into thought,
leaving the sensibility of the spectators to feed on ideas.
Claudel knows the risk. He points out that the French theater, both the classical and the bourgeois, is full of speeches
that sound like legal briefs. "But the heroes of *Soulier* are
not lawyers; they are believers. They do not confront a dialectic proposition or a case to discuss, but—how best to put
it?—they hear a roar! a prohibition uttered once and for all
as by a single burst of the voice, implanted by a single blow
like a bolt on granite: *Non moechaberis.*"[15] The playwright, instead of merely availing himself of the conventional belief in a supernatural order and pointing to it eloquently, must each time recreate that order as something
to be experienced in the theater. The protagonist must *become* a Christian hero; his *knowledge* of the way should be
irrelevant.

Both Claudel and Hofmannsthal have a keener artistic
sense of this problem than Eliot, because they look "to the
theocentric drama of the Middle Ages and of Spain's period
of florescence." Untouched by Aristotelian classicism and
its derivative literary systems of France and Italy, as Curt-

ius points out, this drama best exhibits "the tie between man and God in time and eternity" through the theatrical metaphor of *theatrum mundi*. "In history it saw an 'archive of the ages' in which the peoples of all times and places had entered their memories. Kings and heroes, martyrs and peasants, are actors on the great stage of the world. Immaterial powers intervene in Destiny. Over everything arches the dispensation of divine mercy and wisdom" (Curtius, pp. 143-144). Similarly, in Claudel, the course of history and the accidents of life, which appear to depend on the political will of the Spanish king, *become* parts of God's design. The Guardian Angel must persuade Prouhèze to consent to her death in the African colony of Mogador, allowing her to reinterpret her exile and the king's political will to coincide with her understanding of God's will. In returning to Don Camille and renouncing the consummation of her love on earth, she consents to a sacrifice to "make room for an incited action of Grace,"[16] and so turns the event into a sacramental act, a figure of God's purpose. In this way, the still point, the center around which all action and suffering (man's resistance and ultimate consent) falls into place, becomes meaningful as an experience, sensuously apprehensible, rather than as an idea that must be elucidated before it can be grasped.

Eliot's dramaturgy is different. The agony of the will in his plays is rendered on the level of the intellect and the violence of the act of sacrifice is lodged in the language, lyrically, as in the magnificent chorus of the Women of Canterbury, "Clear the air! clean the sky! wash the wind! take stone from stone and wash them. . . ." When he tries to stun the heathen West End audience dramatically, he misses the mark. Celia Coplestone in *The Cocktail Party* also consents to her death in a remote colony. But Eliot makes a spurious coup de théâtre out of it, when he interrupts the casual conversation in the last act with the particularly gruesome story of Celia's crucifixion "very near an ant-hill"—the completion of her journey to salvation. Compared with the dramatization of the sacrificial act in the plays of Claudel and Hofmannsthal, this moment in the theater strikes one as disingenuous; its effect is so sensational as to become antiseptic.

Can the spirit of man find fulfillment in the world? The question is central in the Christian drama, and the process of learning that it can not, unless it is reborn to a new vision of life, is often tragic because it involves the struggle of the will to deny itself, and of the soul to divest itself of the love of created beings ("Hence the soul cannot be possessed of the divine union, until it has divested itself of the love of created beings"—St. John of the Cross). It is a feature common to Claudel's plays that the high passions of love and conquest turn to ashes or are violently transformed, as God, invisible above the scene of the *theatrum mundi*, asserts his purpose and brings the misguided to a vision of life in which, ultimately, only His will matters. The violence is there, whether human passion is forcibly turned aside, unable to take what belongs to God, or used as an instrument to ensnare the lover. Mesa (in *Break of Noon*), the man once rejected by God, learns to lose himself in passion, crime, and sacrifice, lured to his conversion by an unscrupulous adulteress and, in turn, transforming the nature of her love. They are irresistibly drawn one to the other: one soul and name in two bodies. Prouhèze, inaccessible on earth, becomes in death a lodestar for Rodrigue, transforming his merely human passion until he loses everything but gains the freedom of religious service in anticipation of their reunion. Nor does Claudel minimize the pain of God's elect when, as Wallace Fowlie aptly puts it, they are "violated by the Spirit." Violaine, the martyr-heroine of *The Tidings Brought to Mary*, pure in heart, secure and happy in the beauty of the visible world, learns to bear unexampled afflictions, the pain of calumny, leprosy and blindness, ostracism and death.

Claudel's plays circumvent the argument that the "efficacy" of the Christian faith makes Christian tragedy theoretically impossible, since affliction and pain are sublimated in the promise of salvation. Precisely because his drama stresses the purgation of the will and the extreme cost of denying the self and the world, it cannot be reduced to a dialectic proposition; it is anchored in human experience, not in theological ideas. Claudel as a Christian dramatist is dogmatic on one point: God's attention is never diverted from the spectacle of life and his demands are severe—He writes straight with crooked lines. The alleged incompatibility of the tragic drama with Christianity can be argued only if, as in the mystery cycles, the dramatist imitates the known materials of scriptural history or, as in the medieval *Everyman*, the machinery of salvation is set in motion before an audience of believers. A modern playwright works under different conditions. Once *Murder in the Cathedral* moved out of Canterbury, it lost part of its sacred character, and consequently the fear and the uncertainty of the poor Women of Canterbury loom larger in our consciousness than as a ritual prelude of despair that is overcome by the final hymn of praise. To the Christian, tragedy may be only a historical episode in the greater divine drama; but unless the play specifically declares its action to be a subordinate part of, and subsumed in, a greater metaphysical drama, which it can do only if it retains its liturgical character, it cannot efface the tragic burden on the merely human protagonist who would undergo the supreme trial of his faith.

Besides, the Christian sacrifice, as Claudel conceives it, is an act that involves not only the agent but the fate of others as well. It has social consequences and therefore it is an act of conscience. Eliot's characters seek their salvation peculiarly in isolation. The poet's assumption is that martyrdom brings a potentially greater spiritual and therefore social benefit than any other course of action.

> . . . For the Church is stronger for this action,
> Triumphant in adversity. It is fortified
> By persecution: supreme, so long as men will die for it.
>   (*Murder*, Part II)

And in the case of Celia Coplestone, Eliot takes pleasure in toying with the paradox that her death in Kinkanja, though it appears to be utterly useless, *may* have made a difference to the plague-stricken natives and *does* illuminate the lives

of her former friends in London. In neither instance does
the protagonist directly touch the fate of others. But like
Hofmannsthal, who coined the word *allomatisch* to designate the fateful linking of two individual lives so that one
embodies the other's destiny, Claudel recognizes similar
implications in the act of sacrifice:

> There is deep mystery and an infinite source of tragedy in the
> fact that we are the condition of eternal salvation one for the
> other, that we alone carry within ourselves the key to the soul
> of some one of our brothers, who can be saved only by us, and
> at our own expense.[17]

Thus, despite the invisible presence in his dramatic composition that orders the action according to the design of
Providence, the free human choice is necessary to the fulfillment of that design. But such a choice made by mortal
and fallible men involves a tragic conflict; they know and
do not know what it is to act or suffer. There is the battle
with the recalcitrant will which shuns self-sacrifice, and
the agonizing wager that the implication of others is justifiable. Claudel may thrust the certainty of his own faith at the
audience, but he does not lend any of it to his characters
to ease the pain of their commitment. If Violaine is the exception because she is destined to be a saint, repeating
"in a smaller figure" the mystery of the incarnation, Claudel heaps the greatest afflictions on her to make her worthy
of such a role. His characters suffer and consent (in Eliot's
words) "That the pattern may subsist, that the wheel may
turn and still/ Be forever still." They are "swept" by the
Spirit and toppled and buffeted, in order that they may
learn the part they are playing in the theater of the world.

This is doctrinally and dramatically the opposite of the
attitude of *contemptus mundi* which is exemplified in a play
like Montherlant's *The Master of Santiago* (*Le Maître de
Santiago*). Here a mixture of religious pride and devotion,
a hubris of ethical perfection, causes the protagonist to
turn his back on the world striving for a mystical union with
God. With his daughter he retreats into a life of silence and
isolation, which is an intensely private choice, an escape

from the possibility of human folly and error. He seeks salvation by rejecting life on earth rather than transfiguring it
through a tragic commitment. In Claudel there is no such
shortcut. The divine drama must be played through to its
conclusion here on earth because, to him, it is the deeds and
the tragic suffering of the human actors that attest to the
benevolence of God. In one of his earliest works, the allegorical pageant *The City* (*La Ville*), he puts forth on a
broader scale the idea of a Christian society. In the ruin, the
burning, and the rebuilding of the city, in the shaping of its
new prince, Claudel outlines, rhetorically if not dramatically, the steps by which the tragic events of a people's history may be redeemed in time. The prince is the son of
Coeuvre, the visionary poet turned priest, and Lala, the female temptress who thus becomes the instrument of salvation. Through betrayal, violence and suffering there
emerges a vision of the divine order—this, essentially, is the
tragic rhythm of his drama.

Eliot, of course, knows of this experience too, but holding
to the laws of classical decorum he, rather, has his Guardi-
ans discuss the violent ways of God toward those who respond to his will.

> But what do we know of the terrors of the journey?
> You and I don't know the process by which the human is
> Transhumanised: what do we know
> Of the kind of suffering they must undergo
> On the way of illumination? (Act II)

And after Celia's death, Reilly interprets the event:

> EDWARD. Do you mean that having chosen this form of death
>   She did not suffer as ordinary people suffer?
> REILLY. Not at all what I mean. Rather the contrary.
>   I'd say that she suffered all that we should suffer
>   In fear and pain and loathing—all these together—
>   And reluctance of the body to become a *thing*.
>   I'd say she suffered more, because more conscious
>   Than the rest of us. She paid the highest price
>   In suffering. That is part of the design.
> LAVINIA. Perhaps she had been through greater agony be-
>   forehand.
>   I mean—I know nothing of her last two years.

REILLY. That shows some insight on your part, Mrs. Chamber-
    layne;
   But such experience can only be hinted at
   In myths and images. To speak about it
   We talk of darkness, labyrinths, Minotaur terrors. (Act III)

Eliot simply tells us here (i.e., we are being verbally instructed in these matters) that Celia, having made her
choice of the unknown journey, experiences through her
physical suffering and death a fulfillment of the spirit. In
view of her earlier hopelessness and her inability to love or
be loved, this sacrificial death is like a stepping forth into
the light from the terror of solitude and despair. And to her
friends who hear about her willingness to undergo such
suffering, it is explained as a sacramental act in that unof-
ficially she has entered the communion of saints reaffirming
God's will. But what about the modern-day audience?

The Christian playwright in the modern theater, as Eliot
recognized, ought to be able "to hold the attention, to
arouse the excitement, of people who are not religious as
well as of those who are—or . . . of people who are not consciously and practically religious, as well as of those who
are." Eliot looked for a "reintegration" of religious and
secular drama as a step toward the reintegration of the religious and our ordinary life.[18] But it may well be that the
reaction of these two groups of spectators to the "redemptive pattern" of the Christian drama is not the same. To
those who bring to this drama a living faith in the mercy
and wisdom of Providence, the cruel destiny of the protagonist who seeks his or her salvation at all cost will only reaffirm that faith. Christopher Fry relates the story of his
last meeting with Charles Williams. Williams shouted to
Fry from the tailboard of a moving bus: "When we're dead
we shall have the sensation of having enjoyed life altogether, whatever has happened to us." And he leaned out
once more: "Even if we've been murdered, what a pleasure
to have been capable of it!" Fry's comment is an excellent
characterization of the believer's reaction to this kind of
drama, the positive supervention of a joyous faith in the
purpose of the Creator:

He was not at all saying that everything is for the best in the best of all possible worlds. He was saying—or so it seems to me—that there is an angle of experience where the dark is distilled into light: either here or hereafter, in or out of time: where our tragic fate finds itself with perfect pitch, and goes straight to the key which creation was composed in. And comedy senses and reaches out to this experience. It says, in effect, that, groaning as we may be, we move in the figure of a dance, and, so moving, we trace the outline of the mystery.[19]

But to those who are not religious or are not "consciously and practically religious," the great majority, if we include the passive worshiper whose religious experience does not extend to participation in the joy of martyrdom, who cannot honestly thank God for the spilling of the blood of saints— to them the choice between the soul's despair and the willed self-mortification to escape from despair is a tragic choice. That is not to say that the decision of the protagonist to give up the self is not an authentic decision. It is rather a question of the ordinary spectator's ability to respond to the dramatization of an act of faith. We *feel* the murder of Becket, "an instant eternity of evil and wrong," but we only know that it was a worthwhile act. As modern spectators of the drama of redemption, we occupy the position of the Chorus in *Murder in the Cathedral*. Although we note the Archbishop's resolute calm on the morning of the assassination, we must share the rebuke to his attendant priests:

I give my life
To the Law of God above the Law of Man.
Those who do not the same
How should they know what I do?
How should you know what I do? Yet how much more
Should you know than these madmen beating on the door.

How should we know? Our only possible approach to such knowledge or imaginative sharing in the experience is to absorb the spoken lesson of the Christmas sermon and then, like the Women of Canterbury, instructed by pity and fear, to witness the tragic moment of sacrifice; or, to adapt Christopher Fry's words, "by the experience of tragedy and the intuition of comedy, to make [our] difficult way."

The difficulty of reconciling the knowledge and the experience in dramatic form comes to the surface in Eliot's amusing backward glance at *The Family Reunion*. He concedes that

> we are left in a divided frame of mind, not knowing whether to consider the play the tragedy of the mother or the salvation of the son. The two situations are not reconciled. I find a confirmation of this in the fact that my sympathies now have come to be all with the mother, who seems to me, except perhaps for the chauffeur, the only complete human being in the play; and my hero now strikes me as an insufferable prig.[20]

The difficulty for Eliot twenty years later seems to be that the imposition of a religious intuition on a tragic experience dehumanizes the protagonist and therefore fails to be dramatically convincing. Similarly, Fry's essay on comedy gives a better account than his plays of the dilemma inherent in the religious drama.

> I know that when I set about writing a comedy the idea presents itself to me first of all as tragedy. The characters press on to the theme with all their divisions and perplexities heavy about them; they are already entered for the race to doom, and good and evil are an infernal tangle skinning the fingers that try to unravel them. If the characters were not qualified for tragedy there would be no comedy, and to some extent I have to cross the one before I can light on the other. In a century less flayed and quivering we might reach it more directly; but not now, unless every word we write is going to mock us. A bridge has to be crossed, a thought has to be turned. Somehow the characters have to unmortify themselves; to affirm life and assimilate death and persevere in joy. Their hearts must be as determined as the phoenix; what burns must also light and renew: not by a vulnerable optimism but by a hard-won maturity of delight, by the intuition of comedy, an active patience declaring the solvency of good.[21]

In Shakespearean tragedy the active patience of a Cordelia, "declaring the solvency of good," is no guarantee of joy. The question is whether in the drama, excepting the medieval or the modern mystery play, the characters can "unmortify" themselves, especially in a secular theater and before an audience that brings to the theater its naturalistic and anthropocentric attitudes to life. Eliot's difficulty is that he *refers* to a Christian world view, but does not fully embody it (and thereby trap his audience) in the metaphor of *theatrum mundi*.

But even when the divine will ("the third dimension, the Vertical direction" in Claudel's phrase) is operative in the drama of life, fusing the idea of the eternal order and the experience of temporal disorder on a single plane of representation, the tragic struggle by which men are transformed to play their parts in the eternal design remains in the foreground. Even so orthodox a believer as Claudel or Ugo Betti does not deny that the ceaseless care of Providence in no way preempts the necessity of tragic human choices.

> We were indeed given a final victory and truth. This is sure. But why these landslides around us, then? And still others announce their coming with far-off thundering. Why these defeats here and there? And why, today and perhaps again tomorrow, this flood of cruelty and hatred, greater than ever before in history? What is the dam that gave way? And, on the other hand, this giving way—was it useless? Is this vast perturbation which is in us and in many others, useless too?
> . . . Has the danger ceased to exist; is vigilance useless; is doubt itself forbidden, even though it was allowed Christ when He said, "Remove this cup from me," or when He cried with a loud voice at the ninth hour, "Eli, Eli, lama, sabachthani"? . . . Happy are they who are calm, sure, strong, and no longer need anything, or at least think they don't. But how can we avoid thinking, also, of those who are weak, without faith, and without hope? Is it not true that we must think of them before all?

Betti is concerned with that major portion of the present-day audience that is less likely to respond to the renewal of faith through the agency of martyrs ("who spend their last vigil in self-contemplation, examining with subtle syllogisms their own spiritual experience") than to the dramatic inquiry into their own doubts and anguish, the unfulfilled needs of the human spirit. "The true targets, the dangerous targets of today—that is, certain objections widespread in the world, certain disbeliefs, certain discouragements—are probably beyond the range of fire, and the sacrifices of the Carmelites or of Thomas à Beckett [*sic*] cannot even scratch them."[22]

3

The opening of *The Satin Slipper* comes to grips at once
with the two types of religious drama, first in the sacramental act of the Jesuit priest, who commends his soul to God
in perfect submission to His will, and then in the more difficult case of his brother Rodrigue, who must find his salvation indirectly by way of evil and disorder. The priest is
fastened to the broken mast of a ship sacked by pirates and
drifting on the open sea between the Old World and the
New. He is celebrating his last Mass:

> Lord, I thank You for having so fastened me! And if some-
> times I have found Your commandments painful
>> And my will faced with Your rule
>> Perplexed, restive,
> Today I can hardly be more closely tied to You than I am, and
> I have well scanned each of my limbs, there is not one that
> could turn an inch from You.

*   *   *

> I have given myself to God and now the day of repose and re-
> laxation has come and I may entrust myself to these bonds
> which hold me fast.
> They speak of sacrifice when each choice we make is no
> more than making an almost imperceptible movement of the
> hand.
> But it is evil alone that indeed demands an effort, since it
> is against reality, to separate oneself from those great and per-
> manent forces that involve and embrace us.

And then the prayer for his brother Rodrigue, who has
turned from his first commitment to the service of God:

> . . . and now because he has given up Your novitiate, he imag-
> ines no doubt that he has turned his back on You,
> His task in life, he thinks, is not to be ready and wait, but to
> conquer and possess
> All that he can, as if there were anything that did not belong
> to You and as if he could be anywhere but where You are.
> But, o Lord, it is not so easy to escape You, and if he does not
> come to You by what is light in him, then let him come by what
> is dark in him; if not by what is straight, then by what is errant;
> and if not by what is simple, then
> Let him come to You by that in him which is diffuse, and toil-
> some and entangled,

And if he desires evil, let it be such evil as is only compatible
with good,
And if he desire disorder, such disorder as will cause the
breaking and crumbling of those walls around him which bar
him from salvation,
I speak of him and that multitude with him that is darkly
implicated.
For he is of those who cannot save themselves unless they
save all that mass of men on whom they leave their mark.
You have already taught him what it means to desire, but as
yet he does not suspect what it is to be desired. (First Day,
scene I)[23]

*   *   *

In the two scenes between Prouhèze and the Guardian
Angel (scene XII of the First Day and scene VIII of the
Third Day) as well as the great confrontation scene between
Rodrigue and Prouhèze, Claudel explores the nature of human desire, the romantic, Platonic, and carnal motives
which feed their unconsummated love, and the conversion
of that love into an instrument of faith, forcing Rodrigue to
give his anguished consent as Prouhèze chooses to remain
and die in Mogador. The crucial dramatic moment is the debate between the Angel and Prouhèze, carried on by means
of a sustained metaphor, that of the fisherman and the fish.

GUARDIAN ANGEL. What would you say if I asked you to
    choose between God and Rodrigue?
PROUHÈZE. You . . . you are too cunning an angler.
GUARDIAN ANGEL. Why cunning?
PROUHÈZE. To let me scent the question before the answer is
    ready. Where then would the art of the angler be?
GUARDIAN ANGEL. And yet if I asked the question?
PROUHÈZE. I am deaf! I am deaf! A deaf fish! I am deaf and I
    have heard nothing! (Third Day, scene VIII)

The tactic shifts, moving closer to the concept of a recip-
rocal relation, a common fate (as in the secular drama
Break of Noon). "What," says the Angel, "if you were not
only a catch for me, but a bait?" since there was no other
way to touch this proud man, to make him understand "the
dependence, the necessity, the need" of another upon him.
But—Prouhèze's rejoinder expresses her disbelief in the

paradox—"Man in the arms of a woman forgets God. . . .
Is not love outside the sacrament a sin?"

> GUARDIAN ANGEL. Even sin! Sin also serves!
> PROUHÈZE. Thus it was good that he loves me?
> GUARDIAN ANGEL. It was good that you taught him desire.
> PROUHÈZE. Desire for an illusion? for a shadow which forever
> escapes him?
> GUARDIAN ANGEL. Desire is for that which is, illusion is that
> which is not. Desire by way of illusion
> Is for that which is by way of that which is not. (Third Day,
> scene VIII)

The debate continues as the Angel parries her heartfelt
arguments and translates speculative theology into the
simpler language of faith and love eternal. Thus reversing
the process—now she believes in order that she may understand—he is able to convince her of the efficacy of the Christian sacrifice: "It is in him that you were necessary. . . . A
Prouhèze forever whom death does not destroy." Lodged
like a hook inside Rodrigue's heart, she will draw him
through exile and penance, loss of name and humiliation,
to his deliverance. "For some," as the Angel explains, "the
understanding is enough. It is the spirit that speaks purely
to the spirit./ But for others it is necessary that the flesh
also become gradually evangelized and converted. And
what flesh is more powerful to speak to man than the
flesh of woman?/ Now he will no longer be able to desire
you without at the same time desiring where you are"
(Third Day, scene VIII).

But God's design cannot be fulfilled, despite Prouhèze's
ecstatic consent at the end of this scene, until the last tragic act of their trial is complete. In order to recover her soul
from Rodrigue, she must persuade the uncomprehending
man, viceroy of half the world, to relinquish his claim to her
earthly love and to pronounce his consent to her death. The
scene on board Rodrigue's flagship off the coast of Africa is
climactic. Sitting in state on a great gilded chair, he holds
fast to the promise made so many years ago.

> That promise between your soul and mine by which time for
> one moment stood still,

That promise which you made me, that pledge you took, that
duty which you assumed towards me,
  Is such that death itself can by no means
  Free you from it,
  Such that, if you do not keep it, my soul from
the depths of hell for all eternity will accuse you before
the throne of God.

But Prouhèze has come as an envoy from her earthly purgatory to take back that promise and to offer Rodrigue a far
greater temptation:

What He wills, who possesses me, that alone is what
I will; it is in His will, in whom I am annihilated, that you have
to find me again!

*   *   *

He who has faith has no need of promise.
  Why not believe that word of joy and ask for no other thing
than that word of joy now, since I exist to make it known to
you and no promise but myself!
  I, Rodrigue!
  Myself, myself, Rodrigue, I am your joy! Myself, myself,
myself, Rodrigue, I am your joy!

*   *   *

Take, Rodrigue, take, my heart, take, my love, take this God
who fills me! (Third Day, scene XIII)

In the end, the force of her conviction prevails. Although
Rodrigue has the power physically to liberate her from the
besieged fort of Mogador, he capitulates to a greater power
within. He finds it impossible to command her to stay with
him. Instead, he bows his head and weeps as Doña Prouhèze veils herself from head to foot and escorted by two
black slaves descends into the funeral barge. By concluding
the scene with the shrieks of her abandoned child, Claudel
underscores the pain of her sacrifice which the splendid
rhetoric inspired by her faith cannot mitigate. Despite the
divine promise that ultimately Truth and reality will be one
and the same, the road toward the attainment of that
promise leads through the purgatory of tragic suffering
here on earth. Even Rodrigue's humiliation in the last act

brings him only to the threshold of understanding his life
of desire and conquest as the figure of God's purpose.

Though we never lose sight of the doctrinal goal in
Claudel's theater, we are primarily immersed in the emotional experience of the dramatic action. This is no less true
of a saintly figure like Violaine, who embodies the other-
worldly spirit of Monsanvierge, than of the more ob-
stinately passionate Doña Prouhèze. "The hand of God is
upon me and you cannot defend me!/ O Jacques, we shall
never be man and wife in this world!" The enforced separation of Violaine from her betrothed, who pleads for the
natural blessings of this world, is as painful an act of
renunciation as the release and the sentence of death which
Prouhèze demands of Rodrigue. The onset of leprosy marks
Violaine as the chosen of God, a being set apart for extraordinary suffering. But the ravages of the disease also mark
her as a holy being, as if she wore a costume and mask
giving her other than human characteristics; when on the
eve of Christmas miraculously she revives the child, she
is the bringer of joy touching in a distant analogy the joy
of the Nativity.

In spite of the difference between the protagonists, the experienced prince of the church and the innocent country
girl, *The Tidings Brought to Mary* and *Murder in the
Cathedral* bear a strong resemblance to each other. There
is a rhythm of expectation and fulfillment in both plays.
We share the suspense of the opening chorus:

> We wait, we wait,
> And the saints and martyrs wait, for those who shall be
>   martyrs and saints.
> Destiny waits in the hand of God, shaping the still unshapen:
> I have seen these things in a shaft of sunlight.

And we watch to see how "All things prepare the event." Yet,
what is foreseen comes unexpected. As the tempters shape
Becket's will, confirming him in his rejection of worldly
power, and the fourth tempter challenges him to drive out
the last vestige of pride, so Violaine must resist her sister's

repeated cry, "Give me back my child," until God wills the miracle. But Claudel is not faced with Eliot's problem of dramatizing Becket's inner struggle to consent without damnably willing the way of martyrdom. The archbishop's Christmas sermon is a spiritual preparation so that we may understand the sacramental meaning of the coming event, whereas the reading of the Christmas Office in *The Tidings Brought to Mary* transfigures the visible action on stage. Violaine's simulated labor, climaxed by a stifled cry, becomes an act of universal significance as she takes the living child from under her cloak.

VIOLAINE. A small child is born to us too!

*   *   *

Behold I bring you tidings of great joy. . . . (Act III)

Claudel trusts to the powerful impression of the dramatized action; he seems not to be concerned with those who "are not consciously and practically religious." The staged miracle, *coram populo*, is his characteristically bold way of transmuting idea into sensation.

In contrast, Eliot finds it necessary to rely on (what Coleridge in a different context called) a "credibilizing effect." He has no other means of presenting the "intersection of the timeless/With time." At the end of the Christmas sermon Becket predicts "it is possible that in a short time you may have yet another martyr," and in his agon with the knights and the priests he lets the idea (and his readiness for it) repeatedly intrude in the unfolding drama of his martyrdom.[24] Given the circumstances of this protagonist, the inner struggle "to make perfect [his] will" and the approaching event of his violent death, Eliot cannot bring off the necessary humility of the true martyr "who has become the instrument of God." The idea, discursively, almost didactically stated, that here is an instance when God's design is momentarily completing itself in time, threatens to preempt our more immediate apprehension of the acting out of that design. Only the chorus of the Women of Canterbury preserves the concrete experience of the historical event and its felt religious significance from being lost in doctrinal statement. During Becket's internal strife with the fourth temptation, the Women ironically fear his imminent consent, seeing only the false consequences:

> God is leaving us, God is leaving us, more pang, more pain, than birth or death.

> * * *

> O Thomas Archbishop, save us save us, save yourself that we may be saved;
> Destroy yourself and we are destroyed. (Part I)

And after the first visit of the knights, they understand their tragic implication as sinful creatures in Thomas's death.

> Have I not known, not known
> What was coming to be? It was here, in the kitchen, in the passage,
> In the mews in the barn in the byre in the market place
> In our veins our bowels our skulls as well
> As well as in the consultations of powers.
> What is woven on the loom of fate
> What is woven in the councils of princes
> Is woven also in our veins, our brains,
> Is woven like a pattern of living worms
> In the guts of the women of Canterbury. (Part II)

Eliot was aware that unless the Women were tragically involved in the martyr's death, shamed and soiled by it, learning to accept their "share of the eternal burden,/ The perpetual glory," his work would become simply a pious reenactment of a saint's death. On the one hand he was convinced that all drama, insofar as it was meant to be taken seriously, needed to be exposed to religious ideas. "There is a very profound kind of boredom which is an essential moment in the religious life, the boredom with all living in so far as it has no religious meaning. The capacity for this boredom is latent in everybody, and it can never really be appeased by mere amusement." But on the other hand he understood "that a religious play, to be good, must not be purely religious. If it is, it is simply doing something that the liturgy does better; and the religious play is not a substitute for liturgical observance and ceremonial, but something different. It is a combination of religious with ordinary dramatic interest. . . . In *Everyman* the religious and the dramatic are not merely combined, but wholly fused" (*Religious Drama: Mediaeval and Modern*).

These remarks are, of course, applicable to *Murder in the Cathedral*. The Women of Canterbury, in their despair, counteract but are finally absorbed in Thomas's growing certainty of the role he and they must play in the drama of his martyrdom. Still, in their concluding chorus, they fuse the idea of God's redemptive design (the religious interest) with the shattering experience of the murder (the dramatic interest). While a *Te Deum* is being sung in the distance, they confess their human frailty:

> Forgive us, O Lord, we acknowledge ourselves as type of
>   the common man,
> Of the men and women who shut the door and sit by the fire;
> Who fear the blessing of God, the loneliness of the night
>   of God, the surrender required, the deprivation inflicted;
> Who fear the injustice of men less than the justice of God;
> Who fear the hand at the window, the fire in the thatch,
>   the fist in the tavern, the push into the canal,
> Less than we fear the love of God.
> We acknowledge our trespass, our weakness, our fault;
>   we acknowledge
> That the sin of the world is upon our heads; that the
>   blood of the martyrs and the agony of the saints
> Is upon our heads. (Part II)

In acknowledging themselves as "type of the common man," they extend their experience as ambivalent participants in the event to the spectators: it is in God's design that each man cause the blood of the martyr to flow and yet celebrate the "redemption by blood." Thomas himself may emerge victoriously from his "soul's sickness" and meet death gladly:

> I have had a tremor of bliss, a wink of heaven, a whisper,
> And I would no longer be denied; all things
> Proceed to a joyful consummation. (Part II)

He can "unmortify" himself in the knowledge that he is the chief actor in a divine comedy. But the common man, despite the renewed promise, remains a tragic participant in the event. His faith has been buttressed according to the liturgical structure of the play: the *Dies Irae* is followed by a *Te Deum*. Yet the hymn of praise is fused with the hard-won knowledge that he has been soiled by evil and that, in this world, his faltering spirit must purchase the promise of redemption through fresh pain and suffering.

Claudel and Eliot are obviously aware of the tragic element in these two mystery plays; but they make sure by incorporating part of the liturgy that it is understood to be only the condition of the "sudden painful joy/When the figure of God's purpose is made complete." *Murder in the Cathedral* ends with a *Kyrie*, and *The Tidings Brought to Mary* with voices singing *Gloria in excelsis Deo . . . Laetare Laetare Laetare*, while Mara lifts her child and, with her, makes the sign of the cross over the body of Violaine. Becket and Violaine have died a violent death, yet there is rejoicing over the revelation of God's purpose, and not only despite men's sins but because of them and by means of them. That is the sign of the fruition of the Christian sacrifice.

Claudel worked on his play intermittently from its first version, published in 1892 as *La Jeune Fille Violaine*, until he made a final version for the stage which was published in 1948. *Murder in the Cathedral* was produced and published in 1935. But in revising or critically reconsidering his play, neither poet yielded to the secular pressures of his time. If anything, the immense political and moral crises of the twentieth century strengthened the conviction in both poets that the Christian sacrifice of the elect and the pattern of sin and redemption for the rest of mankind are the most meaningful "perception of an order" in an otherwise senseless reality. Hofmannsthal, on the contrary, struggled with the material of his last play, *The Tower*, for a quarter of a century, determined to test his convictions against the turbulent events of his own time. In the final stage version of the play, which he finished in 1927, two years before his death, the tragic vision prevails over his faith. He found that the purely religious solution to social and moral problems, which was appropriate in the allegorical festival plays and particularly in the mise en scène of *The Salzburg Great Theater of the World*, became inapplicable to the story of his last play.

In the "poetic" version, the text of 1925, Hofmannsthal tried to revert to the metaphor of *theatrum mundi*, raising a historically conceived situation into the realm of myth.[25] The dying hero, Sigismund, leaves the wracked kingdom in the hands of a mythical boy-king leading an army of orphan children, the victims and the only hope of a bloody time, who can restore the world to the ways of peace and brotherly love. Incredible as this solution may seem, following the terrors of the play up to that point, it is yet a powerful symbolic gesture of faith, born out of a sense of despair. It is an invented pattern of redemption, in keeping with the religious and dramatic conception of the world as a stage, but outside the specifically Christian view of sacrifice as a fulfillment of God's design. The play is based on the old story of the prince imprisoned in a tower from the time of his birth because his father fears a prophecy of insurrection and the loss of his throne. Liberated, he steps into a world of corrupted authority and anarchy. But though, in the end, Sigismund has cleansed the world by his personal sacrifice, his strength is only the strength of the impregnable tower (that is, his own self) of which he is still king and master. It is not for him to create a new order out of the shambles of the old; he is the saintly interim king, the sacrificed liberator and deliverer, who may only glimpse the promised land.

The stage version of 1927 goes farther. It effectively isolates the protagonist.[26] Having stirred messianic hopes among the poor and the oppressed—he is the nameless beggar king who comes in chains to deliver them—Sigismund finds that he is locked inside himself, preserving his integrity in a brutal world, but unable to reach out to those who are in need of redemption. In this revised version of *The Tower*, Hofmannsthal answers to a new mandate of poetic justice, dictated by his observation in his own life-time of the collapse of an ancient society and the resultant moral and political chaos. The play is an unflinching his-toric testimony, as well as a moving personal confession, that the tragic event in time may not be part of an eternal design or even capable of being transcended through the mythopoeic power of religious faith. Hofmannsthal shows that the spirit of the chosen, the potential savior, is un-impaired, yet in a world that is forsaken and torn by rebellion and suppression it remains tragically imprisoned. In the face of absolute power it cannot come to fruition outside himself. When it becomes impossible for the Chris-tian playwright to conceive of the world as God's stage, the actors must play their roles in a historic setting subject only to their unregenerate passions and to the superior force of will in others. Sigismund, like the Beggar in *The Salzburg Great Theater of the World*, remembers the condi-tion of his existence; without faith in eternity no true life is possible. But in a world which rests no longer on spiritual foundations, action and suffering has no meaning beyond itself. Hence Sigismund dies, not as a martyr, an instrument of God's will, but as a sheer victim of unrestrained violence. Struck by a marauder's bullet, he is at peace and resigned to his death, but he also recognizes his tragic failure to find his way out of the tower, which is still his prison and the source of his strength. "Bear witness, I was here, though no one has known me."

It is an absolutely hopeless ending. *The Tower* is still recognizably in the tradition of the allegorical theater of the world, the mode of *Everyman* and Calderón. Hofmannsthal used the ancient motif and some of the figures of Calderón's *Life is a Dream* (*La Vida es Sueño*), but in the course of many years, during which he pondered the subject, he radi-cally reshaped the play. In the final version, Sigismund is drawn into the life-and-death struggle among the corrupt powers of this world. He is tested by his father, the king, and later he is tested by the mob; neither power finds

him useful, and neither power recognizes his identity.
He dies inviolable but ineffectual, like an actor on the
world's stage which has been inexplicably deprived of
God's presence. In Hofmannsthal's Christian festival plays,
as in Claudel's theater, dramatic irony is a central and
necessary feature. Although the characters are caught up in
their passions, the audience is at all times privy to the
workings of the divine order through the historical event.
But here the ironic condition of playacting in this sense has
virtually disappeared.

It is only a step from here toward a theater in which the
spectators, as well as the actors, are afflicted with blindness,
not knowing that there is a great void rather than a
superpersonal order operative in our lives. And a generation later we have a theater in which the actors have become paralyzed and disoriented because they are
determined not to give up the idea that what they do *might*
have meaning, if only there were a superpersonal order or
purpose beyond the bare stage of life. This becomes explicit
in Samuel Beckett's new metaphor: The world is Godot's
stage. Godot holds out the promise of his arrival (as
witness and judge) but postpones the fulfillment indefinitely. And so Beckett's two clowns, as they wait for Godot,
embellish the emptiness with remembered fragments of
religious faith.[27]

NOTES

1. "Das alte Spiel von Jedermann" (1912), *Gesammelte Werke*, ed.
Herbert Steiner, *Prosa III*, pp. 115-116.

2. *Selected Essays, 1917-1932* (New York: Harcourt, Brace, 1932),
p. 93.

3. See *Poems and Verse Plays* (New York: Pantheon, 1961) and
Selected Plays and Libretti (New York: Pantheon, 1963), both edited by
Michael Hamburger.

4. *Book of Friends*, in *Selected Prose* (New York: Pantheon, 1952),
p. 350.

5. Every work of art worthy of its name, Hofmannsthal once wrote,
includes the whole of human life.

6. *The Complete Poems and Plays* (New York: Harcourt, Brace, 1952).

7. See above, chapter 6, note 12. Brian Downs cites a parallel passage in Kierkegaard.

8. "Aufzeichnungen zu Reden in Skandinavien," *Prosa III*, p. 351.

9. Paul Claudel, *Tête d'Or* (2e version), *Théâtre*, eds. Jacques Madaule and Jacques Petit, vol. I (Editions Gallimard, 1967).

10. *"Le Soulier de Satin* et le public" (1944), in *Mes Idées sur le théâtre* (Gallimard, 1966), pp. 189-190.

11. "Poetry and Drama," *On Poetry and Poets* (London: Faber and Faber, 1957), p. 87.

12. Ernst Robert Curtius, *European Literature and the Latin Middle Ages*, trans. Willard R. Trask (New York: Pantheon, 1953), p. 142.

13. *Die fürchterliche Bühne Wirklichkeit*; from a poem, *On the Death of the Actor Hermann Müller* (1899). See *Selected Plays and Libretti*, p. xix.

14. Quoted in Curtius, p. 138.

15. "A propos de la première représentation du 'Soulier de Satin' au Théâtre-Français" (1943), *Théâtre*, II (1965), 1474.

16. I am using Jacques Guicharnaud's translation of the phrase. "En nous retirant volontairement, nous faisons place à une action en quelque sorte stimulée de la Grâce, nous lions partie pour un énorme profit avec la Toute-Puissance" (" 'Le Soulier de Satin' et le public"), ibid., p. 1480.

17. *Le Soulier de Satin* (Paris, 1953), Appendix, p. 20, quoted in translation by Guicharnaud, *Modern French Theatre* (New Haven: Yale University Press, 1967), pp. 74-75.

18. *Religious Drama: Mediaeval and Modern* (New York: House of Books, 1954), n. pag., quoted in William V. Spanos, *The Christian Tradition in Modern British Verse Drama: The Poetics of Sacramental Time* (New Brunswick, N. J.: Rutgers University Press, 1967), p. 20.

19. Christopher Fry, "Comedy," *TDR*, 4 (Mar 1960), 77.

20. "Poetry and Drama," p. 84.

21. "Comedy," p. 78.

22. Ugo Betti, "Religion and the Theatre," trans. Gino Rizzo and William Meriwether, *Theatre in the Twentieth Century*, ed. Robert W. Corrigan (New York: Grove, 1963), pp. 117, 120, 121-122. The reference is to *Dialogues des Carmélites* by Georges Bernanos.

23. *Le Soulier de Satin* (version intégrale), *Théâtre*, vol. II (1965).

24. E.g., *Complete Poems and Plays*, pp. 200, 207, 209, 212.

25. *The Tower*, trans. Michael Hamburger, in *Selected Plays and Libretti*.

26. *The Tower* (1927), in *Hugo von Hofmannsthal: Three Plays*, trans. Alfred Schwarz (Detroit: Wayne State University Press, 1966).

27. Ruby Cohn, in *"Theatrum Mundi* and Contemporary Theater," *Comparative Drama*, 1 (spring 1967), 28-35, is largely interested in the role of the audience in the plays of Brecht, Beckett, Genet, and Weiss.

8. *"CONDEMNED TO BE FREE":*
THE WILL IN ACTION AND PARALYSIS

We are dealing once more with a theater of the will. But the theatrical metaphor has changed. The world, rather than being God's stage on which men assume their destined roles, now becomes a universe newly created by a man's act of commitment, the exercise of a purely human freedom.[1] For Eliot, as well as Claudel, "Destiny waits in the hand of God, shaping the still unshapen." Now, destiny is in the hands of man, willing, choosing, acting; and when he does not or cannot act or acts in bad faith, he consigns himself to the peculiar hell of Sartre's *No Exit* (*Huis Clos*). In the Christian drama we witnessed man's agony in coming to God. Now we must be concerned with the pain and the tragic understanding of man having to replace God. In the words of Camus, "Choosing between heaven and a ridiculous fidelity, preferring oneself to eternity or losing oneself in God is the age-old tragedy in which each must play his part."[2] Claudel's conqueror, Rodrigue, turns to God, away from the absurdity of his earthly adventures, while Camus's Caligula makes use of his absolute power to play the absurd part of Fate, to "wear the foolish, unintelligible face of a professional god." The emperor's failure to break through human limits is only an initial exploration of the search for freedom and meaning in an irrational universe; it is a contrast for Camus to "the higher fidelity [of a Sisyphus] that negates the gods and raises rocks."[3] Both Camus and Sartre discover a number of different dramatic, and sometimes tragic, subjects in the attitude of necessary rebellion as well as in the waste of life and value when one accepts an indifferent, absurd universe.

At any rate, appealing to a divine order is merely an evasion of the facts of human existence. Neither for Sartre
nor Camus is unbelief the cause of despair, as of course
it must be for Claudel and Eliot; it is rather the starting
point toward the only meaningful response to the wretched
condition of man and the denial of human values—namely,
revolt. In Christian doctrine, to despair is to be in a state of
sin. But Camus defines the absurd, "which is the metaphysical state of the conscious man," as "sin without
God."[4] These are the premises of Camus's and Sartre's
dramatic explorations of the estate of man. "Existentialism," says Sartre, "is nothing else but an attempt to draw
the full conclusions from a consistently atheistic position."[5]
And Camus speaks of fate as "a human matter, which must
be settled among men."[6] Both writers in their contexts
mean to be optimistic in that they reject passive suffering
and resignation to a higher will. But at the same time, giving to man the power to scorn, to appropriate, and even to
shape his fate, they set the stage for their tragic parables
adapted from myth, history, and politics. In these, man goes
under because he deceives himself as to the nature of an
alien universe in which he counts for nothing. His alternative is to create an intelligible world centered in himself
through a free act of commitment, assuming the burden
of guilt implicit in any choice or action.

Despite the obvious fundamental differences among
them, there are certain motives common to the so-called
existential theater, the Christian drama, and the late plays
of Ibsen. The bid for freedom, deliverance from a state of
captivity or paralysis, the desire to liberate and thereby
define the self by means of an act of the will—the lines
of the drama converge on this central moment in all three
theaters. But if such motives and type actions are comparable, the concepts behind them are not. The human
will in each instance is guided by a different ethic. Ibsen's
demonic heroes are impelled to seek their deliverance from
social responsibilities and impediments of guilt through a
final act of self-fulfillment; but at the moment of consummation and death they alone are witnesses to their own

vision of renewed freedom and power. If, in reasserting their will, they move from resignation to the momentary freedom of revolt, the heroes of the Christian drama move in the opposite direction. In purging their will, they may be said to move from revolt to the freedom of resignation and consent in the will of God. The existential protagonist starts similarly from a forlorn condition. Without hope (which is, however, not to be confused with Christian despair), acknowledging and yet resisting death and the absurdity of life, he proceeds from that awareness to the freedom of being able continuously to shape his existence by choosing to act. In the theater of *his* world he is indeed the "first actor" or protagonist, the sole judge and spectator.

"Man is not *only* social," says Camus in his *Notebooks.* "His death at least belongs to him . . ." (p. 122). Each of these theaters views man primarily in relation to either a "sacred" world or a "world of rebellion,"[7] and considers his fate as being determined by other than social or historical forces. We are familiar with the rejection of history as a determinant in the Christian drama where it serves rather as an instrument of God's purpose. For Camus who posits a metaphysical consciousness which, however, does not lead to God, the problem of treating moral questions outside the pale of history is more acute. He speaks of the Hegelians' basic error in reducing man to history and the effort of German thought to substitute for "human nature" the notion of the "human situation."[8] But, he asks himself, "being in history while referring to values that go beyond history—is it possible, legitimate? . . . " (*Notebooks, 1942-1951*, p. 159). Thus, the real difficulty for atheist existentialism is creating a morality "without reintroducing into historical existence a value foreign to history" (*The Rebel*, p. 249, n. 1). It is one thing to decide to "accept the unintelligibility of the world—and to pay attention to man" or to say that "nothing is determined but what has been lived . . . the future belongs to God neither more nor less than to man"; it is another to create a viable ethic on the basis of this new humanism.[9] Camus argues eloquently in

The Rebel that history alone cannot be a source of values. "It is one occasion, among others, for man to prove the still confused existence of a value that allows him to judge history. Rebellion itself makes us the promise of such a value." Rebellion is, in fact, "the refusal to be treated as an object and to be reduced to simple historical terms. It is the affirmation of a nature common to all men, which eludes the world of power" (p. 250). Yet the nagging question remains: "*Can man alone create his own values? That is the whole problem*" (*Notebooks, 1942-1951*, p. 94). It is a problem perhaps better illuminated by the literary and dramatic imagination than by abstract reasoning. Camus remains a myth maker and storyteller even under the guise of philosopher.

How can man alone create his own values, without trolls to tempt him, like Solness, beyond human limitations and without guardian angels to lure him, like Rodrigue across continents, to his salvation? Camus starts from a rock-bottom position, questioning, in the person of Meursault, all "values" except the existence of the physical universe. For Meursault, the protagonist of his novel *The Stranger* (*L'Étranger*), the overwhelming heat and brilliance of the sun appears to be the immediate cause of the murder he has committed; this makes no sense to anyone because no one will accept a biochemical reaction as a proper explanation of a morally reprehensible act of violence. But as far as Meursault is concerned, the sun and the sand did overwhelm his protoplasm so that he cannot explain in any other way why he fired at a prostrate man. Camus accepts the extreme implications of a naturalistic view of life, that impersonal forces rule the universe including man, and goes one step beyond. Meursault's consciousness is stripped down to where he apprehends everything in phys- ical-sensuous terms; for example, in prison he experiences a moment of hope, but it is registered as a sudden longing to squeeze Marie's shoulders under the silken texture of her dress. All his other relationships and experiences are similarly reduced to the unpredictable flux of pleasant or unpleasant sensations. Hence, to him all human emotions and the behavior based on them are meaningless. "And just then it crossed my mind that one might fire, or not fire— and it would come to absolutely the same thing."[10] Since nothing really matters, everything is legitimized. The shocking indifference of the "outsider" makes us suddenly realize that the naturalists were, at least, outraged by their clinical insights into the world. Their art was an exposé of the forces that hold man in their grip, but it still implied a system of values, if not the traditional ethic of right and wrong. In the world as Meursault apprehends it, all such judgments are considered futile. *The Stranger*, says Camus, describes the nakedness of man facing the ab- surd (*Notebooks*, p. 24).

Only at the conclusion of the novel, on the morning of his expected execution, does Camus's anti-hero find a measure of peace. It is the first reward for the condemned man and the first step in the direction of an ethic that is based neither on the illusion of an eternal life nor on the alibis of history or society.

> It was as if that great rush of anger [his outburst against the prison chaplain] had washed me clean, emptied me of hope, and, gazing up at the dark sky spangled with its signs and stars, for the first time, the first, I laid my heart open to the benign indifference of the universe. To feel it so like myself, indeed, so brotherly, made me realize that I'd been happy, and that I was happy still. For all to be accomplished, for me to feel less lonely, all that remained to hope was that on the day of my execution there should be a huge crowd of spectators and that they should greet me with howls of execration. (p. 154)

Meursault is not exactly an Algerian counterpart to Sisy- phus in his happiness nor does he share the tragic con- sciousness of Oedipus (making, in Camus's word, the "sacred" remark: "I conclude that all is well"); yet on the day of his execution he experiences the sense of freedom which the privation of hope and future restores. It is his first positive feeling lifting him above the life of bodily sensation, and it is a value gained from his sudden, though minimal, awareness of the absurd: "Nothing, nothing had

the least importance, and I knew quite well why" (p. 152).
Meursault is an ordinary man with an ordinary mind. His
observation of the human condition suggests to him only a
fatalism which "levels out" all ideas, choices, actions in
view of the fact that all men are condemned to live and to
end their lives in an irrational, indifferent universe.

Beyond the stolidly pragmatic voice of the Stranger regis-
tering the absurdity of his existence in this world, the
dramatic imagination (in the work of Camus and Sartre)
discovers the logic of other, more passionate, attitudes.
There are first those individuals who are trapped in the
absurd or in their own evasions, unable to extricate themselves from the scenario of hell, as in *The Misunderstanding*
(*Le Malentendu*) and in *No Exit*. At the other extreme,
there are the figures of power, like Caligula and Goetz in
The Devil and the Good Lord (*Le Diable et le Bon Dieu*),
who seek to escape the human predicament by setting
themselves up as arbiters of fate, donning the mask of
God, and arrogating to themselves total freedom of action. Finally, neither slaves nor masters, neither victims nor
oppressors, there are the genuine rebels who face their
tragic dilemmas and thereby create their own, specifically
human, values.

Although Camus and Sartre did not see eye to eye politically and philosophically, they were both concerned with
the drama of man creating his own values, alone and
unaided. They prize their differing brands of humanism,
but each involves his hero in an act of revolt that marks
the progression from the situation of the stranger to that of
the man who conquers reality. *The Flies* (*Les Mouches*)
and *State of Siege* (*État de Siège*) are philosophic parables
that have to do with the struggle for freedom in societies
that have capitulated to the tyranny of nihilism; and while
the two political plays, *Dirty Hands* (*Les Mains sales*)
and *The Just* (*Les Justes*), show in their subject matter
what different situations the two playwrights will characteristically seize upon, yet in another way they complement
one another. In both, the individual, at a tragic cost,
preserves the value of his act against the merely political

expediency of terrorism. Sartre's protagonist pays with his life in order to retain the identity which the act of murder has bestowed upon him; Camus's hero dies willingly on the gallows in order to make of his act of political murder a morally justifiable act of rebellion.

1

The situations in all these dramas are extreme. The characters are criminals, murderers, tyrants, terrorists, and the circumstances in which they are placed border on the grotesque. Though the techniques differ—Sartre disguising his purposes with plausible characterization and realistic dialogue, Camus sometimes barely covering the allegorical import of his plots—both playwrights handle the drama as a moving form of argument; they are more interested in a demonstration of behavior than in behavior itself. When Camus introduces the story of *The Misunderstanding* (in a bare journalistic outline) into the world of *The Stranger*, the difference becomes apparent. Meursault finds a faded newspaper clipping under the mattress of his prison cot which, for lack of anything else to do, he reads over and over again. A man returns after twenty-five years to his native village. Wishing to surprise his mother and sister who run the local hotel, he registers under an assumed name. They kill him for his money, and when his identity is established they commit suicide. On the one hand, Meursault finds the story most unlikely: "The man was asking for trouble; one shouldn't play fool tricks of that sort." Given his no-nonsense attitude toward the world, he is unsympathetic to the victims of a cruel misunderstanding. But in another way, having read the story a thousand times during his imprisonment, he detects its schematic rightness: "It was plausible enough" (p. 100). For Camus that critical verdict is sufficient. If his audience can share the recognition that his story renders an essential truth about life, he feels free to develop it into a dramatic parable of the absurd. *No Exit*, underneath its naturalistic manner, is even more fantastic, but here also our attention is mainly occupied by the play of ideas rather than the melodramatic images and events which embody them.

The setting of both plays is isolated: the small hotel in a drab central European village where well-to-do guests unaccountably disappear and the drawing-room in Second Empire style which is Sartre's hell. Both are concrete images of a philosopher's idea of the universe, which traps its victims and from which there is no escape. What the characters do to each other and say to each other—these are the specific dramatic gestures reflecting man's awareness of his fate; they tell the story of his helplessness and fear, the desire to escape, the recognition of failure, and the abandonment of hope. *The Misunderstanding* and *No Exit* demonstrate the negative aspect of existential philosophy, the marred possibilities of life. Both for Camus and Sartre, the caged victims are, as well, their own jailers and executioners. The characters of *The Misunderstanding*, unlike Sisyphus, surrender to—and enact—the senseless violence and indifference of the universe; they are its irrational human counterpart. And Sartre's trio of damned souls learn that their acts, which define them for what they are, have directly brought into being the hell of mutual torture and dependency.

At one point Camus thought of publishing the play (under an earlier title) as a comedy and *Caligula* as a tragedy. But in the Preface (dated December 1957) to Stuart Gilbert's translation published in America, he encourages the reader to look upon *The Misunderstanding* "as an attempt to create a modern tragedy."[11] Considering the consequences the misunderstanding ceases to be a comic motive in the traditional sense, but rather approaches what we have come to mean by the term "tragic farce." This misunderstanding is not merely an instance of natural human ignorance which causes unforeseen troubles; it is, in fact, the symptom of a deep malaise. The life of crime to which the mother and the sister have become habituated before Jan returns to the village is, in a philosophic sense, a form of self-betrayal, a violence done to their own humanity, which must inevitably lead to the tragic outcome. Therefore the failure to recognize their guest is a modern un-Aristotelian form of *hamartia*, that is to say, not the blindness which is a universal human liability, but the self-induced blindness of those who have blunted their vision by forfeiting all human values in the face of the uncertainty and irrationality of life.

Camus makes a significant distinction between the mother's and the sister's reaction once the error has been discovered. The mother's remorse is mingled with her realization that her grief makes as little sense as the world itself; hence she must kill the rekindled but now intolerable love for the returned son along with herself. The sister, Martha, on the contrary, reconfirms her sterile response to the condition of her existence. She not only despises her mother's talk of crime and punishment, but she also gives evidence of having lost whatever natural saving grace there may be in the human heart: "If I had recognized him, I know now that it would have made no difference." In other words, the failure of recognition is not merely an error committed by a fallible human being; it is a central symbol of the absurd, the "divorce between man and his life."[12] Martha, in effect, becomes the spokesman for the tragic failure to surmount despair. She consents to the absurdity of the world which drives her to senseless crime in search of life and hope. At the moment when Jan has been drugged, his fate made over to "indifferent hands," a moment expressive of the absurdity of life, Martha refuses to let him wake instead of flinging the body into the river. To her the sleeping figure is an emblem of man's fate in the world at large; "this room is made to sleep in and this world to die in."

The lesson of despair becomes explicit in the concluding dialogue between Martha and Jan's wife, Maria. Camus was concerned over the dramatization of the final scene (*Notebooks, 1942-1951*, pp. 26-27, 31-32). In order to give this strange story general validity, the last illusions of evasion or consolation must be proven false. Hence Martha's peroration, her attempt to drive Maria to despair: What has happened was no accident. No one is ever recognized as this world goes. And love is futile for the man who has descended into permanent exile. Therefore pray to God to turn you hard as stone (*qu'il vous fasse semblable à la pierre*); that, after all, is His happiness—to be hard as stone and deaf to all cries for help. Choose either the mindless happiness of stones or the river bottom, where we are waiting for you (Act III, scene 3). The allusion to Camus's interpretation of the myth of Sisyphus is apparent. If suicide is an illegitimate escape, the problem becomes how to push the rock endlessly without becoming *semblable à la pierre*. In this play there is no hero who is thus superior to his fate. In fact, to make the image of futility complete, Maria does raise her arms screaming for God's pity "on those who love each other and are parted," and Camus ends the play with a startling coup de théâtre. The old manservant enters and, answering her call, speaks for the first time. Maria still on her knees repeats her plea for pity and help, and then—perhaps giving voice to the deaf and hardened power that rules the universe, perhaps representing only an old perplexed man—he answers: "*Non!*"[13]

This tableau of the suppliant being rejected serves as a fitting epilogue to Camus's handling of the story. Within the realm of the absurd, it shows the reverse side of the attitude which Camus celebrates in Sisyphus. The hero of the myth undergoes eternal pain, but he also preserves life and his consciousness of its value. It is *he* who rejects the irrational, the Absurd, and by his scorn of gods, his hatred of death, and his passion for life he becomes superior to his fate. "The lucidity that was to constitute his torture at the same time crowns his victory. There is no fate that cannot be surmounted by scorn" (*Sisyphus*, p. 121). In *The Misunderstanding*, however, there is no such lucidity and no such rebellion. The characters are trapped by false hopes and subterfuge which lead to murder and suicide. They consign themselves to the Absurd as the only possible fate in this world. And when Maria seeks to escape the sterile alternatives of death and a nonhuman existence in her ultimate appeal to God ("Oh! mon Dieu! je ne puis vivre dans ce désert!"), the last hope is lost. The deaf servant has found his voice.

The irony of Sartre's drama of pre-existential suffering is that the characters of *No Exit* postulate a supernatural power where there is none. The question here is not that of overcoming an unjust fate or rejecting a superhuman, and therefore inhuman, power that would otherwise rule their lives; it is rather a question of learning that the universe is empty except for what men make of it. It is the difference between the wholly absurd situation of Jan, in Camus's play, drugged and impotent before his fate ("où son destin même lui est étranger, où ses chances de vie sont remises dans des mains indifférentes"), and Garcin's recognition in Sartre's play that by his act of cowardice he has forever lost the power to change his fate ("Ils ne m'oublient pas, eux. . . . je leur ai laissé ma vie entre les mains"). Early in Sartre's play all three characters attempt to evade the knowledge that they have damned themselves and that they must inexorably pronounce judgment upon themselves. As every route of escape is tested in their dialogue and logically blocked, they begin to understand the nature of their self-created prison.

But first they yield to the temptation of regarding themselves as mere victims, having stumbled into a diabolically planned trap. "I tell you they've thought it all out. Down to the last detail. Nothing was left to chance. This room was all set for us"; and later, "Do you think *they* have not known beforehand every word you say?" It is much more difficult to face the reality that by being what they are they have themselves contrived the logic of their suffering. As the sounds and sights of earth fade from consciousness, they are forced to turn to each other to find a solution to the enigma of their common fate. There are no alibis left because what each has done on earth is the unalterable sum of his life which, in turn, is the key to his present behavior. Once they realize that they are the architects as well as the inhabitants of their peculiar hell, they have gained an invaluable insight into this self-contained logic; but, as there is no opportunity of escape so is there none for rebellion. In Sartre's view, the myth of Sisyphus provides no model for the human condition. There are no gods to scorn, no fate to be surmounted. (Zeus in *The Flies* is a politician, a petty tyrant, rather than the source of man's fate.) Either man shapes his own fate in Sartre's universe, which is devoid of supernatural powers, or he consigns himself to the limbo of the uncommitted, unless, as in *No Exit*, he lays himself open to the eternal torture of having to contemplate his human failings through the eyes of the others ("Pas besoin de gril, l'enfer, c'est les Autres"). The horror of the situation lies not only in the eternity before them but as much in the "ineluctable modality" of time, whereby the past is fixed and unchangeable since they are dead and forever defined. That is the meaning of death. That Inès is impervious to the knife elicits a momentary shock of recognition ("Morte? . . . Morte! . . . C'est déja fait, comprends-tu?"), then an explosion of laughter, which dies down as they comprehend the meaning of their plight. Neither defiance nor remorse is possible in a situation in which there is no external system of values that the human will can reject or accept; only a stoic resignation to the finality of death which precludes new choices and redeeming actions, only a perpetual awareness of the self as a fixed object.

In the absence of mirrors, Inès assumes the function of a reflecting glass, at first playfully, sexually, to help Estelle put on make-up and assure her of her existence, though even in this scene the experience is frightening because what Estelle gets is not the familiar "tamed" image of herself. But this is only the prelude to the grim metaphorical play of the mirror of judgment in which one cannot see oneself as one wants to be. That is the moment of reckoning for Garcin. Estelle, who is physically attracted to him, is incapable of understanding his need to be seen, and therefore to see himself, as a man who *cannot* have acted in a cowardly fashion. Inès, on the other hand, understands his need for self-deception. But she, who knows "the price of evil," serves him as a pitiless mirror forcing him to see how his act has defined him and exposing his twofold self-deception. He must pay the price. On earth he chose to see himself as a strong-willed and courageous man; and retaining his faith in that image, he could excuse his

act of cowardice as a single lapse. Now, in his present
situation, having been shot as a deserter, he desperately
needs one of the two women to believe in him in order to
be saved. But hell is the lucidity which uncovers this form
of self-deception, so widely practiced on earth. Inès thus
has it in her power to make him see himself objectively,
not as he wishes to be, but as he really is. Only what a
man does defines his life; there are no other values except
those which he creates by his acts. Each member of the
trio of "inseparables" must therefore fall back upon himself
or herself. They cannot save one another. Yet they are
inextricably linked one to another in this place of the dead
where they perpetually reflect the world of the living and
judge it with the clarity of hindsight.

In Camus the exile, or the stranger, is trapped in a world
in which the human spirit has surrendered to absurdity.
In Sartre's play the human actors have paralyzed themselves through cowardice, crime, and bad faith. Camus's
people typically react by accepting or rebelling against the
irrationality of the fate which is in store for them, whereas
Sartre's discover the hard truth that they are alone and that
by their acts they are directly responsible for their fate.
In *No Exit* the place is hell, and the dead behave as they
did in life until the discovery is made. In *The Misunderstanding* the place is a house which resembles hell, and the
living behave like the damned until their fate is sealed.
The ambiguity in both instances signifies that man has
tragically forfeited his prerogative; none of them can master or reshape their fate at the point at which the playwright
catches them. Neither rebellion nor a fresh commitment
can save them now. The characters in Camus do not possess
the courage of revolt, and Sartre's trio are forever defined as lacking the courage of a positive commitment by
the finality of death.

2

It is not surprising that when these playwrights turn to
the opposite extreme—man in his absolute power im-
personating God—Camus should produce out of the idea of

unlimited freedom a tragedy of failure and nihilistic despair, while Sartre manipulates such a situation into a less than satisfactory tragicomedy of good and evil. Camus's *Caligula* is a much better play than Sartre's *The Devil and the Good Lord* because it pursues the premise to its logical conclusion. It is no less didactic or propositional than Sartre's play, but it takes seriously the logical consequences of total freedom, whereas Sartre treats the questions of responsibility and guilt rhetorically and propels his hero toward a man-made ethic through a series of calculated paradoxes. *The Devil and the Good Lord* is highly entertaining; it also appears to be, as has been suggested,[14] a deliberate reply to Claudel's *The Satin Slipper*, and a tongue-in-cheek reply at that. God's steady pull in the Christian drama is replaced by an impudent experiment. Against the setting of the historical period of the German Reformation, the military commander Goetz playacts the traditional attitudes of Goodness and of Evil and finds little difference between them. Camus, for his part, expressed his animosity toward Claudel succinctly in his Notebooks and left it at that.[15] The image of man as God in *Caligula* is a far too serious matter for polemic.

One thinks of the idea of man replacing God as pure fantasy or as a philosopher's hypothesis tò be followed through as an experimental thought. There are, however, situations in history which may serve the writer as plausible test sites to gauge the results of such an idea. Thus, for example, Caligula, and to a lesser degree Goetz, can impersonate a supreme power acting out the logic of total freedom. Single acts of anarchy prove little in themselves about the exercise of the unencumbered will. The murder of Fyodor Karamazov by his bastard son is an ordinary sordid act of violence, but Ivan's part in it becomes the universal anguish, to the point of madness, of the man who speculates on the notion that if there is no God everything is permitted. Camus cites the case of Sade who in his imagination advances from the role of uninhibited libertine to that of supreme master and God, but indistinguishable in the end from the solitary prisoner in the Bastille

(*The Rebel*, p. 45). This culmination of Sade's fantasy world was for Camus perhaps an actual prognostication of the end of Caligula usurping the place of the Absurd. His reading of Nietzsche reminds us that Caligula's search for something not of this world was illogical to begin with.

> If nothing is true, if the world is without order, then nothing is forbidden; to prohibit an action, there must, in fact, be a standard of values and an aim. But, at the same time, nothing is authorized; there must also be values and aims in order to choose another course of action. . . . The sum total of every possibility does not amount to liberty, but to attempt the impossible amounts to slavery. Chaos is also a form of servitude. Freedom exists only in a world where what is possible is defined at the same time as what is not possible. Without law there is no freedom. (*The Rebel*, p. 71)

Thus, with *Caligula* we return to the question: how can man alone create his own values? The answer is once more negative. He cannot in the way attempted by Caligula. In Camus's words, his is "the story of a superior suicide." It is not the illegitimate suicide of escape, nor the desperate act of Martha and Jan's mother at the end of *The Misunderstanding*. Far from cooperating with the forces that make human life absurd, he decides to master them by becoming their human incarnation, and thereby possibly achieving an unheard-of individual freedom for himself. The death of his sister has taught him the truth that "men die" and that "they are not happy." If he, having the power to do so, were to force men to live by the light of this truth, ordering a famine, replacing epidemics, persecutions, suffering of every kind that ordinarily happen to men in ways they do not understand, would he not thereby conquer fate by his godlike willfulness and so liberate himself from the anguish of living? Thus, he does not accept nor evade his anguish; on the contrary, "faithful to his logic, [he] does what is necessary to arm against him those who will eventually kill him."[16] In this sense, it is a "superior suicide" because, having embarked upon a path of destruction and self-destruction, he follows it consistently and in full consciousness of what he is doing, to the inevitable

end. Camus pictures Caligula, not as a wicked man, though
he pursues the ideal of total freedom at the expense of his
fellow men, but as a man "obsessed with the impossible,"
who finds to his horror that the degradation of all human
values leads to self-hatred and unbearable solitude. "The
sum total of every possibility does not amount to liberty,
but to attempt the impossible amounts to slavery."

Caligula is not mad. Camus calls his discovery that men
die and that they are not happy "a very modest ideology."
But it triggers in the young emperor a passion for life
that bursts forth in one way as a revulsion from the world
as it is, where men accommodate themselves to their fate;
and in another, the way of personal rebellion, as a seem-
ingly mad desire to possess the moon, or happiness, or
immortality—"something, which may perhaps sound demented, but which is not of this world,"—in short, the impossible. The poet, Cherea, understands from the beginning
that Caligula's subjects are not confronting a mad tyrant,
but a deadlier enemy by far. What he fears and loathes
in him is that the emperor knows what he wants; his passion is fed by an idea legitimizing every conceivable act
which he is determined to follow through to the end.
Hence he must be destroyed, not alone for himself, but in
order to annihilate the idea. We are in the world of *Coriolanus*, not that of *Macbeth*. The enormity of Macbeth's
crimes can be grasped and judged as a breach of the known
moral bonds between king and God and king and subject.
Coriolanus, however, *is* sufficient in himself; he deems himself an incarnation of the idea of Rome which, it turns out,
is also to attempt the impossible. He achieves the power
to determine the fate of Rome, but falls before the logic
of his insoluble dilemma. Like the man-god Caligula, he can
be true to his "perfection" only outside the contingencies
of politics; both try to vault above the unstable life of the
human community, but are pulled back down into history
and die a dishonorable death.

Two entries, in the Notebooks, on tragedy are pertinent
here.

> If the world is tragic, if we live torn asunder, it is not so much
> because of tyrants. You and I know that there is a liberty, a
> justice, a deep, shared joy, a common fight against the tyrants.
> When evil dominates, there is no problem. When the adversary
> is wrong, those who are fighting him are free and at peace.
> But the split develops because men equally eager for the good
> of mankind either want it at once or else aim for three genera-
> tions from now, and that is enough to divide them forever.
> When the adversaries are both right, then we enter tragedy.
> . . . (pp. 115-116)

This is the familiar dialectic of modern historical tragedy applied to a political dilemma, possibly that of reconciling
liberty with justice. In an earlier entry, the Hegelian
formula had been expanded and intensified, bringing us
closer to *Caligula*.

> What makes a tragedy is that each of the forces in opposition
> is equally legitimate, has a right to live. Whence a weak
> tragedy: which involves illegitimate forces. Whence a strong
> tragedy: which legitimizes *everything*. (p. 79)

If Caligula were merely a tyrant, there would be no tragedy;
our interest would be confined to when and how he can be
toppled. But, as Cherea recognizes, even Caligula's unlimited exercise of power, though it may seem demented, has
its legitimate goal—to find a way by which he may be
transfigured and the world renewed. The world as it is has
no importance, and he who realizes this gains his freedom.
But on the other side, those who suffer his whimsical cruel-
ties decide that to see the validity of love denied and to
live a life devoid of meaning is worse than losing it. The
issue is not Caligula's cruelty, but the logic of his experiment. Apparently Camus does not doubt its legitimacy;
he has no doubt whatever about the tragic ending: "A day
will come when he will be alone in an empire filled with
the dead and the kinsmen of the dead" (Act II, scene 2).

The last act of the play is indeed the drama of Caligula's
descent into the realm of the dead. It has become clear
that he desires his own destruction. While the physical
signs of his dissolution appear, his mind still plays gro-

tesquely upon the possibility of a splendid and sterile happiness beyond love and pain, a murderous freedom from
memories and illusion, "the godlike enlightenment of the
solitary" (trans. Gilbert; Act IV, scene 12). He is the poet
of death, the only true artist in Rome, because he *lives*
his art. But in the end, after strangling his mistress in a
perverse consummation of his passion, his exultation
changes abruptly and he comprehends his failure. Having
searched for the impossible, he sees nothing in the mirror
except the hated image of himself; in place of utter loneliness, only emptiness; instead of freedom, guilt. Again, this
is not the soul's despair of a tyrant like Macbeth. It is
Caligula's recognition that his ruthless logic has come to
nothing; hence he weeps over his desolation. Then, smash-
ing the mirror, he faces the conspirators and laughs at his
ironic fate: "To history, Caligula! Go down to history!"
(trans. Gilbert). Instead of breaking through the limits of
life and human feeling, instead of the hoped-for abrogation
of time and this world's judgment, he will now go down in
history as another tyrant and madman. But he hurls a last
challenge, and a final vindication, choked in laughter and
blood: "I am still alive!" The idea may have failed, but it
cannot be eradicated. The play, says Camus, is a tragedy of
the intelligence, "the story of the most human and most
tragic of errors" (Preface, p. vi).

One pauses over the phrase "the most human . . . of
errors." But unlikely as it may seem, Caligula *is* a representative tragic hero. He is at once protagonist and antagonist. The man who feels the anguish of being human
and has dreams of freedom and an impossible happiness
is at the same time the cruel man-god, enacting his dreams
regardless of the cost until he must be removed like a
malignant disease. He has the requisite power to rival the
gods in their capriciousness, to choose purposely to become
an unintelligible force determining the fate of his fellow
men; thus he is able to explore in behalf of mankind the
consequences of confronting the irrational world in a new
way—by becoming its irrational master. But therein lies his
error. His rebellion merely duplicates the reign of the ab-

surd and therefore ends in nothingness. "The absurd," says Camus, "has meaning only in so far as it is not agreed to" (*Sisyphus*, p. 31). Only the tension between the human ("my revolt, my freedom, and my passion") and the inhuman ("the unreasonable silence of the world" [p. 64]) holds the promise of a meaningful existence in the face of the absurd. In Caligula the tension collapses at once since he misprizes the human in order to match the cruelty of the gods. The tragedy of his failure is not to be measured by the pain this causes his fellow men, but by the dehumanization and enslavement of mind and spirit which result from a misconceived form of rebellion. Camus intended to, but did not, add the following remark on the proofs of the play: "Well, the tragedy is over. The failure is complete. I turn my head and go away. I took my share in this fight for the impossible. Let us wait for death, knowing in advance that death liberates from nothing" (*Notebooks, 1942-1951*, p. 85).

In contrast, Sartre's hero, Goetz, who plays at being the devil and then one of God's elect, discovers the futility of both roles and claims to have found release in the new kingdom of man. Sartre allows his heroes to liberate themselves not merely from the prescriptive ethic of Christianity but also from the inhibiting idea that man has to come to terms with any superhuman power. "If God exists, man is nothing. If man exists . . ." *The Devil and the Good Lord* is not exactly a model of philosophic reasoning, but it is a dramatic and, in part, ironic celebration of the emptiness of heaven. "Halleluiah! I have delivered us." There is no question here, as there is in *Caligula*, of emulating the gods or of consenting in the irrational quality of life. The "unreasonable silence" of the universe is simply proof that man is alone and, therefore, by definition master of his fate. What Goetz discovers is that he alone was the author of evil in the first part and that he alone invented good in the second; thus only he can accuse himself and absolve himself. Goetz is done with the comedy of Christian brotherhood as well as with the melodrama of doing evil for its own sake. He has shown that both postures can be faked. Now, by choosing to lead men in order to save them, by whatever combination of good and evil this may be accomplished, he demonstrates that man not only can, but must, supplant the idea of God by acting freely and responsibly.

At this point, Sartre is more persuasive in declaring man's independence than imagining the terrifying burden of his freedom. The furies fling themselves shrieking after Orestes at the conclusion of *The Flies*. The play ends there, and all we know is that Zeus has been toppled. In *The Devil and the Good Lord* there is the opportunity to ask, What then? But in the tumult of the action the interesting questions about the emancipated individual get lost. There is one indication of the frightening consequence of the idea that man is alone. "Let Him damn me a thousand times, provided He exists." It is a brief, desperate counterstatement, quickly swept aside. Again, Sartre's doctrinal conduct of the play causes him to overlook the implications of Goetz's inability to love, knowing that heaven is an empty hole. Camus perceives in the "torn or dead souls" of *The Possessed* (both the novel and his dramatization) the suffering and aridity of modern man and a prophecy of twentieth-century nihilism. But Sartre's ethics and politics are far too rigorous to allow such an admixture of sentiment. Goetz notes his inability to love in the poignant scene with Hilda, but he puts the question behind him as he ends "the comedy of Good" and proceeds in his purpose of saving the peasants like a modern social engineer, discoursing on the inseparability of good and evil under an empty sky. Far from being messianic ("the kingdom of man is beginning") or exhilarating, it is a surprisingly banal ending to an otherwise witty play.

Caligula and *The Devil and the Good Lord* have distinct historical settings that serve, however, mainly as useful arenas in which to test a hypothetical situation: what if man discovered that, since God does not exist, every conceivable action was legitimate? Caligula rues the course he has chosen which leads to nothing. He finds to his horror that his freedom is not the right one. Goetz, on the other hand, feels himself imbued with a new sense of reality once he has sloughed off all moral presuppositions and can rededicate himself, if necessary, to evil in order to accomplish the good. In the end he no longer merely plays the role of the devil. Since all men are alone, prompted neither by God nor by the devil, he is free, in fact he is compelled, to assume responsibility for his actions. But here the play breaks off with a rhetorical flourish. Sartre is still satisfied with bringing his protagonist only to the threshold of existential independence.

3

The Flies, when it was produced in 1943 in occupied France, was regarded more as an act of politics than a landmark of Sartre's philosophical ideas.[17] As such, the demythologizing of the story of Orestes ended with a flourish too, and properly so for the occasion. Zeus was shown up as a petty tyrant, or perhaps more precisely and philosophically as a nonentity. Under the circumstances, the question of what happens to Orestes after his stirring exit was felt to be impertinent. The liberation of the people of Argos was at least as important as defining the nature of Orestes' burden, as he strides off stage. Yet today the play still stands on its own, apart from the political context of its original production, as an important statement in Sartre's work. We may read it, in relation to Camus's *State of Siege*, as a modern political drama having to do with liberty and the revolt against the totalitarian state. We must also look at it as a drama having to do with man's challenge to God, his assumption of authority over his own fate by emancipating himself from traditional religious and moral ideologies. Like *The Family Reunion* (1939) it deals with the exile's return, his conquest, and departure. In this sense, Eliot's play, as well as Giraudoux' *Electra* (1937) to which Sartre alludes, forms a cognate background and foil to *The Flies*.

The Orestes of the ancient legends and the versions of the Greek dramatists was a figure of vengeance, and in Aeschy-

lus' *Oresteia* his deed became a cause célèbre for a new
dispensation of justice. Zeus himself stood behind Apollo's
directive, his championship of the matricide, and Athene's
final judgment. Sartre reverses both motives in his play in
the interest of his theme. He creates a new Orestes who
comes to Argos, but not because he is of the race of Atreus
and therefore doomed to commit his crime, or "entangled
in his destiny," as Electra imagines him, "like a disem-
boweled horse with his legs entangled in his entrails so
that whichever way he moves he tears them out" (Act II,
Tableau I, scene 4).[18] Rather, he arrives like a curious
traveler, a cultivated upper middle-class Corinthian-
Parisian youth returning as a stranger to the inhospitable
country town which happened to be his birthplace. The
Orestes figure who fulfills his destiny by avenging the murder of his father is a tragic hero in the classic sense.
The modern Orestes of Sartre who *chooses* to commit the
crime in order to acquire a destiny is tragic in another
sense. He is the dispossessed prince laying claim, not to
the throne occupied by a usurper, but to the collective guilt
of his people. By this act of moral daring, he wants to be
a savior king to his people, but "a king without a kingdom
and without subjects." And when Zeus cynically performs
the role of the Creator of the Universe, in an electronic
parody of the voice of God out of the whirlwind in the
Book of Job, the modern Orestes becomes the dispossessed
youth laying claim to the freedom of Man: ". . . You are
the king of the gods, the king of stones and stars, the king
of the waves of the sea. But you are not the king of man"
(Act III, scene 2). The new dispensation of justice must
be earned just as painfully and this time in defiance of God.

　　Orestes' rebellion is defined by the nature of his antagonists, Aegisthus and Zeus, and by the contrast between
Electra's behavior and his own. King and God have made
of Argos a city where fear and remorse have become civic
virtues. It is the model of man in political and moral
bondage. There is no question here of searching out a hidden crime. Aegisthus has institutionalized the public admission of all crimes and repentance for them, and chief among

them the murder of Agamemnon. That event has become
the occasion for the annual ceremony for the dead.[19] The
celebration of the unappeasable dead and the inexpiable
crime approaches a kind of necrophilia which is the psychological equivalent of total self-abasement. Aegisthus and
Zeus use these rites to enslave the people of Argos through
guilt and terror. But though Electra's defiant dance of joy
on the temple steps—"I am not afraid of my dead, and yours
are nothing to me" (Act II, Tableau I, scene 3)—is a bold
challenge to their tyranny, it can be only partially successful. Zeus intervenes with a simple miracle, and she is
banished from Argos. Electra is capable only of a gesture
of moral resistance which is quickly put down.

The episode is a preparation for Orestes' full and positive
involvement. It is a foil to his radical act of revolt: the killing of Aegisthus and Clytemnestra and the lifting of the
curse from the people of Argos. Zeus remains powerless
in the face of his free choice to take the crime and the
burden of responsibility upon himself. It is significant
that Orestes' motives are unintelligible to Electra. For, unlike her brother, she is locked in the cycle of vengeance,
self-hatred, and unending remorse; following the crime
she needs the torture of the furies to bear up under her
sense of guilt. Electra's reaction to the accomplished act of
revenge separates her life from his and underlines dramatically what his commitment means. Besides, the emphatic
contrast is Sartre's assertion of the difference between his
reading of the human challenge to the injustice of the gods
and that of Giraudoux.

The difference is enlightening. The voice of Giraudoux'
Electra is a prewar voice, condemning the complacency of
men and nations, founded as it is on concealed injustice
and crime. The phrases are those of the editorial writer—
"an assault on human dignity," "infecting a nation," "corrupting its loyalty." On a deeper level she prosecutes the
collusion between the gods and men in pursuit of happiness: "In this country of mine, concern for justice is not the
gods' business. The gods are artists. A beautiful light from
a conflagration, beautiful grass on a battle field, such is

their justice. A magnificent repentance for a crime is the gods' verdict on your [Aegisthus'] case. I don't accept it" (trans. Winifred Smith; Act II, scene 8). But Electra's stubborn will to force justice and truth upon the city results in its destruction. The final irony of Giraudoux' version is that the furies have gradually taken on her shape and intend to pursue Orestes to the point of madness or suicide until he will curse his sister.

The reversal is poignant, but since it is brought about gratuitously (rather than logically from the premises of the story) only to give expression to Giraudoux' urbane pessimism, the paramount impression is the paradox of Electra's fate. She stands alone at the end, an agent of justice but resembling the furies in their mindless violence. In contrast, in an earlier play, *Judith*, Giraudoux had been able to fashion a tragedy out of the distortion of human values. Judith resists the role of martyr which is imposed upon her partly as holy prophecy and partly to vindicate the chauvinists and theocrats of her nation. She kills Holofernes for reasons of her own, but must assume her place in the official legend. It is the conspiracy of fanatical men and a jealous God in collusion which violates her spirit. In both plays Giraudoux shows the rebellious will of his heroines broken, their values dissipated, while a cruder (supernaturally sanctioned) necessity prevails. The infernal machinery which, according to Cocteau's play (*La Machine infernale*, 1934), operates with terrifying efficiency behind the lives of men is attenuated in the hands of Giraudoux to a merely deplorable malevolent force which spoils the fruition of what is instinctively good in man. Giraudoux' particular form of intellectual irony plays constantly over the texture of his drama. But the points scored do not amount to a radical defiance; they are verbal protests preceding the inevitable loss and resignation. In contrast, Sartre's irony is satirical; it is part of the assault on the vulnerable reign of Zeus.

The choices are clear in Sartre's play. Orestes kills Aegisthus and his mother swiftly and deliberately, not for revenge, but as a necessary act of commitment transforming the detached stranger suddenly into the guilty murderer deeply implicated in the fate of his race and of his city. As he takes possession of his life, he is struck simultaneously by the heavy burden he has taken upon himself and the freedom he has gained by doing so. Sartre's Electra experiences the opposite extreme. Orestes' existential transfiguration is incomprehensible to her whose life has been dedicated to hatred and the idea of revenge. Now that the revenge has been accomplished she is devoid of hatred as well as any other feeling except fear. But in Sartre's view she fears Orestes more than the furies. A man who leaves behind him all ordinary human emotions, who declares himself outside the divine law, outside nature, utterly alone, who glories in his crime because it set him free, determined to seek his own way and to be a savior to his community by taking its sins and its remorse upon him—such a man is frightening. Yet such a man, choosing this bitter and dangerous path in order to find an unknown but free existence on the other side of despair, is also a tragic rebel: "The words which I speak are too big for my mouth; they tear it. The destiny which I carry is too heavy for my youth; it has shattered it" (Act III, scene 2). Electra cannot participate in this rite of existential salvation. Her infatuation with her role of avenger is no victory at all. Having aged overnight and taken on the dead eyes of Clytemnestra, she accepts the known way of admitting her guilt and propitiating the dead. Her failure lies in herself; thus separated from Orestes, she is by implication Sartre's verdict on the heroine of Giraudoux.

In *The Flies* Sartre could still indulge in a kind of theoretical purity. The discovery that man is free and can therefore create his fate was—translated into practical terms—a call to a new life, a way of resisting political and moral subjugation, through acting and taking responsibility for one's acts. But by the time the war was over, the world had begun to learn the horrors that had occurred. *The Condemned of Altona* (*Les Séquestrés d'Altona*, 1959) incorporates Sartre's consciousness of a greater catastrophe, a more stupendous moral crisis, than resulted from the defeat of France. In view of the experience of the world war and later of Algeria, he must now deal with guilt as an ineradicable stain.[20] In *The Flies* guilt and remorse had been a publicly cultivated instrument of oppression, part of an age-old myth that must be shaken off by an act of rebellion. *Altona* has to do with another world in which, as in Miller's *After the Fall*, deliverance does not come in the form of a secular redemption or liberation of the human spirit, but is attainable only in a tragic confrontation of the evil of which man is capable. It is therefore far less programmatic than *The Flies*. The difference for the protagonists is due in part to the change in venue from Argos (Paris 1943) to postwar Germany.

If Orestes seeks by his crime to become personally "engaged" and is thus able to pit his free will against the power of Zeus, Franz von Gerlach, the ex-Nazi officer, conscious of his war crimes but seeking to evade his responsibility, must find his tragic deliverance in the opposite direction. The fiction of the inexpiable crime and the unappeasable dead invented by Zeus to enslave the Argives is now a reality; and the father-God figure of this play, old Gerlach, the Nazi industrialist, is enveloped in the guilt of his son. "He created me in his image," says Franz, "unless he has become the image of what he created" (Act II).[21] Thus, the hero of *The Condemned of Altona* terminates his self-imposed protective exile; he abandons the elaborate self-justifications and after thirteen years descends from his room to face old Gerlach. There is no defiance and liberation "after the fall"; they pronounce self-judgment and join in a double suicide, Franz, the "butcher of Smolensk" and old Gerlach (or Zeus, or war-time Germany), the author of his life and fate.

If Orestes' act of commitment is the norm of behavior for the engaged existentialist hero, the conclusion of *Altona* illustrates commitment of the will to end a life of crime and injustice, as if the stalemate situation of *No Exit* had been broken to allow the condemned the freedom to redefine themselves in death. Orestes voluntarily assumes the guilt of Argos and goes out into the world presumably to shape his life. Franz returns from the war unable to shoulder the accumulated guilt of his life and that of his time until he is willing to face his conscience. It is a far less sanguine view of the exercise of human freedom since the choice is now limited to self-deception and self-judgment. Sartre says that there is an "actual liberation in the two suicides"; that is to say, the act of engagement is the breaking of the moral stasis through self-awareness and death. He protests that he does not want the play to be confused with a *drame bourgeois* which after all "exists only for the purpose of eliminating the problem it deals with."[22] Thus the play is also "an act of personal engagement" for the artist and should be by implication an act of engagement for the audience. Yet, the matter of guilt and conscience, engagement, liberation bears a greater resemblance to the corresponding acts in a play like *Rosmersholm* than to the existential ethic of Orestes in *The Flies*. Liberation has obviously a different meaning in *The Flies*. It is a question, to return to Camus's phrase, of man's being able to create his own values alone. Orestes' crime liberates him. In *Altona* Sartre is forced back to a more traditional view. After thirteen years of concealment, Franz and his father openly implicate each other in their heinous crimes. The double suicide attempts to resolve an unyielding moral crisis, since Franz cannot resume life in a resurrected and prosperous Germany and Gerlach holds himself responsible for the inhumanity of his son. If it is an act of liberation, one ought to consider that it is so by virtue of their returning to and judging themselves by commonly accepted values. It is as though Zeus and Orestes together capitulated before the invisible bar of human justice in order to expiate their crimes.

With Harry, Lord Monchensey, in *The Family Reunion*, we return to a version of the Orestes figure whose anguish and deep sense of guilt is the threshold to the road to freedom. He too has his crime, in a manner of speaking, and he has his furies. But beyond that he reveals to us the Christian consciousness of sin and expiation, which goes far deeper than the superstitious fear of the unappeasable dead in *The Flies*. Orestes masters anguish and remorse, but Harry's search reveals a life that "begins to seem just part of some huge disaster,/ Some monstrous mistake and aberration/ Of all men, of the world, which I cannot put in order" (Part II, scene 1). In an English country house the furies become "*divine* instruments" and "hounds of heaven,"[23] pointing inexorably to "the filthiness, that lies a little deeper . . ." and driving the hero to an existential pursuit of liberation "somewhere on the other side of despair." While Orestes comes to Argos, appropriates the flies and leaves again, trailing them as the inescapable burden of his new life, the cost of his freedom, Harry has been running from the furies to the safety of his home, only to find them there ("No! you were already here before I arrived"). The dramatic action of *The Family Reunion* is to find out what had happened at Wishwood in order to understand what has happened to him. Once he does, the decision is made "in a moment of clarity,"

> not to run away, but to pursue,
> Not to avoid being found, but to seek.

He knows that he must seek liberation from "a world of fugitives" (Part II, scene 2).

Thus he, too, marches out, but following "the bright angels." What is there for him on the other side of despair? A hoped-for redemption through the experience of a different order of reality and the certainty of an ordeal which, though unknowable in his individual life, has its antecedents in the experience of men:

> I have not yet had the precise directions.
> Where does one go from a world of insanity?
> Somewhere on the other side of despair.
> To the worship in the desert, the thirst and deprivation,
> A stony sanctuary and a primitive altar,
> The heat of the sun and the icy vigil,
> A care over lives of humble people,
> The lesson of ignorance, of incurable diseases.
> Such things are possible. It is love and terror
> Of what waits and wants me, and will not let me fall. (Part II, scene 2)

Orestes' life-to-be is similarly uncharted. The difference, however, is that he will have to shape it with each choice he makes. He will create his role in a continuous drama in which he stands at the center. Harry, on the other hand, has relinquished the direction of his individual will to assume his part in the *theatrum mundi* ("I shall have to learn. . . . I have not yet had the precise directions"). The furies, the chthonic powers, are merely in the foreground to lead him to despair and, transformed into "divine instruments," to lead him out of despair. Behind them, as becomes clear in his dialogues with Agatha, there is, however dimly apprehended, a providential power.

It is a sign of his "election" that he feels the necessity of rebelling against, and abandoning, the life which his mother has preserved at Wishwood. This is no mystery to the common-sense mind of his valet, Downing:

> I think I understand his Lordship better than anybody;
> And I have a kind of feeling that his Lordship won't need me
> Very long now. I can't give you any reasons.
> But to show you what I mean, though you'd hardly credit it,
> I've always said, whatever happened to his Lordship
> Was just a kind of preparation for something else.
> I've no gift of language, but I'm sure of what I mean:
> We most of us seem to live according to circumstance,
> But with people like him, there's something inside them
> That accounts for what happens to them. (Part II, scene 3)

But it becomes a problem for the modern playwright to dramatize this insight. The concept of election, or the operation of grace in the individual life, is tantamount to a deliverance *from* tragedy, as is the beneficence of the gods operating on a larger scale in *The Eumenides*. The subject of Eliot's and Sartre's dramas is the passing of the frontier into another world, into another order of reality. Both Orestes and Harry march right out of the domain of tragedy, expecting an ordeal which is adumbrated philosophically in one play and through religious imagery in the other. Both protagonists meet an old self and are prepared to shed it, and both playwrights are interested in such a transformation by means of a deed or a commitment which causes their heroes to shoulder a heavy burden but at the same time delivers them from the despair and destruction of tragedy. Tragedy itself is, so to speak, redeemed, as Karl Jaspers argues in *Tragedy is not enough* (1953). It becomes past and is made "the foundation of real life which is now no longer tragic." It is conquered by "the awareness of a larger context of fundamental reality."

Harry's exclamation, "You have not seen/ What I have seen," thus points beyond tragedy. One recalls Hamlet who, after seeing the Ghost, moves into the heart of tragedy by becoming inextricably involved in the murderous game of revenge. He is the anguished figure of the dispossessed prince (like Orestes) who begins to look himself like an apparition, "As if he had been loosed out of hell/ To speak of horrors" (II, i). Following the nunnery scene Ophelia is moved to exclaim "O, what a noble mind is here o'erthrown!/ . . . O, woe is me/ T'have seen what I have seen, see what I see!" (III, i). In the Renaissance tragedy, the Christian humanist assumption that man *is* free to act one way or another is lost in the reality of evil. "Our erected wit," says Sidney in the *Apologie*, "maketh us know what perfection is, and yet our infected will, keepeth us from reaching unto it." The modern Orestes figure, however, trails the furies behind him or, as here, follows the bright angels into a new life, transcending, if not removing, his anguish and thus learning how to *become* free.

It is a difficult subject for a dramatist. Given the recalcitrant mixture of the Orestes story, a modern setting, and a gradually revealed Christian premise, it is not surprising that there is too much mystification in *The Family Reunion* and a deliberately incantatory air of wisdom emanating from Harry and Agatha. It may have been refreshing to hear Eliot's subsequent judgment on his own play, that Harry makes the impression of being a prig and that Amy, who dies at Wishwood, is the more human and sympathetic character. But unless Eliot meant to deny the point of Harry's pilgrimage, it is hard to imagine how he could have otherwise so radically separated him from the complacent and yet frightened world of fugitives. Even Sartre's

Orestes, who leaves the stage like a public hero, cannot escape the mark of the prig in his simpler, and secular, rhetoric about the nature of freedom.

"A play is something which hurls people into an undertaking," said Sartre in "Beyond Bourgeois Theatre."[24] Contrary to the Aristotelian legacy of a theater of passion, which he describes as "a rapid disturbance between two moments of calm," he sees true theater as the staging of an action causing an irreversible change in the world and in oneself. It is always, in other words, a political act of engagement. Despite the gulf separating them, there is an analogy here between Sartre's defiant Orestes and Eliot's "elect" hero; both turn their back on a merely conservative ideology, in order to bring into being a new self and a new world.

4

Camus views the idea of the anti-bourgeois theater differently; not as an instrument of political change or as a model of redemption, but as a means of exploring the choices which life offers in extreme situations. Although he too thinks of action as a radical undertaking, he does not deliver man from its immediate tragic consequences. For him it would be a fabulous evasion of reality if the act of rebellion in the name of the human values did not initiate an unending battle. Thus, he remains within the realm of tragedy as he enacts the struggle for freedom which is, he says, "the only living religion in the century of tyrants and slaves" (Preface, 1957). This is best exemplified in his last original play, *The Just* (1949), which deals with a historical episode at the turn of the century.[25] Here he draws a distinction between rebellion and revolution that goes beyond the corresponding historical analysis in *The Rebel*. Camus, the polemicist, sees the Russian terrorists of 1905 as having resolved for one short moment of history the dilemma which has plagued man up to the present time: how to secure justice without degrading man in the process. But in the play, though his admiration for his fictional counterparts is undiminished, he assesses unflinchingly the tragic cost of their enterprise. His youthful hero, Kaliayev, and his friend, Dora, embody the tragic predicament of the rebel in human terms. The ideal of the rebel prevails over that of the revolutionary; nevertheless, it too exacts a loss of human qualities as it finds concrete expression.

The tragic dilemma of the true rebel is that he is caught between two rival claims, the love (and reverence) for life and the love of justice. In *State of Siege* (1948) the problem was simpler; the play was Camus's response to the wartime experience of absolute political terror. With the help of Jean-Louis Barrault's inventive staging, he had rendered the modern nihilism of a total organization of life and death in the beleaguered city. He was also one of the first to understand the role of the modern-day victim whose very existence in the logic of tyranny is ultimately unjustifiable. (Ionesco's *The Killer* and Miller's *Incident at Vichy*, as we have seen, share the same insight.) The ending is provisional, according to Camus's conviction that there is a deadlock between tyranny and freedom in our time. The Plague is lifted from the city because Diego teaches its men how to fight fear and to revolt. But the Plague goes elsewhere and will return when men become again fearful. The allegory of the city of Cadiz suggests a condition of continuous strife between the natural impulse to life and the inhuman rationale of a total "justice" which is total oppression—in short, state terrorism.

But when terrorism becomes the instrument of revolt, the threat of nihilism, the condoning of murder in the interest of justice, afflicts equally the cause of the oppressed. What both sides have lost sight of is the ultimate value which alone justifies the power play of politics—and that is man and the respect for human life. Against those, the bourgeois nihilists as well as the revolutionary nihilists of our time, who value the idea by which they justify themselves above human life, Camus erects "the purest image of rebellion," the Russian terrorists of 1905, and in particular the hero and heroine of his play. They demonstrate for the last time in our history, says Camus, that real rebellion is a creator of values. In doing so, making a "double sacrifice of their innocence and their life," they become in their momentary triumph over nihilism the tragic heroes par excellence of our time. But once past this unique historical episode, the twentieth century moves on toward the totalitarian revolutions of the left and the right, "unfaithful to man in having surrendered to history" (*The Rebel*, pp. 164, 172-174).

In his extended commentary in *The Rebel* Camus accepts the arithmetic of rebel justice. These "scrupulous assassins," as he calls them, have the insight to admit that murder in the cause of justice is both necessary and inexcusable, and they have the fortitude to admit that therefore they must offer their lives as justification for their acts of terrorism. "A life is paid for by another life, and from these two sacrifices springs the promise of a value" (p. 169). The idea appears first in the *Notebooks, 1942-1951*, but with a partial disclaimer: "The great purity of the terrorist of the Kaliayev type is that for him murder coincides with suicide. . . . A life is paid for by a life. The reasoning is false, but respectable. (A life taken is not worth a life given.) Today, murder by proxy. No one pays" (p. 156). A year later, in 1948, the idea reappears somewhat more schematically: "The limit of rebellious reasoning: to accept killing oneself in order to reject complicity with murder in general" (p. 205). And finally, in 1949: "Any murder to be justified must be balanced with love. For the terrorists the scaffold was the final proof of love" (p. 231). But in the drama of Kaliayev's assassination of the Grand Duke and his resolution to be hanged for the act, "rebellious reasoning" finds its emotional equivalent; it is supplanted by the young man's pain at having to become a murderer and the agonizing joy of feeling redeemed by his death on the scaffold. He, as the protagonist, and Dora, reflecting and articulating their suffering, work out the rationale of the just assassins slowly and painfully. They render for us the rebel destiny as lived experience with its basic contradiction: the risk of becoming dehumanized against the faith that their brand of justice is redemptive and compatible with their belief in the sanctity of human life.

"Can man alone create his own values? That is the

whole problem." The self-determined action and suffering of the men and women of 1905 is the answer which Camus now offers to the question. Their willingness to pay for each act of terrorism is a form of secular martyrdom, a witnessing or reaffirming of their belief in the value of life without hesitating to exact the high price of justice. The difference between the pragmatic logic of revolution and the tragic choice open to rebellion lies in the attitude toward the relation of end to means. It is a question of defining the limits of action.

> When the end is absolute, historically speaking, and when it is believed certain of realization, it is possible to go so far as to sacrifice others. When it is not, only oneself can be sacrificed, in the hazards of a struggle for the common dignity of man. Does the end justify the means? That is possible. But what will justify the end? To that question, which historical thought leaves pending, rebellion replies: the means. (*The Rebel*, p. 292)

It is here that the claims of justice and the value of each individual life come together and qualify one another. Camus sees the statement and the resolution of this central dilemma of our time in the drama of Kaliayev, who proves that "though the revolution is a necessary means, it is not a sufficient end. In this way he elevates man instead of degrading him" (*The Rebel*, p. 172).

Theoretically Kaliayev also solves Camus's second question. "Being in history while referring to values that go beyond history—is it possible, legitimate?" The answer lies again in the rebel's deliberate incurrence of guilt for the sake of justice and his justifying this end by paying with his own life.

> He who accepts death, to pay for a life with a life, no matter what his negations may be, affirms, by doing so, a value that surpasses him in his aspect of an individual in the historical sense. Kaliayev dedicates himself to history until death and, at the moment of dying, places himself above history. In a certain way, it is true, he prefers himself to history. But what should his preference be? Himself, whom he kills without hesitation, or the value he incarnates and makes immortal? The answer is not difficult to guess. Kaliayev and his comrades triumphed over nihilism.

"But," Camus is forced to say in the following section, "this triumph is short-lived: it coincides with death" (*The Rebel*, p. 173).

So much for the philosophical rationale of this historical episode and, by inference, of the action of *The Just*. Camus incorporates his arguments in the play, but beyond that he imaginatively captures the drama of an idea of rebellion which is born in the minds of a small band of youthful idealists and which is consummated in great agony. First, there is Kaliayev's struggle to accomplish the deed and then the necessity of defending it with his life, i.e. transforming it into a value transcending its immediate political significance. He must guard against the revolutionary nihilism which would degrade him by making him a dispensable instrument of murder for a cause allegedly larger than any single life. And on the other hand, in order to demonstrate the moral limits of action, he is forced to choose the commitment which destroys him. Camus points out that Kaliayev doubted to the end, but that this doubt did not prevent him from acting; hence he is "the purest image of rebellion" (*The Rebel*, p. 173). And insofar as the act embraces not only the assassination but also the giving up of his own life to define the limits of what man may do even for justice, he is at the same time the tragic image of rebellion.

"Ah! pity the just!"—the elect who may not partake of human joys, who have only a faint memory of summer, of human happiness and love. "We are not of this world, we are the just," says Dora as Kaliayev sets out on his mission. But the loss goes deeper as their semireligious devotion to an ideal of justice turns them into martyrs, living symbols of the brotherhood of men, however at the cost of suppressing their humanity. "What a horrible taste brotherhood sometimes has!" Kaliayev must harden his heart against the wife of the man he murdered. He must reject her suffering, though he understands it, and refuse her pardon so that he may recover his innocence on the scaffold and thus reaffirm the ideal. And his act of witness in turn causes Dora to seek the double sacrifice of her innocence and her life. She demands to throw the bomb the next time to repeat the testimonial act, to kill and then to be hanged herself "one cold night by the same rope." When she is reminded that the organization does not allow women to do the actual killing, she shrieks: "Am I a woman, now?" In a political "state of siege" life and love must yield in order to establish a morally acceptable idea of revolutionary justice. Paradoxically, she hopes to reconcile her immediate surrender to dehumanization and death with the ultimate value of "a community founded on love and justice" (*The Rebel*, p. 166).

In the course of the play the ideal is made actual, and in the process of enactment its significance is delimited and defined as Kaliayev, in a series of agons, wards off different temptations that would alter the nature of his act. In the first half of the play, the antagonist is the veteran revolutionary, Stepan, who places the revolutionary cause above all other considerations. He triggers the debate which will determine the theoretical justification of violence. Against Stepan's intransigent and destructive nihilism ("I do not love life, but justice which is something higher than life"), Kaliayev gradually formulates the only justification open to an ardent, yet humane person who loves life and has become a terrorist precisely because he loves life. He starts off naively enough with a textbook idealism which is almost frivolous in its simplicity, an amalgam of sincerity and inexperience. "For a whole year I've thought of nothing else. It's for this moment that I have been living and waiting. . . . To die for a cause, that's the only way of proving oneself worthy of it. That is the only justification." Theoretically, in his ruminations at night, the arithmetic of justice is much too easy. "One thought worries me: they have made murderers out of us. But then I think that I am going to die myself, and I calm down again. I smile, you know, and I go back to sleep like a child." But the actual is different from the imagined moment.

The wish that, God willing, hatred may so blind him that he will not have to look in his victim's face does not come true. The presence of the children in the Grand Duke's carriage causes the failure of his mission and necessitates a more serious formulation of the ethical limits of terrorist action. This time the positions are sharply polarized over the definition of the ends of the revolution in terms of the means. Contrary to the opinion of the critics who complained of the lengthy debates in the play, the conflict of ideas is drama of a high order; it produces before us an ideal of conduct tested and shaped by extremes of faith, and it does so concretely and passionately.

On the one hand we have the logical consequences of Stepan's single-minded faith in ultimate justice. "Once we can make up our mind to forget about children, only then, and not until then, will we be masters of the world and the revolution will triumph." In other words there are no limits to the sacrifices that may be demanded for the liberation of Russia and the whole world. Everything is justifiable for the ultimate good of mankind; for that certainty whole generations may have to forfeit their lives. Stepan's revolutionary absolutism is the mirror image of the tyranny of total justice in *State of Siege*; and Kaliayev recognizes it at once:

> KALIAYEV. I am ready to kill in order to overthrow despotism. But behind your words I can see the coming of another despotism, and if that should ever take over, it will make me into a murderer when I am trying to do justice.
>
> STEPAN. What does it matter that you don't feel you are just, as long as justice is being done—even by murderers. You and I, we don't count.

The priority of the abstract idea over the meaningful human act is typical of Stepan's position. It represents a form of nihilism embodied in the figure of Nada in *State of Siege* who easily exchanges the profitless freedom of scorn for the senseless, mechanical administration of total justice; they are the two sides of the same coin. "For us who don't believe in God," Stepan admits later on, "there must be total justice or utter despair."

Kaliayev, for his part, as he prepares for the second attempt on the Grand Duke's life, learns the desperate enterprise of trying to do justice in the world. But in opposing Stepan's incipient despotism, he must try to define the

difficult paradox of committing violence and yet retaining
one's innocence. The key is his love of life and sense
of honor—"the last thing of value left to the poor man."
These are the safeguards against the brutality of terrorism
which justifies itself as serving an ultimate end. "I will
not add to the living injustice for the sake of a dead justice.
. . . No! I have chosen to die so that murder shall not
triumph. I have chosen to be innocent." Camus underlines
the courage of Kaliayev's redefinition of himself as a just
assassin by adding the incident in which Voinov disinte-
grates, not out of fear of his own death, but because he
lacks the moral certainty necessary to take another's life
along with his own. By the time Kaliayev throws the bomb
in earnest, he understands that killing the Grand Duke and
giving his own life in return is a decision which demands
more than bravery and idealism. It springs from a conviction of tragic necessity predicated on the love of man, not
merely on the hatred of injustice. And it is for the sake of
that value that he must defend his deed against those who
would take it from him or cause him to renounce it.

The temptations to falter are subtle during the interval
between the assassination and the execution. Now the antagonist is the shrewd police chief, Skouratov, who means
to discredit the high idealism of brotherhood that fuses the
terrorists by a single motive into a possibly dangerous
revolutionary force. He plans the confrontation scene with
Foka, the imprisoned murderer. A poor victim of social injustice in Kaliayev's view, Foka turns out to be no brother
in the common struggle, but the appointed prison-
hangman, ready to accept a year of freedom for each hanging he performs. The irony does not escape Kaliayev that
the man who some day should have been the benefactor of
his personal act of sacrifice becomes instead his hangman
and indeed regards him as no different from himself, a
hired executioner. Skouratov represents the nihilism of the
state; nonetheless he has insight into the idealistic motive
of his prisoner, the precarious balance of guilt and defiant
innocence in Kaliayev's soul. He dwells on the physical
horror of the Grand Duke's death, but Kaliayev withstands
the attack and the shrewd offer of a pardon.

A far more difficult test awaits Kaliayev when the Grand Duchess enters his cell. Like Skouratov, she stresses the unjustifiable cost of his so-called act of justice, and, more insidiously than Skouratov, she offers her pardon as a value outside history, namely through Christian forgiveness. Their bond is that of suffering, the brotherhood of the murderer and the widow of the murdered. "The others don't understand. They look distressed. And they are, for an hour or two. Then they go off to eat and to sleep. Sleep especially . . . I thought that you must be more like me. You don't sleep, I am sure. And to whom can one speak about the crime if not to the murderer?" She threatens to confound Kaliayev's notion of justice and brotherly love by her presence as the suffering Christian soul, pointing to the *general* injustice in the world and the vileness of man, and seeking refuge in prayer, repentance, and divine forgiveness. If the whole world is empty and cruel, as she says, and the human condition such that the victim as well as the murderer and even the children whom he spared are all unjust, the only value that can sustain life must come from God and the idea of another, eternal, world. Kaliayev rejects this doctrinal assault on the ground that only he himself can judge his act and justify it by keeping faith with his brothers in death. It should be added that Camus, in *The Rebel*, rejects this kind of argument because thus slandering the world amounts to "ratifying historical injustice and the sufferings of man," which is only another form of nihilism (*The Rebel*, p. 249).

With his decision to die unrepentant, Kaliayev's torment comes to an end. He has won his struggle to retain the purity of his ideal. He has established the true limits of action, effacing the stigma of murder. But in a very real sense his act of justice is not brought to completion until his brothers in rebellion wish his death too. The scene of the fifth act shifts back to them in order to register the emotional response to Kaliayev's final moments in the enactment of his ideal. It is, of course, Dora who carries the pathos of the moment, torn between a yearning for love and the conviction that Kaliayev's way is the way of justice. His almost suppliant words to the Grand Duchess, "Let me die," are now echoed as Dora seeks to transcend her own personal agony: "Let him die! [*More softly*] But let him die quickly." Her decision is tragic because, in saying that his brothers must wish his death, she has chosen in favor of her understanding instead of yielding to her natural feelings, and she has done so knowingly in order to complete his sacrifice and to affirm it as an ideal to be emulated by others. She has put behind her the memory of faces and people, becoming in effect a devotee of death for the sake of life: We are "condemned to be greater than ourselves."

But there is an inherent ambiguity in the conclusion which Camus does not shirk. His admiration for this small group of idealists is unconcealed, yet he is honest enough as well as skillful enough as an artist to know that he should not underrate the human cost. Even as she waits for word of Kaliayev's execution, Dora probes the meaning of their act of justice. She is fully aware of the dehumanization attendant on the life of the terrorists; though they die bravely in the struggle, their activity devours their lives—they are no longer men. In the end, Camus shows her making the choice; she does not merely suffer, or submit to, this tragic necessity, but she commits herself to it with a furious and ecstatic dedication. Stepan's voice still fills her with fear that others may come who, mistaking their example, will kill and not pay with their lives. Now, however, as he narrates the details of Kaliayev's execution, her rising determination blots out all moral and political as well as purely human considerations: "Am I a woman, now?" It is an awful transformation we are witnessing as she demands to become the next agent-victim. Stepan yields his place to her: "She is like me, now" ("Elle me ressemble, maintenant"). Camus leaves the statement unchallenged and unexplained. The implication may be that Stepan now understands the high ideal of self-sacrifice; but it also means that she has cut herself off from all human feelings, as he had done, to become an instrument of the revolution. The ambiguity embracing these two contrary and yet complementary impulses defines the tragic role of the just assassin.

Camus in this play describes the contemporary and continuing tragedy of a political "state of siege," when injustice forces individual human beings who love life into that position of ambiguity. But he insists on the difference between his view and that of the existentialists who say "that there is progress in the transition from rebellion to revolution and that the rebel is nothing if he is not revolutionary." On the contrary, says Camus, it is a matter of unavoidable contradiction. "The revolutionary is simultaneously a rebel or he is not a revolutionary, but a policeman and a bureaucrat who turns against rebellion. But if he is a rebel, he ends by taking sides against the revolution. . . . Every revolutionary ends by becoming either an oppressor or a heretic" (*The Rebel*, p. 249). Again, the difference comes down to the question of values. Any political philosophy that limits itself to choices sanctioned by history alone is doomed to such fruitless alternatives. Taking a broader view, Camus remarks, "Atheist existentialism at least wishes to create a morality. This morality is still to be defined. But the real difficulty lies in creating it without reintroducing into historical existence a value foreign to history" (p. 249, n. 1).

These reflections shed light on certain points of common interest between *The Just* and Sartre's *Dirty Hands* (*Les Mains sales*, 1948). Both are political dramas and focus on a moral predicament of our time: namely, the necessity of sacrifice to create and authenticate purely human values. Both protagonists pay with their lives, in an act of free choice, in order to transform murder into a value that transcends the brutality in the one instance and its sheer senselessness in the other. In a world devoid of absolute values the search for justice entails a voluntary giving of the self, not simply in payment for the life taken, but to create such a value—irrationally, imprudently, disregarding the immediate political interest. Kaliayev, as we have seen, does so in order to establish a publicly shared meaning for his act of justice. The case is somewhat different with Hugo in Sartre's play. The struggle there is private and treated in terms of existentialist psychology. In his effort to shed his bourgeois character and become *engagé*, Hugo undertakes a job of political assassination for the party. But he cannot act except under a trivial pretext and at the wrong opportunity, and then almost playacting the scene. Hence the need to reconstruct the meaning of his act, unlike Sartre's earlier hero, Orestes, who kills *in order to* gain the burden of guilt and responsibility. Apart from Sartre's testing of the weaknesses of his modern protagonist, there is however in Hugo's second chance to make sense of his act the possibility of a free choice, and, like Camus's hero, he asserts his humanity and that of his victim in an irrational gesture of revolt. The sudden change of party policy leaves him with an act of murder done for the wrong reason. But instead of adapting himself to the needs of the party, serving a cause allegedly greater than the life of any single man, he declares himself (in the famous final phrase of the play) *non récupérable*, ready to face his own liquidation as a politically useless and dangerous person.

In the context of Sartre's thinking, Hugo's act of murder does not define him existentially until he understands that he has killed a man and not merely a party functionary who has outlived his usefulness and until he assumes full responsibility for the deed. Only by his last decision, made as a free agent, does he gain the moral initiative. Thereby he redeems his victim's name and the meaning of his life, at the cost of his own. But this conclusion points also in the direction of Camus's recognition of the tragic political dilemma of our time. In both plays it is based on the central debate as to whether the point of revolution is an abstract cause, a distant justice to be pursued by whatever means, or an ever-present regard for the worth of human life, namely that of each and every man. Kaliayev and Stepan debate the question as do Hugo and Hoederer in *Dirty Hands*; and Hugo learns the essential lesson from the man he is ordered to kill. Whereas Kaliayev understands his act and what sacrifice it involves, Hugo at first does not know why he acted or what it meant. But he too finds "a value foreign to history," as Camus puts it, and thereby creates a morality.

Camus's *The Just* raises a prior question: Is the search

for justice possible in a world devoid of absolute values, that is, without resorting to the fictitious claims of a philosophy of eternity or the uncertain and dangerous claims of a philosophy of history? The answer is a severely qualified Yes. Camus sets before us a brief historical episode, insisting on the tragic cost of even a momentary victory over injustice. He rejects out of hand the different forms of nihilism which offer solutions without regard for the worth of human life. But even the moment of triumph over nihilism is qualified by the preceding agony of guilt and the inhuman arithmetic that equates murder and suicide. It is the answer of a twentieth-century humanist, clear-sighted and skeptical, who shows us that, left to his own devices, modern man must act to create his own morality, but that in doing so he becomes inescapably a tragic figure.

NOTES

1. "In Russian *volia* means *both* will and freedom." Albert Camus, *Notebooks, 1942-1951*, trans. Justin O'Brien (New York: Knopf, 1965), p. 179. (The quoted phrase in the title of the chapter is Bernard Frechtman's translation in *Existentialism and Human Emotions* [New York: Philosophical Library, 1957], p. 23.)

2. *The Myth of Sisyphus and Other Essays*, trans. Justin O'Brien (New York: Knopf, 1961), p. 83.

3. Ibid., p. 123.

4. Ibid., p. 40.

5. "Existentialism is a Humanism," trans. Philip Mairet, in *Existentialism from Dostoevsky to Sartre*, ed. Walter Kaufmann (New York: Meridian Books, 1957), p. 310.

6. *The Myth of Sisyphus*, p. 122.

7. *The Rebel* (*L'Homme révolté*, 1951), trans. Anthony Bower (New York: Vintage Books, 1956), p. 21.

8. *Notebooks, 1942-1951*, pp. 136, 141, 152. See also *The Rebel*, p. 237: ". . . human nature, to date, has never been able to live by history alone and has always escaped from it by some means."

9. *Notebooks, 1942-1951*, pp. 159, 86, 109.

10. *The Stranger*, trans. Stuart Gilbert (New York: Vintage Books, 1954), p. 72.

11. *Caligula and Three Other Plays* (New York: Knopf, 1966), p. vii.

12. *The Myth of Sisyphus*, p. 6. ". . . Man feels an alien, a stranger. His exile is without remedy. . . ." "The Exile (or Budejovice)" was Camus's original title for the play.

13. *Le Malentendu/Caligula* (Paris: Gallimard, 1947). In the *Notebooks, 1942-1951*, pp. 31-32, Camus writes, "Look for details to strengthen

the symbolism"; fifteen years later, in the Preface to the American edition (1957) he tries to avoid a symbolic explanation of the manservant's role.

14.   Philip Thody, *Jean-Paul Sartre* (New York: Macmillan, 1960), p. 106.

15.   "Claudel. That greedy old man flinging himself at the Communion table to gobble up honors . . . Alas!" (p. 253) and again, "Claudel. Vulgar mind" (p. 258).

16.   Preface, *Caligula and Three Other Plays*, p. vi.

17.   In his preface to the German edition, *Dramen* (Stuttgart: Rowohlt Verlag, 1948), Sartre recalls that the play was intended to show his countrymen the way out of a defeatist and hopeless attitude toward the building of a future as free men.

18.   Jean-Paul Sartre, *Théâtre* (Paris: Gallimard, 1947).

19.   Sartre may have had in mind the propitiatory rites at the tomb of Agamemnon in *The Libation Bearers* and perhaps the tradition that Aegisthus was killed during the festival of the Death-goddess Hera. See Robert Graves, *The Greek Myths* (Penguin Books, 1955), II, 62.

20.   Sartre revealed in his interview with Professor Oreste Pucciani that he meant to write a play about French torture in Algeria, but decided on a German setting in order to get the play produced in Paris. *TDR*, 5 (March 1961), 13-14.

21.   *The Condemned of Altona*, trans. Sylvia and George Leeson (New York: Knopf, 1961).

22.   *TDR*, 5:16.

23.   Letter to E. Martin Browne, quoted in Matthiessen, *The Achievement of T. S. Eliot*, p. 167, and in Spanos, *The Christian Tradition in Modern British Verse Drama*, p. 209.

24.   In Robert W. Corrigan, ed. *Theater in the Twentieth Century* (New York: Grove, 1963), p. 137.

25.   *Les Justes* (Paris: Gallimard, 1950).

PART FOUR

Epilogue—The Devaluation of Life

9. *THE OUTMODED INDIVIDUAL*

The theaters of Sartre and Camus represent the last instance of a world view in which the life of the individual is regarded as a central value. Rejecting the idea that man is subject to time and circumstances conceived as fateful, a pawn in the play of external forces, they invested their heroes with the freedom to act and thus to gain a moral autonomy independent of any sanctions imposed from without. Even when the situation is depicted as hopeless, as in *No Exit* and *The Misunderstanding*, the freedom and the autonomy are forfeited only on account of misdirected choices or a failure of the will; there is never an outright denial that man can act in good faith. Common to both theaters, despite their differences, is the idea of a tragic humanism. It is an affirmation of the worth of human life even in the face of the absurd.

But once the center of attention shifts away from the human actor and fastens on the situation which renders him fearful, disoriented, helpless, his destiny as an individual ceases to matter. We begin to question man's mode of existence: the question then is not what happens to him or what does he do or suffer, but what is he? Reduced to a complex of mechanical reactions and feelings of fear or frustration, he becomes an object of derision even as he transmits the sense of helpless bewilderment to the audience. The farcical element in the postwar theater of Beckett, Ionesco, or Pinter is due to the reduction of the protagonist to the status of a not entirely predictable automaton. Depersonalization may give way to dehumanization, but even that becomes the occasion for a grim amusement accompanying the dreadful realization that the human being is entirely expendable. And in many instances, what is notably absent, as it cannot be in tragedy, is the sense of a loss of value.

307

As a matter of fact, in retrospect the postwar theater can no longer be called an experimental theater, in the sense that it has opened our eyes to things hitherto unperceived. It is not a beginning, but an ending. It ought rather to be viewed as the final phase of a process which has forced us to witness the various traditions of the modern drama being brought logically to their absurd conclusion. The disappearance of the individual from the center of the stage reflects the increasingly tenuous relationship between the individual and the world in which he lives, as well as the universe in which he must justify his reason for being. To the extent that in depicting this situation a loss of value is at least negatively implied, the playwrights still pay their respect to the tragic tradition which they are abandoning in response to the moral climate of their time. In a sense, we have come full circle from the disintegration of the individual in Büchner's tragedies. Hebbel, as we have seen, predicted the dissolution of tragedy into a hybrid form which alone could deal with man's desperate plight in a world devoid of any recognizable moral center, combining the effect of terror and absurdity at one and the same time (see chapter 1).

In the twentieth century, the traditional idea of a structure of human values based on man's "appropriation" of the natural universe for his own needs has come under attack from many quarters. To the scientist the separation of man from nature is a necessary assumption, if he is to be an unbiased observer. But for the modern artist such an estrangement has incalculable consequences. The fact that man is no longer "at home" in the universe and may have to abandon the comfortable fallacy of a moral relation between himself and nature is a revolutionary change, the unsettling effects of which we have been beginning to see and feel in this century. Among others, I. A. Richards directed our attention to the likely consequences for the future of poetry of what he called the *"Neutralisation of Nature,* the transference from the Magical View of the world to the scientific" (*Science and Poetry*, 1926). More recently, Alain Robbe-Grillet has attempted both in his novels and in his theory to draw the necessary conclusions for the artist of the systematic rejection of any kind of anthropomorphism or false humanization of the objects of the world around us. In his essay, "Nature, Humanism, Tragedy" (in *Pour un nouveau roman*, 1963), he tries to show that Camus's conception of the absurd, far from being an endeavor to escape the "tragification" of the universe, is really a version of tragic humanism. The difference between these two writers is symptomatic of the process of depersonalization which marks, as well, the dominant change in the postwar theater. Camus countered the threat of an indifferent universe with the notion that man must, whatever the tragic cost, create his own, purely human, values. That affirmation of life through individual action strikes the postwar dramatists and Robbe-Grillet as an unwarranted, typically humanist rationalization of the state of man, an indulgence in the old persistent fictions with which we have been assuaging our anxiety in an alien universe.

Not only is tragedy, in this view, a relapse into an outdated world-picture; it must be positively avoided, considering the premise that the world cannot be appropriated and interpreted to suit our emotional needs. The epigraph to "Nature, Humanism, Tragedy," a passage from Roland Barthes, summarizes the new attitude:

> Tragedy is merely a means of "recovering" human misery, of subsuming and thereby justifying it in the form of a necessity, a wisdom, or a purification: to refuse this recuperation and to investigate the techniques of not treacherously succumbing to it (nothing is more insidious than tragedy) is today a necessary enterprise. (Trans. Richard Howard)

It is an attitude which indicates not so much a refusal to confront human misery, the object of tragedy, as the determination not to find comfort in a conventional ethical and aesthetic formulation. However, in thus dissolving the relation of man to the universe which defines the condition of his being, the writers of the postwar period have made it impossible for him to understand the nature of his plight, and in denying him the capability (that Camus insists on) to create his own, purely human, morality, they have robbed his life of any claim to value.

This turning away from the realm of individual tragedy toward the dramatization of the impersonal and incomprehensible experience of what it is like to be human can be, at least indirectly, accounted for by the grim events of the mid-twentieth century. While it was once possible to name the incarnations of evil (Satan or pelican daughters or the oppressive forces of society) and thus subsume them in the normative order on and off stage, now the real-life horrors lodged in the consciousness of the spectator derived from an evil that had become nameless, impersonal—banal (as Hannah Arendt called Eichmann's efficiency in transporting the victims to the death camps). Starting from this level of common awareness, the postwar playwright had to invent symbolic equivalents of such states of mind and feeling. Thus, without necessarily alluding directly to the events of his time, he pictured the disintegration of the human personality in other ways and made an inquest into the dissolution of all human values. In his prologue to a production of Brecht's *Baal* in 1926, Hofmannsthal had his actors engage in a good-natured controversy over the idea that the concept of the individual—"This prodigious offspring of the sixteenth century which the nineteenth has fattened to its present size"—was an anachronism of which the twentieth century must rid itself.[1] But what was, in the 1920s, still speculative and subject to debate, or appeared as a satiric parable in Brecht's *A Man's a Man* (*Mann ist Mann*), became a savage historical fact twenty years later when masses of human beings were systematically stripped of personality, reduced to numbers and units, in order to facilitate their extermination. "There are no persons any more, don't you see that?" says the Major in *Incident at Vichy*. "There will never be persons again. . . ." Miller deals with the historical fact. The theatrical metaphors of Beckett spell out in other ways the last steps of the depersonalization and eventual dehumanization of modern man.

1

Brecht is a transitional figure. Between the two world wars he conducted his own "transference from the Magical View of the world to the scientific" by developing the idea of a non-Aristotelian theater, one in which the laws of social change might be shown to be more important than our reaction to the inexorable course of a personal tragedy. Even so, Brecht's response to his time is ambivalent; hence the contradictory effect of such plays as *Life of Galileo* (produced in three versions, 1943, 1947, 1955) and *Mother Courage* (*Mutter Courage und ihre Kinder*, produced in 1941). He is aware of the ongoing process of depersonalization, (in Gerald Weales' phrase) of "the uncertain figure of the individual in a face-dissolving society, world, universe";[2] and in demonstrating again and again, sardonically, that man as man does not represent a value any longer, that he is easily changed and absorbed by the demands of the world around him, Brecht tries to turn us away from our interest in the fate of the individual. But he does not on that account deny the value of human life as such or fail to condemn man's inhumanity to man. Rather, as in his most nearly tragic plays, he is profoundly concerned with elucidating the false social values engendered by the false choices which human beings make.

Outside the plays he talks tough, accusing his protagonists, like a public prosecutor in the court of history, of far-reaching crimes. Mother Courage follows the war for profit. She pays the price; but though, by the end, she has lost her children, one by one, and most of her possessions, she has still learned nothing. Thus the institution of war perpetuates itself. Galileo commits the "original sin" of all modern science by making science "pure" of social significance and becoming indifferent to the social implications of his work. By 1947 Brecht can say that "the atom bomb both as a technical and a social phenomenon is the classic end product of his scientific achievement and his social failing."[3] Yet Courage in particular, but also Galileo, appears tragic to audiences and readers—contrary to Brecht's theoretic intentions—because what comes through strongly is the view that the individual destiny constitutes still a paramount value. It does so for itself; that is to say, a life defeated or destroyed (Courage's vitality, Galileo's appetite for free and useful inquiry), despite the broad didactic intent, is felt as a tragic loss. Moreover, in its wake it also leaves the wreckage of a potentially better world, which is a universal loss. Seen in this fashion, is the general effect upon an audience really different from that of traditional tragedy?

Actually, it may be idle to prolong the debate as to whether Brecht did or did not produce something resembling tragic drama in spite of his intentions. The fact is that he thought the twentieth century needed a different kind of drama, one whose primary purpose would be to expose at last the character of human society and to show that it can be changed. "In an age whose science knows how to change nature to such an extent that the world appears to have become almost inhabitable," he writes in 1955, "man cannot much longer be described to other men as a victim, as an object of an unknown but fixed environment. From the vantage point of a ball being tossed about, the laws of motion are hardly conceivable."[4] He admits that the epic, non-Aristotelian, dramatic style may not be the only one appropriate to this purpose; but one thing has become clear: today's world can be described accurately to a modern-day audience only if it is shown to be capable of change. Thus Brecht agrees with Walter Benjamin's remark, though it may be an oversimplification, that the "hero" of the play is not Galileo, but the people. He hopes that he has shown how the society extorts from its individual members what it needs from them. Under the circumstances it is hardly a question of entirely praising or entirely condemning Galileo's conduct in the play.[5] The end, after all, is not to suffer the destruction of the individual but to show clearly the mistaken choices of men in the crucial moments when the laws of social life stand revealed. Such a drama consists, then, of a series of transitory, i.e., not at all inevitable, tragic paradoxes, dilemmas, demonstrating how the world goes and that it need not be that way. The protagonist does not engage our feelings nor our attention exclusively on account of his personal fate. He is, nonetheless, a commanding figure and, in what he does and suffers, he is a powerful dramatic means of directing our attention to a social tragedy in its full historic perspective.

Brecht's new conception of theater, as he makes amply clear in the lecture of 1939-1940 entitled "On Experimental Theatre," is actually an extension of the modern social drama, but at the same time a revolt against the techniques of nineteenth-century realism, which had become a conventional means of hypnotizing the audience. How, he asks, can the theater be turned "from a place of illusions to a place of experiences?" How can the theater help the man of this century to understand and master the world he lives in? Once again art must be assimilated to the new knowledge we have gained, but this time, unlike the naturalists, the artist must make "models of how men live together that would enable the spectator to understand his social environment and both rationally and emotionally to master it."[6] But does not such an aim cancel the possibility of any tragic effect? If the fate of the hero is not determined by unalterable conditions (his individual character on the one hand and on the other, the given social structure or a universally accepted moral law), how can a spectator be made to feel the tragic hopelessness of an irremediable situation? In the non-Aristotelian theater, answers Brecht's spokesman in a brief discussion of the tragic effect, he cannot and should not. That is not to say, however, that no tragic effect is possible. To create such an effect is not the particular interest of Brecht's dramaturgy. But if it arises incidentally, though the focus is on the historicity, the temporary and therefore changeable social basis, of the situation, a tragic effect is admissible.[7] It would be false to equate Brecht's insistence that the social basis of men's lives is alterable with a facile optimism. There is no indifference to human misery, and though the dramatic representation makes it clear that the protagonist had an alternative course of action open to him (as is the case with

Galileo and Mother Courage), the choice that is actually made, considering its consequences, can surely affect the spectator tragically.

Brecht's comments, over the years, about the case of Galileo demonstrate the shift in emphasis. In 1939 we get a downright laconic statement. The "Life of Galileo" is no tragedy. "The play shows the beginning of a new age and attempts to revise a few preconceived ideas about the beginning of a new age." The reference is, of course, to the rise of modern science. But during his work on the California version of the play (in collaboration with Charles Laughton) the atomic age "made its debut in Hiroshima," and overnight the biography of the founder of the new physics appeared in a different light. "The object of the research scientist is 'pure' research; the product of his research is less pure." In Brecht's subsequent remarks the fourteenth scene (scene 13 in the California version) is lifted into prominence, particularly Galileo's self-condemnation. He "proves" to Andrea "analytically" that the most valuable work can never outweigh the harm done by his betrayal of humanity. In the first version his recantation in the face of the pressure applied by the Church enables him to finish the *Discorsi* and smuggle the work out of the country, a cunning victory over the forces of reaction. By contrast, in the California version Galileo interrupts Andrea's praise of him to prove that the recantation was a crime not redeemed by the importance of his book. In effect, Galileo enriched the sciences of astronomy and physics while, at the same time, he deprived them of the greater part of their social significance. Instead of discrediting the reactionary power of the Church and inaugurating an age of reason, his capitulation resulted in a separation of scientific progress from the needs of the people. "In the end he pursues his scientific studies like a vice, furtively and probably with a bad conscience."[8]

Although Brecht specifies that he would not wish Galileo's self-castigation to arouse an audience's sympathy, such a full awareness that a lifetime of extraordinary promise ended in personal failure is nothing less than a tragic recognition on the part of the old, half-blind genius held in captivity by the feudal authorities. Beyond that, the play displays a new, and public, mode of tragic awareness. Like the Greek drama, it stresses the stake that the community of men has in the agon between the individual discovering new facts that alter men's understanding of their world and the established interests of the power structure. Only, for the modern audience the significance of the conflict depends on as yet incalculable historical events. For the moment, in view of the direction of the scientific enterprise, once the chance was missed to make its discoveries beneficial to life in society, the play points in the direction of tragedy. Galileo is a martyr manqué. His mission, his original vision, has failed. He is, in Brecht's view, the fountainhead of the scientific and technological sweep over modern life, the new "church" in possession of the "truth," but still cut loose from any sense of social responsibility. Historically, then, modern science is "the legitimate daughter of the Church"; it has emancipated itself and has turned against its mother. In fact, it has taken her place. Therefore, in the original conflict between the seventeenth-century intellectual and the establishment, Brecht was not interested in any of the religious issues involved. The dignitaries of the Church are to be played merely like men in power, like our bankers and senators, in clerical costume.[9]

This is a new form of open-ended historical-social drama. It is different from the realistic historical tragedy, described in chapter 3, because Brecht sees historical incidents as unique, transitory events associated with particular periods which may be overtaken by the subsequent course of history and are therefore subject to criticism from the point of view of the immediately following period.[10] This "historicization" (*Historisierung*) makes it impossible to consider a tragic dialectic between the individual and the institution, as in the case of Saint Joan, ending in an inevitable catastrophe. For Brecht such incidents are merely models of behavior from which one can learn in order to change the situation. Shaw's comic epilogue "historicizes" the event, too; but Brecht makes the historical

perspective a part of his dramaturgy throughout the play.
Galileo is open to criticism from each generation, because
fresh historical circumstances demand newly formed attitudes. Right now, the consequences of his act make his
choice tragic as well as enlightening in its issue. The point
is that there is no inherent "tragic" split in his nature. He
acted according to his natural inclinations, which combined
an unquenchable, instinctive thirst for new knowledge
("no less voluptuous or dictatorial than the instinct for
procreation") with an entirely human desire for pleasure
and well-being. It is the consequent events which determine the moral quality of his act. The objection that
Brecht misconstrues history, that he overestimates the
significance of Galileo's decision, may be just; but it is not
quite to the point. His many polemical remarks to the contrary, Brecht is first and foremost an artist whose business
is playing, and that is still to show "the very age and body
of the time his form and pressure." To that end he may,
quite legitimately, make history fictitious and then, to
drive home his point, alienate the sympathies of the spectators by "historicizing" his fiction, i.e., causing them to
assess Galileo's act and his awareness of what is at stake
from the vantage point of the atomic age.

Two short essays on the epic theater clarify Brecht's
attitude toward the role of the individual in the process of
historical development. The new dramaturgy must take
cognizance of the fact that the individual has become a
more indeterminate phenomenon, whereas the social mass
moves according to laws of causal necessity. For the dramatist, predictions with respect to the individual are becoming less certain. At any rate, his interest lies in the movements of society as a whole; here he hopes to be able to
make predictions of a satisfactory sort. Not that a law of
causality is no longer applicable to the individual. Only,
"in certain situations we must expect more than a single
answer, reaction, or mode of behavior; we must expect a
Yes *and* a No. Both sides must to some extent appear to
have an adequate basis and motive. The attention of the
spectator, his interest in causality, must be focused on the
movements of masses of individuals according to law."[11]

It follows that Brecht's "dramaturgy applies to the single spectator only insofar as he is a member of society. It demonstrates that the way men live together depends on the society as a whole." The "great individual" has not disappeared from reality or from literature. But he has lost his independence. The roles have switched. As the single man has become more indeterminate and dependent, which was formerly the condition of the mass of the people, so now the society has become more autonomous, less dependent on the individual.[12]

Galileo's role is that of the great man, who, in Brecht's imagination, *might* have ushered in a new age of reason, while Mother Courage belongs to the mass of the common people. Both are shown as exercising the individual's prerogative of choosing between alternative courses of action. Yet both, in the end, must yield their independence before the inescapable law of causality. In both instances our interest in the individual's fate should theoretically shift in the direction of the condition of the society as a whole. Galileo's final self-incrimination points the way. But Mother Courage proves to be a more troublesome case to Brecht the theorist.

So pronounced is her misfortune that she engages the audience's sympathy even in the later amended versions, where Brecht's efforts at historicizing prove only partially successful. A series of notes and changes in the text, from the première in Zürich in 1941 to the performance in Göttingen in 1956, the year of his death, attest to Brecht's frustration at the persistent "misunderstanding" of his play. Referring to the original production in the Züricher Schauspielhaus, he complained that even in the middle of the second world war the bourgeois press could speak of a "Niobe tragedy" and "the truly moving vitality of the maternal animal."[13] Apparently the production left the impression of a "picture of war as a natural disaster, an unavoidable blow of fate," and "Courage's business activity, her keenness to get her cut, her willingness to take risks, as a 'perfectly natural', 'eternally human' way of behaving, so that she was left without any alternative." The opening scene must have failed to make the crucial point that Courage had traveled far in her cart to follow the war, that her participation in the war was "voluntary" and "active." The audience fell back upon the ordinary stock responses: "Courage as the representative of the 'little people' who get 'caught up' in the war because 'there's nothing they can do about it', they are 'powerless in the hands of fate', etc."[14]

Brecht made changes in order to prevent the petty-bourgeois audience from identifying too closely with the petty-bourgeois Courage. For example, in the Zürich production Courage demonstrates her humanity, tearing shirts from her stock of merchandise into strips to bandage the wounded, though at the same time she gives vent to her outraged feelings as a businesswoman. In the Berlin production of 1949, Brecht practically removes the conflict of feelings, creating an almost repugnant scene. Courage blocks the entrance to the canteen, refusing to give up her merchandise, so that Kattrin threatens her with a wooden plank and the Chaplain lifts her bodily off the steps to get at the linen shirts. The most pointed alteration came after the Munich production of 1950 when Brecht added a line to the last scene, as Courage in the midst of total devastation yokes herself to her cart: "I must start up my business again." She believes in the war until the very end, says Brecht in a political note, historicizing the event. She does not even understand that it takes a large pair of scissors to get one's cut from the war. The spectators expect wrongly that the sufferer would learn from his misfortunes. "As long as the common mass is the *object* of politics, it cannot regard what happens to it as an experiment, but only as its fate; it learns as little from a catastrophe as the guinea pig learns about biology." Hence the playwright is not obliged to make his protagonist see clearly at the end; he wants to make the spectators see.[15]

"Misfortune alone is a bad teacher"—the apothegm points in two directions. Courage herself has learned nothing, which is the bitter lesson of the play. As for the German audiences in 1949 and the following years, they did not see the crimes of Mother Courage, her active participation, her profiteering; they saw only her failure, her suffering. And that is the way they looked at Hitler's war in which they had taken an active part. It was a bad war, and now they suffered. In his final note, for the production in Göttingen in 1956, Brecht once more points the lesson, this time in relation to the "economic miracle" of the mid-1950s. Now it is especially important to play Courage as the businesswoman who wants to get her share from the war. She mistakes her business mentality for the mentality of motherhood, but it destroys her children, one after another.[16] On each occasion, Brecht relentlessly underlines the continuing social tragedy that as Courage has learned nothing, so the audiences trying to escape his condemnation have learned nothing, for their part. If we took his comments to heart, presumably an anti-war audience, enraged by Mother Courage's behavior, may some day see the play for what it was meant to be: a monumental *Lehrstück*.

But it is not that. One may see *The Good Woman of Setzuan* (*Der gute Mensch von Sezuan*) as an example of a mature play in which the central paradox clearly demonstrates Brecht's moral judgment. Callousness and goodness are the two sides of the same coin. The good deeds of Shen Te are made possible only through the callous deeds of Shui Ta—"a devastating testimony," says Brecht, "of the unfortunate state of this world."[17] The paradox remains deliberately unresolved, leaving us with something more than regret that the generous impulses of a genuinely good human being must come to nothing. The ending is sardonic as well as tragic as the impotent, self-satisfied gods withdraw from a world of moral desolation. *Mother Courage*, lacking the quality of a clear-cut parable, presents a more complicated case. Here, despite Brecht's alterations and his numerous notes indicating the way he wants the play to be understood, we are faced with built-in ambivalences, which reflect Brecht's own unresolved attitudes toward his protagonist.

First, as to the name of Mutter Courage. The denotative English equivalent *courage* is not enough. In the German

patois—for example as in the phrase, "Die hat eine Courage!"—the word carries the connotations of presumption,
gall, recklessness which strongly qualify the sense of heroic
courage. When she tells the sergeant at the opening of the
play how she got the name, driving her cart through an
artillery barrage because her fifty loaves of bread were beginning to spoil, Brecht's irony is obvious. Hers is the courage of desperation when she is faced with what she regards as intolerable alternatives. Under ordinary circumstances she opts for safety and survival, capitulation rather
than heroism. However, Brecht's dramatic imagination is
so vivid that we mistake his purpose. Because she is
shrewd, stubborn, businesslike and has a sense of humor,
the audience quickly focuses attention on these attributes
in the conventional way of sympathetic identification. She
is one of "us" trying to survive in a dangerous world. But,
as in *Galileo*, Brecht wants at the same time to subordinate
character to the unfolding of an idea: "That in wars little
people have no part in big business. That war, which is a
continuation of business by other means, makes the human
virtues fatal, even for those who possess them. That no
sacrifice is too great to do away with war."[18] Brecht might
have easily made an exemplum out of the story of Mother
Courage by showing her merely as the "hyena of the battle
field" (as the Chaplain calls her in scene 8), criminally living off the war, afraid of peace, destroying her children one
by one. But he does not want to go that far.

The fullness of her stage life as a character makes it
impossible to view her actions as "demonstrations" of social situations where the alternatives are clearly visible to
the jury-audience. And Brecht appears to acquiesce in the
resultant ambivalence. In the beginning she follows the
war, coming all the way from Bavaria, for profit. But as
the war spreads everywhere—in the wake of the armies she
has twice traversed Bavaria—the choice of participating or
withdrawing has been eliminated; she is faced with the
problem of sheer survival. The illusion that doing business
she can beat the war has brought her face to face with the
reality of doing business in order to survive the war. Even-

tually the cart symbolizes her life line in a sea of devastation, as well as the weight which pulls her down to destruction. Her pragmatic ethic, which Brecht condemns, becomes her only means of self-preservation. Thus, more so than Galileo, Courage still stands at the center as a tragic individual. Her suffering does not displace, but rather broadens the narrow lesson that one cannot live off war without paying in return. Brecht may have admitted as much when he wrote: "Experience shows that many actresses playing Courage find it easier and more congenial to play this final scene simply for its tragedy. This is no service to the playwright. He doesn't want to detract from the tragedy, but there is something that he wants to add: the warning that Courage has learnt *nothing*."[19]

Helene Weigel may have been able to play Courage "hard and angry"; i.e., the *actress* was angry while representing a tough and cunning tradeswoman, who loses her children to the war and yet keeps on believing in the profits that can be made out of the war. But as the play stands, it leaves our feelings and our understanding divided. Despite his politically motivated remarks on the occasion of the several productions since 1941, Brecht may well have *intended* to catch his audiences in a dilemma. Commenting on the powerful scene in which the dumb Kattrin sits on the roof, beating the drum to alarm the neighboring town until she is shot down, he makes the parenthetical remark: "Those who have compassion for the many, must not have any for the few."[20] Kattrin weighs the danger to the intimidated, timeserving farmer and his family and to the threatened destruction of the canteen against the welfare of the sleeping townspeople. She looks down unmoved and continues to beat the drum. Brecht's remark characteristically directs our attention and our feelings toward the mass of people rather than the individual. Applied to the play as a whole, it would point to the social tragedy that men do not learn anything from the catastrophe of war. Courage's individual suffering may move us, but it must also anger us if we have any compassion for the many. That is the way Helene Weigel played the part, demonstrating that Courage has learned nothing and hoping that the audience has learned something by observing her.

Brecht's own compassion for the many rules out the exclusive concern with an individual fate and the traditional dramatic devices that ensure an audience's hypnotic reaction to a personal tragedy. But though the interest in the historical situation is supposed to supervene, he places man still in a central position. The actor's choices have far-reaching human consequences; however, we are invited to judge his actions with respect to the general welfare rather than simply his own. There is a measure of depersonalization, at least in intention, in that man is to be shown as "a variable function of the milieu and the milieu as a variable function of man."[21] Yet Brecht holds firmly to the view that man as social being is of supreme concern and that the drama ought to be an instrument for understanding and improving his existence in this world.

2

If, according to Brecht, our concern over the individual must yield to our compassion for the many, that social consciousness disappears now altogether, and in its place arises a dispiriting theatrical metaphor to account for the condition of man: he becomes an involuntary player forced into the role of a victim, justifiably fearful, paranoiac, hunted down to his death or his simple disappearance in a script not of his own devising. In the different forms of postwar theater which have as their common point of origin Beckett's *Waiting for Godot*, man has lost his importance as an individual as well as a social being. At this point in the discussion, two plays in particular, both composed in the spirit of parody—where tragic action is purposely trivialized and burlesqued—may serve us as models to illustrate the general trend: the questioning of the significance of an individual's life as a central value, and its correlative, the playwright's felt need to shy away from, or as in this instance, to invert, the conventional presuppositions of tragedy about the nature of man.

Dürrenmatt describes *The Visit of the Old Lady (Der Besuch der alten Dame*, 1956) as a tragic comedy, more precisely as a comedy which ends tragically. But neither term is used in the traditional sense. Humor and wit, which we associate with comedy, have been replaced by the grotesque; whereas terror and pity have been turned into horror and contempt. What happens to Ill is a bitter travesty of the ancient scapegoat motif. As in the Greek tragedy, the community has indeed a stake in the fate of the hero. But the idea has been perverted, reducing his life to a commodity which can be sold for the common weal. Dürrenmatt's parody extends even to his notes to the play. He is aware of the implicit (and he makes a few explicit) allusions to the life of the polis and our archetypal reactions to guilt, revenge, and expiation. Yet, to gain his desired effect, he recommends a humane, sorrowful, even humorous reading of an admittedly vicious "comedy"; in short, the descent to the level of the inhuman should be made comprehensible as the result of mere human weakness. Even Ill's own family "is not evil, only weak like all the rest."[22] Traditionally, such weakness in the face of temptation has always been a major tragic motif. Dürrenmatt insists, however, that the twentieth century can no longer respond to the clear assumption of tragedy that man has a sense of responsibility and personal guilt.[23]

He allows the victim, Ill, a measure of understanding of his guilt in order to deprive him ultimately of his instinct of self-preservation. But the evil of the hunters, Claire Zachanassian who demands revenge in the name of justice, and the townspeople who cannot resist the temptation of a billion in bounty, is partially disguised by Dürrenmatt's fantastic theatrical inventiveness. He is able to exhibit the gradual deterioration of the community's superficial moral sense as a behavior pattern not really unexpected in ordinary people. One gets the impression that there is something natural, almost self-evident, in their dwindling resistance. Although he concedes that Claire Zachanassian dwells outside the human order, like an unchangeable, heathen idol turning to stone, he tries to naturalize that image of a merciless goddess of fate by grant-

ing her a kind of vicious charm and even "humor"; she is
remote toward other men, as well as herself, being well
able to purchase them like merchandise ("Anmerkung
zum 'Besuch'," p. 182). Actually her appearance, the arti-
ficial limb and the manikins that constitute her entourage,
is the outward physiognomy of a dehumanized character.
What Dürrenmatt is pleased to call humor and comedy is
really the essence of the grotesque: we recognize the monstrous though it is hidden under a cover of near-ludicrous
absurdity.

The implication of this strategy is that the modern mass
audience has become immune to the effects of tragedy, its
formal rehearsal of the most painful experiences of the
community, but that it can be trapped into witnessing even
the most outrageous spectacle of human behavior by means
of comic distortion or a parody of the tragic. The grotesque,
says Dürrenmatt in his "Note on Comedy," is an extreme
form of stylization which enables the writer artificially to
create distance toward the problems of his own time. "I
could therefore imagine a horrible grotesque of the second
world war, but *not yet* a tragedy since we cannot yet have
the necessary distance for it."[24] And in his best-known essay, "Problems of the Theater," he argues that to mirror
such a world is to depict, not tragic heroes, but an enormous disaster which is all but senseless. In the complex
structure of the modern state, one can see the victim, but
the powers that set the tragic events in motion are anony-
mous, impenetrable. "Creon's secretaries take charge and
settle the case of Antigone" ("Theaterprobleme," pp. 119-
120). Under these circumstances, the playwright resorts
to parody and the grotesque to give palpable shape to the
things that have lost their name and shape. For Dürrenmatt, "Ill's death is at once meaningful and meaningless.
It would be alone meaningful in the mythical realm of an
ancient polis, but the story happens to take place in Güllen.
At the present time" ("Anmerkung zum 'Besuch'," p. 182).
That is to say, it derives its meaning at the present time by
virtue of the parodist's allusion to the ancient hero as
scapegoat, which only points up the mockery of Ill's

ritual death, since it brings to the community neither a re-
dressing of the balance of justice nor a removal of the taint
of crime. It does bring wealth and material well-being. In
this sense the grotesque mimicry of the ancient sacrifice,
followed by the caricature of a Greek tragic chorus of
thanksgiving, renders the story both meaningful and meaningless.

The shock effect of Dürrenmatt's tragic comedy is great.
Like Brecht, he does not deny the experience of the tragic
moment, when we share the desperation and the terror of
the victim, though pure tragedy as a genre is to him no
longer possible. Rather the tragic experience may arise out
of comedy which, he thinks, is the only feasible approach
to the modern world ("Theaterprobleme," pp. 122-123).
He gives a similar rationale of his recent (and in my judgment, supererogatory) adaptation of Strindberg's *Dance
of Death:* "A bourgeois domestic tragedy has been turned
into a comedy about bourgeois domestic tragedies: 'Play
Strindberg'."[25] In other words, a tragic action becomes the
object of a comic play. That is one link between the two
plays which I have chosen as models of a growing skeptical attitude toward the significance of the individual's fate
in the modern world. In both instances, *The Visit* and
Rosencrantz & Guildenstern Are Dead, there is an allusion
to a monumental tragic act from an essentially comic perspective. As soon as man is conceived of as expendable, he
becomes a pathetic or a farcical figure, and the devaluation of life brings with it a flight from tragedy.

Another link between the two plays has to do with the
theatrical metaphor which is operative in *The Visit,* but
less pronounced than in *Rosencrantz & Guildenstern.* The
idea of the world as a stage upon which men play their
parts has its sources in pagan antiquity and the Christian
Middle Ages; and as we have seen, the idea of God
watching the human players as they fulfill their fate, the
Christian use of *theatrum mundi,* has been revived in the
modern theater by Hofmannsthal and Claudel.[26] Tragic
heroes like Richard II and Hamlet define themselves at
critical moments in terms of the difference between acting

and playacting, making use of the theatrical metaphor in a secular sense as well. But the situation in the two plays under consideration is different. The protagonists are also transformed into players. They are, however, marked for destruction in a scenario which unfolds around them step by step, while no one is watching except the audience, which knows the "reality" of their fate.

Dürrenmatt compares Claire Zachanassian to a cruel heroine of Greek tragedy, Medea perhaps; but evidently her role transcends the human power of exacting vengeance. She creates a grotesque version of *theatrum mundi*, sitting on her hotel balcony overlooking the stage and waiting for the temptation to take its effect on the human agents below. Replacing the God of the sacred drama, she impersonates Nemesis setting in motion her own scenario and observing how the players assume their expected roles. Ill's life takes on the character of a stage existence as he wanders through a changing mise en scène; it becomes the obstacle to a satisfactory dramatic resolution of Claire Zachanassian's plot. And finally when his life is snuffed out, Güllen celebrates its good fortune and the goddess of vengeance leaves her world-stage, ceremoniously taking the coffin with her like a piece of captured stage property. Ill, as actor and victim in the virtually predictable plot, knows and fears the outcome, yet gradually he is resigned to the ending of a senseless life. The suspense here is greater than that afforded by surprise; it is the suspense of a dreaded expectation to be fulfilled.

Symbolizing man's helpless existence, the play-metaphor generates the whole design and the language of *Rosencrantz & Guildenstern*. Stoppard takes two instantly recognizable yet almost proverbially minor fictional characters and places them on a stage, intimating at the outset that they represent two Elizabethan gentlemen. They act and speak at first as if they were figures imitated from real life. He permits them, according to dramatic convention, to assume that they are men of flesh and blood, situated in an as yet unspecified context. As the play progresses, they discover, however, that they are indeed fictional characters, who possess only a stage-life which simply ceases when their play-destiny overtakes them. The audience, on the other hand, soon observes that Rosencrantz and Guildenstern are located at any given moment, not in their own coherent world of space and time, but always with reference to the world of *Hamlet*. Although in Stoppard's theater they are stage center, we know that they are borrowed actors from a play being produced in an adjacent theater. Being neither imitated nor freshly invented, they are characters who have no claim to an independent fictional existence as protagonists or antagonists in a story of their own. They simply enact their involuntary roles at the edge of a more important play—but still a play.

Put simply, they represent the disoriented life of ordinary men. Nothing of importance really happens to them; yet they "get caught up" in a scheme they do not understand and find themselves at last on a boat, apparently free to move about but being taken ineluctably in a given direction. "We've travelled too far, and our momentum has taken over; we move idly towards eternity, without possibility of reprieve or hope of explanation" (Act III).[27] Still, the fatalism does not seem altogether threatening to us, partly because their incessant clowning dissolves each moment of rising panic in laughter, and chiefly because the pervasive comic irony mitigates the feeling of fear. Like *The Visit* but for other reasons, this story is at once meaningful and meaningless, threatening and harmless. On the one hand, we recognize our own uncertainties, the failure of the reassuring laws of probability, our inability to pluck out the heart of the mystery; we all are "born with an intuition of mortality. . . . there's only one direction, and time is its only measure" (Act II)—that is the human condition. On the other hand, we look with amusement, perhaps condescension, i.e. from a safe distance, upon two blundering figures on the stage, and we are privy to what is a mystery to them, namely what roles they must play and what their fate will be. We know they are "only" players, originally figments of Shakespeare's imagination. But what if Stoppard is right? what if that is the tragicomic condition of man?

The audience is always involved in the play-metaphor,

although it would dearly wish to evade it. Instinctively, we sympathize with Rosencrantz & Guildenstern's claim that they are "entitled to some direction," to an identity of their own. But the professional Player is there to disabuse them, and by extension the audience, of the commonplace assumption that they are people with a right to an independent existence. As an actor, he identifies life with make-believe action; the intervals are weariness and survival on the road. He is there to convert Rosencrantz and Guildenstern to the truth that they too are actors. The Player strikes a pose.

> GUIL: Well . . . aren't you going to change into your costume?
> PLAYER: I never change out of it, sir.
> GUIL: Always in character.
> PLAYER: That's it.
>   *Pause.*
> GUIL: Aren't you going to—come *on*?
> PLAYER: I *am* on.
> GUIL: But if you *are* on, you can't *come* on. *Can* you?
> PLAYER: I *start* on. (Act I)

At this point Guildenstern does not yet suspect that the Player and his troupe of actors foreshadow his own destiny. Ever since the messenger had brought the summons to the court of Claudius, he had been prepared for direction, for a hint of the role he was to play. No wonder then at his outrage that these players, hardly "the abstract and brief chronicles of the time" but rather a group of obscene mountebanks and perverts, should spoil (or, worse still, presume to represent) the mysterious function he is supposed to fulfill. The Tragedians—"a comic pornographer and a rabble of prostitutes"—invite him not merely to watch their performance, but at a somewhat higher price to "get caught up in the action": a double entendre touching not only our two anti-heroes, but the audience as well.

"It is *written*," says the Player, as if engaged in a parody of *theatrum mundi*, and we enact the script. And despite Guildenstern's (and by implication, the audience's) protest against this melodramatic version of life and death, the disconcerting fact dawns on us that this may well be the most plausible description of how most of us play our parts. But the illusion of having choice and purpose is difficult to give up. Stoppard defines man, not as the object of imitated dramatic action, but as a player who enacts a script without knowing the synopsis, waiting for the outcome which is out of his control. Again, the Player instructs Guildenstern: "We're tragedians, you see. We follow directions—there is no *choice* involved. The bad end unhappily, the good unluckily. That is what tragedy means" (Act II). In his more desperate moments, Guildenstern begins to realize his flimsy hold on reality. "Give us this day our daily mask. . . . We've been caught up" (Act I). "Give us this day our daily cue. . . . We act on scraps of information . . . sifting half-remembered directions that we can hardly separate from instinct" (Act III). He is learning the truth of the Player's knowledge, that "uncertainty is the normal state," and that therefore an actor must always be ready to improvise.

It is a farcical situation, this bumbling discovery by Rosencrantz and Guildenstern that they are not able to fall back on their personality and character to save themselves, but that they have been caught up as actors in the intrigues of *Hamlet*. Nonetheless, the tragic overtones should be equally evident in a successful production. Behind the farce lurks the historical reality recorded in Miller's *Incident at Vichy*: "There are no persons any more. . . . There will never be persons again." Stoppard, however, contents himself with exploring the psychological consequences of the annihilation of personality. The relatively lighthearted realization of the theatrical metaphor at the hands of the Player and his Tragedians turns suddenly sour, the only time that his self-assurance is shaken. "You left us. . . . You don't understand the humiliation of it—to be tricked out of the single assumption which makes our existence viable—that somebody is *watching*. . . . We're actors. . . . We pledged our identities, secure in the conventions of our trade, that someone would be watching. And then, gradually, no one was. We were caught, high and dry." The degradation of being made ludicrous, like "demented chil-

dren mincing about in clothes that no one ever wore,
speaking as no man ever spoke, swearing love in wigs and
rhymed couplets, killing each other with wooden swords,
hollow protestations of faith hurled after empty promises
of vengeance," has a much more serious consequence:
the act of make-believe as such, without the consent and
faith of an audience, is emptied of meaning. And going
beyond that, the Player admits to an existential predicament: the unwatched actor does not exist. "Don't you
see?! We're *actors*—we're the opposite of people!" (Act II).
Rosencrantz and Guildenstern "recoil nonplussed," because with this pathetic exclamation he has made them
see the true nature of the play-metaphor.

At the end of the play, Rosencrantz and Guildenstern
vanish; they too cease to exist, though not for the lack of
an audience. They have performed their roles and are no
longer needed. Stoppard gives serious attention also to this
aspect of the play-metaphor. Their complete puzzlement as
to what is wanted of them leads to the following fatalistic
reasoning:

> GUIL: Wheels have been set in motion, and they have their own
> pace, to which we are . . . condemned. Each move is dic-
> tated by the previous one—that is the meaning of order. If we
> start being arbitrary it'll just be a shambles: at least, let us
> hope so. Because if we happened, just happened to dis-
> cover, or even suspect, that our spontaneity was part of their
> order, we'd know that we were lost. (Act II)

But no logic or tactic can solve their problem because being players they have no choice. Except once. Here Stoppard expands on the meager account of their journey to be
found in *Hamlet*. They read Claudius' letter entrusted to
them and discover that Hamlet has been condemned to
death. This is the only moment when Stoppard allows them
a glimpse of direction and purpose—and gives them a choice.
But they fail to take advantage of the only opportunity to
control the course of events.

Their dialogue is a classic exercise in prevarication. It
would be too much to say that they *choose* not to tell Hamlet of the contents of the letter; rather they *do not* choose

to interfere in what now seems to be a plausible chain of events in which they are deeply implicated. In Shakespeare's play they are marginal characters whose willingness, like that of Polonius, to meddle in great affairs seals their fate.

> HAMLET. Why, man, they did make love to this
>   employment!
> They are not near my conscience; their defeat
> Does by their own insinuation grow.
> 'Tis dangerous when the baser nature comes
> Between the pass and fell incensed points
> Of mighty opposites. (V, ii, 57-62)

Stoppard views the incident from the vantage point of two disoriented and frightened characters, who are now half convinced that they are players in a tragic charade and whose only concern is to escape unharmed. If they had been conceived as free agents, their failure to act at this point would be morally reprehensible. What Stoppard is saying is that the opportunity to act, the momentary sense of direction and identity, is an illusion. They are bound to participate in the still mysterious conclusion of the scenario. Hence the mockery of justice and logic—

> ROS: . . . We're his *friends.*
> GUIL: How do you know?
> ROS: From our young days brought up with him.
> GUIL: You've only got their word for it.
> ROS: But that's what we depend on.

—is only a wry comment on the irrelevance of moral obligations when a more basic existential question is at stake. Who are they to interfere with an unknown and threatening order of events which at last promises to draw toward its conclusion? Stripped of will and identity, man plays his role to the end and disappears from the scene.

> GUIL (*quietly*): Where we went wrong was getting on a boat. We can move, of course, change direction, rattle about, but our movement is contained within a larger one that carries us along as inexorably as the wind and current. . . .
> ROS: They had it in for us, didn't they? Right from the beginning. Who'd have thought that we were so important?

GUIL: But why? Was it all for this? Who are we that so much should converge on our little deaths? (*In anguish to the PLAYER:*) Who are *we?*
PLAYER: You are Rosencrantz and Guildenstern. That's enough. (Act III)

If the question lacks the authentic tone of anguish, it is because Stoppard's comic play-metaphor consigns it to insignificance before it is asked. Besides, we have heard earlier voices ask more desperate questions and answer them more desperately. "In the post-Pirandellian world of ambiguous relationship between person and rǫle," writes Ruby Cohn, "Beckett twists Descartes' 'I think, therefore I am' to 'I play, but am I?' "[28]

NOTES

1. *Das Theater des Neuen.* See Alfred Schwarz, "A Prologue to Brecht's *Baal,*" *TDR*, 6 (Sep 1961), 111-122.

2. "Brecht and the Drama of Ideas," *Ideas in the Drama*, ed. John Gassner (New York: Columbia University Press, 1964), p. 129.

3. "Preis oder Verdammung des Galilei?" *Gesammelte Werke* (Frankfurt am Main: Suhrkamp Verlag, 1967), XVII, 1109.

4. "Kann die heutige Welt durch Theater wiedergegeben werden?" Ibid., XVI, 930.

5. Ibid., XVII, 1109.

6. "Über experimentelles Theater," ibid., XV, 295, 305.

7. ["Dreigespräch über das Tragische,"] ibid., XV, 309-313.

8. Ibid., XVII, 1106, 1108-1110, 1112, 1129-1133.

9. Ibid., XVII, 1110-1112, 1125.

10. "Kurze Beschreibung einer neuen Technik der Schauspielkunst, die einen Verfremdungseffekt hervorbringt," ibid., XV, 347.

11. "Die Kausalität in nichtaristotelischer Dramatik," ibid., XV, 279-280.

12. "Grenzen der nichtaristotelischen Dramatik," ibid., XV, 282-283.

13. Ibid., IV, 1439.

14. From the "Couragemodell," in *Theaterarbeit* (1952), trans. John Willett, in *Brecht on Theatre* (New York: Hill and Wang, 1964), pp. 220-221. One wonders, however, how he could expect an audience (which he describes as consisting largely of German emigrants), though devoted to antifascist and pacifist principles, to respond to his antiwar sentiment in the middle of a total war fought against Nazi Germany.

15. *Gesammelte Werke*, IV, 1443; XVII, 1150.

16. Ibid., XVII, 1148, 1150.

17. Ibid., XVII, 1160.

18. Ibid., XVII, 1138.

19. *Theaterarbeit*, pp. 298-299, quoted in Willett, p. 221.

20. "Der Stein beginnt zu reden," *Gesammelte Werke*, XVII, 1140.

21. "Verfremdungseffekte in der chinesischen Schauspielkunst" (*Der Messingkauf, 1937-1951*), ibid., XVI, 628.

22. "Anmerkung zum 'Besuch der alten Dame'," *Theaterschriften und Reden*, ed. Elisabeth Brock-Sulzer (Zürich: Im Verlag der Arche, 1966), p. 183.

23. "Theaterprobleme," ibid., p. 122.

24. "Anmerkung zur Komödie," ibid., p. 136.

25. See Dürrenmatt's end note to *Play Strindberg: Totentanz nach August Strindberg* (Zürich: Verlag der Arche, 1969).

26. See chapter 7, p. 233, and note 12.

27. Tom Stoppard, *Rosencrantz & Guildenstern Are Dead* (New York: Grove, 1967).

28. *Currents in Contemporary Drama* (Bloomington: Indiana University Press, 1969), p. 232.

10. *CONDEMNED TO EXIST*

Although Rosencrantz and Guildenstern mirror the uncertainty, disorientation, and fear of the ordinary man caught up in an action beyond his understanding, the play bypasses the more radical questions touching on the nature of existence. In this respect it is mainly an entertaining spin-off from the world of Vladimir and Estragon; in that world the question, What is it like to *be*? is answered by an invitation to watch ourselves wait. There is no way of bringing Stoppard's dramatic metaphor to fruition except to descend to literalism, i.e. to turn off the spotlights and cause Rosencrantz and Guildenstern simply to vanish. It is a more serious business to express what Ionesco calls "the ontological void."[1] Unaccommodated man, Poor Tom himself, not Edgar in disguise, now makes his reappearance on the modern stage (he first appeared as Woyzeck), a figure in whom we can contemplate a reality distorted, diminished, and at last reduced to nothingness.

Contrary to Rosencrantz and Guildenstern, the maids of Jean Genet's play know exactly what roles to assume in their ritual "psychodrama" (Sartre's term). They play their game of impersonation to the hilt in order to give vent to their repressed feelings of hatred and adoration. In *The Maids* (*Les Bonnes*, 1948, 1954; first performed, 1946), moreover, the play-metaphor permits Claire and Solange to intensify their experience of degradation and their need for vengeance. By changing into Madame-Claire and Claire-Solange, they can act out their psychological tensions more frankly and brutally than their position allows. As long as their existence is completely defined as servants to Madame, they are nothing in themselves; that is to say, to the question, "Who are we?" there is no answer eman-

334

ating from or initiated by a sense of self. But the reality
they create through play and improvisation is, to begin
with, unsatisfactory because it is impermanent. Whenever
Madame returns, the game must be broken off. They can
achieve a true sense of being only by killing Madame, or,
failing that, killing one the other in a ritual murder-suicide
which links them in a fabricated, yet irreversibly fixed reality. "We'll be that eternal couple . . . of the criminal and
the saint.—We'll be saved. . ." (trans. Bernard Frechtman).

Claire and Solange are, then, not only the actors, but also
the authors and spectators of their tragic drama, rehearsing
the intolerable situation in order to master it. But though
their transformation fills them with ecstatic joy—not to
speak of the brutal pleasure of vengeance and masochistic
suffering—it is an empty triumph. In the final scene, they
skip the preliminary stages in order to proceed directly to
the climactic moment of the game. At that moment the
make-believe situation becomes a new reality for them in
which they celebrate their new identities: "We're alone in
the world. Nothing exists but the altar where one of the
two maids is about to immolate herself." They are released
and transfigured. "We are beautiful, joyous, drunk, and
free!" But the tragic fact remains that the maids have been
denied the possibility of a life that is not a fantasy. Genet's
compassion for the outcast is balanced by a sober irony.
The ceremony is the only way of salvation, but it is also a
grand self-deception, at once heroic and naive: "It's God
who's listening to us. We know that it's for Him that the
last act is to be performed, but we mustn't forewarn Him.
We'll play it to the hilt" (trans. Bernard Frechtman).

Ionesco and Beckett go further. Removing the possibility of release even through self-deception, they involve not
only their characters but the audience as well in the drama
of a devaluated existence and a diminishing reality without
reprieve. The maids raise themselves out of the limbo of
virtual nonentity to a consciousness of a new self, though
at the cost of their lives. Ionesco and Beckett take us in the
opposite direction: actors and audience are locked in a
mutual contemplation of the collapse of being itself. While

Brecht had tried to "historicize" the individual act in order to direct our attention to the fate of society as a whole,
here the individual is "dehistoricized," severed from his
social context in history, to mark the desperate plight of his
"non-social self."[2] This is the key to Ionesco's and Beckett's
almost lyric use of the theater (a histrionic lyricism) to bind
actor and audience in a shared consciousness of the essential condition of man. If we take tragedy, in the traditional
way, to be the rehearsal of our worst fears in order that we
may master them, or at least try to understand and accommodate disorder within a provisional framework of order,
the theaters of Ionesco and Beckett demonstrate that such
mastery is impossible, such an attempt at understanding is
vain, and that therefore we can only create absurd gestures
of collapse to indicate what it feels like to exist in the twentieth-century theater of the world. The nightmares of history have resulted in a nightmare of individual and collective consciousness which cannot be accommodated to
anything else because there is nothing else. That is Poor
Tom's insoluble dilemma on the modern stage.

When Ionesco writes, "To become fully conscious of the
atrocious and to laugh at it is to master the atrocious," he
means something less than gaining upon the threat of
chaos, or mastering the incomprehensible evil by making
it comprehensible. In another context, he had written, "The
unendurable admits of no solution, and only the unendurable is profoundly tragic, profoundly comic and essentially theatrical" (pp. 206, 52). The problem is how to give
shape and objective validity to such despair. Ionesco hopes
that if he succeeds in "materializing" on stage "the unseen presence of our inner fears" (p. 63) his personal anguish will be expressive of everyone's anguish:

> By expressing my deepest obsessions, I express my deepest
> humanity. I become one with all others, spontaneously, over
> and above all the barriers of caste and different psychologies.
> I express my solitude and become one with all other solitudes;
> my joy at existing or my surprise at being are those of everyone
> even if, for the moment, everyone refuses to recognize it. (p.
> 87)

In his early plays, Ionesco was above all concerned with inventing a theatrical language that would externalize his personal (and, one might add, not particularly novel) feelings of bewilderment at the contradictory aspects of human existence: that we are social beings and yet utterly alone; that the "joy at existing" is matched by a feeling of emptiness; that material presence is negated by spiritual absence; solidity by evanescence. The paradox of life itself is that man is destroyed by time, "by the fact of living" (p. 222).

> "What is all this?" I wonder. "What does it all mean?" And out of this state of mind ["a mixture of anguish and euphoria"], which seems to spring from the most fundamental part of my nature, is strangely born at times a feeling that everything is comic and derisory, at others a feeling of despair that the world should be so utterly ephemeral and precarious, as if it all existed and did not exist at one and the same time, as if it lay somewhere between being and not being: and that is the origin of my tragic farces, *The Chairs*, for example, in which I myself would find it difficult to say whether some of the characters exist or not, whether the real is truer than the unreal or the reverse. (p. 196)

The uncertainty of existence leaves him simply perplexed; yet in the short plays of the 1950s he created a series of brilliantly executed confessions of his comic despair.

Ionesco's theater is predominantly comic because it grows directly out of his ambivalent and provocatively subjective view of the world. At first, he professes not to be able to separate comic from tragic in his experience. "Wonder [L'étonnement] is my basic emotional reaction to the world. Not tragic—all right; then comic perhaps, strangely comic indeed, derisory, this world of ours. And yet if I take a closer look at it, a kind of searing pain takes hold of me" (p. 295). This type of experience is described in several places: what appears to be a strange, implausible, even nonsensical universe when viewed from the outside, in a state of detachment, causes him intense distress when he realizes that it is the sole reality of his existence. But the comic impulse prevails. Looking back upon his work, Ionesco singles out this gift of detaching himself from the

world as the reason why he can view even the painful aspects of man's existence as comic in their improbability
(p. 179). He is nothing if not coy in his description of the unexpected effects of his first plays upon the audiences. They
laughed at *The Bald Soprano* when he thought he had written the "Tragedy of Language." They found the sadistic
business of *The Lesson* highly amusing. Conversely, the
"classic vaudeville situation" of *The Chairs* struck them
as peculiarly macabre (pp. 131-132). The fact is, of course,
that the audiences respond precisely to Ionesco's manipulation of his ambivalent feelings in any given situation.
However, his detached view is not a substitute for an objective universal view of the human predicament (such as
Beckett's); therefore, he succeeds in achieving only a detached recognition on our part of his particular version of
an incomprehensible universe. Since he exaggerates, or
makes grotesque in other ways, the precarious nature of
our existence, the audience laughs. It recognizes its image,
but so enlarged or frantically distorted that it fails
to share Ionesco's submerged anguish.

If indeed, as Ionesco claims, the writing of *The Bald Soprano* (*La Cantatrice chauve*, 1948; first performed, 1950)
was attended by physical anguish, nausea and vertigo,
why is so little of that transmitted to the audience in performance? Why does the "Tragedy of Language," or (in
Jean Vannier's more precise description) the "destruction
of language" which ushers us into the "Kingdom of Terror," namely "the tragic silence which is that of the solitude of his beings,"[3] make us laugh? Because his characters are so far stripped of thought, emotion, personality,
having lost their identity in the world of the impersonal,
that we presume to watch them from a safe distance. Ionesco writes the comedy of dehumanization. By translating the
breakdown of communication into the automatic give and
take of the English Language Manual, he calls attention to
his detached comic view of man totally lost (or to use his
own word, "steeped") in his social environment. The only
indication of his terror comes in the end when the tone of
petit bourgeois complacency rises to a pitch of incoherent

madness. He speaks of this as "a kind of collapse of reality" (pp. 252, 253). But because this typical rhythm or pattern of intensification reflects the eminently subjective
response of a sensitive mentality, we feel free to stand
back and laugh (perhaps cruelly) both at the comic side of
his discomfiture and the grotesque expression of his terror. Ionesco's plays, as he never tires of saying, are about
himself struggling to find theatrical equivalents for his own
states of mind and feeling. That is really the point of his
elaborate self-justifications in the *Notes and Counter Notes*,
as well as his speculations about the relation of comedy to
tragedy.

Hence he belabors the problem of how to get from his
intensely subjective apprehension of the world to a more
universal, tragic vision. He declares that Beckett, in contrast to Brecht, is essentially tragic because he brings the
whole of the human condition into play, not man in this or
that society, because he poses the problem of the ultimate
ends of man. Although Ionesco ranges himself on the side
of Beckett in his concern with the "authentic reality in
which man is integrated" (p. 195), there is this difference
to be observed between them. Ionesco does not possess
Beckett's objectivity and therefore not his universality. It
does not escape him that he can speak of *Endgame* in the
same breath with the lamentations of Job (Job "that contemporary of Beckett") or the tragedies of Sophocles and
Shakespeare (pp. 223, 96), whereas his own plays (with
the possible exception of *The Killer* and *Exit the King*)
hardly grasp the "essentially tragic human reality" (p. 335)
in any universal sense. Rather they tend to fluctuate between derisive laughter at his caricatures of human behavior and sudden pain when he discovers that his invented
situations accurately render his own desolation. He follows
the rhythm of his intuitions and feelings instead of the
logic of the invented dramatic situation.

> Ah! Molière! Of course, he is a master for all of us—in spite of
> his realism. . . . But when these older writers use the comic
> and mix it with the tragic, in the end their characters are no
> longer funny: it is the tragic that prevails. In my plays it is just

the opposite: they start by being comic, are tragic for a moment and end up in comedy or tragi-comedy. (p. 176)[4]

Beckett's comedy, on the other hand, is integral to his
tragic vision. It does not compete with it (as is the case in
Ionesco's tragic farce), but forms a part of the general
rhythm of the play: the stalemate of *Waiting for Godot* or
the descent to nothingness in *Endgame* and *Happy Days*.
Nor are any of the celebrated enigmas of Beckett's drama—
the identity of Godot or Clov's discovery of the small boy—
evidence of his personal bewilderment or subjective ex-
pressions of his uncertainty in the face of an incomprehensible universe. Though rationally inexplicable, they are
in each instance part of the objective tragic reality depicted
in the play, relating to the fate of the *protagonists*. In fact,
Beckett fulfills Ionesco's theoretical idea of tragedy, the
creation of a mythical cosmos and a "pure drama" of universal significance that reproduces "the permanently destructive and self-destructive pattern of existence itself:
pure reality, non-logical and non-psychological . . ." (p.
298).[5] But, writing in 1953, he admits ruefully, to make such
a world which is peculiarly *one's own* communicable and
identifiable to others is perhaps impossible. A set of contrasting definitions sheds light on the difficulty:

> The tragic: when the whole destiny of man is summarized
> in one model situation (with or without divine transcen-
> dence).
> The dramatic: a particular case, particular circumstances
> and a particular destiny.
> The tragic: destiny in a general or collective sense; a revela-
> tion of the human condition.
> I myself participate in a drama: I see reflected there *my
> own* case (the painful things that happen on the stage can
> happen to me).
> Tragedy: what happens on the stage can happen to *us*. It
> can concern *us all* (and no longer just *myself*). (p. 303)

Ionesco is aware that he falls short of achieving such an
absolute tragic action of universal significance. Twice, he
thinks, he has come close to it. In connection with *The
Killer* he describes a universal dramatic situation that approaches "pure reality":

> But are we not all moving toward death? Death is really the end, the goal of all existence. Death does not have to be buttressed by any ideology. To live is to die and to kill: every creature defends itself by killing, kills to live. . . .
> Do we perhaps feel in a confused sort of way, regardless of ideology, that we cannot help being, at one and the same time, both killer and killed, governor and governed, the instrument and the victim of all-conquering death?[6]

And *Rhinoceros* strikes him as "a fairly *objective* description of the growth of fanaticism, of the birth of a totalitarianism that grows, propagates, conquers, transforms a whole world and, naturally, being totalitarian, transforms it totally" (p. 290; [my emphasis]). Although the play is a farce, according to Ionesco (a tragic farce, in Barrault's production, and quite oppressive), above all, it is a tragedy. "One man helplessly sees his whole world transformed and can do nothing to stop it: he no longer knows if he is right or wrong; he struggles but without hope; he is the last of his species. He is lost" (p. 289). But it is only rarely that Ionesco manages to create a "model situation" reflecting the human condition on a large scale or posing "the problem of the ultimate ends of man."

For the most part, his talent, contrary to Beckett's, leads him to what Francis Fergusson called the partial perspectives of the modern theater, "highly developed fragments of [the] great mirror."[7] He only touches upon the tragic reality underneath the comic surface of life. The conformist, the ideologist, the purely social or "sociologized" man negates his humanity and thus becomes an object of derision; but insofar as in organized society man is reduced to his function in that organization, he is alienated from other men (p. 124). Concealed under the comic picture of a life emptied of meaning lies the horror of solitude. The insight is sharply realized, for example, in the automatic chatter of *The Bald Soprano* and in several other plays; but typically it has the limitations of a theatrical essay upon one of his favorite themes: that it is the human condition which governs the social condition, not the other way around (p. 143). More ambitiously, as in the masterpiece among his short plays, *The Chairs* (*Les Chaises*, 1951), he tries to

deprive us of our sense of the real. The apparently harmless hallucination, begun in the spirit of vaudeville, progressively reveals the "gaps in reality." The proliferation
of chairs to accommodate the invisible guests suggests a
more than physical absence; and at last he succeeds in expressing the void, "the unreality of the real. Original
chaos" (pp. 267-268). But, as he points out in "La tragédie
du langage," the tragic character does not change; he is
wrecked; he is himself, he is *real*. Comic characters, on the
other hand, are people who do not exist (pp. 253-254).

That the Smiths and the Martins in *The Bald Soprano*
are perfectly interchangeable, because of "the absence of
an inner life," makes them comical in the way that puppets
can be taken as abominable imitations of humanity. Accel-
erate their mechanical babble to the point of incoherence,
and their behavior becomes painful, a kind of threatening
disorder. Although Ionesco had in mind at least two explo-
sive endings, involving the audience in a scene of mayhem,
extending as it were the "collapse of reality" from the
stage to the auditorium, circumstances forced upon him the
more brilliant idea of returning to the opening scene as
the curtain slowly falls. Thus the comic spirit supervenes.
The Martins take the place of the Smiths, easily assuming
the identity of any member of the "universal petite bour-
geoisie"; they are people who are nothing in themselves,
therefore they do not exist. The loss of identity, the absence of real people, in *The Chairs* is a decidedly more serious matter. Now Ionesco looks beneath the surface of actual existence and finds a void, an emptiness that "grows
and devours everything" (p. 264). The frantic stage business, the fabricated dialogue with the absent crowd of
guests—the whole grotesque effort to conceal the failure of a
lifetime (perhaps of a civilization) and to push back the encroaching emptiness, inevitably breaks down. But again,
face to face with the terrifying void, Ionesco truncates his
statement by arranging a convulsive, farcical ending: the
Old Man and the Old Woman attain their false apotheosis
by leaping into the abysmal water outside, in a double suicide, and the Orator, who was to deliver the Old Man's

message of salvation to the assembled guests, only gurgles and scrawls inarticulately. Ionesco's vision stops short because he is perplexed by what he has discovered; the tragic "unreality of the real" is a condition of chaos with which he cannot deal in a meaningful way.

2

But where Ionesco stops, perplexed, Beckett begins his patient inquest into the way we play out the endgame because that is all we *can* do. The desert landscape or the room surrounded by the void becomes Beckett's *Spielraum*, the arena of his most telling theatrical metaphors for the disintegration of life. Ionesco's short plays take us rapidly from the absurd to the terrific at which point the drama is simply arrested because it can be no longer sustained. Even in the longer, baldly allegorical plays, *Rhinoceros* and *Exit the King*, Ionesco simply registers the fact of dehumanization or dissolution; he does not render the experience of a declining and ultimately meaningless existence. Bérenger is brought to the point where he cannot justify his existence before the Killer. But significantly the merely helpless concluding line of *The Killer*, "What can we do?" has its counterpart in the opening statement of *Waiting for Godot*, "Nothing to be done." This is where Beckett's plays begin, with variations to indicate what each self-conscious player, about to play a segment of his life, thinks there is in store for him: "Finished, it's finished, nearly finished, it must be nearly finished," says Clov at the beginning of *Endgame*; and Winnie, half-way buried, starts her monologue with the disarmingly ironical exclamation, "Another heavenly day."

For Beckett the "unreality of the real" is man's normal state of being while he playacts the static or waning remnant of his life. Stoppard's play-metaphor ends in a melodramatic joke; it is the ineluctable fate of Rosencrantz and Guildenstern to disappear into the world of *Hamlet*. As a version of man's tragicomic existence, the metaphor offers Stoppard opportunities to exercise his sharp wit, but ultimately it forces him into an unsatisfactory conclusion.

Beckett's vision is at once more radical and true to our experience. He takes the *theatrum mundi* concept as seriously as do the orthodox Christian dramatists in the modern theater except that his actors play under a vacant heaven.[8] They are observed, but only by themselves and by spectators whom they implicate as witnesses and participants in the game of waiting, waiting either for the dim possibility of release or for the end to come. Thus the stage-life of his actors is not merely an imitation of "real" life; it constitutes a reality, that of playing which is Beckett's analogue for living. For the duration of the performance it *is* a segment of human existence, inasmuch as his actors are trapped on a specific stage, each a desolate image of the world. Jacques Guicharnaud shows why the play-metaphor is essential in Beckett's work: "Life consists in pretending to live—just as children pretend that they fly or are animals —yet we have nothing more than our lives. Thus there is a correspondence between our lives in the world and the essence of theatre, in which, paradoxically, what is performed is both reality and a game and requires both participation and detachment. Clearly, Beckett's vision of life is made for the stage."[9]

Purely theatrical, Beckett's drama is nonetheless without conflict. Situated in no theodicy or society, his characters encounter no antagonist; they do not assert themselves against an idea or an institution, suffering a defeat in the process. They simply suffer their existence. As Robbe-Grillet has pointed out, with regard to Didi and Gogo, "We grasp at once, as we watch them, this major function of theatrical representation: to show of what the fact of *being there* consists. For it is this, precisely, which we had not yet seen on a stage, or in any case which we had not seen so clearly, with so few concessions. . . . In Beckett's play . . . everything happens as if the two tramps were on stage *without having a role*" (trans. Richard Howard).[10] In trying so hard to give themselves the impression that they exist, they assault our complacent assumption that existence is its own justification. Their plight is ours, and while they *are there* improvising games, trying to imitate the act of

living, waiting for Godot, they force us to share the tragic
consciousness that that is all we can do. In this theater the
spectator must abandon whatever roles he ordinarily plays
in order to participate in the tragicomic crisis of being: he
can laugh at the antics of Didi and Gogo, who seek to pass
the time, but he knows that for him, too, Godot (in Guicharnaud's phrase) is "systematically absent." In this theater
he too is caught in time conceived as an eternal present, a
perpetual interim; he learns that he is destined to lead a
provisional existence defined as waiting for Godot—a messianic hope perpetually deferred.

On the second day, while Estragon is asleep, Vladimir
does not question the boy as he did on the first day. He
anticipates the expected answers. "It wasn't you came
yesterday."—"This is your first time."—"You have a message from Mr. Godot."—"He won't come this evening."—
"But he'll come to-morrow."—"Without fail." Yet to admit
outright that Godot does not come because he does not exist would be tantamount to removing the only reason for
prolonging the illusory pretense of living. It would be to
face an unendurable reality. Vladimir approaches momentarily the awareness of such a reality, provoked by Pozzo's
birth-grave image:

> Astride of a grave and a difficult birth. Down in the hole, lin-
> geringly, the grave-digger puts on the forceps. We have time
> to grow old. The air is full of our cries. (*He listens.*) But habit
> is a great deadener. (*He looks again at Estragon.*) At me too
> someone is looking, of me too someone is saying, He is sleep-
> ing, he knows nothing, let him sleep on. (*Pause.*)
> I can't go on! (*Pause.*) What have I said?
> *He goes feverishly to and fro, halts finally at extreme left,
> broods. Enter Boy right.* (Act II)

Ascertaining the expected answer that Godot will not
come, he seems to prefer the illusion to the suspected reality. Actually there is no choice. Both Vladimir and Estragon claim that they cannot go on like this, but they do.
Since they cannot *not be*, there is no alternative. Unlike
the Old Man and the Old Woman in *The Chairs*, who commit suicide ecstatically confirming the delusion of their

lives, Vladimir and Estragon (he perhaps more dimly) comprehend the "unreality of the real" and know that to exist is to be condemned to go through the motions of waiting for Godot. Their playing annihilates memory and the consciousness of time and saves them from the unbearable confrontation with nothingness; it is their only resource against absolute insignificance.

Their tenderness for each other in their misery reinforces the inclination to pity. Our horror is reserved for the image of humanity presented by Pozzo and Lucky, who do not wait for Godot. Pozzo assumes his existence; hence he acts and suffers. But, curiously enough, the outrageous world of power and degradation, the stuff of which tragedies are made, is here reduced to the position of an interlude, a show, a form of diversion for the two protagonist-clowns; and they participate in it only marginally. The dynamism of Pozzo's shallow life is as futile as the static existence of Vladimir and Estragon, with the difference that the former does not know that his life is meaningless, whereas they possess an ironic awareness that they are building flimsy bridges across the void: "We always find something, eh Didi, to give us the impression we exist?" Pozzo's display of brute power is followed by brute suffering in the second act, a shocking demonstration of the sudden collapse of what passes for human strength and certainty: "I woke up one fine day as blind as Fortune," says Pozzo. "Sometimes I wonder if I'm not still asleep." In the way he handles the two modes of life as foils to each other, Beckett suggests that the moral and social questions provoked by the spectacle of Pozzo and Lucky, important as they may once have been, really do not constitute the essential drama of the human spirit. The cry for pity rises from both sides.

ESTRAGON: (*stopping, brandishing his fists, at the top of his voice*). God have pity on me!
VLADIMIR: (*vexed*). And me?
ESTRAGON: On me! On me! Pity! On me!
Enter Pozzo and Lucky. Pozzo is blind.

As they lie helpless on the ground, Pozzo calls for help and then for pity. The juxtaposition is underscored by Estragon's astonishment: *"We* help *him?"* Humanity reenacting the violent relationship of Cain and Abel can no longer arouse either terror or pity. Vladimir's rhetoric is meant to fall on deaf ears.

> To all mankind they were addressed, those cries for help still ringing in our ears! But at this place, at this moment of time, all mankind is us, whether we like it or not. Let us make the most of it, before it is too late! Let us represent worthily for once the foul brood to which a cruel fate consigned us! What do you say?
> *(Estragon says nothing.)* (Act II)

Once Pozzo is on his feet, he continues his savage treatment of Lucky, though it is the latter now who guides him. They simply stumble on and on, falling from time to time and going on when they can. The victims of time and mutability, they only pass across the world-stage on which Vladimir and Estragon keep a timeless vigil and live a changeless existence, hoping to be saved.

The world-stage of *Waiting for Godot* merely registers the fate of Pozzo and Lucky, a caricature of those who "live" in the world of affairs and of strife. But what is unfolded between their first entrance and their last exit leaves no more than a faint momentary impression on Vladimir:

> Was I sleeping, while the others suffered? Am I sleeping now? To-morrow, when I wake, or think I do, what shall I say of to-day? That with Estragon my friend, at this place, until the fall of night, I waited for Godot? That Pozzo passed, with his carrier, and that he spoke to us? Probably. But in all that what truth will there be?

Presently the Boy makes his appearance and the episode is forgotten, or displaced by the predominant truth that other than waiting there is nothing to be done. The play is tragicomic in the sense that it pictures the human consciousness as incapable of admitting that Godot does not exist. The fear of that reality is always there; and compared with such a threat to existence, the uncertainty and suffering in the world of affairs are known facts of life that can be borne with resignation. But on the other hand, if the absence of Godot means merely that he has not come, there is hope, though forever unrealized. Man has acquired a specifically tragicomic fate: He is not strong enough, in the manner of the tragic hero, to face his despair; instead, he turns away and redefines his senseless existence as a passive waiting, indefinitely, and filling up the time with games, fearful of the intervals of emptiness. As onlookers we find such self-delusion both comic and pitiable until we realize, perhaps in the second act, that the tragic reality for us too can be concealed only by a constant effort at comic improvisation. We all play, in various ways, to avoid the pain of consciousness.

If the stage-existence of Didi and Gogo, playing to pass the time, is equivalent to the human condition, it is so only in a universe where the concept of Godot can still be postulated. Hamm and Clov, trapped on the stage of *Endgame* (*Fin de partie*, 1957), also embody a condition of immobility but because they are waiting for the end. They do not try to avoid, they cultivate the awareness that Godot does not exist. They also play, but only in a futile effort to prolong the irresistible decline. Their stage-existence is not an indefinite repetition amounting to stasis; it eventuates in the end of playing as such, the loss of the game, the likelihood of extinction. The relationship of master and servant is here not alone meant to reflect the world of power and exploitation (as with Pozzo and Lucky); it is qualified by the consciousness on both parts that they are the remnants of humanity, that there are no further resources in the human player to effectuate change or to arrest the inevitable process of disintegration.

Beckett translates the ontological drama into physical terms. The spiritual anguish merges into the physical, almost undifferentiated:

HAMM . . . Last night I saw inside my breast. There was a
  big sore.
CLOV Pah! You saw your heart.
HAMM No, it was living. (*Pause. Anguished*) Clov!
CLOV Yes.

HAMM What's happening?
CLOV Something is taking its course. (*Pause*)
HAMM Clov!
CLOV (*Impatiently*) What is it?
HAMM We're not beginning to . . . to . . . mean something?
CLOV Mean something! You and I, mean something! (*Brief laugh*) Ah that's a good one!
HAMM I wonder. (*Pause*) Imagine if a rational being came back to earth, wouldn't he be liable to get ideas into his head if he observed us long enough. . . . (*Vehemently*) To think perhaps it won't all have been for nothing!
CLOV (*Anguished, scratching himself*) I have a flea!

. . . .

HAMM (*Very perturbed*) But humanity might start from there all over again! Catch him, for the love of God!

In Hamm, there is both a fear of and a desire for extinction. Yet, as in *Godot* it is impossible for the tramps to leave since to exist is to wait, so here it is impossible to die: Hamm and Clov know that to exist is to be condemned to endure the irresistible decay of the material universe, the condition of entropy.[11] As a metaphor of man's life their stage existence describes only a segment of the road toward total immobility, loss of motion, loss of energy; it points in the direction of an ending, but does not come to an end. The desire to be done with this farcical existence is balanced by the realization that, wretched as it may be, as long as there is still the semblance of life, the exercise of the will, motion, self-consciousness, the end, which is nonbeing, nothingness, is held in abeyance. Pozzo's and Vladimir's more elaborate birth-grave image of life as a *slow* instant is here replaced by the experience of a gradual wasting away of the substance and hence even of the sense of being. But Hamm's self-consciousness during the process and his readiness to play the game, to discard and to make the last moves, redeem the event from insignificance.

He is like Prospero (another self-conscious actor) come to the end of time, facing a universal dissolution. Beckett invites the comparison (explicitly in the English version) with the line: "Our revels now are ended."[12] But the differences between Prospero's conception of the end and

Hamm's are instructive. They measure the distance from
a time and a theater in which a shattering insight,

> The cloud-capp'd towers, the gorgeous palaces,
> The solemn temples, the great globe itself,
> Yea, all which it inherit, shall dissolve,
> And, like this insubstantial pageant faded,
> Leave not a rack behind,

can be turned to prayer and a call for mercy. In Beckett's
theater the apocalyptic rhetoric is less grand. There are
simply no more bicycle wheels, painkillers, sugarplums.
Prayer to Our Father is futile because "He doesn't exist!"
and as for Hamm's natural father, the "accursed progeni-
tor," he sinks back into his bin with a curse on his lips.

Prospero averts potential tragedy with the help of magic,
and then rids himself of the instruments of power. He
strips away levels of illusion, ending the ideal world of the
wedding masque, burying his staff and drowning his book,
and finally the illusion of the stage itself when he steps
before the English audience to speak the Epilogue. The
existential experience he reveals to us in this sequence is
the consciousness of human frailty, everyman's need for
mercy when all illusions are discarded. Addressing the
audience directly, the costumed actor and the fellow mortal
speak as one:

> Now I want
> Spirits to enforce, art to enchant;
> And my ending is despair
> Unless I be reliev'd by prayer,
> Which pierces so that it assaults
> Mercy itself and frees all faults.

No such break in illusion is possible, or even necessary,
in *Endgame*, since for Beckett the reality of existence is
identical with the act of playing the endgame, the king
trapped on the chess board or the actor trapped on the
stage. If Shakespeare is skeptical of his own art as a means
to salvation, Beckett agrees. But we *must* play, in his

view; that is all we can do, and we do what we can. In composing and narrating the story of his life, Hamm tries to create an alternative, and perhaps plausible, reality to account for his situation, but it can only prolong the endgame for a while. Like Prospero's masque, it is no substitute for the facts of existence, which must at last be faced. Thus, in his epilogue, Hamm discards his gaff, his whistle, and his toy dog; tries a little poetry to capture his plight in words and to savor their cadence—"You cried for night; it falls: now cry in darkness. (*Pause*) Nicely put, that"; resumes his story and gives it up; and having called out twice to his Father, in mimicry of the suffering Son, spreads his handkerchief over his face and resigns himself to a posture of immobility. In contrast to Prospero, his is the anguish of a devalued being in a decayed world, without hope of reprieve.

But while in *Endgame* we still witness the act of self-perception and Hamm's need to express his anguish by playing several roles, in the companion piece of 1957, *Act without Words I* (*Acte sans paroles I*), there is only the stimulus to action and the futile effort preceding the final tableau of the actor, immobile, lying on his side, in the foetal position. Beckett has reduced existence to the image of man inhabiting an empty stage. If his view of an exhausted universe is accepted, he has brought us to the ultimate tragic subject: the necessity of suffering an existence to which (though it is patently absurd) man clings tenaciously because he will not give up even his uncertain sense of self. He cannot help the general decay nor his own deterioration, but instinctively he pits what is left to him, his self-consciousness, against the threat of nonbeing: "One day you'll be blind, like me," says Hamm. "You'll be sitting there, a speck in the void, in the dark, for ever, like me." It is the horror of nothingness, of nonentity, that gives Beckett's protagonists their ludicrous, yet none the less admirable, persistence in their desperation. Theirs is the ultimate *human* commitment, in that it is not a commitment to *this* action or *that*, provoking tragic consequences, but more radically to the enterprise of enduring the given interval, before the end, with a certain integrity.

And Beckett demands a similar commitment from the
artist, a confirmation of his desperate eschatology together
with the assertion that intellect and imagination must give
expression to it—a tragic paradox. ". . . I speak of an art
. . . weary of its puny exploits, weary of pretending to be
able, of being able, of doing a little better the same old
thing . . . [and preferring] the expression that there is
nothing to express, nothing with which to express, nothing
from which to express, no power to express, no desire to express, together with the obligation to express." When his
interlocutor objects, "But that is a violently extreme and
personal point of view, . . ." Beckett does not reply.[13]
What is there to reply? The last phrase, "together with the
obligation to express," spells the difference between a
nihilistic and a tragic sense of life. One imagines that
Büchner would not have replied to the objection that his
hero's paranoiac visions represented a violently extreme
and personal point of view and had therefore no objective
validity. We have come full circle from Woyzeck to Hamm.

Though Büchner stands at the threshold of the modern
social drama, his play already anticipates the tragic questions concerning man's "non-social self." His imagination
could conceive of a social and psychological deprivation so
strong that it destroys his hero's sense of his own existence.
Woyzeck's anguish, expressing itself in images of violence
and desolation, becomes the center of consciousness in
the play so that the spectators begin to share his perceptions:

> WOYZECK. It's nature, Herr Doctor, when nature is no
> more. . . .
> DOCTOR. What! when nature is no more?
> WOYZECK. When nature is no more, that is when—it's all
> done with, and the world has turned so dark that you have
> to grope for it with your hands, and you think it runs be-
> tween your fingers like a spider web. Ah, when something is
> and yet is not! . . .[14]

For Büchner, Woyzeck's total estrangement, his experience of the unreality of the real, is not alone the result of a
mental aberration. He generalizes the vision of the death

of the natural world in the story of the old woman in which the abandoned child searches over the whole universe—sun, moon, and stars—only to find it deserted and in a state of decomposition. But while Büchner's images of emptiness and darkness and insubstantiality hover in an area between hallucination and plausible surmise, they have become matter-of-fact statements in Beckett's play. There is no more nature, though that is momentarily disputed. Outside all is "corpsed." The seeds do not sprout. Mother Pegg is extinguished; she has died of darkness.

There is a *controlled* nihilism evident in both writers. It seeks to find expression in Woyzeck's cataclysmic visions and in the grotesque oppressive figures that constitute his social world. His suffering is animal-like. He cannot master it through intellect and speech. But it is none the less significant. In his barely articulate victim, Büchner successfully associates the degradation of human life with the imagery of a dying universe. We get a similar effect in Clov's epilogue:

> I say to myself—sometimes, Clov, you must learn to suffer better than that if you want them to weary of punishing you—one day. I say to myself—sometimes, Clov, you must be there better than that if you want them to let you go—one day. But I feel too old, and too far, to form new habits. Good, it'll never end, I'll never go. (*Pause*) Then one day, suddenly, it ends, it changes, I don't understand, it dies, or it's me, I don't understand, that either. I ask the words that remain—sleeping, waking, morning, evening. They have nothing to say. (*Pause*) I open the door of the cell and go. I am so bowed I only see my feet, if I open my eyes, and between my legs a little trail of black dust. I say to myself that the earth is extinguished, though I never saw it lit. (*Pause*) It's easy going. (*Pause*) When I fall I'll weep for happiness. (*Pause. He goes towards door*).

But in Hamm, the king, the storyteller, the self-conscious actor, the human sensibility struggles against the encroaching void until he concedes defeat. Like Beckett's artist, he feels "the obligation to express"; it is the last specifically human act possible, and the more keenly the mind perceives the general degradation, the more it becomes aware of its suffering. Such an awareness is a tem-

porary saving grace—it gives the illusion of momentary control—until even expression is no longer possible. When
Hamm suspects that Clov has left and that he is totally
isolated, the prospective speck in the void, he lapses into
silence and immobility.

> (. . . *He sniffs. Soft*) Clov! (*Long pause*) No? Good. (*He takes
> out the handkerchief*) Since that's the way we're playing
> it . . . (*He unfolds handkerchief*) . . . let's play it that way
> . . . (*He unfolds*) . . . and speak no more about it . . . (*He
> finishes unfolding*) . . . speak no more. (*He holds handker-
> chief spread out before him*) Old stancher! (*Pause*) You . . .
> remain. (*Pause. He covers his face with handkerchief, lowers
> his arms to armrests, remains motionless. Brief tableau*)
>   Curtain

Hamm is of course wrong. During the entire concluding
monologue, Clov stands by the door, dressed for the road,
but not moving. He keeps his eyes fixed on Hamm till the
end.

Beckett is not dramatizing the end of the world or the end
of time or the end of man. He is creating a theatrical metaphor for man suffering an existence which is in the process
of continuous devaluation, and to the anguished cry,
"What's happening?" there is only the answer, "Something
is taking its course." As for the unspoken tragic question,
"Is man no more than this?" the play answers in the affirmative, except that on the modern stage Poor Tom, though
blind and lame, understands his condition and plays his
role of everyman in the center of the stage.

It is clear that with this play Beckett undercuts all other
tragic theaters. If his metaphor is given credence, if we do
not simply reject his point of view as "violently extreme
and personal," all other instances of tragic predicaments,
inescapable dilemmas, unavoidable conflicts become
supererogatory. Beckett's theater tests man's capacity to
endure the one misfortune—that he exists at all. Because of
the horror of nothingness he is locked in the course of his
declining existence by necessity. Beckett's subject, the imminent collapse of being itself, reaches the extreme point
of tragic consciousness. But with the two mimes entitled

Act without Words he has begun to move, both in the actor and the spectator, beyond the feeling of anguish to the verge of negative withdrawal. We look, but cease to feel and that is the end of tragedy. (Lear: "Yet you see how this world goes." Gloucester: "I see it feelingly.") Unless we are made to care about, or wish to understand, the loss involved in a devaluated existence, the play no longer touches us with fear or pain, but rather calls attention to itself as an exercise in thinking up symbolic attitudes of despair. And then the obligation to express can be no longer the last refuge from nothingness.

NOTES

1. Eugène Ionesco, *Notes et contre-notes* (Editions Gallimard, 1966), p. 266 (" 'Le vide' ontologique, ou l'*absence*" with reference to *The Chairs*). All subsequent references will be to this edition. The translations are those of Donald Watson, *Notes and Counter Notes* (New York: Grove, 1964).

2. "L'extra-social: c'est là où l'homme est profondément seul." Ibid., pp. 196, 274.

3. Jean Vannier, "A Theatre of Language," *TDR*, 7 (spring 1963), 184-185.

4. "Entretien avec Édith Mora" (1960), *Notes et contre-notes*, p. 176. In the same interview, he was asked (pursuing a figurative example he had introduced), "Are you then sometimes the 'patient' at the same time as the physician, or rather the surgeon, in your comedies?" and he replied significantly, "Oh! I have always made fun of myself in my writing! It must however, be admitted that this happens far less often now and that I take myself more and more seriously when I talk about what I do" (p. 179).

5. See "Notes sur le théâtre, 1953," ibid., pp. 297-300.

6. "Avant-première pour *Tueur sans gages*," ibid., p. 230.

7. *The Idea of a Theater* (Princeton, 1949), p. 145.

8. See Ruby Cohn, *"Theatrum Mundi* and Contemporary Theater," *Comp D*, 1 (spring 1967), 28-35.

9. *Modern French Theatre* (New Haven: Yale University Press, 1969), p. 251.

10. Alain Robbe-Grillet, *Pour un nouveau roman* (Paris: Les Éditions de Minuit, 1963), p. 103.

11. On the theme of entropy, see David H. Hesla, *The Shape of Chaos: An Interpretation of the Art of Samuel Beckett* (Minneapolis: University of Minnesota Press, 1971), pp. 155-159.

12. See Ruby Cohn, *Samuel Beckett: The Comic Gamut* (New Brunswick: Rutgers University Press, 1962), pp. 236-237.

13. "Three Dialogues" by Samuel Beckett and Georges Duthuit, I "Tal Coat" in *Samuel Beckett: A Collection of Critical Essays*, ed. Martin Esslin (Englewood Cliffs, N.J.: Prentice-Hall, 1965), p. 17.

14. Manuscript fragment (Woyzeck, Doctor), *Sämtliche Werke und Briefe*, ed. Werner R. Lehmann, I, 369.

INDEX

357